TRANSLATING LIFE

Studies in Transpositional Aesthetics

LIVERPOOL ENGLISH TEXTS AND STUDIES

General editors: JONATHAN BATE and BERNARD BEATTY

*

Byron and the Limits of Fiction
edited by BERNARD BEATTY and VINCENT NEWEY
Volume 22. 1988. 304pp. ISBN 0-85323-026-9

Literature and Nationalism
edited by VINCENT NEWEY and ANN THOMPSON
Volume 23. 1991. 296pp. ISBN 0-85323-057-9

Reading Rochester
edited by EDWARD BURNS
Volume 24. 1995. 240pp. ISBN 0-85323-038-2 (cased), 0-85323-309-8 (paper)

Thomas Gray: Contemporary Essays
edited by W. B. HUTCHINGS and WILLIAM RUDDICK
Volume 25. 1993. 287pp. ISBN 0-85323-268-7

Nearly Too Much: The Poetry of J. H. Prynne
by N. H. REEVE and RICHARD KERRIDGE
Volume 26. 1995. 224pp. ISBN 0-85323-840-5 (cased), 0-85323-850-2 (paper)

A Quest for Home: Reading Robert Southey
by CHRISTOPHER J. P. SMITH
Volume 27. 1996. 256pp. ISBN 0-85323-511-2 (cased), 0-85323-521-X (paper)

Outcasts from Eden: Ideas of Landscape in British Poetry since 1945
by EDWARD PICOT
Volume 28. 1997. 344pp. ISBN 0-85323 531-7 (cased), 0-85323-541-4 (paper)

The Plays of Lord Byron
edited by ROBERT F. GLECKNER and BERNARD BEATTY
Volume 29. 1997. 400pp. ISBN 0-85323-881-2 (cased), 0-85323-891-X (paper)

Sea-Mark: The Metaphorical Voyage, Spenser to Milton
by PHILIP EDWARDS
Volume 30. 1997. 240pp. ISBN 0-85323-512-0 (cased), 0-85323-522-8 (paper)

Passionate Intellect: The Poetry of Charles Tomlinson
by MICHAEL KIRKHAM
Volume 31. 1999. 320pp. ISBN 0-85323-534-0 (cased), 0-85323-553-8 (paper)

'The New Poet': Novelty and Tradition in Spenser's Complaints
by RICHARD DANSON BROWN
Volume 32. 1999. 320p. ISBN 0-85323-803-3 (cased), 0-85323-813-8 (paper)

TRANSLATING LIFE:
Studies in Transpositional Aesthetics

Edited by
SHIRLEY CHEW &
ALISTAIR STEAD
University of Leeds

LIVERPOOL UNIVERSITY PRESS

First published 1999 by
LIVERPOOL UNIVERSITY PRESS
Liverpool L69 3BX

British Library Cataloguing-in-Publication Data
A British Library CIP Record is available

ISBN 0-85323-674-7 (hardback)
0-85323-684-4 (paperback)
Typeset in 10.5/12.5 Stempel Garamond
by BBR, Sheffield
Printed by Alden Press, Oxford

TO
INGA-STINA EWBANK

Acknowledgements

The editors thank Elizabeth Paget for invaluable secretarial assistance; and are indebted to the Witt Library, Courtauld Institute of Art, University of London, for permission to reproduce the photographs after page 248 illustrating 'Thackeray and the "Old Masters"'.

Contents

Introduction

SHIRLEY CHEW and
ALISTAIR STEAD

'Translation it is that openeth the window, to let in the light'
Miles Smith, Preface to King James version of the Bible

This volume, comprising many individual but conceptually interrelated studies, sets out to multiply perspectives on the concept of translation, making it intellectually generative, an invaluable prompter to reinterpretation of texts and fresh theoretical reflections on pertinent critical issues. Mindful that the ideally singular light radiating from translation as conceived by the translators of the King James Bible might actually be refracted through manifold interpretations, our twenty-two collaborators read and reread through what we would call the prism of translation, shedding on the concept and the texts, to bend one of Philip Larkin's luminous epithets, a 'many-angled light'.

The identification of reading with translation has by now a distinguished literary pedigree (one thinks of a line of modern writers from Proust to Calvino who have either claimed that reading entails an act of translation or, more challengingly, that translation is the only proper way to read a text).[1] 'Reading is already translation, and translation is translation for the second time,' wrote Hans-Georg Gadamer,[2] and this is dynamically related to writing, also seen by Proust as, ideally, translation.[3] 'In the act of writing, the author is producing a complicated translation of the "text" of the world; we generate a second translation in our attempt to return to the "native tongue of reality".'[4] Others have gone on to multiply the number of translations involved in these writings and readings, notably Octavio Paz and Jacques Derrida,[5] so that perception, speech, writing, reading, criticism, all participate in the same interpretative act. But the basis of translation proper, and of the interpretations of and through translation included in this book, remains the same: that close reading of texts on which translation has always to depend.

Translation and Transposition

Whatever the temporary inflection we give to the word, translation is a linguistically and culturally central process, comprising, grandly, 'the transforming principle at the heart of all literary activity',[6] but also more pragmatically, as Susan Bassnett has argued throughout her many important contributions to Translation Studies, it is reading and writing across linguistic and cultural boundaries.[7] Where these essays deal with translation in a restricted sense, that is, interlingual transcoding (as in Andrew Wawn or Jonathan Bate), it is not 'routine information transfer' but 'literary' or, more inclusively, 'literary-philosophic translation' which is under consideration.[8] In a provocative and fertile phrase, George Steiner has called translation 'that exact art of metamorphic duplicities':[9] 'exact' in its heroic (exacting) search for semantic and functional equivalence between different languages and cultures; 'metamorphic' in its acceptance that not only is that quest for identity of meaning quixotic, necessitating changes, but that changes are creatively essential if the transfer is to be successful, with the original text finding its afterlife in the 'transformation' toward which '"translation" always tends'.[10] It is perhaps significant that, after Shakespeare, it is Ovid, the much-translated writer on 'translations', the *Metamorphoses*, who is most frequently cited in these essays.

In this volume, translation is widely understood in its transferred or metaphorical senses, most fundamentally as a process of change or a passage from one state to another, as is made most explicit in Stanley Wells's study of (not coincidentally Ovidian) *A Midsummer Night's Dream*. Indeed, translation is itself commonly identified with metaphor by many writers on translation (Willis Barnstone, Fritz Senn, Salman Rushdie in *Shame*) and writers in this volume will draw on this tradition. In his discussion of *Rites of Passage*, Steven Connor plays with the image of voyage or passage, an image which has often enabled discussion of metaphor and translation alike.[11] Translation, as Michael Wood puts it, is 'travel between meanings'[12] and metaphor, as Elizabethan rhetoricians like George Puttenham knew, is 'the figure of transport'.[13] More than one contributor to this book reminds us that etymologically both metaphor and translation (*translatio*) signify 'a carrying across'. As John Paul Riquelme reminds us, metaphor, like translation, involves the practice of substitution. It is 'the uneasy equivalence between two concepts that results when we try substituting words for one another. This equivalence is uneasy because it can never be exact; there is always a residue of meaning left over or a new meaning added in the act of substitution.'[14] And if the analogy with metaphor is sustained, then William H. Gass's acute observation that the terms of the metaphor, its tenor and vehicle, 'are inspecting one another—they interact—the figure is drawn both ways'[15] may be read into the give-and-take of the act of translating, the alternations of submission and domination, of restitution and innovation. If translation constitutes a commentary upon or innovatory increment to the original text, then translation can only take place in a language whose transformations are informed and fuelled by contact with the source.

Translation is a carrying across of meaning from one language to another. The traffic may be in subsets of the receptor language rather than between foreign and familiar tongues, that is, it can be an *intralingual* transfer, and the text may exhibit 'the capacity to move between idioms, to translate',[16] and effect conversions between classes, cultures, races, genders, or sexual orientations. But semantic transportation, whether active or passive, may be easily correlated to the literal or transferred senses of the migration of writers or characters from one place to another, underlining the point that in these essays the translating under consideration may be the activity of either the writer or the projected character, or both, and bringing to the fore the potentiality for cultural resignification, where a classic is read in a totally alien environment (the Bible by the Ganges, Virgil on the Nebraskan plains), even for cultural shock, where, as in *The Satanic Verses*, there is 'the transposition' of 'sacred names into profane spaces'.[17]

The subtitle of the volume calls attention to a term nearly related, if not identical, to translation: *transposition*, or the act of moving persons or things from one place to another. Anthony Burgess's stated preference for the German word for translation, *übersetzung*, 'which implies "setting a thing over there"', brings out the dynamic likeness of the two concepts.[18] Hard-and-fast distinctions between terms for linguistic and cultural transferences are not easy to agree upon. Nevertheless, what may be gained by summoning up transposition as more than a handy synonym is the foregrounding of two senses that seem particularly applicable to discussions proceeding in this book. On the one hand, transposition seems to be intimately related, in the contexts of its widespread use, to the sheer mechanics of the act of translation, whether considered as literal or figurative, frequently implying detailed restructuring and strategic resequencing. On the other, it is attached to the ambitious, inventive relocation or transplantation of whole works or discourses, which brings the past into the present in what Declan Kibberd calls a 'dynamic constellation',[19] and/or makes culturally remote works familiar, and/or makes an intermedial or intergeneric transfer. Something of the large claims of the latter sense underpin Barnstone's affirmation that all literary translation is 'creative transposition' (following Roman Jakobson's conclusion that translation of poetry always had to be such),[20] and certainly they confirm the reference to those more than linguistic transcodings of Shakespeare involving 'cultural, rhetorical, and theatrical transpositions', which the editors of *European Shakespeares* have often found unjustly neglected by researchers.[21] The former sense predominates in John Barton's usage here, in the interview with Mark Batty about 'Translation as Adaptation'. He is thinking of transposition as a subordinate translational process, as the theatrically effective reordering of portions of a playtext in the process of adaptation.

Conversely, Gérard Genette in *Palimpsestes*, his vast inventory of transpositional techniques, reserves the term for the 'serious' (as opposed to ludic or satiric) transformation of an antecedent text, for instance, Thomas Mann's reworking of the Faust legends as *Dr Faustus* or Joyce's replaying of the *Odyssey* in *Ulysses.* With such we might compare the spatial and temporal resitings/recitings of cultural myths such as William Hazlitt's Regency Pygmalion, or James Joyce's Dublin Hamlet. But, Genette also admits, translation, mere interlingual transfer, is the most conspicuous and frequent mode of transposition, or *hypertextual* transformation.[22] Transposition may also be the term most readily invoked to describe interdiscursive or intersemiotic translation, as when one work of art interprets or emulates another.[23] Transpositions can be from play into opera (as in Benjamin Britten's *A Midsummer Night's Dream*), or from play into film (as in Laurence Olivier's version of *Henry V*); they can translate the discursiveness of theory into the enactments of fiction (as in the debate on aesthetic autonomy in Henry James's *The Tragic Muse* explored by Richard Salmon).

Genette's transpositions are part of the greatly expanded study of intertextuality in the latter part of the twentieth century. Our contributors have for the most part found that their take on translation is an intertextual one, in the spirit of current emphases within literary, literary-theoretical and translation studies, and in accordance with Inga-Stina Ewbank's conviction that translation 'is one form of re-writing, and needs to be thought about and studied as such'.[24] Every text may be considered a translation, or, as Terry Eagleton has put it, 'a set of determinate transformations of other, preceding and surrounding texts of which it may not even be consciously aware'.[25] But, whether intertextuality is understood as culturally determined, following Roland Barthes's famous definition, in 'The Death of the Author', of the text as 'made up of a variety of writings, none of them original',[26] or intentionally constructed, all these linguistic transcodings, adaptations, versions, imitations, parodies, settings, transformations, transpositions, involve some revision of the source, or the kind of engagement in covert or overt dialogue with another text—going under the name of 'conversation' (Montaigne) in Bate's work on Elizabethan translations of Ovid and John Barnard's on Hazlitt's refashioning of Ovid's and Rousseau's Pygmalion (the transpositions, it need hardly be said, are often multiple)—which takes place, say, in James's confrontation with Paterian aestheticism in the figure of Gabriel Nash in *The Tragic Muse*.

Major Emphases

George Steiner's conception of the translator as '*un interprète*—a life-giving performer'[27] and Jonathan Miller's characterization of the afterlife of the dramatic work as 'subsequent performances'[28] proffer a most suitably dramatic figure for much of the emphasis within the arguments of this book on translation as performative. Thus translation often gets discussed as a form of realization or an enactment. It is used like this, for example, in Geoffrey Hill's admiration for Wordsworth's translation of 'ethos into activity' in 'Michael', and in David Fairer's subtle analyses of the ways in which his eighteenth-century sentimental translators re-enact the Fall and play their self-conscious part in a sentimental economy. But there is a significant proportion of these essays which understand performance less metaphorically, taking translation as, for instance, 'theatrical re-enactment'.[29] This pragmatic emphasis on specific function informs the discussions of the actualities of transference from page to stage (and vice versa) or, exchanging kinds of performance, from stage to screen (as in the theatrically attuned pieces by Martin Banham and Eldred Jones on Shakespeare in Krio, by Lynette Hunter and Peter Lichtenfels on interpretation of character in *Romeo and Juliet*, by Sir Peter Hall and John Barton on the 'uneasy equivalence' of adapting and directing works from Shakespeare to Beckett, by Wells and by David Lindley on aspects of productions of *A Midsummer Night's Dream* and *The Tempest* respectively, by Richard Brown on the putative impress of productions of *Troilus and Cressida* and *A Midsummer Night's Dream* on *Ulysses*, by Peter Holland on the part played by *Hamlet* in Russian culture, and by Martin Butler on the political resonances of a wartime film version of *Henry V*).

Sometimes the focus is on *self-translation* as a self-dramatization, which may in some discussions exemplify that simultaneous losing and finding of the self in performance that characterizes the successful theatrical translations of the actual Helena Faucit or James's fictional Miriam Rooth, and the poetic and fictional impersonations of Robert Browning's dramatic monologues about Renaissance artists (Kelvin Everest) and of W. M. Thackeray's artist-hero Clive Newcome (Leonée Ormond). Others tend to write of self-translations as more problematic self-mythologizings, whether it is in the 'textual impersonations' of Naipaul (as an ambivalent English pastoralist) or in the Russian Hamlets of Turgenev and Chekhov, and the Irish Shakespeare of Joyce's Stephen Dedalus, a tradition reaching back at least as far as the beginnings of the European novel in *Don Quixote*, whose hero 'determined to call himself Don Quixote'. Eventually, and somewhat exemplarily, Don Quixote will admit defeat and re-word himself more humbly, but not before we have grasped that a double action proceeds: the translator has been translated. Translation may then be conceived as both active and passive, a process of changing and being changed, which may have its living counterpart in the 'mutual translation' of Shakespeare and Helena Faucit or produce the complex compliment/complement of 'Morris's translation of Iceland' meeting 'Iceland's translation of Morris' through the mediation of Wawn's translation into English of Matthías Jochumsson. Finally, it may reflect on the all-important role of the reader *qua* translator too.

Shakespeare's use of translation is most often metaphoric and this use is concentrated in *A Midsummer Night's Dream*, whose various inflections of the word and cognate processes are explored with exceptional clarity and force by Wells. That Shakespeare should appear so many times as instance and inspiration in this volume, from *Romeo and Juliet* to *The Tempest*, seems wholly appropriate where translation (and its performativity) is the dominant theme. For, as Inga-Stina Ewbank has reminded us, in her compelling and civilized investigation into a Shakespeare transported to, and enriching, other cultures, 'Shakespeare Translation as Cultural Exchange',[30] the broadest and most discriminating senses are to be attached to the term, from 'exchange' to 'transmigration', from 'collusion' to 'adaptation', and, above all, 'cultural re-writing'. Thus her essay affords a natural introduction to reflections in this volume on such matters as what happens to Shakespeare when twentieth-century African dramatists translate him into their dialects and incorporate him into their cultural work, or how he is recreated in the image of a Victorian playwright by a nineteenth-century popular actress. Within such accounts of Shakespearean metamorphoses, we may also encounter the puzzling fact of 'transworld identity' (which posits the possibility of survival of sameness in difference that both metaphor and translation entertain) in studies of the Russian Hamlets of Turgenev and Chekhov and Eastern European Hamlets of Heiner Müller and Andrzej Wajda (Holland), of the German Hamlet of Goethe and the Irish Hamlet of James Joyce (Brown) broached by Inga-Stina's attention in the essay to Brecht's German and Ibsen's Norwegian Coriolanus and so to the refractions of Dr Stockmann, the protagonist of *An Enemy of the People*, in theatrical and cinematic versions by Arthur Miller and Satyajit Ray.

'In questions of translation, poetics readily slides into politics.' So translation may be viewed in Inga-Stina's terms as 'a collusive re-creation',[31] a reworking or adaptation of the original text that is inevitably freighted with historical and cultural values. First of all, it may be observed that in translation cultural gains can easily outweigh linguistic losses, something readily apparent when translation functions as a mode of cultural transmission: William Morris's versions of Icelandic sagas circulates the literary wealth of a small nation and extends the range of the receptor language's literature, just as Ovid metamorphosed into Elizabethan English and Flemish Symbolism pastiched in Allan Hollinghurst find further distinct lives for varieties of Roman and Belgian art. Translation as 'the staging of cultural difference'[32] may be most clearly witnessed perhaps where the re-creations take place across languages and mores in colonial and postcolonial contexts (in the African dramatists' strategic appropriation of 'political' plays like *Julius Caesar* in Banham and Jones; in the translated V. S. Naipaul's migrant transpositional vision of England in Shirley Chew). The translation of canonical literature proves particularly useful in promoting political critiques. So

Shakespeare translations in pre-Revolutionary Russia or in a post-Stalinist Eastern Europe may hold the mirror up to an oppressive culture and function as Steiner's 'Aesopian' language, to transmit political truths unacceptable to the cultural hegemony or authoritarian regime. Less obviously, as Brown points out, the pacifist tendency of *Ulysses* (1922) may be detected in the transposition of the Shakespearean anatomy of Trojan war in *Troilus and Cressida*, revived in wartime Zurich, to a pre-war Dublin. Butler's exploration of the ways in which Olivier's conversion of *Henry V* into cinematic terms also mediates between different historical moments (1415, 1600, and 1944) and constitutes a subtly political reading of temporal translations—a mapping of one period on another, such as we find, too, in the doubling of the *fins de siècle* in Hollinghurst's *The Folding Star*—as well as a major instance of a study of intersemiotic translation.

Translation may also be politically charged as gendered rewriting. Writing on Ibsen, Inga-Stina Ewbank has drawn attention to the bilingualism of women obliged to translate from and into the dominant male discourse,[33] and the theme is enforced by Maggie Humm who considers Zora Neale Hurston's bilingualism, though it is chiefly a straddling of the borders between the Black South's orality and the White North's literariness, as eminently 'feminine'.[34] Humm would maintain that 'translation is often the conscious subject of women's writing', and that many, though not all, women writers (and hence their women characters) focus on the activity of translation as a way of subverting patriarchal culture.[35] Gail Marshall's analysis of Faucit's rewriting and performing of Shakespearean women confirms the gendered interest in translation but denies the radical political agenda. During Leonée Ormond's examination of Thackeray's transpositions of his aesthetic responses to the Old Masters into the attitudes of the hero of *The Newcomes*, she furnishes a remarkable instance of the marriageable heroine's explicit translation of a painting into her keen awareness of an imminent commodification which identifies women with *objets d'art*. All the novel's paintings have been produced by men, of course, and more conspicuous among these essays is scrutiny of the manifestly 'male text': Barnard's designation of the doomed heterosexual romance of Hazlitt's *Liber Amoris* could apply just as well to the equally blighted homosexual romance of Hollinghurst's second novel discussed by Alistair Stead. In the latter there is evidence of some transgendered revisions of heterosexual paradigms, such as the notorious *Lolita* and the less celebrated *Bruges-La-Morte*, that plays between the received straight and gay readings of experience. Indeed, Bate's intriguing reformulation of Elizabethan translation as hybrid, or 'hermaphroditic', seems to suggest a fusion or compounding of old and new textual elements rather than any absolute division between source and fresh invention.

Some of the essays included in this volume, albeit to varying degrees engaged in analysis of transformational techniques, choose to put the emphasis on issues, philosophical, ethical, political, cultural and aesthetic, which subtend the translational process. Fairer, for example, notably explores what problematic body-mind relation lies behind the inscription of the transient moment of 'sentimental translation' (the translation into affecting words of non-verbal signs such as gesture and facial expression) in fictions of eighteenth-century Sensibility, while offering an elaborate taxonomy of the principles on which the semantic transfer from subject to object is made. On the other hand, Everest's focus is deliberately not so much on a literary criticism of Browning's monologues on Italian Renaissance (more especially Florentine) art, as on how these Italian historical and artistic circumstances provide materials for English cultural debate. Thus he is able to address the question: 'what is involved in the process of cultural translation by which one set of historically specific forms can provide material for quite different and historically remote cultural conditions and thereby functions as the vehicle for a new expression.' Hill defends, with typical scruple and suggestiveness, the need for delicate translation of vital terms, close attention to semantic shifts, as essential to his comparative assaying of the moral soundness of the ethical language deployed by John Ruskin, William Wordsworth and G. M. Hopkins. Salmon's concern with the usefulness of Adorno's ideas on aesthetic autonomy as a model for an important reassessment of nineteenth-century aestheticism draws out the ambiguous implications of any idea of translation of life into art, and challengingly proposes that such aestheticism, 'through its characteristic manipulation of normative cultural and epistemological boundaries, might well be defined as an aesthetic of transpositionality'.

The title of this collection of essays, so variously addressing issues of translation, deliberately equivocates. It most obviously refers to the transformational process implicit in any aesthetic project, the rendering of life-experience into artistic form, a translation, as Julia Kristeva (with Beckett in mind) has phrased it, 'between an affective life and a personal language'.[36] Less obviously, perhaps, it alludes to a life spent in the business of (literary) translation. So, while individual essays may incline more to one pole than the other, they cohere in one way because they tend to combine, in differing proportions, the general concerns of the first sense with the more restricted focus on the second. But, in another, they cohere as indirect homage to a major exponent of the translating life, one who, as an expatriate in England and the USA, has been faced with the necessity of direct translation and has, in the course of a very distinguished academic career, been enthusiastically engaged in the professional practice of literary and dramatic translation and the study of its metaphorical extensions. This book, we trust, will serve as a tribute to Professor Inga-Stina Ewbank, the distinguished Swedish scholar, critic, teacher and translator, reflecting in the provenance of the contributors the principal loci of her academic career (Liverpool, London, and Leeds) and in the range of their topics the principal fields of her intellectual passions and achievements: Shakespeare and his contemporaries, Victorian and Modern literature. Here the offerings of her close collaborators in the theatre, Sir Peter Hall and John Barton, recognize particularly eloquently and affectionately the outstanding part she has played in helping to bring home to English audiences the power and the glory of the Scandinavian drama, of plays by Ibsen as well as by her beloved compatriot Strindberg. If the study of translation, as Susan Bassnett wisely avers, 'can teach us a great deal not only about other literatures, but also about our own',[37] then Inga-Stina has, through an exemplarily interdependent practice of both creative translation and the study of translation, made an immense and widely acknowledged contribution to our knowledge of other literatures and our own, and also puts in delightful question what is and is not our own. To this remarkable 'life-giving performer', so versed in the arts of life, we dedicate this book, looking forward to many 'subsequent performances'.

NOTES

1. Marcel Proust, 'Time Regained', *Remembrance of Things Past*, III, trans. Andreas Mayor (London: Chatto and Windus, 1981), pp. 948–49; Italo Calvino, '*Tradurre e il vero modo di leggere un testo*', *Saggi 1945–1985*, II (Milano: Mondadori, 1995), pp. 1825–31.
2. Hans-Georg Gadamer, 'To what extent does language prescribe thought?', quoted by John Paul Riquelme, 'The Use of Translation and the Use of Criticism', in Fritz Senn, *Joyce's Dislocutions: Essays on Reading as Translation*, ed. John Paul Riquelme (Baltimore and London: Johns Hopkins University Press, 1984), p. xv.
3. Proust, 'Time Regained', p. 926.
4. Donald P. Spence, *Narrative Truth and Historical Truth: Meaning and Interpretation in Psychoanalysis* (New York and London: W. W. Norton & Co, 1982), p. 49.
5. Octavio Paz, *Traducción: literatura y literalidad* (Barcelona: Tasquets, 1971), pp. 7–19; Jacques Derrida in *Difference in Translation*, ed. and trans. Joseph F. Graham (Ithaca and London: Cornell University Press, 1985).
6. Willis Barnstone, *The Poetics of Translation: History, Theory, Practice* (New Haven and London: Yale University Press, 1993), p. 8.
7. See Susan Bassnett, *Translation Studies* (London and New York: Methuen, 1980); 'Transcending Frontiers: Tales of Travellers and Translators', Inaugural Lecture, Centre for British and Comparative Cultural Studies, University of Warwick, 1993; 'Questions of Culture and Identity', Keynote Address at 1996 Women Writers' Workshop, Gresham College.
8. Willis Barnstone, *The Poetics of Translation*, p. 4; George Steiner, 'The Feast of Dissemination', *On Translation: A Symposium* in *The Times Literary Supplement* (14 October 1983), p. 1117.
9. George Steiner, 'The Feast of Dissemination', p. 1117.
10. George Steiner, *After Babel: Aspects of Language and Translation*, second edition (London: Oxford University Press, 1975), p. 426. Cf. Octavio Paz, *Traducción*, p. 10.

11. Steven Connor, *The English Novel in History, 1950–1995* (London and New York: Routledge, 1996), pp. 155–56.

12. Michael Wood, *The Magician's Doubts: Nabokov and the Risks of Fiction* (London: Chatto and Windus, 1994), p. 51.

13. George Puttenham, *The Arte of English Poesie* 1589 (Menston: The Scolar Press, 1968), ch. xvi, p. 149.

14. John Paul Riquelme, 'The Use of Translation and the Use of Criticism' in Fritz Senn, *Joyce's Dislocutions*, p. xix.

15. William H. Gass, 'In Terms of the Toenail: Fiction and the Figures of Life', *Fiction and the Figures of Life* (New York: Vintage, 1972), pp. 67–68.

16. David Trotter, writing on *Middlemarch*, in 'George Eliot, Joyce and Cambridge', Letter in *London Review of Books*, 7–20 May 1981, p. 4.

17. Homi K. Bhabha, 'How Newness Enters the World', *The Location of Culture* (London: Routledge, 1994), p. 225.

18. Anthony Burgess, 'Bless thee, Burgess, thou art translated', abridged version of the inaugural 'European Lecture' delivered at the Cheltenham Festival of Literature, *The Independent*, 27 November 1993, p. 31.

19. Declan Kiberd, 'Translating Tradition', *Inventing Ireland* (Cambridge, MA: Harvard University Press, 1996), p. 629.

20. Roman Jakobson, 'On Linguistic Aspects of Translation', in *On Translation*, ed. Reuben A. Brower (Cambridge, MA: Harvard University Press, 1959), p. 238.

21. 'Introduction', *European Shakespeares: Translating Shakespeare in the Romantic Age*, ed. Dirk Delabastita and Lieven D'Hulst (Amsterdam/ Philadelphia: John Benjamins, 1993), p. 15.

22. Gérard Genette, *Palimpsestes* (Paris: Seuil, 1982), pp. 36, 237, and pp. 238–39.

23. Cf. David Scott, *Pictorialist Poetics: Poetry and the Visual Arts in Nineteenth-Century France* (Cambridge: Cambridge University Press, 1988). Ch. 5, 'The Art of Transposition', discusses the translation of visual into literary, more particularly poetic, forms, the '*transposition d'art*'.

24. Inga-Stina Ewbank, 'Shakespeare Translation as Cultural Exchange', *Shakespeare Survey*, 48 (1995), 1–12 (p. 7).

25. Terry Eagleton, 'Translation and Transformation', *Stand*, 19, no. 3, 1978, p. 73.

26. Roland Barthes, *Image–Music–Text*, trans. Stephen Heath (London: Fontana, 1977), pp. 142–48.

27. George Steiner, *After Babel*, p. 28.

28. Jonathan Miller, *Subsequent Performances* (London: Faber, 1986).

29. David Johnston, 'Text and Ideotext: Translation and Adaptation for the Stage', *The Knowledges of the Translator: From Literary Interpretation to Machine Classification*, eds Malcolm Coulthard and Patricia Anne Odber de Baubeta (Lewiston: Edwin Mellen Press, 1996), p. 252.

30. Inga-Stina Ewbank, 'Shakespeare Translation', p. 5.

31. Inga-Stina Ewbank, 'Shakespeare Translation', p. 6.

32. Homi K. Bhabha, 'How Newness Enters the World', p. 227.

33. Inga-Stina Ewbank, 'Ibsen and the Language of Women', in *Women Writing and Writing about Women*, ed. Mary Jacobus (London: Croom Helm, 1979), pp. 114–32 (p. 128).

34. Maggie Humm, *Border Traffic: Strategies of Contemporary Women Writers* (Manchester: Manchester University Press, 1991), pp. 94–95.

35. Maggie Humm, *Border Traffic*, p. 105. See Luise von Flotow, *Translation and Gender: Translating in the 'Era of Feminism'* (Manchester and St Jerome, Ottawa: University of Ottawa Press, 1997), for a fuller theoretical and historical account of women in translation.

36. Margaret Waller, 'An Interview with Julia Kristeva' (trans. Richard Macksey), *Intertextuality and Contemporary American Fiction*, eds Patrick O'Donnell and Robert Con Davie (Baltimore and London: Johns Hopkins University Press, 1989), p. 293.

37. Susan Bassnett, 'Nothing lost, nothing sacred', *The Times Literary Supplement*, 6 September 1996, p. 10.

Translations in *A Midsummer Night's Dream*

STANLEY WELLS

A Midsummer Night's Dream is profoundly and constantly—though also delicately and humorously—concerned with processes of change, of translation from one state to another, and its audience is frequently made aware that for human beings translation—any kind of translation—is likely to be a difficult process requiring that obstacles be overcome, and that it may involve loss as well as gain. The most prominent, and most frequently discussed, aspect of translation in the play is from the unmarried to the married state. In no other play by Shakespeare is the process of courtship leading to marriage so central a concern. Almost all his comedies portray attempts to overcome obstacles to marriage, but at the end of most of them marriage is deferred, not accomplished. This play, however, opens with preparations for marriage, continues with the story of wooings at first thwarted but then successfully concluded, and ends with the celebration of not one but three marriages. But the transition from the unmarried to the married state is not the only form of translation with which the play is concerned, and I shall consider the idea less in relation to the lovers than to the labourers, or mechanicals, and especially Bottom. 'Bless thee, Bottom, bless thee', says Peter Quince at a climactic moment, 'Thou art translated' (III.i.113). But Bottom is a translator as well. I shall look at both roles, and I start with the passive rather than the active.

At the moment of his translation, Bottom's appearance wearing an ass's head comes to Quince and his fellows as a total, and unwelcome, surprise. It is a surprise for the audience, too, though one for which there has been, in Shakespeare's usual manner, a good deal of subtextual preparation. We know of Oberon's plot to drop the liquor of love-in-idleness on Titania's eyes so that

> The next thing then she waking looks upon—
> Be it on lion, bear, or wolf, or bull,
> On meddling monkey, or on busy ape—
> She shall pursue it with the soul of love. (II.i.179–82)[1]

We have seen him squeeze the juice on her eyes with the invocation,

> What thou seest when thou dost wake,
> Do it for thy true love take;
> Love and languish for his sake.
> Be it ounce, or cat, or bear,
> Pard, or boar with bristled hair,
> In thy eye that shall appear,
> When thou wak'st, it is thy dear.
> Wake when some vile thing is near. (II.ii.33–40)

More recently, we have seen Robin Goodfellow moving invisibly among the mechanicals at their rehearsal, looking for mischief—'I'll be an auditor—/ An actor too, perhaps, if I see cause'—and then following Bottom off stage with the threat that at his re-entry he will appear 'A stranger Pyramus than e'er played here'. Bottom, in training to translate himself into Pyramus, has gone supposedly into the hawthorn-brake that serves him and his fellows as a tiring-house, but presumably, in Shakespeare's theatre, into the actual tiring-house. He re-enters a few moments later '*with the Asse head*', as the Folio direction has it, and speaking the ironically appropriate words, 'If I were fair, fair Thisbe, I were only thine' (II.ii.98).

Around thirty different animals have so far been named in the play, but Shakespeare has cunningly refrained from having anyone speak of an ass until the moment of Bottom's translation. For the audience, this is a moment that permits a reaction at least partly comic: we see now where Oberon's plot is leading, it seems appropriate enough that Bottom, like his close relative Dogberry, should be writ down an ass,[2] and we have the pleasure of observing the theatrical mechanics of the transformation. A history of asses' heads in *A Midsummer Night's Dream* would form an entertaining chapter of theatre history in itself. Trevor R. Griffiths provides a concise survey in his 'Shakespeare in Production' edition,[3] and the variety of expedients that have been adopted, ranging from realistic full heads with working ears and mouths to mere skull caps with ears attached, bears witness to the fact that this is not an easy moment to bring off effectively. Partly this is because Shakespeare, as often in his early plays, does little to integrate action into dialogue. The translation of Bottom into an ass is abrupt; nor is it total. Bottom needs to look enough like an ass for us to sympathize with those who believe him to have been transformed, but at the same time the actor has to be perceptible enough for us to register facial expression.

William C. Carroll, in his excellent study *The Metamorphoses of Shakespearean Comedy*, describes Bottom's translation as 'the only onstage physical man-to-beast transformation in all of Shakespeare's plays',[4] but of course it is not an 'on-stage transformation', which would be impossible to achieve in the theatre, at least without technical means that were not at Shakespeare's disposal. Bottom has to go off stage to don the ass's head, and from the neck downwards he remains the actor playing Bottom. At the moment of his reappearance everything depends on visual effect, and although for the audience the effect may be comic, for Quince and his fellows it is one of consternation. A nice balance needs to be struck. If we are to have any sense that Bottom's colleagues have reason to be frightened we must at least momentarily share their fear. In their simplicity, Bottom's friends believe that he truly has been metamorphosed as the result of supernatural agency. 'O monstrous! O strange! We are haunted. Pray, masters; fly, masters: help!' says Quince on first seeing the man-ass, and he and his fellows (possibly but not certainly with Bottom too[5]) run off in a fear which will be all the more genuinely funny if it also seems real. And then Robin exults in his success in words which portray himself as the arch shape-changer; for him, translation is effortless:

> I'll follow you, I'll lead you about a round,
>   Through bog, through bush, through brake, through brier.

> Sometimes a horse I'll be, sometime a hound,
>   A hog, a headless bear, sometime a fire,
> And neigh, and bark, and grunt, and roar, and burn,
> Like horse, hound, hog, bear, fire at every turn. (III.i.101–06)

As the bolder of the mechanicals recover their nerve, they lurk back to test the evidence of their eyes. First is Snout:

> O Bottom, thou art changed. What do I see on thee?

And then Quince:

> Bless thee, Bottom, bless thee. Thou art translated.

There is an element of potential paradox in the wording of this reaction. Quince does not say, 'Bless me, here's a donkey, where has Bottom gone?', but unequivocally addresses what he sees as 'Bottom'. Bottom may be 'translated', but he is not transmuted. Just as a passage of prose or verse translated into a different language both is and is not what it originally was, so, to Quince, Bottom is still recognizably Bottom; similarly, the volumes of Ovid's *Metamorphoses*, both in the original Latin and in Golding's English version which no doubt lay open on Shakespeare's desk as he wrote, were recognizable to him as things that both are and are not the same.

The word 'translated' would have had a range of possible meanings for Shakespeare's early audiences. Of course it could mean 'rendered from one language into another', as on Golding's title page—'translated oute of/ *Latin into English meeter, by A-r/*thur Golding Gentleman', but that is only metaphorically appropriate here. It could signify simply 'changed' in one way or another, but the fact that Snout has already used that word suggests an element of intensification in Quince's usage. The word could also have more elevated senses, including 'transformed' or 'transmuted', and even 'carried or conveyed to heaven without death', and the hint of the supernatural would have been supported by Quince's exhortation to his companions to pray, and by his words 'Bless thee, bless thee', which might well have been heard as more than a conventional expression of good wishes, and might indeed have been emphasized by Quince's making the sign of the cross and/or falling to his knees. The brief episode may then have been given—may still be given—a quality of awe and wonder as the result of the verbal and gestural reactions of those who witness it.

The fact is that more than one sense of the word 'translated' is felt simultaneously here. To Bottom's fellows, he is changed yet remains Bottom, rather as the story of Pyramus and Thisbe is still the same story whether it is told in Latin or in English, or in narrative or dramatic form. On one level Bottom is, we might say, a simile rather than a metaphor. To himself, he is a bilingual edition, with the original at the foot of the page and the translation at the head: he is Bottom to the extent that he has recognized his friends and can apparently speak to them in their own language (though there may be some question about this, since Shakespeare cannot avoid using this language if he is to remain in communication with his audience, and Bottom's fellows do not respond directly to what he says); but he is an ass to the extent that on his next appearance he has a longing for 'good dry oats' and a 'bottle of hay'. And out of this incongruity much mirth comes.

For Titania, however, Bottom is translated in the most elevated sense of the word: roused from her drugged sleep by his singing, she asks what angel has woken her from her flowery bed, while acknowledging that he has enough dregs of mortality in him for her to need to 'purge' his 'mortal grossness' so that he may 'like an airy spirit go'. For her, his translation resembles that of a literary work which so far transcends the original as to constitute an entirely new creation, like, perhaps, *The Rubáiyát of Omar Khayyám*. And Bottom, too, readily accepts a sense of new identity, very much as does Christopher Sly in the Induction to *The Taming of the Shrew*; just as Sly is ministered by the Lord's servants, so Bottom yields to the pleasurable attentions of Titania's attendant fairies, Peaseblossom, Cobweb, Mote and Mustardseed. But Titania belongs to the world of spirits, not of mortal beings, and Bottom, thus translated, enters her exalted sphere. Though Titania and her fairies address him still as a mortal he enjoys immortal privileges. Paul Hardwick beautifully conveyed this in Peter Hall's 1962 Stratford production, of which

The Times wrote that he was 'quietly discovering unexpected truths about life, as when he accepts modestly but with respectful rapture the embraces of Titania and the homage of her fairy attendants'.[6]

Whether Bottom's privileges include physical union with the fairy queen has been a debating point among critics. David Young thought not,[7] but Carroll, citing Titania's words 'Tie up my lover's tongue, bring him silently', remarks 'I find this last line explicit: Titania is tired of Bottom's voice, and wants him now to perform.'[8] Directors of recent productions—some taking their cue from Jan Kott's well-known assessment of the sexual equipment of the ass: 'Since antiquity and up to the Renaissance the ass was credited with the strongest sexual potency and among all the quadrupeds is supposed to have the longest and hardest phallus'[9]—have been only too ready to agree. Perhaps the best-known image of Peter Brook's famous production is the photograph of David Waller as Bottom with another actor's forearm, fist clenched, rampant between his legs, a moment which in the theatre brought the first part of the play to an exultant conclusion as confetti fluttered down and the band played a snatch of Mendelssohn's wedding march.

Later directors have been even more explicit, representing before the tiring-house wall action which Shakespeare's audience was at the most expected to imagine happening behind it. In Adrian Noble's Stratford version of 1994, for example, Titania beckoned Bottom into the large upturned umbrella that represented her bower, and as it ascended we were treated to the sight of Desmond Barrit's ample posterior lunging energetically up and down in a manner that left the relationship unequivocally sexual. Critics have taken the same tack, to such an extent that 1994 saw the publication of an article by T. B. Boecher entitled 'Bestial Buggery in *A Midsummer Night's Dream*' and beginning with the words 'Although no one has paid much sustained attention to the fact, *A Midsummer Night's Dream* is patently about bestiality.'[10] This substantial, well written and scholarly piece is supported by an Appendix, 'Bestiality and the Law in Renaissance England', providing statistical tables on 'Indictments for bestial buggery in the reigns of Elizabeth I and James I' and

'Animals abused in English Renaissance bestiality indictments'. (The author manfully suppresses any disappointment he may have felt that the list includes no asses.)

The emphasis upon sexuality has no doubt occurred as the result of a reaction against sentimentalizing interpretations, but perhaps it is not unreasonable to suggest that the winsome phrase 'Bestial buggery' affords, to say the least, an imprecise response to the text's tonal register. Even critics heavily committed to a post-Freudian approach have demurred. Though there is truth in Boecher's claim that 'the spectacle of Titania and Bottom embracing and sleeping together comes as close to enacted sexual intercourse as any scene in Shakespearean comedy', intercourse is at most to be inferred; we should perhaps remember that Bottom is not really an ass and that Titania is a fairy, and that she has declared her intention to turn Bottom into the likeness of 'an airy spirit' by purging his 'mortal grossness'—words not quoted by Boecher. And, whatever Titania's fantasies may be, Bottom gives no signs of actively sharing them. He may acquiesce in her embraces, but even Jan Kott has dissociated himself from Brook's emphasis upon sexuality, remarking that 'in the spectacle staged by Peter Brook and many of his followers which emphasizes Titania's sexual fascination with a monstrous phallus (*mea culpa!*), the carnival ritual of Bottom's adventure is altogether lost'. Bottom, says Kott, 'appreciates being treated as a very important person, but is more interested in the frugal pleasure of eating than in the bodily charms of Titania'.[11] And James L. Calderwood has written 'Surely a good part of Oberon's punishment of Titania centres in the physical and metaphysical impossibility of a fairy Queen to couple with an ass.'[12] To which it is worth adding that if the coupling does occur, Oberon has connived in his own cuckolding. If Bottom and Titania do make love, they do it as fairies—or, to quote another of Titania's epithets for Bottom—as angels do. However that may be.

It is also relevant that the relationship is presented as occurring in a dream—or, to use the word that both Titania and Bottom deploy, in a vision. The actor has the opportunity to convey something of this by a shift in consciousness during Bottom's scenes in the fairy court. More, I suppose, than any other character in Shakespeare, Bottom has often been played by performers associated with music hall and popular theatre—Stanley Holloway and James Cagney, Frankie Howerd and Tommy Steele among them. There is no reason why the comic skills of such performers should not be harnessed to the role, and some of them, such as Frankie Howerd, appear to have revealed new sides to their talent in doing so. But the potential range of the role fits it also for the talents of great actors of the 'legitimate' theatre, as Ralph Richardson appears to have demonstrated particularly in these scenes in an Old Vic production of 1931. According to James Agate,

> In the fairy scenes he abandoned clowning in favour of a dim consciousness of a rarer world and of being at court there. This was new to me, and if Mr Richardson had not the ripeness of some of the old actors, his acting here was an agreeable change from the familiar refusal to alternate fruitiness with anything else. Most of the old players seem to have thought that Bottom, with the ass's head on, was the same Bottom only funnier. Shakespeare says he was 'translated', and Mr Richardson translated him.[13]

'Twenty years later', as Griffiths notes, Richardson's 'performance was still being invoked as a benchmark':

> no one before Richardson, and no one after him either, guessed that there was in this weaver so deep a well of abused poetry, such an ineradicable vision of uncomprehended wonder.[14]

For Titania, Bottom's presence at her court is a fantasy induced by Oberon's love potion, and when Oberon has achieved his aim of subduing her and persuading her to return the Indian boy, he reverses the potion's effect. Bottom, still in his (possibly postcoital) sleep, has to be translated back from ass to man, and this translation takes place on stage, as Robin removes the ass-head at Oberon's behest. For the audience the effect is instantaneous, but Bottom, like the lovers, sleeps on, receding from our consciousness through Oberon and Titania's dance of reconciliation, the formal entry of Theseus with Hippolyta and 'all his train', the awakening of the lovers, Theseus's overriding of Egeus's objections to the marriage of Hermia and Lysander, and the lovers' reflections on their dream.

When Bottom wakes it seems at first that no time has elapsed since his translation: 'When my cue comes, call me, and I will answer.' But then he remembers he has had a dream, and starts to try to recall it. He fails, as we all fail when we try to translate our dreams into language. But he knows he has had an experience 'past the wit of man' to translate. He alone among the mortals of the play has had direct communion with the inhabitants of fairyland. He alone has been translated into a higher sphere, if only temporarily.

But the lovers, if they have not actually seen inhabitants of the fairy world, have been unknowingly touched by it and, like Bottom, undergo a form of translation. Roused by Theseus's hunting horns, they have given classic poetic expression to the sensation of being suspended between sleep and waking, between the unconscious world of dreams and earthly reality, in lines that figure Quince's state of mind on beholding the translated Bottom—and which, we might also suggest, portray the state of mind of a translator struggling to formulate, in a new language, thoughts that have already reached poetic form in the language from which he is translating:

> *Demetrius:* These things seem small and undistinguishable,
> Like far-off mountains turnèd into clouds.
> *Hermia:* Methinks I see these things with parted eye,
> When everything seems double.
> *Helena:* So methinks,
> And I have found Demetrius like a jewel,
> Mine own and not mine own.
> *Demetrius:* It seems to me
> That yet we sleep, we dream. (IV.i.186–92)

To the lover, the beloved is both a possession and something that can never be possessed, just as a poem is something that can be translated yet never loses its own perfection of identity. It is a paradox that lies at the heart of artistic creation; no wonder Benjamin Britten makes a vocal quartet based on this dialogue a highspot of his opera, dwelling repeatedly and lovingly on the phrase 'mine own, and not mine own'. Here a great composer was translating Shakespeare's portrayal of translation in an act of what Inga-Stina Ewbank has called 'collusive re-creation' which, characteristically of good translation, adds a new dimension to the original.[15]

Bottom's struggle to dredge from the ooze of his subconscious mind the jewels that lie there embedded is more effortful but no less genuine. At first he thinks no time has passed, then simply that he has slept:

> When my cue comes, call me, and I will answer … God's my life, stolen hence, and left me asleep?

But then the wisp of a memory supervenes:

> I have had a most rare vision. I have had a dream past the wit of man to say what dream it was. Man is but an ass if he go about to expound this dream.

Bottom's metaphorical use of the word 'ass' appears to trigger his residual memory of the state of being in which he believed himself truly to be an ass.

> Methought I was—there is no man can tell what. Methought I was, and methought I had—but man is but a patched fool if he will offer to say what methought I had.
> (IV.i.205–06)

The effort at translation is too great, and he abandons it. But the effort has been made, and it is the sense this gives us that Bottom, for all his asininity, is—like Caliban—capable of having, and of trying to put into words, a vision which lifts the role from clownishness to greatness. At least it does if the actor lets it. It did in 1853, when Samuel Phelps played Bottom:

> He was still a man subdued, but subdued by the sudden plunge into a state of unfathomable wonder. His dream clings about him, he cannot sever the real from the unreal, and still we are made to feel that his reality itself is but a fiction.[16]

In some productions, Bottom has discovered about his person a tangible reminder of his dream life—a wisp of hay or a flower, for example.[17] I remember a production in Victorian style at Nottingham when Bottom's departure after his 'dream' was most touchingly marked with that phrase from Mendelssohn's incidental music which has a dying fall symbolizing the power of dream.

But not all actors approach the speech in so romantic a fashion. Everything rests on the nuance given to the words 'methought I had' and the pause that follows. The innocent, and once traditional, interpretation is that Bottom is simply recalling his ass's ears. But directors keen to demonstrate explicit sexual awareness allow their actor, by facial expression or gesture, a leer, a wiggle, or a movement of the hand, to imply that Bottom is coyly avoiding saying 'methought I "had" Titania', or 'methought I had a penis of the proportions ascribed by Jan Kott to the ass'; Desmond Barrit's peering down the front of his pants at this point in Adrian Noble's production meant even more to members of the audience who remembered Jan Kott's remark than to those who did not. One cannot say that this is wrong; but one can say that by narrowing the focus on to the physical it denies the spirituality of Bottom's translation—renders it, so to speak, with a four-letter word.

Bottom's last speech before vanishing into the hawthorn brake is given in the character of Pyramus; his translation comes as an involuntary interruption to a willed attempt at another kind of translation on which he and his fellows were engaged at the moment of his ascent into asininity. When we first see them they are embarking on the task of translating into stage action the pre-existing script of *The Most Lamentable Comedy and Most Cruel Death of Pyramus and Thisbe*, and we are left in no doubt that they find the task difficult. The first stage is the assignment of the roles into which each of the performers will endeavour to translate himself, and this introduces the need for deliberate physical transformation. Flute as Thisbe may, Quince tells him, hide his incipient beard—if it truly exists—with a mask; and Bottom boasts of a virtuosic capacity to modulate his voice according to the varied demands of the roles, from Thisbe to

Lion, that he aspires to undertake. He appears, too, to have access to a rich collection of false beards (which in some productions he has brought with him).[18]

Once rehearsals get under way, the actors discover that before the text of the play can be translated into stage action certain modifications must be made in order to fit it for performance 'before the Duke' and his ladies. There are episodes, such as Pyramus's drawing a sword to kill himself, 'that will never please'. Starveling fears that the problem can be solved only by cutting the text: 'I believe we must leave the killing out, when all is done.' But Bottom proposes instead to make an addition to the text: 'Write me a prologue, and let the prologue seem to say we will do no harm with our swords, and that Pyramus is not killed indeed.' Additional lines must be written, too, to mitigate the terror of Lion's appearance, and as the rehearsal proceeds the need becomes apparent even to write in two additional characters, Moonshine and Wall, each of them to be represented by an actor who will make adjustments to his personal appearance in the attempt to 'disfigure, or present' the character.

The rehearsal scenes in *A Midsummer Night's Dream* offer a copybook demonstration by Shakespeare himself of the instability of the dramatic text. As the Folio text of the play shows (in its changes of word and stage directions from the Quarto text, in its substitution of one character—Egeus—for another—Philostrate—in the last act, and in its re-allocation of certain lines of dialogue), in the course of its translation from authorial manuscript to promptbook Shakespeare's own text underwent exactly the same kinds of changes, if on a smaller scale, as the play within the play. This makes it all the more surprising that scholars were so long resistant to the notion that variant texts of Shakespeare's plays demonstrate theatrical revision; and the fact that we cannot be sure whether Peter Quince, who makes himself responsible for the additions to the text of *Pyramus and Thisbe*, is the original author of the play, or merely its director with a talent, like some modern directors—John Barton is the most distinguished example—for literary pastiche, reflects our uncertainty whether changes in the texts of Shakespeare's own plays were made by Shakespeare himself, by members of his company, or collectively.

The actors' attempts to translate their text into action are hampered in part by their literalism, and by their expectations of a similar literalism in their audience. The ladies, they fear, will be so totally illuded by what they see that they will take it for reality, so a prologue must assure them, not only that 'Pyramus is not killed indeed', but that Pyramus is not Pyramus 'but Bottom the weaver'; similarly Snug must tell the ladies that he is 'a man, as other men are', and 'indeed name his name, and tell them plainly he is Snug the joiner'. And their audience cannot be relied upon to imagine the moonlight by which Pyramus and Thisbe meet, and the wall through which they talk—as Shakespeare's own audience was required to imagine the moonlight by which Oberon has met Titania, and, so far as we can tell, the 'orchard wall' that Romeo is said to have overleapt in *Romeo and Juliet* (II.i.5)—but must be confronted with an actor in the person of Moonshine and Wall. This literalism is akin to that of a literary translator who, in an over-zealous effort to render a text's substance, fails to convey its spirit. It can be amended only by imagination, and Shakespeare is careful to preface Theseus's wedding entertainment with the discussion between the Duke and Hippolyta about the power of imagination. This is offered as a reaction to the lovers' account of their enchanted night, and Theseus's view—perhaps surprisingly in view of attitudes he will later express—is sceptical; it is Hippolyta who acknowledges that the transformation in the lovers bears witness, not simply to fancy, but to the transmuting power of imagination:

> all the story of the night told over,
> And all their minds transfigured so together,
> More witnesseth than fancy's images,
> And grows to something of great constancy. (V.i.23–26)

In the play's terms, then, a real-life translation has been successfully effected. We are about to see whether the fictional translation of text into performance will similarly succeed; and the omens are not good.

The potentially damaging effects of unskilful theatrical translation are made apparent even in advance of the performance in the reported reactions of Philostrate (or Egeus) to the rehearsal which he has attended as part of the auditioning procedure for the wedding festivities. The ineptitude of the writing and the unfitness of the players have resulted in an involuntary change of genre, the transformation of a tragedy into a comedy:

> in all the play
> There is not one word apt, one player fitted.
> And 'tragical', my noble lord, it is,
> For Pyramus therein doth kill himself,
> Which when I saw rehearsed, I must confess,
> Made mine eyes water; but more merry tears
> The passion of loud laughter never shed. (V.i.64–70)

In spite of this warning Theseus persists in asking for the play to be performed, and does so in lines anticipative of audience response theory in their suggestion that the spectator has a part to play in the success of the performance. Egeus warns him that the mechanicals' play is

> nothing, nothing in the world,
> Unless you can find sport in their intents
> Extremely stretched, and conned with cruel pain
> To do you service. (V.i.78–81)

But Theseus rejects the warning, with a courtly expression of charity:

> never anything can be amiss
> When simpleness and duty tender it. (V.i.82–83)

Theseus's readiness to exercise imagination may seem surprising after the long speech in which he has spoken dismissively of its powers, but the theme is insistently developed in response to Hippolyta's complaint that she loves 'not to see wretchedness o'er charged,/ And duty in his service perishing'. Theseus proclaims himself as the ideal member of an audience, comparing the efforts of amateur actors to those of 'great clerks'—people, presumably, such as rectors of Elizabethan universities delivering addresses of welcome to their sovereign—who, overwhelmed by the occasion, 'Make periods in the midst of sentences', exactly as Quince is about to do in his delivery of his Prologue. Theseus can, he claims, 'read as much' 'in the modesty of fearful duty' 'as from the rattling tongue/ Of saucy and audacious eloquence'. He rams home the moral with almost priggish ostentation, as if to shame the theatre audience into comparable charity. Shakespeare is preparing us for both the comic incompetence of Bottom and his fellows and the paradoxical skill of the real-life actors who will be required to impersonate incompetence. The audience, like Theseus, has its part to play in the translation process, and Shakespeare not merely tells us but demonstrates that meaning can be apprehended even in a translation so bad that on the surface it means the opposite of what is intended. Although the 'periods' that Quince, shivering and pale, makes in the midst of *his* 'premeditated' sentences cause him to say the opposite of what he means—'All for your delight/ We are not here'—both Theseus and we are able to 'take' what he 'mistake[s]'. His lines simultaneously convey opposed meanings, rather as the translated Bottom both is and is not Bottom, with the result that his audience may both laugh at his ineptitude yet appreciate the good will that lies behind it.

The rehearsal scenes have revealed to us only a few lines of the text of the tragedy. As the performance progresses, it becomes clear that this text is comically inadequate as a translation into dramatic terms of the story of Pyramus and Thisbe. Layers of translation here are complex. The story is a pre-existing one both for the mechanicals and for Shakespeare. Many members of the original audience, too, would have known it. Shakespeare had certainly read it both in the original Latin and in Golding's translation. We are given no clue whether Bottom and his fellows are supposed to have created the script themselves (except for the interpolated lines) or to have purchased a script from the Athenian equivalent of Samuel French. They cannot certainly be held responsible for its ineptitudes. Nevertheless, they are responsible for using it. Part of the comedy, that is, derives from their unawareness of the bathetic inadequacies of the translation into verse drama of the tragic tale they enact—and a director may make something of this unawareness.

Shakespeare, on the other hand, *is* responsible for the badness of the script, and is indeed to be congratulated on it. This is good bad writing—in other words, excellent parody both of Golding's translation (which Shakespeare seems to have regarded with amused admiration, or admiring amusement) and of the literary and dramatic conventions of the interlude writers.[19] In part, the criticisms of the onstage audience are directed at the inadequacies of the script: 'This is the silliest stuff that ever I heard', says Hippolyta. But the spectators are highly conscious, too, of the performers' failure to translate this script convincingly: 'he hath played on this prologue like a child on a recorder—a sound, but not in government.' Indeed they seem to make little distinction between script and performance, in this perhaps reflecting the Elizabethan theatrical scene, where an audience probably considered a play as a company event in which the writer was simply one member of the company, and may have been performing in his own play. Frequently, that is to say, playgoers went, not to see a group of players interpret a script with which they were already familiar, but to enjoy an entirely new event, an experience that was simultaneously literary, dramatic and theatrical.

As the play scene progresses, the mechanicals' efforts at translation sink to ever deeper levels of ineptitude which can be salvaged only by massive doses of good humour, tolerance, and imagination from its onlookers. Primarily, it represents the mechanicals' efforts at active translation, but it climaxes in a representation of passive translation which takes us back to the point earlier in the play at which we saw Bottom turned into an ass. At that point he was rehearsing the role of Pyramus. Now, enacting that role in a manner that, Theseus is to say, might well prove *him* an ass (V.i.306), he finds himself required to represent the character in the process of a translation from the corporeal to the spiritual state, such as he had himself undergone, at least in the eyes of his fellows and of Titania, within the hawthorn brake. After stabbing himself, he describes his elevation:

> Now am I dead,
> Now am I fled,
> My soul is in the sky.
> Tongue, lose thy light,
> Moon, take thy flight,
> Now die, die, die, die, die. (V.i.296–301)

But even here the translation is not complete; before long Bottom arises from the dead to offer an epilogue or a bergomask dance.

One of Shakespeare's most striking uses of the concept of translation occurs in *As You Like It*, when Amiens congratulates Duke Senior on his capacity to 'translate the stubbornness of fortune/ Into so quiet and so sweet a style' (II.i.19–20). It is striking because it encapsulates the very process of comedy itself, a process that is often, as in *A Midsummer Night's Dream*, symbolized by the overcoming of obstacles to marriage. It is a process that can be accomplished only through the exercise of imagination. The last act of *A Midsummer Night's Dream* recapitulates in comic form the turmoils that the lovers have experienced in their efforts at translation, reminds us that fortune can be stubborn; but as bedtime approaches, Oberon and his train, in their blessing on the house, invoke for us the quietness and sweetness that can come with the translation to the married state. And at the very end Robin Goodfellow, calling for our active imaginative collaboration, invites us to think that we 'have but slumbered here,/ While these visions did appear'. Like Bottom, we have been granted a vision; and also like him, we shall be asses if we try to expound it. Men cannot translate dreams into language; but in this play Shakespeare comes pretty close to doing so.

NOTES

1. Quotations and references are to the Oxford *Complete Works*, General Editors, Stanley Wells and Gary Taylor (Oxford: Oxford University Press, 1986, etc).
2. So David P. Young, *Something of Great Constancy: The Art of 'A Midsummer Night's Dream'* (New Haven and London: Yale University Press, 1966), p. 157: 'Bottom changed to an ass is but a short step, a revelation of inner qualities already familiar to us.' Bottom resembles Dogberry in his good qualities, too; both are men of good will.
3. *A Midsummer Night's Dream*, ed. Trevor R. Griffiths (Cambridge: Cambridge University Press, 1996).

4. William C. Carroll, *The Metamorphoses of Shakespearean Comedy* (Princeton, NJ: Princeton University Press), p. 148.

5. See the note to III.i.100 in Peter Holland's Oxford Shakespeare edition (Oxford: Oxford University Press, 1994).

6. *The Times*, 18 April 1962. I owe this reference, and helpful comments, to Roger Warren.

7. Young, *Something of Great Constancy*, p. 157: 'just as the "marriage" is probably never consummated, so is the transformation incomplete'.

8. Carroll, *Metamorphoses*, p. 152.

9. Jan Kott, *The Bottom Translation*, trans. Daniel Miedzyrzecka and Lillian Vallee (Evanston, IL: Northwestern University Press, 1987).

10. T. B. Boecher, 'Bestial Buggery in *A Midsummer Night's Dream*', in *The Production of English Renaissance Culture*, eds D. L. Miller *et al.* (Ithaca and London: Cornell University Press, 1994), pp. 123–50.

11. Kott, *The Bottom Translation*, p. 52.

12. James L. Calderwood, *A Midsummer Night's Dream*, Twayne's New Critical Introductions to Shakespeare (Hemel Hempstead: Harvester Wheatsheaf, 1992), p. 63.

13. *The Sunday Times*, 8 November 1931, quoted by Griffiths, *A Midsummer Night's Dream*, p. 53.

14. Griffiths, *A Midsummer Night's Dream*, p. 60.

15. Inga-Stina Ewbank, 'Shakespeare Translation as Cultural Exchange', *Shakespeare Survey*, 48 (1995), 1–12.

16. Henry Morley, *The Journal of a London Playgoer, 1851–1866* (London: George Routledge, 1866, repr. 1891), pp. 60-61.

17. Various treatments are discussed in Griffiths's note to IV.i.197–211.

18. Griffiths, *A Midsummer Night's Dream*, note to I.ii.71–78.

19. The burlesque elements of the play are discussed in J. W. Robinson, 'Palpable Hot Ice: Dramatic Burlesque in *A Midsummer Night's Dream*', *Studies in Philology*, 61 (1964), 192–204.

Elizabethan Translation: the Art of the Hermaphrodite

JONATHAN BATE

> **Hermaphrodite:** a human being or animal combining characteristics of both sexes; figuratively, a person or thing combining two opposite qualities or functions (usage dating from late Middle English); also, a homosexual, an effeminate man (late sixteenth-century usage, now rare).[1]

The Elizabethans seem to have had a peculiar interest in hybrids, in the crossing of boundaries and the mixture of opposites. Shakespearean comedy celebrates the quasi-hermaphroditic boy actor playing the part of a girl who then dresses as a boy (Rosalind, Viola). The first published version of *The Faerie Queene* ends with the coupling of Amoret and her beloved Sir Scudamour: fused together in 'long embracement', they are 'growne together quite', so that

> Had ye them seene, ye would have surely thought,
> That they had beene that faire *Hermaphrodite*,
> Which that rich *Romane* of white marble wrought,
> And in his costly Bath causd to bee site.[2]

Two beings becoming one in the act of lovemaking is nature's supreme transformation. One and one makes one, and, out of that one, another, a third, is created—or, in the special case which is Shakespeare's speciality, two others, a pair of twins, are created. Spenser's choice of image, though, is from art, not nature: the fused Amoret and Scudamour are compared to a beautifully wrought statue of a hermaphrodite, not an actual hermaphrodite. Nature's transformation is imaged by means of the artist's work of transformation. A statue is both nature (a chunk of marble) and art (a form realized by the work of the artist). It is itself a kind of hermaphrodite.

The Elizabethans were as attentive to any work of art's intensity of artfulness—its *energia*, as Sir Philip Sidney had it—as they were to its truth to nature (its *mimesis*).[3] We might even say that they celebrated an aesthetics of hermaphroditism. After all, what is the key to Shakespeare's endurance if not his extraordinary capacity to appeal to so many different dispositions that he seems to answer perfectly to the definition of the hermaphrodite: 'a person or thing combining two opposite qualities or functions'? The combination of opposites is the Shakespearean hallmark which has variously been called his 'negative capability', his 'seventh-type ambiguity', his 'principle of indetermination'.[4]

If Shakespeare had a kindred spirit in sixteenth-century Europe, if there was a mind which resembled Will's even as it worked in a different medium, that spirit, that mind surely belonged to Michel de Montaigne. 'Shakespearean contradictions', writes Stephen Greenblatt, 'are more often reminiscent of the capacious spirit of Montaigne, who refused any systematic order that would betray his sense of reality.'[5] One of the contradictions represented by both Montaigne and Shakespeare is that they had minds of supreme originality, yet they were both committed to an art of translation. The vast majority of Shakespeare's works are translations—in the sense of Latin *translationes*, carryings across—of the writings of others, whether chroniclers and historians, or classical poets, or romancers and old playwrights. As for Montaigne, almost all his essays are woven together into a tapestry of allusions and quotations, redeployments of the wisdom of his admired masters among the classics.

Montaigne was as fluent in Latin as he was in French, so he could read his beloved Seneca and Ovid—whom Shakespeare also loved and freely translated—with ease in their original tongue. But Greek was a much harder matter: Plutarch, says Montaigne, only became a favourite 'since he spake French', that is to say, since the appearance of translations of his *Lives* (1559) and *Moralia* (1572) by Jacques Amyot, bishop of Auxerre. Contemporaneous scholars criticized Amyot for his philological inaccuracies, but Montaigne knew by instinct that Father Jacques had caught the spirit of his original:

> I have no skill of the Greeke, but I see thorowout al his translation a sense so closely-joynted, and so pithily-continued, that either he hath assuredly understood and inned the very imagination, and the true conceit of the Author, or having through a long and continuall conversation, lively planted in his minde a generall Idea of that of *Plutarke*, he hath at least lent him nothing that doth belye him, or mis-seeme him.[6]

True translation, Montaigne implies, is an art less of philological exactitude than of creative conversation. The true translator 'ins' or enters the imagination of the foreign author in order to convey the 'Idea' of him (in the platonic sense of the word), whilst at the same time he produces 'closely-joynted' sense and pithy phraseology that are worthy of his own language. Amyot is to be thanked for presenting to his country the invaluable gift of Plutarch. In 1579, Sir Thomas North passed the gift on to the English nation by, to adapt Montaigne's phrase, teaching Plutarch to speak English. In so doing, he made possible the Roman plays of Shakespeare.

In Elizabethan England the 'conversation' was such that translation and original creation were not readily distinguishable from one another. Nowhere is this hybridity more apparent than in the bejewelled body of late sixteenth-century erotic narrative poems that are based on stories in the *Metamorphoses*. With their appearance, Ovid may be said to have spoken English. Where the tendency of literary translation in the 1560s to 1580s had been to focus on the dignifying of the English tongue and the appropriation of high Roman values, the genre of erotic narrative poem or 'minor epic' may be read as a reaction against the literature of exemplary history, patriotism and ethical severity, exactly as Ovid himself wrote in reaction against Virgil's elevated Augustanism.[7]

In the Elizabethan Ovidian tradition of which Marlowe's *Hero and Leander* and Shakespeare's *Venus and Adonis* are the most celebrated products, *amor* overrides *virtus*. Love is confusing and painful, but desire also proves to be comic and undignified.

'Perverse it shall be where it shows most toward', says Shakespeare's Venus in her curse on love (*Venus and Adonis*, 1157): contrariness is the key. That contrariness returns us to the idea of doubleness and hence to the hermaphrodite. Marlowe's Leander has the charms of both boy and girl: he is a kind of hermaphrodite. Given what we know of Marlowe's own life, the other late sixteenth-century meaning of the word, homosexual, may be relevant here. Shakespeare's Adonis has a similarly double identity, and indeed Shakespeare made use of Ovid's story of the origin of the Hermaphrodite, as well as the narratives of Adonis and of Narcissus, when writing his poem. I would suggest, then, that it was what I have called the aesthetics of hermaphroditism that drew the witty poets of the 1590s to this body of Ovidian material.

The aesthetic of hermaphroditism is true to the spirit of Ovid and Montaigne. The compositional method is a hybrid of adaptation and new creation—Montaigne's combination of entering the very imagination of an admired source whilst simultaneously stretching the expressive capabilities of one's own native tongue. And the way of looking at the world is also double: often wry, ironic, detached and sceptical, yet when it really matters passionately committed to human vitality with all its foibles.

Late-Elizabethan erotic Ovidian narrative poetry is hermaphroditic at the level of both content and form: in content, because of its relaxed exploration of sexual ambivalence; in form, *because a translation is itself hermaphroditic*. A translated line is written by two authors, the original and the translator. In Montaigne's term, the translator 'ins'—has intercourse with, we might go so far as to say—the original. When Spenser compares Amoret and Scudamour to 'two senceles stocks in long embracement', he fuses himself hermaphroditically with Ovid, who wrote

> *velut, si quis conducat cortice ramos,*
> *crescendo iungi pariterque adolescere cernit,*
> *sic ubi conplexu coierunt membra tenaci*

> Like as if a man should in one barke beholde
> Two twigges both growing into one and still togither holde:

Even so when through hir hugging and hir grasping of the
tother
The members of them mingled were and fastned both
togither. (Arthur Golding's 1567 translation)[8]

This image occurs at the climax of Ovid's story of the mythical origin of the Hermaphrodite. Hermaphroditus, as his hybrid name reveals, is a son of Hermes and Aphrodite. He bathes in a fountain—hence the bath context for Spenser's statue—and Salmacis, the nymph who is its presiding spirit, falls in love with him. Like those other lovely boys, Adonis and Narcissus, Hermaphroditus rejects love. But girl grabs boy, the gods relent, and the two beings are fused into one.

Fittingly, the genre of Ovidian erotic verse came to its climax with an Englishing of this story, published in 1602. Though published anonymously, *Salmacis and Hermaphroditus* is generally regarded as a youthful work of the dramatist Francis Beaumont.[9] It is equally fitting that the poem should have been written by a half-member of the most famous hermaphroditic writing team in English theatre history, Beaumont and Fletcher. Given that *Venus and Adonis* is the obvious model for Beaumont's poem, and that the career of the writer of that poem ended in the hybridity of 'Shakespeare and Fletcher'—hermaphroditic author of *Henry VIII*, *The Two Noble Kinsmen* and the lost *Cardenio*—we could almost indulge in a Shakespearean multiplication and say that the poem is not only by 'Beaumont and Ovid', but also by 'Beaumont and Shakespeare'.

Beaumont's poem is a free translation, interspersed with digressions, of the story that forms lines 274 to 388 of the fourth book of Ovid's *Metamorphoses*. I want to argue here that one of the hermaphroditic qualities of the original Hermaphroditus story is its susceptibility to opposite interpretations. Contained within the Ovidian narrative is a moralized reading—which appealed to Arthur Golding's Puritan leanings—in which the story is an admonition against effeminacy. But also contained within it is a ludic and erotic reading—which appealed to Beaumont's fertile *energia*—in which the story is an unabashed celebration of polymorphous sexuality.

On the surface, the story of Salmacis and Hermaphroditus is

admonitory. The pool of Salmacis is associated with ill fame ('*infamis*'), enervation ('*enervet*') and impure power ('*incesto*' in the final line of the Ovidian narrative is suggestive of an extreme of transgressive hybridity). But, shimmering as Ovid's surface always is, he always asks the reader to stir the waters of the pool.

A cardinal principle in reading the *Metamorphoses* is that we must attend to the teller as well as the tale. Consider, for example, Book Ten. It is a series of tales of destructive love and rapacious female desire, but this is not so much because Ovid thinks love is always destructive and female desire always rapacious as because the narrator, Orpheus, has turned against womankind after his loss of Eurydice. In order to read Salmacis and Hermaphroditus, then, we need to move out from the story itself and consider its context in Book Four of the *Metamorphoses*. A contextualized reading will look very different from the superficially admonitory one. I think that Beaumont perceived this and used it as licence for his celebratory reworking of the narrative.

Ovid's Salmacis and Hermaphroditus is one of a series of intricately interlocked narratives. The narrators of the first half of Book Four of the *Metamorphoses* are the daughters of Minyas. They represent the principle of *resistance to Bacchus*. So what does it mean to resist Bacchus (Dionysus)? The daughters are introduced at the beginning of Book Four; the second half of Book Three has told the story of Pentheus, who has shown the same resistance. At this point in the *Metamorphoses*, Ovid is writing under the strong influence of the most Dionysiac of tragedians, Euripides. To discover the meaning of the resistance, we need to consider what Bacchus means for Ovid.

Upon the arrival of Bacchus, people mingle together and rush out from the city. The influence of the god represents transgression of reason, law and restraint, neglect of the values of civility (*civitas*). Bacchus represents loss of individual identity and social place. He stands for mixing—hermaphroditing, if you will—of gender, ages, ranks. His spirit is that of *conjunction*, a behavioural phenomenon which Ovid renders by means of a grammatical technique, namely the suffix of conjunction. In Latin you can say 'and' either through *et* in the position of the English conjunction or by adding *que* to the end of one of the terms you wish to link. With the arrival of Bacchus in Book Three, Ovid introduces a riot of conjunctions:

> *turba ruit, mixtaeque viris matresque nurusque*
> *vulgusque proceresque ignota ad sacra feruntur.*
> (*Met.* III.529–30)

> The folke runne flocking out by heapes, men, Mayds, and wives togither
> The noble men and rascall sorte ran gadding also thither,
> The Orgies of this unknowne God full fondely to performe. (Golding, III.667–69)

In a stratified society like Ovid's Rome, where distinctions of gender, age and rank (patrician versus plebeian) are the glue that holds the communal order in place, it is dangerous to celebrate these conjunctions. The release and conjunction of women represent a special affront to Roman manhood (*virtus*). Bacchic rites are associated with what Pentheus scornfully calls '*femineae voces*', women's voices (536), rendered by Golding as 'sheepish shriekes of simple women fray'. The bacchantes are emblems of an alternative female power, bearing the thyrsus instead of the arms which are the mark of the male. When Agave hunts down her own son Pentheus, he invokes their ancestor Actaeon, whose demise at the hands of female power has been narrated earlier in Book Three. This book, then, is framed by the paired dismemberments of hunter and legislator.

At the end of the book, Pentheus's severed head and shredded body admonish the people of Thebes into worship of Bacchus. Early in Book Four there will be another of those riots of conjunction. Ovid displays his *energia* by accumulating more *ques* than you would have imagined possible, fusing different groups of women and multiplying names for the god (Golding's English version, alas, can do nothing to convey the effect):

> *parent matresque nurusque*
> *telasque calathosque infectaque pensa reponunt*

turaque dant Bacchumque vocant Bromiumque Lyaeumque
ignigenamque satumque iterum solumque bimatrem ... etc.
(*Met.* IV.9–12)

The women straight both yong and olde doe thereunto obay.
Their yarne, their baskets, and their flax unsponne aside they lay,
And burne to *Bacchus* frankinsence. Whome solemly they call
By all the names and titles high that may to him befall.
As *Bromius*, and *Lyëus* eke, begotten of the flame,
Twice borne, the sole and only childe that of two mothers came. (Golding, IV.11–15)

As the only being who is the child of two mothers (‘*bimatrem*’), Bacchus is an appropriate presider over the book of the Hermaphrodite.

But the book has actually begun with a woman who refuses to set aside her work and follow him into the wild: ‘*At non Alcithoe Minyeias*’ (IV.1); but *not* Alcithoë, daughter of Minyas. She and her sisters dedicate themselves to Pallas, who is a divinity of Greece as opposed to the alien realm represented by Bacchus’ oriental origins, a god of the mind as opposed to the bacchanalian body, a female god with traditionally male qualities as opposed to the male god who associates with the female. The daughters of Minyas remain indoors, within woman’s traditional sphere; they sew, that is to say, they undertake traditional women’s work.

Take woman outside her sphere and you will enter the world of desire and sexual temptation. Surprisingly, in Book Three Ovid had not emphasized the sexual aspect of Pentheus’s attraction to Bacchus—he didn’t follow Euripides down the way of cross-dressing. I suggest that this was so that he could withhold the association of Bacchus with dangerous sexual freedom until Book Four, displacing it from Pentheus and making it the unifying theme of the narratives of the daughters of Minyas.

The first of the tales they tell whilst they ply their household tasks in wilful oblivion of the bacchanalia beyond, is that of Pyramus and Thisbe. But this turns out to be a story which rebounds against their own ideology. The values of *civitas*—the marriage bond associated with the economic security of the household, not with sexual desire—are embodied in the parental prohibition which sends the lovers outside the city walls, into the space of Bacchus. The *energia* of the story is stoked by sustained imagery of fire, ardour, burning love. Desire speaks through the chink in the wall of the body-politic. To leave the city is to break down the wall of civic restraint. The lovers meet at a royal ancestral tomb, the dead Ninus (Bottom's Ninny) thus becoming a figure of buried patriarchy. Admittedly, the narrative only allows Pyramus and Thisbe to come together in death; Alcithoë blocks desire through the agency of the lion. But behind the narratorial denial is an Ovidian celebration of union, again rendered by means of verbal play: the closing words of the tale are '*una requiescit in urna*' (IV.166). The funeral urn's doubling of the lovers' unity celebrates the bond of mutual desire. The superficial meaning of the narrative is that the desire for two to become one is fatal—Renaissance commentators moralized it as a warning against the force of heady young love that goes against parental will—but to see only this in the story of Pyramus and Thisbe would be as if to proffer an anti-Romeo and Juliet reading of their play or a reading of *A Midsummer Night's Dream* that takes the side of Egeus.

According to the hermeneutic of the daughters of Minyas, if two-into-one desire is mortal, then many-into-one desire, as encouraged by Bacchus, is much, much worse. After one sister tells of Pyramus and Thisbe, the next begins with Mars enmeshed in the snares of Venus, the archetypal narrative of female sexual wiles destroying male strength. She then relates how even the sun has been infected by desire ('*cepit amor Solem*', IV.170), narrating a story in which the natural order is triply subverted: Sol enters the apartment of the lovely Leucothoë at night, whereas he should belong to the day, and he snatches a burning kiss whilst metamorphosed into the form of the girl's mother, thus transgressing the orders of both gender and family. The second sister's linked narratives of desire and death lead to a debate among the daughters of Minyas as to whether the gods truly do have metamorphic power. They conclude that some do, but Bacchus does not. At this point, the final sister, Alcithoë, is called upon to tell her tale. Its specific context, then, is a denial of Bacchus' powers. Its subject-matter is that same fear which motivated Pentheus in the previous book: that Bacchus would be the bringer of effeminization.

The *locus* is the pool that effeminizes. Inevitably, it carries the memory of other pools of which we have heard in Book Three: those of Narcissus and of Diana in the Actaeon story, where the unified male self embodied in the figure of the hunter is scattered by the hounds of his own desire. Alcithoë is a worker. She does not approve of Salmacis, nymph of the pool, because the latter is a figure of *ease* ('*otia*' is reiterated in lines 307 and 309). Alcithoë thus reads Salmacis as a dangerous enchantress who weakens man, brings work to a halt, and bends gender. In all these respects, Salmacis is a representative of forces which are manifestly bacchic.

Alcithoë's negative reading is apparent from her comparisons of Salmacis to a serpent, an octopus and choking ivy ('*serpens*', '*polypus*', '*hederae*', IV.362–66). The serpent and the ivy are themselves insignia of the bacchic thyrsis. But does Ovid—does the poem itself—endorse the narrator's negative reading? Isn't the key to the story the author's pleasure in his reversal of literary convention and thus implicitly of civil tradition and order? Ovid seems to take particular delight in his swerve away from prescribed gender roles, as when he offers a gender-reversed improvisation on Odysseus' praise of Nausicaa (*Odyssey*, IV.149ff.). Poets usually undress their women bit by bit, enumerating a succession of body-parts; Ovid frequently does so himself, as, for instance, in the Arethusa narrative (*Met*. V.572ff.). But here he makes the woman the watcher. He reverses the blazon and has Hermaphroditus strip off with a becoming blush (IV.330).

The blazon is a much-favoured poetic device because it is self-performing: the undressing enacts that image-by-image, metaphor-by-metaphor, progression which is the poet's own art. In his description of Hermaphroditus, Ovid's instinct as an artist is to take pleasure in imaging the metamorphosis of a male body into an artwork. His loveliest simile is of Hermaphroditus swimming,

in liquidis translucet aquis, ut eburnea si quis
signa tegat claro vel candida lilia vitro (*Met*. IV.354–55)

And rowing with his hands and legges swimmes in the
water cleare:
Through which his bodie faire and white doth glistringly
appeare,
As if a man an Ivorie Image or a Lillie white
Should overlay or close with glasse that were most pure
and bright. (Golding, IV.436–39)

Into the mayne part of the cristall flood.
Like Iv'ry then his snowy body was,
Or a white Lilly in a cristall glasse.
(Beaumont, *Salmacis and Hermaphroditus*, 862–64)[10]

(As is usually the case, the plainer translation of Beaumont is truer to the original than the fussy Golding.)

It is at this point that Salmacis starts seducing Hermaphroditus. The image of ivory has suggested an analogy with Pygmalion and his statue. The artist's implements—sculpting tool, writing stylus, rhetorical voice—are themselves instruments of seduction. Narratives of this kind always drive us towards *union*. Ovid's linguistic triumph on this occasion, analogous to the '*una*'/'*urna*' play at the climax of Pyramus and Thisbe, is his placing of the word '*una*' alone at the line-opening when the moment of conjunction is finally reached. The word is 'one' alone (notice also how '*mixta*' takes us back to the idea of bacchic minglings), an enactment of achieved hermaphroditism:

nam mixta duorum
corpora iunguntur, faciesque inducitur illis
una. (*Met*. IV.373–75)

The bodies of them twaine
Were mixt and joyned both in one. To both them did
remaine
One countnance. (Golding, IV.462–64)

And in one body they began to grow. (Beaumont, 902)

(The economy of Latin allows a compression that neither translator can quite achieve in English, where '*una*' has to become 'one countnance' or 'one body'.) To Ovid and his readers, this hermaphroditic 'one' will surely seem not a figure of debilitation, as Alcithoë intends it to be, but a recovery of that lost original unitary gender which is mythologically imagined in Plato's *Symposium*.

Alcithoë's reading is most firmly undermined by the action following her story, in which art is metamorphosed into nature: the cloths which the daughters of Minyas have been weaving are transformed into vines of ivy. The presence of the vine signals the advent of Bacchus into the very chamber of the girls who have denied him. He takes on Pygmalion's role of animating an artwork. By the same account, he animates the poem. So it is that the text perforce endorses him and, by implication, Salmacis. The daughters of Minyas, meanwhile, are metamorphosed into bats, symbolic of darkness and the opposite of Bacchus' sunshine rites. If we look at Book Four as a whole, the hermeneutic of Alcithoë and her sisters is turned upside-down: the Pyramus and Thisbe story will be read as a celebration of the transgression of parental and civil control, Salmacis and Hermaphroditus taken as a celebration of gender reversal and fusion.

Since the translator's own art is hermaphroditic—transformational, fusional—it is perhaps to be expected that in loosely Englishing the story of Salmacis and Hermaphroditus, Francis Beaumont followed the anti-Alcithoën reading. 'My wanton lines doe treate of amorous love', he begins (*Salmacis and Hermaphroditus*, line 1). Instead of condemning wantonness in the manner of Alcithoë, the lines proclaim their own allegiance to it. Together with the sexual freedom goes a freedom in the translator's handling of his source material. In the world of this poem, even the goddess Diana falls in love with Hermaphroditus: had he not run away, Beaumont informs us, she would have ceased to be a maid. In another added incident, a nymph steals Hermaphroditus' clothes whilst he is bathing, in order to gaze longer on his nakedness. Where in Ovid the sole focus is Salmacis' desire, in Beaumont the body of Hermaphroditus is the object of universal desire.

Beaumont undertakes an expansive improvisation upon relatively slender materials. In his version, Jove is in love with Salmacis. The girl wants to become a star (don't we all, dear?). Jove goes to ask Astraea to grant this, in a sequence which provides the opportunity for some local satire on the difficulty of gaining access to Justice, a frequent late-Elizabethan complaint. One of the respects in which good translation always has the doubleness of the hermaphroditic aesthetic is that it looks to its own time whilst being true to the spirit of its original.

Astraea, however, is in the midst of sorting out the dispute between Venus, Mars and Vulcan. This allusion to one of the other stories told by the daughters of Minyas suggests Beaumont's alertness to the shape of Ovid's fourth book.[11] Venus reacts tetchily to the arrival of Jove. She doesn't want Salmacis to be a star, for fear the beauty of the nymph will outshine her own light. So she gets Vulcan to agree that if Salmacis is raised to the skies, he will stop supplying Jove with thunderbolts. Fearing the loss of his principal weapon, Jove renounces desire in the name of power. But, as a parting gesture, he doubles the proportions of Salmacis's already considerable beauty. 'This have I heard, but yet scarce thought it true', interjects Beaumont's narratorial voice (356), marking the sequence out as one of his insertions into the original. Only after this (lines 361ff.) does he begin to translate Ovid quite closely. But the joins are for the most part seamless: *Salmacis and Hermaphroditus* is itself a hermaphroditic poem because you cannot readily distinguish between the lines originated by one person, Beaumont, and those translated from another, Ovid.

Before following Ovid to the moment of union, Beaumont inserts a further invented story, which offers an explanation as to how Salmacis and Hermaphroditus came to the same pool. It again ties their narrative to the wider context of Ovid's third and fourth books, since it concerns

an uncouth accident of love
Betwixt great Phoebus and the sonne of Jove,
Light-headed Bacchus: (407–09)

In accordance with the principle that both partners in the central narrative are objects of multiple desire, Bacchus has seen Salmacis and fallen in love with her. He nearly seduces or rapes her, but Phoebus intervenes to save her maidenhead.[12] Bacchus is annoyed, so he goes to Mercury, who has long been hostile to 'that great commaunder of the West,/ Bright-fac't Apollo' (496–97). Mercury steals up and filches the wheels of Apollo's sun-chariot. So Apollo has to go to Salmacis and say that if she can get the wheels back, she will be rewarded with the loveliest boy in the world. She succeeds, and that's the reason why gorgeous girl and lovely boy came to meet at the pool. Beaumont, in true Ovidian fashion, has invented a new myth-within-the-myth. Apollo rides out of the story, whipping his horses to catch up on lost time—that's why the sun dips and reels in red-hot brightness towards the end of the day, then sinks to cool off in the sea—leaving the reader to turn attention to Salmacis' seduction of Hermaphroditus.

Beaumont reverts to his Ovidian text, but expands upon the seduction speech, as Shakespeare had done in *Venus and Adonis* and Marlowe in *Hero and Leander*. Salmacis warns Hermaphroditus of the dangers of resistance to love by reminding him of the watery fate of Narcissus, whom we have met in Ovid's third book. Beaumont's Salmacis woos with 'manly boldnesse', even wishing that she could initiate the act that 'Jove and Læda did' (716, 723). You must not resist love, she says, for everyone feels it, even the gods: 'All know the story of Leucothoë' (770). A negative *exemplum* narrated by the daughters of Minyas in Ovid becomes a positive *exemplum* cited by Salmacis in Beaumont. Such switching of poles is of a piece with the hermaphroditic aesthetic which reaches its height when conventional gender roles are reversed. The girl puts her hand on the man's breast, blazons him, gazes on his nakedness as he bathes. Here Beaumont translates Ovid closely, but when it comes to the final merging there are some significant changes and omissions:

'vicimus et meus est' exclamat nais, et omni
veste procul iacta mediis inmittitur undis,
pugnantemque tenet, luctantiaque oscula carpit,
subiectatque manus, invitaque pectora tangit,
et nunc hac iuveni, nunc circumfunditur illac;

denique nitentem contra elabique volentem
implicat ut serpens, quam regia sustinet ales
sublimemque rapit: pendens caput illa pedesque
adligat et cauda spatiantes inplicat alas;
utve solent hederae longos intexere truncos,
utque sub aequoribus deprensum polypus hostem
continet ex omni dimissis parte flagellis.
perstat Atlantiades sperataque gaudia nymphae
denegat; illa premit commissaque corpore toto
sicut inhaerebat, 'pugnes licet, inprobe,' dixit,
'non tamen effugies. ita, di, iubeatis, et istum
nulla dies a me nec me deducat ab isto.'
vota suos habuere deos; name mixta duorum
corpora iunguntur, faciesque inducitur illis
una. velut, si quis conducat cortice ramos,
crescendo iungi pariterque adolescere cernit,
sec ubi conplexu coierunt membra tenaci,
nec duo sunt et forma duplex, nec femina dici
nec puer ut possit, neutrumque et utrumque videntur.
(*Met.* IV.356–79)

Then rose the water-Nymph from where she lay,
As having wonne the glory of the day,
And her light garments cast from off her skin.
Hee's mine, she cry'd; and so leapt spritely in.
The flattering Ivy who did ever see
Inclaspe the huge trunke of an aged tree,
Let him behold the young boy as he stands,
Inclasp in wanton Salmacis's hands,
Betwixt those Iv'ry armes she lockt him fast,
Striving to get away, till at the last:
Fondling, she sayd, why striv'st thou to be gone?
Why shouldst thou so desire to be alone?
Thy cheeke is never fayre, when none is by:
For what is red and white, but to the eye?
And for that cause the heavens are darke at night,
Because all creatures close their weary sight;
For there's no mortall can so earely rise,
But still the morning waytes upon his eyes.

The earely-rising and soone-singing Larke
Can never chaunt her sweete notes in the darke;
For sleepe she ne're so little or so long,
Yet still the morning will attend her song,
All creatures that beneath bright Cinthia be,
Have appetite unto society;
The overflowing waves would have a bound
Within the confines of the spacious ground,
And all their shady currents would be plaste
In hollow of the solitary vaste,
But that they lothe to let their soft streames sing,
Where none can heare their gentle murmuring.
Yet still the boy, regardlesse what she sayd,
Struggled apace to overswimme the mayd.
Which when the Nymph perceiv'd, she 'gan to say:
Struggle thou mayst, but never get away.
So graunt, just gods, that never day may see
The separation twixt this boy and mee.
The gods did heare her pray'r and feele her woe;
And in one body they began to grow.
She felt his youthfull bloud in every vaine;
And he felt hers warme his cold brest againe.
And ever since was womens love so blest,
That it will draw bloud from the strongest brest.
Nor man nor mayd now could they be esteem'd:
Neither, and either, might they well be deem'd.

(Beaumont, 865–908)

The entwining ivy becomes a witness to the action instead of a simile for Salmacis' wiles. Salmacis herself becomes ivory instead of ivy, and in so doing she is metaphorically fused to Hermaphroditus, for he has already been compared to ivory (*Met.* IV.354; Beaumont, 863, quoted earlier). Beaumont does not translate lines 361–69. Instead, he replaces them with the persuasion to love that makes up his lines 876–94. The serpent and the octopus are thus written out, and in their place a lark is written in. Beaumont's insertion is a celebration of 'appetite', of 'society', of 'overflowing' and escaped confines, of singing, of a recognition of the other. He has Salmacis speak of beauty's need for reflection in another's eye, but this is a reciprocating eye, not a prying one like those of Actaeon and Pentheus. The whole sequence is radiant with the light of Bacchus.

The gods then grant the union, and the pool is transformed, but the final lines suggest a benign metamorphosis, not the debilitating effeminacy with which the daughters of Minyas have tarred the waters: 'And since that time who in that fountaine swimmes,/ A mayden smoothnesse seyzeth halfe his limmes' (921–22). The pool is blest, not cursed. It brings smoothness, not weakness. Allegorically, woman's love is blest because it can draw blood from the strongest male breast (906). The implication is that, far from enervating the body politic, female desire can civilize by assuaging male aggression.

Beaumont's translation is an unashamed celebration of the amorous and the bacchic, the ek-static. It is, to use Montaigne's idiom, a 'conversation' not with the admonitory letter of the tale, as laid down by the daughters of Minyas, but with the creative spirit infused into the verse by Ovid. To follow Montaigne again: Beaumont lends Ovid nothing that belies or mis-seems him. Salmacis has had her will: she has won her argument against 'separation' and in favour of an appetite for society, for dalliance, for sexual union, for conjunction. She has become an admirable hermaphrodite. '*Neutrumque et utrumque videntur*', 'Neither, and either, might they well be deem'd': this should also be what we say of the great translations, when it is asked whether they have been created by an original author or a translator.

Art is a translation of life into special languages with codes of their own. Great art speaks to many different lives because it is responsive to further translations. From one formal medium to another: as when Shakespeare turns an Ovidian tale or a Plutarchan history into a play. From one language to another: as when Florio translates Montaigne or Schlegel translates Shakespeare. From one age to another: as when Ovid's anti-Augustanism speaks to the socially mobile and quick-witted Elizabethans, or when the polymorphous sexual play of 1590s erotic verse speaks to the spirit of sexual freedom and camp which quickened the 1990s. These further translations take their life from a hermaphroditic mingling of multiple agencies—not only translators in the strict sense of bilingual talents, but also all writers and painters, actors and directors, readers and interpreters, who are bold enough to 'in' the very imagination and the true conceit of the authors they admire.

NOTES

1. Definitions based on those in the *New Shorter Oxford English Dictionary*.
2. Edmund Spenser, *The Faerie Queene*, 1590 text, III.xii.46.
3. Sidney, *An Apology for Poetry*, ed. Geoffrey Shepherd (Manchester: Manchester University Press, 1973), *mimesis*: p. 101, *energia*: p. 138. Sidney's English equivalent for the latter term is 'forcibleness'.
4. On these terms, see 'The Laws of the Shakespearean Universe', Ch. 10 of my *The Genius of Shakespeare* (London: Picador; New York: Oxford University Press, 1997).
5. Greenblatt *et al.*, *The Norton Shakespeare based on the Oxford Edition* (New York and London: Norton, 1997), p. 60.
6. 'To morrow is a new day', in *The Essayes of Montaigne*, trans. John Florio (1603), II, 4 (New York: Modern Library, 1933), 320.
7. For introductions to Elizabethan erotic narrative verse, see William Keach, *Elizabethan Erotic Narratives: Irony and Pathos in the Ovidian Poetry of Shakespeare, Marlowe, and their Contemporaries* (New Brunswick: Rutgers University Press, 1977), and Ch. 2 of my *Shakespeare and Ovid* (Oxford: Clarendon Press, 1993). On the historical and political orientation of earlier Elizabethan translation, see C. H. Conley, *The First English Translators of the Classics* (New Haven: Yale University Press, 1927) and Eleanor Rosenberg, *Leicester: Patron of Letters* (New York: Columbia University Press, 1955).
8. *Metamorphoses*, IV.375–77. All Ovid quotations are from the 3rd Loeb edition (London: Heinemann; Cambridge, MA: Harvard University Press, 1977). Golding's 1567 translation quoted from *Shakespeare's Ovid, being Arthur Golding's Translation of the Metamorphoses*, ed. W. H. D. Rouse (London: Centaur Press, [1904] 1961), IV.464–67. All quotations from Golding are from this edition.
9. The poem was reprinted in 1640 with a firm attribution to Beaumont.
10. Quotations from the text in *Elizabethan Minor Epics*, ed. Elizabeth Story Donno (New York: Columbia University Press; London: Routledge and Kegan Paul, 1963).

11. As does a passage in which Phoebus Apollo, the sun god, slips out from the bed of Leucothoë in order to dally with Salmacis. Leucothoë was the unfortunate girl in the tale told by Leuconoë, the second daughter of Minyas. The near-doubling of names between narrator and protagonist is another aspect of Book Four's broader interest in quasi-hermaphroditic fusion of identities.

12. Renaissance mythographers tended to conflate Sol and Phoebus Apollo into a single figure of the sun god. The identification suggests that the subnarrative here offers a parallel with, but also a variation upon, Sol's intervention in Leuconoë's story of Leucothoë: in that sequence of Ovid's fourth book, Sol is both a seducer/rapist and a protector, whereas here those roles are divided between Bacchus and Phoebus.

From Stage to Page: Character through Theatre Practices in *Romeo and Juliet*

LYNETTE HUNTER
and PETER LICHTENFELS

The question that we would like to open up in this essay is how can we talk about 'character'. Working together on an edition of *Romeo and Juliet*, one of us being a theatre director and the other a literary critic, we have found that an area where vocabularies clash most often is that of attributing motivation to the characters' roles. This emerges most clearly in the translation of these roles from the page to the stage but attribution of motives can be informed by a reversed translation from stage practice to reading strategy. Such attribution immediately calls into play the recent critiques in literary criticism of individuality made by discourse studies, the developing field of 'subjectivity' or subject positions within ideology, or the recent emergence of standpoint theory to discuss authenticity and autobiography.[1] 'Character' is in effect a highly problematic term, generating accusations of unselfconscious essentialism. Possibly the most telling critique has been that of Margreta de Grazia and Peter Stallybrass, who argue that characters are all too often 'imagined as having developed prior to and independent of the plays in which they appear and as speaking a language that reflects this experiential and psychological history'.[2] So it has to be said, that our underlying concern with 'translation' is one that transposes between the vocabularies of the theatre and those of the literary critic. However, in this essay what we would like specifically to explore are methods that the actor uses for translating a part from the page into an engaged and engaging individual on the stage. In so doing, we hope to address some of the unease felt by literary critics who dismiss 'character' as a matter of 'filling up stage prefixes'.[3]

The theatre director and the actor have to find reasons for everything the part tells them is done on stage and frequently turn to 'character'. This is particularly important with a play that offers conventionally recognizable roles, that encourage the audience to expect specific habits and movements of behaviour, as many of Shakespeare's plays do in drawing on medieval typology. But no part, however conventional, can be effectively acted by way of habit or tricks of the trade, and productions are always in danger of reducing type to stereotype. Moreover, the familiarity or distance that the people in a modern audience have from a particular type can play a large part in how much they themselves want to invest that type with character. *Romeo and Juliet* is a play of intense generic diversity, with types from the Petrarchan sonnet, from Commedia dell'Arte, and from the Latin satirists, continually disrupting the narrative flow and threatening to reduce it to farce. Indeed, Quarto one (Q1) focuses so clearly on the central romantic narrative that it shuts out the larger world of social and political commentary which Quarto two (Q2) makes available, and can easily slip from tragic dimensions into cliché.[4] The whole question of whether Q1 was 'transposed' into Q2, or the other way around, is of course a major issue in Shakespearean studies.[5] But what is clear is that the two versions of the play offer different approaches to character, and they offer differing resources to the actor developing an individual, with Q2 resolutely undermining any sense of a singular identity. In this essay we will focus on the resources found in Q2, and for two specific parts that are often reduced to stereotype.

We would argue that, like some readings, many productions founder on the idea of type and stereotype, by refusing to look past the superficial convention that predicts why the parts do certain things toward the work that actors have to do on finding out why they are doing and saying those particular things. Characters in Shakespeare's plays are frequently types that are delineated by historical studies either in contemporary theatrical traditions or in the many Early Modern books on conduct; but, by stereotype, we want to connote the often crude anachronistic reduction of type to predictable portrayal of habitual behaviour that can occur both in the theatre and in criticism. The generic instability of *Romeo and Juliet* asks the director and the actors to work on character, to use an old-fashioned phrase, to bring the parts to life, that is, to translate from page to stage by reinvention rather than by mere copying. For a director, character is a mask to be inhabited by a person. Character is brought alive through breath. Because the text poses structures to be resolved by breath, there has to be a person involved.[6] Directors may realize that they are producing fictions, but as a director you cannot read the text as a fiction alone because that does not solve the problem that, to let the line of words live, it has to pass through people.[7] No good actor makes the mistake of thinking that their character is a 'real' person but the text is brought alive by way of real people. If the character moves an audience, it is the actor playing the role who produces that effect. There is a point where directors and actors lose the definition of the words 'character' and 'actor' and work differently from the literary critic.

This essay will go on to look at a few scenes with parts based on types that are, to varying degrees, recognizable in twentieth-century drama, the Friar and more particularly the Nurse, and which are played with varying frequency as conventional and predictable. The exploration will look at how the process of acting and directing can insist on character rather than stereotype. It will be carried out by close technical analysis of the details of a few scenes, both their textual qualities and how these translate into potential performance, and how that translation can reinform the page of literary criticism. The kinds of transpositional strategies that we will be discussing belong to work found in rehearsal, in which actors have to acquire, primarily through breath, and therefore in their bodies, their physical presence, movement and voice, and also, in response to the presence of other people on stage, physiological memory of a large number of actions and speakings that have generated reasons for the words and movements. The introductory study of the Friar will foreground work on breath, and the more extended analysis of the Nurse will extend from breath into interaction with other characters.

When actors play a part, they need that physical memory[8] so that they can, at one and the same time, have the experience to perform, push the character through their bodies, and play the line as if it is the first time it is uttered and they do not know what will happen next. As Cicely Berry says, acting is 'at its best when the thoughts are discovered at the moment of speaking'.[9] The actors' task is to let the words surprise them every time they are played, so that they acquire what we refer to as 'weight'. Weight is not necessarily significance but a potential for the constitution of meaning. Actors who are not putting themselves through the present moment of the words will leave those words dead, and therefore dead for the audience. On stage, an actor only has enough time for the task at hand, and all the work in rehearsal has simply been preparation for getting that double-edged freedom of finding the word in performance. All the strategies discussed below are, therefore, in preparation for acting and, if at times they move toward finding motivation and at others precisely toward disrupting it, once on stage actors have to be able to perform the motivation of character moment by moment,[10] surprising themselves with the reasons released by the words and action.

The Friar in *Romeo and Juliet* is probably the part most often reduced to stereotype, and the lines for this character are among the most frequently cut from modern productions. We would here like to focus on an analysis of I.iii to introduce some of the ways in which rehearsal skills for developing a part through breath can help the actor to work on character, to effect a creative transposition from the type of the text to the moving presence of a theatrical actualization. The sententiousness of the Friar's vocabulary and the rhyming couplets in which he initially speaks are difficult to work with in the theatre. They can lead easily to a cliché of the boring, fusty, platitudinous priest. In the earlier sources the Friar is possibly like this, but Shakespeare changes the role, shortens it, makes it more to the point, and still leaves the actor with a lot of work to do. Actors faced with this work need to discover the reasons in the language for themselves, they have to find out how to inhabit the words.[11] To inhabit the words the actor needs to work in rehearsal with intonation, stress, resonance and the sheer physicality of sound, so that a word, or words, become part of the musculature. Available to them is a range of strategy and technique: argument, genre, line length, punctuation (controversial, but actors use it), rhyme, and word-specifics such as particular clusters of consonants and vowel sounds. All of these may alert one to the weight of the line, although not necessarily to its significance, which is sometimes for the audience alone. That the actor can escape consciously conveying significance is anathema to most literary critics, and difficult to explain. However, we will attempt to describe part of the process as we discuss some of the rehearsal practices.

From the (disputed) quatrain 'The grey-ey'd morn ...' to Romeo's salutation 'Good morrow, father ...',[12] the Friar moves from homiletic reasoning to a central moral, to the pragmatic everyday of the Capulets and Montagues. The movement is a procedure for persuasion: like a prayer, and more certainly like a sermon, as if the Friar is pursuing a collocation of reasonings from wholeness, to balance, to predominance and break-up. The speech has a choric function because it tells the story of the two families again, but also tells this particular story as one of mistaken virtue that can provide justification for vice. It foretells the ending with its reference to medicine and poison that 'stays all senses with the heart' (22), a foretelling that infuses the entire scene, with Romeo then asking for the Friar's help and holy physic (47–48), saying later that he will 'bury love' (78). It contains one possible mistake: that the grave is not always a womb that can issue children, as we find from the ending of the play—unless the deaths do bring about peace.

At the same time, the entire scene is in couplets which pose a theatrical problem which requires a theatrical solution. When dealing with rhyming couplets, a common danger is that the actor gets taken over by the rhyme and does not inhabit the words. Therefore you have to treat the potentially predictable couplet rhyme as if it is an accident, not fore-ordained, and focus on the physicality of what is being said, or on the response to another actor that is wanted, with the couplet providing parallel significance often associated with musicality.[13] To work on this the actor may, for example, concentrate on the clusters of sound in the lines, as in the couplet 'The earth that's natures' mother is her tomb:/ What is her burying grave, that is her womb' (5–6). One unusual rehearsal strategy, that derives from Cicely Berry's detailed work on linguistic experiment[14] and focuses on breath, is to say the lines only with their vowel sounds or only with their consonants, keeping the stress of the words and giving the silent 'e' an 'eh' sound. This would render the lines, as vowel sounds, thus:

e ea a a u eh o e i e oo /
a i e u yi a eh a i e oo

and, as consonants:

th ts n t r s m th r s h r t mb /
wh t s h r b r ng gr v t s h r w mb

In phonetics the vowel sounds would be rendered as:

i: ɜ: æ eɪ ə ʌ ə ɪ ɜ: u:
ɒ ɪ ɜ: e i: ɪ eɪ æ ɪ ɜ: u:

and the consonants as:

ð θ ð ts n tʃ z m ð z h t m
w t z h b r j ŋ gr v ð ṭz h w m

Initially it might be observed that there are many vowel sounds that are different, but there is an internal rhythm of 'nature' / 'mother' / 'is her' in the first line. The balance of the second line around the comma leaves it more self-contained than the first, especially in the matching of 'What is her ...' with 'that is her ...', and in the movement from the polysyllabic 'burying' to the monosyllabic 'womb'. In addition, the phonetics points out a balance emerging around 'nature's' and 'mother is'. Yet there are cross-references between the two lines that insist on wider connections, in 'that's' and 'that is', and particularly in the internal sounds, clearly indicated by the phonetics, of 'is her' and, in the second line, 'is her ... is her', and, of course, 'tomb' and 'womb'. The actors, unlike the phoneticist, sound the silent 'e' when undertaking this exercise to render the context for the consonants when they are enunciated on their own, but the phonetics indicate further elements, which actors might feel in their muscles or which they might miss. The two lines of consonants contain the repeated pattern of 't z h' with 'w' and 'd' in three different arrangements over the two lines, which an audience might interpret as conveying meaning. Further, the balance point of the second line hovers over the back consonants in 'ying' of 'burying', with whose deep resonance, it could be argued, we have significant cultural associations.

This kind of analysis makes the literary critic want to point out that the structure of the sound carries meaning. In doing so, we are of course arguing about significance from personal experience of sound and rhythm. But however tempting it is to carry out such a literary analysis, and one could argue that it is analogous to the reading of metaphor and just as valuable in its social specificity, the point of displaying the exercise on paper is to give readers, who may not be familiar with it, a sense of a technique available to the actor. A feeling for how the exercise works, and how it empties the words of conventional meaning for the actor, cannot be reached unless it is carried out by saying the lines of vowels and consonants aloud. If the exercise is carried out over a number of lines, say at least five, the sheer difficulty of saying simply the consonants out loud requires extraordinary physical exertion since the breath has to carry the gaps of the vowels. The vowels themselves are easier on the body but need exceptional attention to nuances of shift.[15] The entire procedure does two things: it releases potentially new meaning to which the actor may pay attention, but, more importantly, when the actor goes back to saying the lines as a whole, the words acquire definition as objects that may or may not convey significance. The breakdown into the variousness of sound emphasizes the complexity of each phrase, so the couplets do not sink into sameness.

Such tightly formulated couplets are typical of the Friar's speech until he reaches the part in his soliloquy that begins to involve the two families. Here we find the first run-over line, where the grammar forces you into the next line at 'encamp them still/ In man ...', from which point the balance of his words is far less consistent. Because the end of a line functions in the same way as punctuation, run-over lines like full stops, commas and other textual markings clearly structure the way an actor develops the shape of the verse. In general, lightly punctuated lines put the responsibility for shape far more on the actor and, similarly, a run-over line pulls the anchor on significance and releases energy.[16] But the actor may gain most energy for the couplets when responding to others on stage, as here when the Friar talks with Romeo. One of the indications of their particular intimacy is the way they handle the sententiousness and variability of the couplet. This is a development of the previous scene which Juliet and Romeo conclude in couplets, and even share the final couplet; at the same time it recalls their first meeting which is all in couplets. It also underlines Romeo's personal skill in picking up the verbal techniques of those with whom he is intimate. As the scene develops, Romeo acquires the Friar's sententious couplets wherever there is a grammatically complete set of two lines (41–42, 49–50, 81–82), but speaks more usually in enjambements (45–47, 55–57 …). Similarly the Friar, when he first responds to Romeo's admission that he wants to marry Juliet, is infected by his hesitation. His speech is full of apostrophes buying him time, and metaphors that do not help his argument, full of run-on or travelling couplets (62–63, 63–64, 65–66) that gradually settle back down into sententious couplets (67–68), as he reasserts his position as teacher chiding an errant pupil. As so often in Shakespeare's dialogue, one character's words tell you how another is behaving so, a few lines later, Romeo says 'I pray thee chide me not …' (81). The two move on to share several half-lines equally[17] as the Friar attempts to identify with Romeo, saying 'come young waverer, come and go', wavering himself as he says it, and 'I'll thy assistant be' rather than teacher, as if he is renegotiating his position and status. Underlying this verse exchange is an implicit argument that, because Romeo has given up Rosaline on the Friar's advice, he has implicated him in his choice of Juliet.

The Friar in this scene can be read as tedious or as proof of the limits of rhetoric, but neither of these is a sensible proposition to put to an actor who has to deal with the reality that you cannot have a 'boring' character on stage being boring for very long.[18] It is possible to make a boring character funny by foregrounding that quality but, on the whole, this is not the position of the Friar. Hence he has to have a more densely inhabited character to make the words work, to effect the creative translation that will satisfy the audience. The actor must work with the interaction between the words and the body, and one way of doing so is through breath. What is undoubtedly the result is a sense of an individual to whom the other actors on stage, and the audience, can attribute motivation. This is not a matter of hanging a coat on the correct peg, but of responding to the engagement that the actor has in translating from page to stage, and constructing the common ground that allows us to value their actions.

Like the Friar, the Nurse can offer a clearly identifiable type, but, unlike the Friar, the type is one with which British audiences at least still feel familiar: possibly the loyal family retainer but, more likely, because of her overt sexuality, the warmhearted 'easy' woman, possibly a whore.[19] Thomas Overbury's 'Macquerela, in Plain English, a Bawd' describes a woman so similar to the Nurse that either Overbury had seen the play, or Shakespeare and he are using the same Theophrastan source. A bawd is an older woman, once a prostitute, who now acts as a facilitator or go-between for other women. Yet to play the Nurse to type would quickly pall into stereotype unless you had an extremely good comic actor. The sheer extent of her presence in the play means that the part may well have been played by a good actor, but there is more to the character than type. The text gives her a specific characterization in what is called 'the Nurse's delay'[20] which occurs in every single one of her speaking scenes and in her command, or lack of it, over register and appropriateness of speech.

The first occasion, I.iii, in which the audience meets her, she is played alongside the mother and Juliet, the mother saying at the start that she wants to talk in secret with Juliet but then changing her mind and in the process alerting the Nurse to some important decision. That she grasps what the mother will later say about marriage is indicated by her arriving at the line, 'I might live to see thee married once' (61), at the end of her long storytelling. The Nurse begins with a series of stories about her own life, and about the young Juliet. Once again Q1 provides just the first bare narrative, while Q2 encourages the Nurse to tell the story of Juliet's falling over as a child twice, each time rather differently. The first time the story is told, it is shaped by way of apostrophes of a religious kind, which can be played not simply as garrulous interjections, but as if to give her time to think of how to narrate. The result is circular, jerky, leaving lots of gaps. But the second time the story is told, it is far better constructed, to the point and shorter; the Nurse is in control of it. Watching this process helps the audience to understand that the Nurse, as she later proves, has little control over formal devices for narrating, arguing and even speaking, Yes, the story is comic in a gently titillating way, but it also represents the Nurse's way of dealing with anticipated loss, telling Juliet how she became a substitute for her own daughter, how Juliet's presence carries memories of her own husband, how she will miss Juliet.

The Nurse's anecdotal, autobiographical narration works in contrast to the mother's formality and highly conceitful language. Once her long story is done, the scene begins to work by way of the tension between two rhythms, one being to do with status and the other with sexuality. The mother names Paris as the best catch of Verona, and the Nurse says, 'Lady, such a man/ As all the world—' (75–76), stopping herself as if to prevent an indiscretion about his behaviour, and re-routing her comment into 'why, he's a man of wax' (76), with its sexual play on 'wax'. The mother interjects that Verona 'hath not such a flower' (77), and the Nurse immediately picks up 'he's a flower, in faith a very flower', where 'flower' suggests the sexually mature. And following the mother's long development (not in Q1) of how lovers are like books, the Nurse deflates the conceit saying 'No less, nay bigger. Women grow by men' (95). What gets established in this scene is the Nurse's humour and sexuality, as well as her love for Juliet and the way she works hand in hand with Juliet's mother, even though in a different register. We also learn about the difficulty that she has with narration, which leads to her loose autobiographical prose with its air of an informal conversation. This in turn tells us about the way the Nurse controls the pace of the scene because of her need to work on ways of narrating. But none of these elements answer the question why she has such difficulty, and this is a central issue for the actor playing the part.

There is a similar need to listen to the Nurse's potential control over pace in II.iv when she meets Mercutio, Benvolio and Romeo on the street the day after the ball. The Nurse is hurt, affronted and embarrassed by Mercutio's rudeness toward her, and despite Romeo's attempts to defend Mercutio and apologize for him, she is released into a tirade of anger. At first she directs this toward her manservant, who turns it back toward her, which makes her even more angry. Humiliated even by her own servant, she says, 'What she [Juliet] bid me say, I will keep to myself' (161–62). Throughout these two angry speeches, the Nurse is abrupt, full of short sentences and rough language. She stops and starts as if she cannot find the words to express herself yet recognizes that she cannot just remain silent. When Romeo attempts to 'protest', she interrupts him, but why does she do so? The actor could look to motivation and suggest that it is because she wants to turn his protest into a proposition, or because she is being sarcastic, or because she thinks he has succeeded in making his 'protest'. Certainly the interruption ends with 'which, as I take it, is a gentlemanlike offer' (175) as if, after her failure to control the situation earlier, when she was undefended by Romeo, she is not to determine the destination of his protest. But it may also be part of her delaying tactics.

Romeo does go on to propose marriage and tries to pay her for her actions as a go-between, to buy her off, but she does not at first take the money, presumably just because she does not want Romeo to think she is a bawd. Only when Romeo gives her some practical instructions does she begin to come round and shift the rhythm of her speech toward something more emollient, with 'Now God in Heaven bless thee' (190). The speech then moves back into her earlier voice as she begins to bring in her autobiographical reminiscences, 'When 'twas a little prating thing ...' (196), and finally she explains to Romeo what he is up against in Paris, and what Juliet actually feels. In other words, she has come to trust him because he has proved that he can act, is not just words, and she has got involved personally with him. They conclude the scene with a shared joke. As with the earlier scene, she delays getting to the point until she can control her words, but here also we see her delaying until she has tested the person she speaks to and can trust them to treat her properly. The Nurse's delay is not merely a humorous stylistic feature, but an integral part of her strategy for dealing with her vulnerable position as a servant.

The return to the Nurse's earlier voice is an addition found in Q2, not in Q1, and unlike the Friar's opening scene which remains largely unchanged, the Nurse's addition allows for much fuller characterization, insisting that the actor inhabits the part rather than play to conventional expectation. Literary critics often object to taking the parts as characters and arguing from motivation or individuality because, to do so, assumptions have to be made about 'individuality' which may not be appropriate. However, critics also seem less worried by taking the parts as types, or even as stereotypes, and arguing from functionality or convention or their role in a particular generic context, even though, to do so, similar assumptions have to be made about 'role'. Certainly to take the parts as 'subject positions' and argue from subjectivity, or the effects of repression by ideology, is to assume many aspects of ideology and discourse that are just as open to discussion as a consideration of the parts as characters.

The actor, however, has to find reasons in breath, musculature, rhythm, response, interaction and movement, reasons drawn from the experience and training of their bodies. When we think about our bodies, the words we use are tied to convention, habit and discourse, but the actor's body does not necessarily translate the memory of experience in the same way. The actor has to be able to draw on energy that makes sense in terms of bodily capacities and abilities.[21] The character of the Nurse here, and in the scenes immediately following, can attempt a tight control over the pace of speech and response, which is partly premeditative when, for example, she tests Romeo, and partly because she is waiting to assess response, and partly because she needs the time to find the way to say what she has to say.

Throughout II.v the Nurse employs the same tactics, with Juliet now rather than Romeo. By delaying the news Juliet wants she slows Juliet down, at the same time testing the strength of her feelings. At the end of her lengthy complaints, the Nurse suddenly says 'where is your mother', drawing Juliet's attention to her mother's opinion but also reminding us of the responsibility that devolves on the Nurse in the mother's absence. Like many of her breathless apostrophes, the interjection is directed toward things she recognizes but which she finds difficult to control because of her position as a woman and a servant. Even more complaining slows the pace before she delivers her message at last and moves for the first time into rather formal verse, concluding with a rhyming couplet of her own and then a shared couplet with Juliet.[22] As she moves into verse she also takes her place among people in the play whose actions affect others and must be reckoned with.[23] The structure of II.v provides the pattern for III.ii, the next scene between the Nurse and Juliet, where Juliet's long soliloquy after the Nurse's entry and slow revelation of what has happened displays greater maturity as the Nurse shows less control. The Nurse plays the confusion of 'we are undone' and 'whoever would have thought it', indicating that she thinks she has made a misjudgment. In effect, she is panicking; after all within two to three hours of sending Juliet to the Friar to be married, she has gone for the rope ladder, seen Tybalt dead as she was returning, and heard the news of Romeo's banishment. Given her role in their relationship, she must be afraid that she will be held responsible. She cannot tell Juliet the truth directly, but also she is testing Juliet's responses, playing out the grief. First she lets Juliet think Romeo is dead, and only tells Juliet about Tybalt when Juliet says she wants to die (59–60),[24] after which she explains that Romeo is banished for Tybalt's death.

Despite maintaining her control over the pace of the scene, the actor has good indications that the part is changing and that the Nurse is increasingly out of her depth. The Nurse's habitual speech patterns are filled with interruptions, their rhythm changes all the time and proceeds in stops and starts, so that, when she moves into language that is sustained in any way, it is unusual, it alerts us to a different mode. Here in III.ii, we find the excessive repetition of 'he's dead, he's dead, he's dead', followed by the balanced line, 'We are undone, lady, we are undone', and the varied repetition of 'he's gone, he's kill'd, he's dead'. Her speech goes from interruption to repetition very quickly, and the actor can easily get trapped inside the regularity of the repetitive iambics or attempt to get out of them by playing that regularity as a comic feature. It requires a different kind of energy to work on variousness in the rhythm to make the words carry weight, and, when this happens, we see the actor in a different way.[25]

The difference in the Nurse's energy carries over onto Juliet herself, and an instructive example of the different interaction that actors develop in translating from the page comes from a comparison between Q1 and Q2. After the Nurse has told Juliet about Romeo's banishment, she has in Q1 a set piece, 'There's no trust,/ No faith, no honesty in men' (85–86), but little else until she asks Juliet to go to her family. Upon Juliet's threatening to commit suicide, she offers to take a message to Romeo. In Q2 the set piece occurs after a much extended speech by Juliet condemning Romeo's action, so that it seems to reinforce her feeling. As a result, Juliet's about-face attack on the Nurse for saying such things shows the young woman radically changing her mind. This abrupt reversal also causes the Nurse, in Q2, to point out, 'Will you speak well of him that kill'd your cousin?' (96), which sets up Juliet's logical claim that 'My husband lives, that Tybalt would have slain' (105), again only in Q2. In Q2 Juliet matures into a reasoning and complex woman of tragic proportions around the added wordplay (44–50) on 'eye', 'I' and 'ay' in which she questions her existence. This follows on immediately from the dense cluster of 'o's in the Nurse's 'O Romeo, Romeo,/ Who ever would have thought it? Romeo!' (41–42), 'o' forming part of a field of sound that recurs throughout the play particularly when indicating the limitations of language to communicate. Juliet's 'I' is part of a reasoned inquiry, the Nurse's 'o' is a well of absence/presence.

In Q2 the Nurse's role changes because she is responding to a different character. She is no longer a substitute mother or older retainer who gives advice, but a servant from whom Juliet has begun to distance herself not only because of the Nurse's perceived criticism of Romeo, but also because of Juliet's rapid transition into an adult. The Nurse moves from a position where she holds power and information to a position where Juliet is arguing with her and taking responsibility for herself. Juliet moves into her suicide threat by way of rhyming couplets that indicate her formality and seriousness. Yet although the Nurse is frightened, she continues to be involved, agreeing to take Juliet's ring to Romeo in order to stop her killing herself.

The next scene of any note between the Nurse and Juliet occurs at III.v, when Lord and Lady Capulet try to convince Juliet to marry Paris. The Nurse says nothing at all until Juliet goes on her knees to her father and the father responds brutally. At this point the Nurse tries to deflect the anger onto herself, but is told by Capulet, 'Hold your tongue' (170). Capulet's power is such that even after he leaves, when Juliet tries to get her mother to talk to her, the reply is, 'Talk not to me, for I'll not speak a word' (202). Alone with the Nurse, Juliet asks her three times for advice, and when the Nurse finally breaks her silence, she withholds any emotional warmth, calls her 'Madam', and tells her to marry Paris. Juliet cross-examines her and, after she has left, says, 'Go counsellor./ Thou and my bosom henceforth shall be twain' (239–40). And the Nurse says nothing more to her either in IV.ii or IV.iii, even though the stage directions say that she is present on stage. The actor must ask why this talkative woman is silenced. If you work through the tensions of status, responsibility, parental and substitute position, then perhaps there is a reason for it in Juliet's emotional distance. The stories that the Nurse has told to gain emotional proximity are no longer necessary. Certainly, she is no more in a position of power with respect to Juliet. The function of testing the character is now no longer appropriate. Nor does she again transgress the wishes of Juliet's mother and father. Therefore there is no need to listen for the response in order to assess her own situation and its potential dangers.

The final scenes the Nurse participates in cluster around Juliet's false death, in a way that points up what the play does with type quite clearly. IV.iv arrives in precipitous contrast to the darkness of the preceding scene in which Juliet talks of death prior to taking the drug, and moves the action into an excess of farce. The Nurse controls the register of the dialogue, which is one of banter and sexual excitement that she is familiar with. Capulet sounds very like the three young men in I.iv as he orders the servants about, and cries fatefully, 'Make haste, make haste', when he orders the Nurse to wake up Juliet. Throughout the scene the audience forgets about Juliet for a while and enters the world of the family, only to be thrown back, still carried on the Nurse's excitement, to IV.v in which the Nurse has returned fully to the vocabulary and the short sentence structure of her first scene.

The calling back of this energy brings back the time prior to all the unexpected events which have taken place between Juliet and Romeo. The Nurse's actions restore a sense of normality that completely erases Romeo, as she speaks partly to the audience, including them in her excitement and sexual anticipation (10). Her energy becomes anxiety with 'I must needs wake you …' (14), and then panic with 'Lady! Lady! Lady!/ Alas, alas! Help, Help! My lady's dead' (14–15), these repetitions recalling the energy of III.ii where she laments the death of Tybalt, her best friend.[26] Again, because she is without control over words and, as if not wanting to bring the news, possibly fearful that her part may be found out, when Lady Capulet asks her twice what is the matter, the Nurse cannot explain. She just points, and cries, 'O lamentable day!' (17), 'Look, look! O heavy day!' (18). Lady Capulet moves directly into the Nurse's register, saying, 'O me, O me! My child, my only life …' (19). When the father appears, the Nurse does tell him, 'She's dead, deceas'd! She's dead! Alack the day!' (23). The mother immediately reverses the line, echoing the Nurse's lament in III.ii, 'Alack the day! She's dead, she's dead, she's dead!' (24). Lord Capulet responds with very controlled language, but paradoxically complains that death 'will not let me speak' (32), as if his words have no significance.

From the moment the Friar, Paris and the musicians enter, the family goes into a formal lamentation that is almost choric in its distance from the events. It is as if the scene has shifted from the personal and familial out to the public, so that there has to be a display of grief. Each character regains formal control over register except the Nurse, whose speech reiterates the field of 'o's she earlier spoke on Tybalt's death: 'O woe! O woeful, woeful, woeful day …' (49–54). The production of the 'o', coming from the depth of the body, is one of the actor's most difficult tasks. It is associated in many acting traditions with the deepest level of breath, below the solar plexus, and with the fullest sound that humans can make because of what it does to the shape of the mouth and because of the resonance it achieves.[27] The 'o' is what you mean to say before you go on to articulate anything, so each 'o' is specific to what is going to follow. An 'o' is the sound of what the actor will next shape. Deprived of any narration, the actor's playing can translate the Nurse into a character, tragic because without language, or into a stereotype in a melodrama of an inevitable and predictable story, and the lamentation offers similar opportunities.

The formal lamentation, which comes from nowhere like the Queen Mab speech and is just as generically disruptive, proceeds from the Father, through Paris (depending on Q1 or Q2), Lady Capulet, the Nurse, Paris again, and then starts up once more with the Father. With the circle beginning again, the Father's speech becomes emotional, excessive, repetitive like the Nurse's, as he says, 'O child, O child!'. And at this point the Friar intervenes, either because he perceives the words taking over Capulet as they do with Mercutio, or because he sees the grief becoming competitive. The scene is taken right out of a Commedia dell'Arte scene where this would be expected. Indeed, the scene can be played as if it were farce. But if the parts are not played seriously, with the actors trying fully to inhabit them as characters, the roles are devalued; and the audience will not care about the characters if they are simply fools.

The function of the scene is partly to present Juliet's death first, and as valuable, with people grieving over it, so that it is out of the way and there is space later on to develop Romeo's death. But the fact that it is structured on a generically disruptive element of Commedia dell'Arte alerts the audience to the effect of a 'play within a play' that asks them to take the generically comic and potentially stereotypical as serious and complex. In other words, the audience watches a comedic scene played seriously. The scene is placed between two others, IV.iv, and the second part of IV.v, that through their excessive farce and comedic aspects underline that it is played against the expectation of structure. This positioning carries forward the intercutting of the tragic with the comic from IV.iii to IV.iv to IV.v, where the comic scenes make the audience forget what has happened immediately before, where they halt the flow of the tragic narrative before swinging back and forth between tragic and comic, so that the play has no inevitable momentum until Act V. To play the scene as Commedia dell'Arte is possible although difficult. It produces immediate comic satisfaction but works against the internal rhythms of the drama that balance here in a tragicomic mix between the opening and closing movements of comedy and tragedy respectively. Types can make a shortlived impact on the audience through stereotypical playing but without an attempt to motivate them as actual human beings, as characters, they become mere appendages and lose the energy that situates the central narrative within a social context.

Character is a problem for literary critics primarily because it has come to imply fixity. In the theatre character is necessarily not a fixed entity but is always subject to translation, worked on in rehearsal, and changed in performance. Even the phrase 'character actor' signifies an actor who has created a particular type which is infused with new life every time it is played. Yet we have all seen acting where that work is not carried out to any considerable extent, so that the actor reproduces habitual movements and inflections upon which they have come to depend and which render the character flat and stereotypical, translating from the page to the stage by mere repetition rather than reinvention. Farce is a relatively stable genre of theatre in which there are many types: played well it is exhilarating but most often it falls flat. Shakespeare's plays are at the other end of the spectrum and are frequently generically unstable. *Romeo and Juliet* is particularly so, and consistently plays *with* and *off* type rather than *in* type. Many productions deal with its instability by fixing on the recognizable types and the central romantic narrative, but this will not bring the play to life.

We could say the same for literary criticism: that the critic has to allow the words to work with them rather than simply bringing a set of ideas to the text and gridding them down onto it so that it forms a desired pattern. But the relationship of the critic with their audience is different from the relationship between the actor/director and their audience. Both perform a response to the text, but the theatre audience rarely looks for a 'correct' interpretation. An actor may find reasons for a character to do something, but the members of the audience attribute their own motivation to what they see. Criticism, however, carries the weight of potential 'truth' in its examinations of the text, and this is why critics get worried about character, in case discussion of character closes off response by implying a true and therefore final interpretation. Certainly criticism needs a better vocabulary for looking at character and attributing motivation because 'character' is such a rich field for engaging with the text. What we have attempted in a very preliminary way in this essay is to turn to theatre practices for help, to translate back from the stage to the page. Either way, the joy of Shakespeare is that whether actor or critic, you make discoveries all the time, and meaning in these characters is never resolved.

NOTES

1. The work of Diane Macdonnell, *Theories of Discourse* (Oxford: Basil Blackwell, 1986), of Judith Butler, *Bodies That Matter: on the Discursive Limits of 'Sex'* (London: Routledge, 1993), and of Lorraine Code, *Rhetorical Spaces in Gendered Locations* (London: Routledge, 1995), respectively outline recent critiques of essentialist notions of character. For Shakespeare studies the work of Catherine Belsey attends to all the areas, and her *The Subject of Tragedy: Identity and Difference in Renaissance Tragedy* (London: Methuen, 1985) has generated the most comprehensive rethinking of the category of character in the plays.

2. Margreta de Grazia and Peter Stallybrass, 'The Materiality of the "Shakespearean Text"', *Shakespeare Quarterly*, 44 (1993), 267. For a comprehensive critique of essentialist approaches to character in studies of *Romeo and Juliet*, which draws largely on the tradition following A. C. Bradley's *Oxford Lectures on Poetry* (London, 1905), but which also looks at earlier

critics such as Mrs Jameson's *Characteristics of Women, Moral, Poetical, and Historical* (London: Saunders and Otley, 1832) whose overlap of theatrical and textual elements tends to produce an apparently naive account of motivation, see Fleur Rothschild, *Recovering 'Romeo and Juliet', A Study of Critical Responses to the Play from 1597* (University of London doctorate, 1997).

3. See, for example, Harry Berger, 'What did the King know and when did he know it? Shakespearean Discourses and Psychoanalysis', *South Atlantic Quarterly*, 88 (1989), 811–62. See also R. Cloud, 'What's the Bastard's Name?', in *Shakespeare's Speech-Headings: Speaking the Speech in Shakespeare's Plays*, ed. G. Walton Williams (London: Associated University Presses, 1997), p. 135.

4. For example, the production from the Lyric Hammersmith, in 1995, did precisely this.

5. See for example Kathleen Irace, *Reforming the 'Bad' Quartos: Performance and Provenance of Six Shakespearean First Editions* (London: Associated University Presses, 1994).

6. See Patsy Rodenburg, *The Need for Words* (London: Methuen, 1993), p. 148, where she claims that 'Breathing is speaking'.

7. John Barton, *Playing Shakespeare* (London: Methuen, 1984). He notes that 'the language is the character', p. 59.

8. This is akin to what Patsy Rodenburg calls 'owning' a text by letting it take root in us. See *The Actor Speaks* (London: Methuen, 1997), pp. 210–11.

9. Cicely Berry, *The Actor and his Text* (London: Virgin, 1987), pp. 104–05.

10. The concept of acting in the moment is described in Barton, *Playing Shakespeare*, p. 50.

11. The sense of 'inhabiting' the text here is close to Berry's 'attending to the word' which she describes as feeling 'the energy and texture of each word complete and fulfilled before you allow yourself to go on to the next' (*The Actor and his Text*, p. 158).

12. All line references to *Romeo and Juliet* that are quoted in the essay are taken from Brian Gibbons' Arden edition (London: Routledge, 1980): act and scene numbers are not repeated after the first designation.

13. See Kristin Linklater, *Freeing Shakespeare's Voice* (New York: Theatre Communications Group, 1992), p. 145.

14. For example, Berry, *The Actor and his Text*, pp. 95–98.

15. There is considerable debate about the effects of this exercise. See, for example, Linklater who says that 'vibrations of consonants travel through skin and muscle and bone to the senses, while vowels have direct access to the solar plexus, making them more immediately emotional', (*Freeing Shakespeare's Voice*, p. 19). In contrast, Berry notes the different

effects of the sounds in terms of the patterning found in the vowels and the 'muscular strength' of the consonants (*The Actor and his Text*, p. 152). Rodenburg suggests that vowels open one up to emotion (*The Need for Words*, p. 192).

16. Although potentially reductive, the effect of punctuation on verse-speaking is described clearly in Linklater, *Freeing Shakespeare's Voice*, p. 48.

17. As Barton suggests, equal sharing of lines indicates quite a different rhythm and relationship than short lines which suggest a pause between each speech (*Playing Shakespeare*, p. 152).

18. For an eloquent account of the problem of set-speeches and the 'boredom' quotient, see Barton, *Playing Shakespeare*, pp. 86–87.

19. Sexuality of course is not a characteristic of a 'good' woman in Western culture.

20. The first reference to this effect comes from B. Cardullo, 'The Nurse's Delay in *Romeo and Juliet*', *CEA Critic, College English Association*, 1983, Vol. 46, Pt 1–2, pp. 30–31.

21. This has to do with bodily 'readiness' as described by Rodenburg, *The Actor Speaks*, p. 8.

22. Rhyming couplets function partly by indicating the control that the character has over what has happened in the scene, see Barton, *Playing Shakespeare*, p. 157.

23. Linklater discusses the way that characters with speech that rhymes must be assumed to have the wit to exploit and manipulate meaning (*Freeing Shakespeare's Voice*, p. 150).

24. The Nurse uses exactly the same vocabulary for Tybalt that she had for Romeo in the earlier scene, calling him courteous and an 'honest gentleman', 'the best friend I had' (III.ii.61).

25. See Barton, who says 'It's a great trap with Shakespeare's text if you get on to one note, one tone and one tempo', and the actor always has to look within the text for variety (*Playing Shakespeare*, p. 51).

26. Rodenburg comments that 'a finely wrought text will have these changes and rhythm shifts built into it' (*The Actor Speaks*, p. 170).

27. Rodenburg notes that 'the lower we breathe a word, the deeper its effect on us' (*The Need for Words*, p. 150).

Translating the Elizabethan Theatre: the Politics of Nostalgia in Olivier's *Henry V*

MARTIN BUTLER

A curious and revealing detail in the Globe theatre sequence which opens Laurence Olivier's film of *Henry V* is the repeated introduction of a stage boy, who holds up placards indicating the title and locations of the play we are about to see. The first placard informs us that this is 'The Chronicle History of Henry the Fift with his battel fought at Agin Court in France', and subsequent placards announce locations as an 'ANTE CHAMBER IN KING HENRY'S PALACE' and 'THE BOAR'S HEAD'. Generally speaking, the film's invention of this boy is in keeping with the archaeological thrust of its opening sequence, which represents *Henry V* as it might have been staged in a reconstructed theatre of 1600. Olivier, or his text editor Alan Dent, could conceivably have known that written labels had been used as location indicators in some Elizabethan playhouses, since the practice was extensively discussed by W. J. Lawrence in an essay of 1912 which had long been incorporated into theatre historiography.[1] However, Olivier's management of the labels, with a boy carrying placards, is quite different from that described by Lawrence, as is the labels' aesthetic effect. The first placard is directly transcribed from the title page of the 1600 Quarto, to the extent of carrying over some of its pre-modern spellings. It thereby guarantees that the ensuing film is authentically based on Shakespeare's text, though at the risk, even before the performance starts, of implicitly conceding the priority of print. The other placards are even further removed from Elizabethan labels, as they are clearly indebted to the literary markers of location which had been institutionalized in Shakespeare editing from the eighteenth century onwards. Like (for example) 'Rouen, a room in the palace' or 'Another part of the battlefield', their combination of specificity and vagueness echoes the difficulties encountered by early editors when looking for descriptors which adequately expressed the conventions of Elizabethan stagecraft in terms that met expectations derived from the scenic practice of their own theatres. Presumably Olivier's placards were intended to help cinema-goers of 1944 orient themselves within a forgotten set of performance conventions, but to today's audiences (more familiarized as we are to the codes of the open stage) they seem uncomfortable intrusions in the supposedly coherent archaeology of the Globe. They are a reminder that this reconstruction which aspires to seem self-sustaining is in fact mediated, both aesthetically and temporally. Evoking a semiotics of performance deriving from presuppositions which are later and more readerly than those of Elizabethan playhouses, the stage boy and his placards inadvertently disclose Olivier's recreation of the Globe as itself an act of historical translation.[2]

Olivier's *Henry V* has often been discussed in terms of its aesthetic transpositions, from script to screenplay, word to image, theatre to film. I want to focus more on its temporal translations, the elisions and supplementations—like this invented stage boy—that mark it as mediating in complex ways between different historical moments. Such faultlines are recurrent in *Henry V*, and pose besetting interpretive difficulties over the film's sense of its own historicity. For example, it is hard now to be sure whether the stage boy and his placards would have been felt as a discontinuity in 1944, or whether the small awkwardness that we register was invisible to the first audiences. The ironic applause which greets his third appearance suggests he had already begun to seem otiose, but perhaps in 1944 he appeared just one more detail in a picturesque but essentially unproblematic fantasy of life in the Shakespearean theatre. And if Olivier's translation of an earlier age into the terms of 1944 inevitably generated dislocations of this kind, faultlines are created under reverse pressure through our modern loss of connectivity with Olivier's historical moment. *Henry V* arrives today journeying from a past which, though still relatively recent, is gradually beginning to ossify into history, so that the film now looks increasingly like a time capsule, its recreation of an earlier age overwritten with assumptions and attitudes from a mid-twentieth century which is itself fast coming to feel as remote as Olivier's 'age of Elizabeth'. As a consequence, modern understanding of the movie's significance as a reading of *Henry V* is complicated by the fact of its own pastness. Manifestly, our experience of the film is very different from 1944's: for one thing, we have lost that sense which original audiences had of living through a turning point in history. But, in many other less dramatic (though no less pervasive) ways, the period resonances which *Henry V* inadvertently bears within present us with problems of adjudication between its different levels of anachronism, making it difficult for us to separate those things which the film (so to speak) consciously knows from those assumptions which it inhabits but of which it is effectively unconscious.

Of course, it was a central part of Olivier's patriotic enterprise to treat historical difference with cavalier boldness. His *mise en scène* leaps effortlessly over time, mapping 1944 onto 1600 and 1415 with no appreciable sense of strain. Such conflations begin at the outset, with the dedication to the Allied commandos and airborne troops, announcing Olivier's intention of celebrating 'the spirit of their ancestors' as if the courage needed in the Normandy landings could be collapsed directly into that shown at Agincourt. Similarly, in the famous establishing shot tracking over the roofs of Elizabethan London, the intervening past was deftly erased, and audiences surrounded by the devastation of the Blitz were restored to a capital city so clean-cut that it looked (as James Agate sourly remarked) as 'if half the population had been house-painters'.[3] Such rapid and irresistible telescopings invoke a view of Shakespeare as the classic universal, a writer whose cultural authority is bound up with his ability to float triumphantly free from marks of historical embedment, yet this assumption is implicitly at odds with the film's historicizing project, its all too conspicuous appropriation of Shakespeare in the service of timely national aspirations. It is not altogether surprising, then, if *Henry V*'s apparently seamless surface turns out in practice to be marked by tensions that are half-hidden but vexatious. In this respect, the stage boy with his anachronistic placards is symptomatic of adjustments between competing frameworks which *Henry V* was constantly having to make, and which, however brilliantly finessed, are still intrinsic to its complex effect. Those devices which in 1944 managed the film's aesthetic and historical translations are, fifty years on, testimony to elisions that it can never completely accomplish.

I want to suggest that these considerations press with particular force on the Globe theatre scenes, a sequence which once had (and perhaps still has) an extraordinary subliminal effect on modern imaginings of Shakespeare's theatre. Though the main pleasure for the earliest spectators was *Henry V*'s resonant but reassuring allusions to current anxieties, they must also have incidentally absorbed the densely detailed representation of Elizabethan playgoing which it incorporates. This makes Olivier's Globe easily the single most influential recreation of a Shakespearean playhouse to date: even the newly reconstructed Globe which has just opened in London will take many years before it is as imprinted on the collective mind as Olivier's version. Yet Olivier's Globe is a very divided image and carries the hallmarks of its moment of production, not least because the handling of these framing scenes is in some measure self-contradictory. On the one hand, Olivier represents the Globe staging as visibly inferior to modern performances. The players make mistakes, the acting style is artificial, and the audience is a constant and sometimes troubling presence. This creates a scenario in which the move out of the Globe into fully cinematic space is felt as a triumph of the new, liberation into an aesthetic that is seemingly more contemporary and realistic, and in which Henry's authority over his army appears more naturalized and complete. But at the same time, the Globe world is also enviably unified and inclusive, a happy democracy with which cinema spectators are invited to identify, and which projects an attractive image of a society free from external threats and internally at one with itself. This view of Shakespeare's theatre suggests a nostalgia for a pseudo-historical utopia, so that when cinema eventually triumphs over playhouse the cost is, potentially, an acknowledgment of the loss of such mythical Elizabethan plenitude. These polarities define the aesthetic and ideological oppositions between which Olivier's Globe is somewhat ambivalently poised. The film's project is to bring the two positions into satisfactory relation, but they are also points of tension between which it oscillates. They express the social and aesthetic contradictions that the film aims to reconcile but which, I want to suggest, remain powerful and unacknowledged.

Olivier's recreation of the Globe has often been taken as a simple historical pastiche, a colourful spectacle along the lines of 'life ran very high in those days'.[4] Certainly it belongs to the 'nut-cracking Elizabethans' school of theatre history, and its idea of the Globe, by any archaeological standard, involves some glaring impurities. Nonetheless, at root this opening sequence is surprisingly respectful of what in 1944 was taken for historical authenticity, and it makes a real attempt to present an informed image of Shakespeare's theatre. The Globe scenes may be high-spirited, but they draw demonstrably on the current state of knowledge concerning Elizabethan playhouses. They even incorporate matters that would have signified only to the initiated: for example, the camera's momentary hesitation as it tracks over the London roofs and appears to be heading into the 'wrong' Bankside arena, only to correct itself and make for the Globe, probably alludes to the reversed labelling of the Globe and the Beargarden in Hollar's 1644 'Long View' of London, signalling the film's simultaneous dependence on and transcendence of an imperfect historical record. These scenes present a pointedly defamiliarized picture of Elizabethan stage practice, foregrounding defunct conventions that underline the historical specificity of Shakespeare's theatre and its differences from modern stages. The boys who play women's parts are shown backstage, shaving and stuffing their bodices with oranges. Spectators sit on stage in full view of the audience. Business is devised to make the presence of the book-keeper felt, such as the little joke when he intervenes after a stagehand strikes the wrong time on a clock. The outdoor staging is emphasized when the heavens open during the Eastcheap scene, which sends the audience scurrying for cover. Most interesting of all, because presented on the margins and scarcely visible in the camera's rapid panning, the Globe's admission arrangements are scrupulously reproduced. Gatherers stand at the main door and the entrances to the galleries, taking pennies off the spectators as they arrive, exactly as they would have done in Shakespeare's day. If Olivier's Globe is a fantasy in which audiences and players enjoy an idealized immediacy of contact, the foundations of that fantasy turn out to be surprisingly material. For all its utopian resonances, this Globe is an economic enterprise, and is subject to laws of supply and demand (as we shall see) in more ways than one.

The early twentieth century saw considerable enthusiasm for rebuilding 'Shakespeare's' playhouse, and prior to Olivier's film several real-life reconstructions had already been attempted. Edwin Lutyens designed a half-size Globe for the Earl's Court show in 1912, another was built at the Chicago World Fair in 1933, and plans for a London Globe were developed, but never carried through, before the war. Such projects paralleled experiments (such as William Poel's) with simplified staging, but their recreation of Elizabethan conditions rarely went beyond pastiche: for example, the Earl's Court playhouse was part of an idealizing Edwardian 'theme park' of Shakespeare's England, while the proposed London Globe was frankly a hybrid, in which an Elizabethan thrust stage would have been grafted into a modern proscenium arch theatre.[5] But even serious academic scholarship was subject to comparable uncertainties. In the same period, through the work of historians like E. K. Chambers, George Fullmer Reynolds and John Cranford Adams, playhouse archaeology became a growth area for dedicated research, and a temporary culmination was reached in 1942 with Adams's study *The Globe Playhouse: Its Design and Equipment*. With its measurements to the last inch and its compellingly specific illustrations, Adams's book was much the most persuasive architectural description of the Globe yet published, but despite its detail it was promptly subjected by George Reynolds to devastating attack. Reynolds criticized Adams for using evidence for Globe staging drawn indiscriminately from plays written for different theatres, for conveying an air of certainty over matters where evidence was lacking, and most importantly, for failures in historical perspective: he accused Adams of covertly importing modern expectations about naturalistic consistency and illusionistic realism into a theatre which had not yet heard of such things. For Reynolds, Adams's archaeology was unreliable as history, as it had been irretrievably muddled with a modernist aesthetic.[6]

Olivier's Globe is almost certainly indebted to Adams's. In some ways his reconstruction does diverge: it lacks the pillars and heavens over the platform, omits the stage railings, and its tiring-house façade is flat rather than articulated—changes which reinforce the feeling of audience intimacy. But like Adams's Globe, Olivier's is an eight-sided polygon, with two bays per side.[7] The arrangement of the tiring-house upper level strongly recollects Adams, with its long balcony, flanking bay windows and music room above. Some aspects of Globe furnishing come from Adams, particularly the rushes strewn for the Boar's Head scene (a practice Adams discusses at length), and the little wicket in the door behind the book-keeper (a detail Adams had conjectured and which Olivier foregrounds by inventing business that allows the book-keeper to communicate through it with the tiring-house). And crucially, Olivier's arrangement of the main stage is very close to Adams's, as he is especially respectful of Adams's view of the relationship between main stage and inner stage. This was a crucial point on which Adams and Reynolds clashed. Reynolds argued that, although modern historians often assumed Elizabethan theatres had inner stages, reliable evidence was lacking, and belief in their existence was fostered by theatre historians' inability to imagine Elizabethan actors staging interior scenes without some kind of mimetic indoor space.[8] Adams, though, thought the inner stage was a substantial room opening into the tiring-house, and built it prominently into his designs. For him, this inner space (which he called the study), and the gallery area over it (the chamber), dominated the stage and had central functions in Elizabethan stagecraft. His reconstructions assume that all interior scenes would have been played in one of these two key locations.

Olivier avoided some of these pitfalls by adopting an elaborately non-naturalistic playing style in his Elizabethan scenes, thereby marking off his Globe as a special historicized space. Nonetheless, he followed Adams in considering the chamber as the tiring-house's main structural feature, and in using the inner and upper stages as locations for interior action, despite the obvious shortcomings they have within his more rhetorically oriented aesthetic. The opening dialogue between Canterbury and Ely is performed from the balcony, set with table and chair to resemble a room (as Adams envisaged), but such is the bishops' distance from the spectators that they soon turn every speech outwards and declaim, effectively undermining any achieved illusion of place.[9] In the following court scene, Henry sits in the chamber in his chair of state, but he rapidly abandons that removed position in order to adopt more commanding postures at the centre of the platform. And in the final seconds, the play returns to the Globe to reveal the whole court grouped inside the inner stage, despite the ridiculously cramped conditions into which this thrusts them. At such moments, the film records a tension between Olivier's brilliantly intuitive understanding of the rhetorical and performative aspects of Shakespeare's language, and the residually naturalistic assumptions about Elizabethan stage space he inherited from a misleading archaeology. The Globe's architecture seems exact, yet the handling of its acting areas is curiously at odds with the strengths of the verse as Olivier performs it. Further, Olivier elaborates on this stagecraft by adding to his inner stage a set of painted curtains showing different designs—a coat of arms, a tavern wall, a view of Southampton—which the Chorus draws at moments when locations alter. There are no precedents for stage curtains in Shakespeare's day, and their use to mark scene changes seems overtly to hybridize Elizabethan conditions with practices derived from modern theatres.[10] Though effectively employed, they signal a lack of confidence in the Globe's ability to convey a fully realistic or symbolic sense of location. For all Olivier's panache as an Elizabethan player, the Globe in which he acts carries the hallmarks of conflicting antiquarian and theatrical assumptions specific to 1944.[11]

Into this complexly determined space, Olivier introduces a scenario of his own devising: for, in his version, the story of *Henry V*'s first performance turns out to be a hegemonic struggle between player and public, in which spectator is, eventually though not certainly, subordinated to actor. In considering Olivier's image of his Globe audience it is necessary, again, to register just how much it was shaped by competing modern histories. In many late-Victorian and Edwardian accounts, Elizabethan audiences were described with a combination of amusement and distaste, admired for their supposed lack of inhibition but disparaged as being not quite good enough for Shakespeare. At the most negative, as in Robert Bridges's extraordinary essay of 1907, they were an unworthy mob, primitive, ignorant and brutal. Simon Shepherd and Peter Womack have explored the ideological basis of this prejudice, arguing that the category of the uneducated 'groundling' came into prominence in theatre historiography as the social roots of the Victorian theatre narrowed, and that it was increasingly invoked by defenders of a 'high' culture who wanted to rescue their national poet from associations with a now problematic populism.[12] But by the mid-twentieth century new social priorities were beginning to tell, one instance of which was Alfred Harbage's study *Shakespeare's Audience* (1941), which reviewed the historical evidence afresh and decided Shakespeare's spectators had formed the ideal imaginative community. Harbage called the Globe 'a democratic institution in an intensely undemocratic age', in which for the price of a penny 'cheerful and decent folk', subtended by a 'common humanity', participated equally with their betters in these great occasions.[13] His projection of contemporary ideals onto the Elizabethan past has been much qualified by later historians, but his new myth of Shakespeare's democratic and decent public, with its optimistic and broadly left-leaning liberalism, held the field into the 1980s.[14] Though written in America, Harbage's book exemplifies the consequences for theatre historiography of complex cultural and political changes which were equally working to transform wartime England.

For all their exuberance, Olivier's Globe spectators are not alien exotics or estranged Others. Rather, they are recognizably 1940s cinema-goers in fancy dress, whose theatre-going is the occasion for ordinary sociable activities like eating and making love. In the yard the vendors with their trays bring cinema usherettes irresistibly to mind, and the connection is made by the long-shot from the gallery at the Chorus's first appearance, the point of view for which is defined by a young man eating an apple and a courting couple with their arms around each other, for all the world as if at the back of the circle. The audience in this Globe is evidently a society which communicates easily within itself, for women in the upper galleries converse playfully with men below, while a courtly gentleman who does not belong in the yard still moves through it without discomfort. There is, though, a clear hierarchy between spectators in different areas, for which some historical warrant existed. Olivier's more respectable, middle-class playgoers gravitate to the galleries. Their bearing is restrained, and this is where (with the exception of the fruit-sellers) all the female spectators belong. Wealthy and ostentatiously-dressed gentlemen make up the playgoers sitting on the stage. They are treated deferentially by the players, and some at least have servants with them (when the rain begins, one gentleman remains on the stage under a cloak held by his man). The spectators in the yard, however, comprise the ordinary sort of people. Their group is exclusively male and tightly packed, and most, though not all, of the disruptive behaviour comes from them. This audience is both inclusive and carefully differentiated, and the theatre dynamic, as Olivier depicts it, derives from the interaction between its three groups.

Most discussions of the audience and its response to the performance focus on Olivier's decision to present the bishops as incompetent actors, comically incapable of articulating the complexities of the Salic Law, thereby provoking the crowd's ridicule. It is usually felt that this prepares us for the displacement of a theatrical aesthetic by a cinematic one, and that politically it was necessary since a film designed to help the war effort could not admit the problematic justifications which Shakespeare offers for the French campaign. Harry Geduld says Olivier could not acknowledge the bishops' 'duplicities and complex motivations', and guyed the Salic Law passage so as to distract attention from its speciousness: 'somehow or other Henry's forthcoming campaign seems to have been "justified" without our noticing precisely how'.[15] But while broadly true, this fails to recognize how politically self-aware Olivier's reading is. Although severely cut, his opening dialogue retains the bishops' preoccupation with money, and while Canterbury and Ely make fools of themselves, they exchange looks at the point when Henry seems to have made up his mind which clearly signal their satisfaction with the way things have gone. For all its patriotism, Olivier's film accommodates the perception that even in a heroic enterprise everyone might not share the same public-spirited reasons for wanting war, and registers that the bishops' motives would not have survived serious interrogation.

But if Olivier's French campaign avoids mere jingoism, what I want to focus on here is the encompassing social scenario that the early exchanges are used to express, the allegory of relations within and around the theatrical community which Olivier builds into his Globe scenes. In the opening dialogue in the gallery, it rapidly becomes evident that the bishops attract hostility not simply for their bad performances but for their unfriendly opinions of Falstaff. In some inserted lines, adapted from *2 Henry IV*, Canterbury narrates Henry's reformation and its consequences for characters from former plays:[16]

> Sir John Falstaff,
> And all his company along with him,
> He banished, under pain of death
> Not to come near his person by ten mile.

The audience cheer at Falstaff's name but boo the news of his banishment, and for a moment there is serious disruption as the playhouse seems on the verge of a revolt. Canterbury restores order only by standing and rebuking the crowd directly like a preacher, yet the exclusion of this popular but subversive figure is plainly deplored and the bishops are distinctly embarrassed. The episode divests them of what little authority they have and Ely's praise of the reformed king, 'We are blessed in the change', is greeted by a jeering echo from one spectator. By allowing the bishops to lose audience credibility, this insertion seems designed to foreground the potential self-assertiveness of the playgoers and the implications of their commercial ability to command what they want. Faced with an audience demanding a more comedic and potentially more subversive play, the bishops lose out aesthetically and politically. Not only are their performances undermined as performances, so too is their status as clerics, their ideological function within the mimesis. The audience 'rebellion' puts into question the aesthetic economy of the Globe and the social relationships which as an institution it fosters. It takes Olivier's Henry, consummate player as well as consummate king, to regain the confidence of the unpredictable playhouse majority.

In contrast to the bishops' unhappy experience, the following scene, in which Olivier plays 'Burbage' playing Henry, establishes the compelling magnetism of his bearing in the playhouse. His arrival is greeted with resounding applause, and his conduct on the stage has a seemingly effortless grace. He is a charismatic presence who fuses the many-headed audience into a triumphant unity, and his Globe scene is filmed with a preponderance of medium-length shots from platform level, so that spectators in the galleries, stage and arena are at last brought together within the same visual frame. The Salic Law episode and the interview with the French ambassador showcase his easy confidence in his part and his almost uncanny ability to catch the playhouse mood, a theatrical instinct which is underlined by numerous displays of his rhetorical power. Of many examples, perhaps the most striking is the contrived but memorable moment after the disclosure of the tennis balls. Here Henry first looks disconcerted by the Dauphin's insult, then smiles ironically at the joke and slowly replaces that look with an intimidating stare, all this change being accompanied by gasps from the crowd which underline its effectiveness as political threat and histrionic performance. It seems evident that Burbage/Henry fulfils a collective need for persuasive action both at a political and a theatrical level. Nonetheless, it still remains curious that, given the film's patriotic purpose, these early scenes choose to establish his kingly credentials through a scenario focused primarily on domestic politics. The legitimacy of his rule is validated less in relation to a declared enemy overseas than to the potentially unruly public at home.

The consequences of this emerge in two ways. First, there is a functional ambiguity about the sanction Henry's kingship bears, the source from which his authority derives. The Globe sequence makes it seem as if authority is natural in him, an innate kingly bearing, but also that it rests on considerable labour, a discipline through which public confidence is earned. After dismissing the ambassador, Henry displays his self-belief by tossing his crown with casual accuracy onto a finial of his throne, but the backstage view before his entrance has shown him coughing nervously, disclosing that his nonchalance is produced by immense and dedicated artifice. Such doubleness is intrinsic to the Chinese-box structure of the Globe scenes. Within the mimesis Henry is the all-competent king, but, insofar as he is only an actor, kingship is recognized as something he has seriously to work at. This device is nicely calculated for a wartime audience that needed to feel its leaders could be trusted, but it effectively sidesteps the question of the genealogy of Henry's power. It is impossible to know how far his authority is 'natural', something he has because of who he is, and how far it is meritocratic, a sanction he earns through the crowd's approval. There is a striking contrast here with Kenneth Branagh's *Henry V* (1989), a film produced in a culture which no longer believes in innate authority, and in which the elaboration of Henry's fitness for rule has become the story's entire purpose. Olivier's film does not have such doubts and need not admit that a legitimate English ruler could be anything other than kingly. Even so, it dwells on the competence of Henry's performance, and thereby admits a hesitation about the genetics by which his authority is derived.

Secondly, there is considerable ambiguity around the politics of Henry's relationship with the crowd, and the nature of the power of which in the Globe he is master. His sanction as player/king is bound up with his rapport with the spectators, so that he seems simultaneously a popular actor and a popular monarch. But he also has (in the strong sense) a *command* over the audience's affections: he has only to enter the stage for everyone to brighten, and he seems able almost to conjure authority out of them. This ambiguity most appears when he takes their applause, stepping out of the illusion as he repeatedly does and bowing deferentially to the spectators. At such moments we have the teasing image of a king humbling himself before his people, even though the cue for their approval is the superbly manipulative performance which has produced the plaudits. Where does power reside in this: with the people who applaud, or the player who wrings applause from them? For all Henry's elaborately acted deference, it seems evident that his authority is established all the more emphatically for the gestures of submissiveness in which it is couched. Presenting a command which is expressed as if it were obedience, the Globe scenes allow Henry to be seen from two perspectives at once, making him both the mere servant of his people and an all-competent master over them. This monarch manages to be entirely absolute while still remaining only ever the people's representative.

At this distance, it is difficult to know whether or not the film is conscious about its delicate handling of Henry's authority, or even whether, if remarked upon in 1944, it would have been felt as contradictory. In one recent essay, Graham Holderness has forcefully argued that these tensions were strategic and allowed Olivier to insinuate a latent radicalism, his attentiveness to the King's theatricality qualifying his film's overt patriotism. Noting how the film makes Henry's performance visible as a performance, Holderness suggests it thereby 'incorporates some of the aesthetic devices which work within Shakespeare's drama to undermine the play's traditionalist and official ideology', its appreciation of the constructedness of kingship demystifying the roots of Henry's power, permitting his rhetoric of rule to be scrutinized, and blocking a reading of his character in terms of a simple holistic naturalism.[17] Certainly Holderness is right to draw attention to these aspects of the *mise en scène*, particularly in contrast with Kenneth Branagh's privatized and sentimentalized *Henry V*, in which the King's personal identity is presented as simply 'authentic' and immunized against any such interrogation. But this reading involves telescoping 1990s critical perspectives back into the 1940s, and, however much Olivier seems to fall on a Brechtian *Verfremdungseffekt* before it was naturalized in English theatre performance, it is questionable whether in 1944 this would have made for an implicit radicalism. On the contrary, even though the film registers that the king is only ever an actor, it seems to relish his histrionic capacities, so that the stress on his rhetoric reinforces his power rather than calling it into question. Olivier's insertion of a gap between player and king may anticipate the conventions of epic theatre, but it is worked out so as to make for a sort of conservative demystification. Though in the 1990s such devices would call Henry's legitimacy into question, in the 1940s they seem to provoke admiration for the star who performed with such aplomb.

What sanctions Henry's power and allows him to appear a self-confident king even while the mechanics of his performance are exposed is, I think, the implied consumer economy into which Olivier delicately embeds his Globe. The film steps around the playhouse's problematic democracy by inflecting the company's relations with its public along lines that seem poised ambiguously between a residually Victorian actor-manager structure and a modern, Hollywoodized star system. In Olivier's Globe, audience enthusiasms are focused on individual players as star performers. 'Burbage' is the big name and receives the loudest plaudits, but the rest of the company likewise have an immediate and charged contact with their audience. From the Chorus downwards, virtually every actor's appearance is rapturously welcomed, and the players reply with extra-dramatic acknowledgements, bowing and smiling as if responding to their public's adulation—so much so that the performance is constantly being held up by eruptions of applause. In this arrangement, the potentially unsettling self-assertiveness of an Elizabethan participatory democracy is channelled into the more governable enthusiasms of the entertainment industry, and Henry's absolute command is established without its seeming to contradict either the playhouse's notionally collective ethos or his company's inner collegiality. Within the company structure

Henry is first among equals, but every player receives some credit, and there is a striking absence of horizontal competitiveness. The players bow politely to one another, and underlying actorly bonds are suggested even in the non-Globe scenes, such as the silent but appreciative looks that Henry and Mountjoy exchange in their last meeting before Agincourt. Even a measure of incompetence is tolerated, for in the tiring-house Henry enthusiastically pumps Canterbury's hand, despite that unfortunate gentleman's disaster with the Salic Law: the company's collegiality projects a sense of overriding common purpose that echoes Angus Calder's account of wartime Britain as a period in which people learned how to lead themselves.[18] At the same time, the idealized intimacy between player and spectator allows the audience to feel that they, too, are part of the team and that Henry's performance empowers them, projecting the will of the playhouse majority as law. In fact, this is an illusion, since the spectators' participation is based on their status as paying consumers, and in practice they do not get the one character whom they most wish to see (Falstaff): they are customers rather than masters. Nonetheless, Olivier's Globe is arranged so that each customer feels himself a king, or is at least permitted temporarily to imagine that he were.

However, instabilities arise in this system if tensions between stars appear, as this opens the possibility that the supposedly unified aesthetic event conceals unspoken class fractures. From this angle, the destabilizing factor is the underplot, since not only do Pistol and his companions project the attitudes of those within the mimesis who feel a less than complete stake in Henry's expedition, but theatrically they belong to a different and competing universe. At least this is how Olivier handles them, for the first Boar's Head scene is treated as a rerun of the episode with the bishops, only this time the crowd get exactly what they want. Pistol in person proves to be just as big a draw as Falstaff. He provokes riotous responses from the spectators, who push and jostle to be near the stage, and he exploits their enthusiasm with effrontery, egging them on and gagging shamelessly. It's not so much what he does, which is little enough, as the mere fact of his presence that generates the excitement. As verbal comedy Olivier's Boar's Head scene is practically incomprehensible, but Pistol has only to move about the stage for his audience to erupt in a frenzy of enthusiasm, for all the world as if this actor were being mobbed by devoted fans. Pretty clearly, a class antagonism is being established here. Pistol is very definitely low comedy, while the ham-acting Nym, Bardolph with his silly stutter, and the leering and cackling Mrs Quickly belong frankly to the world of music hall. It's not surprising, then, that Falstaff, when he is shown on his deathbed, turns out to be the popular comedian George Robey,[19] nor that Pistol's performance is directed almost entirely to the ordinary folk in the yard. One of the incidental consequences of having rain break out during this episode is that, with the exception of the gentleman with the cloak, all the elite spectators retreat to the shelter of the tiring-house, leaving the heroes of the yard wet but very much in command.

It has often been remarked that Olivier's Henry lacks any real opponent. His Dauphin is a braggart, the French king is an imbecile and, anyway, since the 'real' French were allies they could not be represented as irreconcilable enemies. They are chased from the field, but there are few signs of lasting rancour. Mountjoy always treats Henry with respect, and Burgundy's elegy for the land refers to devastations which in 1944 were of concern to English and French alike. Instead, the role of Henry's structural antagonist devolves through the invented Globe scenes onto Pistol.[20] As Pistol, Olivier cast the slightly larger than life English actor Robert Newton, who here turns in one of his barnstorming performances along the lines of Bill Sykes or Long John Silver, Pistol as goggle-eyed, spastically-gangling turkey-cock. This inspired choice means that Newton effectively competes with Olivier for visibility. No other actor in the film has quite the same presence, and certainly none of the English soldiers, who are all an eminently forgettable lot. As Pistol strides offstage at the end of the Boar's Head scene, waving bountifully to his cheering admirers, it is difficult not to register a momentary reminiscence of the popular acclaim which Henry enjoyed only minutes before: the comparison passingly acknowledges that the king's power, seemingly so unique, has in the playhouse much the same sources and sanctions as the clown's. Perhaps it is not surprising, then, that this is the point at which the film takes leave of the Globe, since any further opportunity of comparing the two players' performances would almost certainly have posed awkward questions about Henry's authority, and Newton is not permitted to destabilize the film any further since in the scenes beyond the Globe his role is severely reduced. In fact, an early version of the shooting script would have allowed Pistol his protest against Bardolph's hanging and a more violent final confrontation with Fluellen, but in the event such details were written out, while the troublesome scene with Monsieur Le Fer was cut from the outset.[21] Pistol's theatrical subversion is 'corrected' by the transforming aesthetic of cinema, which successfully overwrites the vulgar comedy of music hall with Henry's more decorous patriotic romance.

Nonetheless, whenever Pistol appears he continues to complicate the diegesis as he always carries a whiff of the Globe with him. He wears the same feathers he had worn in the playhouse, holds his body in eccentric postures, and uses exaggerated mannerisms which run counter to the more naturalistic environment into which the rest of the film has moved.[22] At his final appearance, in the leek scene, he is humiliated by Fluellen, but he still functions latently as a royal travesty whose activities reflect obliquely on the King. Conspicuously, he wears the Constable's armour—evidently a looted trophy, but one which only moments before we had seen won in single combat by Henry himself—and he seduces French women and runs off with their families' property, actions which are in keeping with his character but which parodically pre-echo the advantages that only in the next scene Henry will be taking with Katherine. Banished from the ending, Pistol nonetheless preserves his volatility and wit—there is none of the demonization that Branagh visits on his Pistol, whose degraded final appearance testifies how far he has travelled from the King—and his farewell lines are spoken direct to camera, a privilege afforded elsewhere in Olivier's film only to Henry and the Chorus. Given the film's triumphant conclusion, it is difficult to know how conscious or unconscious these potential parallels are. Disappearing into the snowy French countryside,

Pistol is dismissed without exactly being suppressed, and he remains a rogue refraction of Henry, not the gallery's hero but the yard's. He reminds us of less fitting ways of seeing Henry's victory, and measures how much the harmonies of the ending depend on careful managing of the robust enthusiasms of the Globe.

As Olivier's film moves gradually away from the Globe, an increasingly naturalistic aesthetic comes into play, so that by the time we reach Agincourt, Henry has acquired a fully-fledged interiority (expressed in his eve-of-battle soliloquy presented in voice-over), and the action has moved into totally cinematic space. On the one occasion Henry encounters Pistol, among the tents before Agincourt, the contrast between his relaxed demeanour and Pistol's zaniness establishes how confidently he moves within these new horizons. But, despite this progressive transformation, Henry's status as monarch continues to draw implicitly on the theatrical investments established in the Globe scenes. Even in 'real' space Henry speaks with great rhetorical self-awareness, and uses an elaborate and formal repertoire of hand gestures which repeats the overtly oratorical body language he had displayed in the theatre, reinforcing the underlying continuities between his presentation within the Globe and without. Both 'Once more unto the breach' and 'Crispin Crispianus' are filmed so as to recollect the tennis balls speech, in a single take with the camera craning away as Henry's volume rises. In terms of the visual relationships that it creates, 'Crispin Crispianus' is an almost exact replay of the tennis balls: the camera follows a gesturing Henry as he walks through his army and climbs into an elevated position, while his men collect around him virtually as if we were back in the Globe yard. The nicest example of this interchange between cinematic naturalism and theatrical artifice comes in the final defiant interview with Mountjoy, during which Henry's horse unexpectedly starts to turn, and he has to pull it back and lean forward to calm it without disrupting his complex rhetorical speech. With no sign of losing grip on his role, Henry regains control of the animal and, as he reaches his peroration, he clips it with his heels so it obediently carries him away from

Mountjoy and out of the frame. Any other director would have retaken this shot, but the moment with the frisky steed brilliantly exemplifies the way that, outside the Globe, Olivier renders Henry's political power as theatrical power naturalized. The rebellious horse incorporates an unpredictable reality into the seamless artifice of Olivier's performance, neatly subordinating nature to art, and it invites us to read Henry's authority as valorized by the theatrical command glimpsed momentarily through the interstices of a more naturalized cinematic aesthetic. On Agincourt field Henry has a power now represented as natural, but which continues to draw on the political scenarios played out in the Globe.

In theatricalizing Henry's power in this way, Olivier provided himself with a mechanism which allowed him to manage the difficult task of translating the personalized heroics of Shakespeare's monarch into the rather different social configurations of 1944. On the surface, *Henry V* tells a story of triumphant British kingship. It shows a single hero asserting his innate authority, making himself the centre of his people's political desires and focusing their energies into an irresistible national will. Closer inspection, though, reveals a more complex attitude towards Henry's enterprise, and some anxiety about the social conspectus it requires. Henry's power is derived ambivalently from his own abilities and from the audience to whom he owes a double-edged loyalty, while the incipiently democratic tendencies of the theatrical community are recognized but distanced: in the playhouse Henry ambiguously serves and presides, at one and the same time the spectators' representative and their master. Eventually liberated from the Globe, he moves into spaces where his power appears more self-authorizing and complete, but even here underlying reminiscences of the theatre continue to suggest alternative genealogies for the authority he seems so effortlessly to command. In this world Pistol is no longer a threat, but he is a character stamped out of the same coin as Henry, who reminds us of the relationships on which the monarch's power rests. Agincourt may seem a fantasy of inexorable British success, but it has been generated in the Globe by a complex economy of assertiveness and subordination.

Whether such fractures would have been visible in 1944 is another question. The most recent commentator on *Henry V* has called it 'an almost entirely positive film', in which internal antagonisms are swept aside in a display of collective accord.[23] This judgement is undoubtedly correct, as the need for wartime unity meant that *Henry V* had inevitably to project a confident mood. And yet if the film's *telos* is necessarily towards integration, it is, as I have been trying to suggest, complicated by adjustments which register tensions in the imagined community that it invents, and which from our vantage point are eloquent of the historical changes that were already working to transform the wartime consensus. The version of the Globe which Olivier translated from his sources may have served a society in need of images projecting unity, solidarity and common purpose, but—as at the margins it seems fitfully to acknowledge—it was an image itself on the brink of yet more radical translations.

NOTES

1. W. J. Lawrence, 'Title and locality boards on the pre-Restoration stage', in *The Elizabethan Playhouse and Other Studies*, 1st series (Stratford-upon-Avon: The Shakespeare Head Press, 1912), pp. 41–71. Well before 1944 Edmund Chambers had cast doubt on the general applicability of Lawrence's evidence, emphasizing that it did not seem valid for the staging practice of public playhouses like the Globe (*The Elizabethan Stage* [4 vols, Oxford: Clarendon Press, 1923], 3: 127n).

2. Of course, another source for these placards might well be the speech and location labels of the silent cinema. See also the thoughtful brief account of these scenes by Douglas Lanier in 'Drowning the book: *Prospero's Books* and the textual Shakespeare', in *Shakespeare, Theory, and Performance*, ed. J. C. Bulman (London: Routledge, 1996), pp. 192–93.

3. Quoted by Russell Jackson, 'Two films of *Henry V*: frames and stories', in *The Show Within: Dramatic and Other Insets*, ed. F. Laroque (2 vols, Montpellier: Publications de Université Paul-Valéry, 1992), 1: 186.

4. From a 1944 review by James Agee, quoted in Harry M. Geduld, *Filmguide to 'Henry V'* (Bloomington: Indiana University Press, 1973), p. 28.

5. See the illustration in A. Gurr and J. Orrell, *Rebuilding Shakespeare's*

Globe (London: Weidenfeld and Nicolson, 1989), p. 32. These early reconstructions are discussed in *Rebuilding Shakespeare's Globe*, pp. 29–34; A. Gurr, 'Shakespeare's Globe: A history of reconstructions and some reasons for trying', in *Shakespeare's Globe Rebuilt*, eds J. R. Mulryne and M. Shewring (Cambridge: Cambridge University Press, 1997), pp. 27–47; and M. F. O'Connor, 'Theatre of the Empire: "Shakespeare's England" at Earl's Court, 1912', in *Shakespeare Reproduced: The Text in History and Ideology*, eds J. E. Howard and M. F. O'Connor (London: Methuen, 1987), pp. 68–98.

6. For Reynolds' critiques, see *The Journal of English and Germanic Philology*, 42 (1943), 122–26, and *Shakespeare Survey*, 4 (1951), 98–99.

7. The assumption that the Globe was octagonal was to be demolished by I. A. Shapiro in 1948. See Gurr, 'Shakespeare's Globe: A history of reconstructions', p. 38.

8. Reynolds, *The Staging of Elizabethan Plays at the Red Bull Theater, 1605–1625* (New York: Modern Language Association of America, 1940).

9. The handling of the death of Falstaff, though strictly outside the Globe sequence, also reinforces the association between balcony and upper rooms.

10. A similar arrangement was used by Ben Iden Payne in his experiments with 'modified Elizabethan staging' in America in the 1930s: see B. Iden Payne, *A Life in a Wooden O* (New Haven: Yale University Press, 1977), pp. 164–65.

11. A similar point could be made about Olivier's handling of music in the Globe. The music cues are almost certainly more elaborate than those that would have obtained in Shakespeare's theatre, and the musicians are led by a conductor who has no place in a 1600 Globe. These details are reflective of more modern theatre practices.

12. S. Shepherd and P. Womack, *English Drama: A Cultural History* (Oxford: Blackwell, 1996), pp. 110–21.

13. A. Harbage, *Shakespeare's Audience* (New York: Columbia University Press, 1941), pp. 11, 158, 162.

14. The major critique is by A. J. Cook, *Shakespeare's Privileged Playgoers* (Princeton: Princeton University Press, 1981). See also M. Butler, *Theatre and Crisis 1632–1642* (Cambridge: Cambridge University Press, 1984), pp. 293–306; and A. Gurr, *Playgoing in Shakespeare's London* (Cambridge: Cambridge University Press, 1987).

15. *Filmguide to 'Henry V'*, pp. 28–29; and compare J. N. Loehlin, *'Henry V': Shakespeare in Performance* (Manchester: Manchester University Press, 1996), pp. 31–33.

16. This passage is a conflation of *2 Henry IV*, V.v.63–65 and 91–92 (Riverside).

17. G. Holderness, *Shakespeare Recycled* (Hemel Hempstead: Harvester Wheatsheaf, 1992), p. 186.

18. A. Calder, *The People's War: Britain 1939–45* (London: Cape, 1969).

19. Robey had in fact played Falstaff in a 1934 production of *1 Henry IV* at His Majesty's (*The London Stage 1930–1939*, ed. J. P. Wearing, 3 vols [Metuchen, NJ: The Scarecrow Press, 1990], 2: 697). It is noticeable how many commentators on the film are embarrassed by the vulgarity of this scene, which seems to them out of keeping with the proper Shakespearean dignity: for example, Geduld, *Filmguide to 'Henry V'*, pp. 30–31.

20. In this respect, Olivier anticipates some of the perspectives developed in postwar Shakespearean criticism, for example Anne Righter's (Anne Barton's) theatre-centred reading of *Henry V* in *Shakespeare and the Idea of the Play* (London: Chatto & Windus, 1962).

21. See Ace G. Pilkington, *Screening Shakespeare: From Richard II to Henry V* (Newark, DE: University of Delaware Press, 1991), pp. 105–06.

22. On this point, see Anthony Davies, *Filming Shakespeare's Plays* (Cambridge: Cambridge University Press, 1988), p. 32; and Jackson, 'Two films of *Henry V*', p. 190.

23. Loehlin, '*Henry V*', p. 48.

Tempestuous Transformations

DAVID LINDLEY

If it is true, as Dennis Kennedy observes in *Looking at Shakespeare*, that 'the visual history of performance ... has been mostly excluded from Shakespeare studies', then it is even more the case that the history of the music which has accompanied successive productions has been virtually totally ignored. However, if 'there is a clear relationship between what a production looks like and what its spectators accept as its statement and value',[1] the same must be true of the aural world generated by musical accompaniment. Less completely pervasive than the visual, physical setting of a performance, and much more prominent in some plays than others, music, although a somewhat neglected medium of translation, is simultaneously capable of giving significant emotional charge to particular actions and moments in a performance, of underscoring its larger direction and purposes, and renegotiating relations between text (the past) and performance (the present).

The Tempest is a particularly useful play through which to explore the contribution music can make to the translation of the text from page to stage. It is Shakespeare's most musical play, and scholars have debated over many years the significance of the contribution which music makes to the play's thematic preoccupations, whether as a symbol of harmony and concord, or as an aspect of Prospero's manipulative magic arts.[2] Yet in recent studies of the play in performance the music gets scant attention.[3] With the information made available by the publication of *A Shakespeare Music Catalogue*,[4] the time seems right to integrate consideration of music into *The Tempest*'s stage history, and this essay aims to make some preliminary exploration of the issues that such an effort raises. I am not concerned here to discuss the ways in which Shakespeare's play has been transposed, from the

Restoration to the present, into a more or less thoroughgoing operatic mode,[5] nor do I explore the potentially fascinating ways in which settings of portions of the text, or composition of pieces alluding to it, form a history of commentary parallel to the much more frequently examined literary penumbra of works inspired by the play.[6] Instead, I want to consider, through a very few examples, some of the ways in which the play might be formed and transformed through the music chosen or composed to accompany its performance.

There is, of course, a pervasive problem in such an undertaking, in that the survival of the music actually used in performances is partial, to say the least. The *Shakespeare Music Catalogue* itself is in many ways a record of ghosts, of scores that have not survived and are known only through the traces left on theatrical programmes. Theatrical companies' archives are frequently haphazard in their preservation of musical scores, and even when music is published it will tend to be only the set pieces from the score—Honegger's *Prélude pour 'La Tempête'*,[7] or Tippett's *Songs for Ariel*,[8] for example—which find their way into print, and they will often be rearranged to suit the concert performance at which they are aimed, as is the case with the suites which Sibelius produced from his 1926 score. Though this is a problem that attends all aspects of performance history,[9] enough remains to make the enterprise worth undertaking.

The history of incidental music for the play involves not only shifts in musical styles, but significant transformations in assumptions about what function music serves in the theatre. As a point of departure, therefore, it is useful first to consider the sound-world that might have been created at the work's initial performances. The musical resources available to Shakespeare's company were relatively limited. In the public playhouses it seems likely that a mixed or 'broken' consort of players of plucked and bowed strings together with flute or recorder formed the basic ensemble, supplemented with trumpets and drums for fanfares and the like, with the possibility of buying in extra musicians from the city or the court for particular performances or special effects. In the private playhouses the ensemble was larger, and, more significantly, it was the custom in these theatres for instrumentalists to provide musical entertainment before the performance began, and then to perform between the acts of the play. After the King's Men took over the Blackfriars theatre in 1608, it is probable that they adopted the practice of musical interludes, and it is likely that they then transported it back to the Globe.[10] It would certainly seem that *The Tempest* was designed in Acts,[11] and therefore that music was performed between them. At first sight, then, it might appear that, apart from a difference in scale, there is a continuity between the deployment of musical resources in the early seventeenth-century playhouse and the provision of entr'acte music by composers such as Sullivan (in 1864),[12] or Sibelius (in 1926).[13] It is extremely unlikely, however, that the entr'actes in Shakespeare's theatre would have been in any way specific to the particular play being performed. It must rather have been independent and detachable entertainment—like that provided by the instrumental ensembles who performed light music in the intervals of repertory theatre performances up and down the country until at least the early 1960s. It was part of the experience of going to the theatre, rather than essential to the experience of a particular play. In later performances entr'actes might, of course, function primarily as 'cover' for the changing of large and cumbersome naturalistic settings from scene to scene, but in both the Sullivan and the Sibelius scores such music is designed very clearly to be appropriate to the scenes which precede or follow it. It is music which aspires to the condition of the tone poems on Shakespearean themes by Romantic composers such as Berlioz, Tchaikovsky or Elgar,[14] like them, in effect, attempting a translation of the dramatic action into the medium of music, producing a self-contained parallel to the play which it accompanies. But these large-scale scores, which also extensively supplemented the music cues embodied in the text, raise a number of more general issues.

In the Shakespearean theatre music is almost always assumed to be heard by the actors onstage as well as by the audience. The apparent exception in *The Tempest*, II.i, where Antonio and Sebastian hear nothing of the 'solemn music' which lulls the other lords to sleep, is making a symbolic point—that these are characters whose insensibility marks them out as fit for 'treasons, stratagems and spoils', as Lorenzo puts it in *The Merchant of Venice*, V.i.84. We recognize its symbolic import precisely because it is such a notable exception to the normal, quasi-naturalistic rule. From the eighteenth century onwards, however, the possibility of music being provided for the ears of the audience alone, as an underlining or emotional characterization of words and actions on stage, is readily accepted, even though its expansiveness could sometimes be the cause of complaint. A reviewer of Beerbohm Tree's 1904 performance, for example, testily observed: 'As the cast always speaks to musical accompaniment, generally slow, it is surprising that they make a single speech intelligible.'[15] But in general the practice has continued to be customary in the twentieth century. John Wooldridge's music for the 1951 Royal Shakespeare Company production, for example, supplies brief chordal progressions played on tremolando strings to underscore many points in Prospero's long narration of past history in I.ii, in order to intensify for the audience the sense of agitation in his recollection of Antonio's trespass, and much the same is true of Davey's score for the 1993 RSC staging. But such instrumental underlining raises pointedly the question that Ferdinand asks on his first entrance: 'Where should this music be?' (I.ii.388)[16]

At one level *The Tempest*, set in an island 'full of noises,/ Sounds, and sweet airs' (III.ii.133), seems to offer *carte blanche* to the composer. All music can be taken by the audience simply as an emanation of the spirit of this magical place and seems, therefore, to need no particular justification. But yet the question of musical agency is vital to the reading of the play. Music actually called for by the text almost always causes something to happen. It puts characters to sleep,[17] wakes them up, or moves them about the island, and it functions as a means of Prospero's control of characters and action. Once music moves into its own freestanding space then that clear sense of music as generated for a narrative purpose is fundamentally altered. Instead, the nature of the music becomes a sign of the purposes of the producer, contributing to the audience's sense of the directorial translation of the text, and it is accepted by them as the normal currency of emotional coercion and commentary that they understand and respond to within the habitual semiotic systems of film and television.

In Sibelius's score the detachment of music from human agency is taken much further, since the opening representation of a storm at sea, wonderfully dramatic and atmospheric as it is, actually substituted in performance for the first scene of the play. It is a thoroughgoing translation of text into another medium, supplanting rather than supplementing the written word. There was, of course, precedent for avoiding the difficulties of staging the quasi-realistic tempest by such translation. Thomas Linley did so in 1777, where a vivid orchestral storm accompanied a chorus (words probably by Sheridan), 'Arise! ye spirits of the storm.' F. R. Benson, in at least some of the performances he gave at the Shakespeare Memorial Theatre between 1891 and 1911, substituted for the opening scene Haydn's *Der Sturm*, a work for chorus and orchestra unrelated to Shakespeare's text.[18] The storm scene is, of course, notoriously difficult to bring off onstage, and all manner of strategies have been attempted—from the full-blown realism of the 1934 Bridges Adams performance at Stratford where 'the reeling ship finally plunges beneath the spouting waves amid all the fury of the elements',[19] through the elaborate theatricality of Giorgio Strehler's Milan performance, where a blue silk cloth was manipulated by sixteen hidden operators to simulate the waves,[20] to minimalist stagings, as in Hytner's and Hall's 1988 productions at the RSC and National Theatre. But one of the central questions every production must decide is whether to make an explicit contrast of mode between the apparent naturalism of the opening shipwreck, and the following scene which moves us unambiguously into the realm of Prospero's 'art'. It has been frequently the practice in recent years to have Prospero or Ariel onstage during at least part of the opening scene, indicating to the audience from the outset that this is a 'magic' tempest. In 1951 at Stratford, for example, 'when the ship begins to founder, Prospero is already there, and the wreck is visibly the product of his imagination',[21] and, in Sam Mendes's production at the RSC in 1993, the play and the tempest itself were set in motion by Ariel entering to swing a lantern suspended at the front of the stage.[22] Substituting music for action, as in Sibelius's storm prelude, ducks completely the problem of staging, but in so doing it unequivocally turns the storm into a symbolic event. It becomes something that must be 'produced' within the audience's imagination—even supplied by them from their memory of the text—and since, as Auden tersely observed, 'Music cannot imitate nature: a musical storm always sounds like the wrath of Zeus',[23] it locates the storm as neither naturalistic, nor yet the product of Prospero's magic powers. Such an extreme translation of theatrical into musical expression decisively places music itself at the centre of the audience's experience and understanding of the play-world.

In a recent performance directed by the Romanian Silviu Purcarete,[24] in place of the storm scene the characters from the ship paraded wordlessly through the audience as they gathered outside the auditorium, and then screamed as they went into the theatre. As the audience followed them inside, they were greeted by a stage swimming in coloured light (representing the sea), with Prospero in eighteenth-century costume standing upstage, and a few phrases uttered in his voice amplified over a soundtrack composed by Vaile Sirli. The 'real' world was left explicitly outside the theatre, in the foyer, and the world of the play was thereby defined 'as a space of dream and of music'.[25]

Sumptuous, rich scores of the kind Sullivan and Sibelius supplied, or Benson and Beerbohm Tree assembled from assorted existing music, carry many implications and bring with them a number of practical consequences. In the first place, their very scale emphasizes clearly enough that the music the audience hears is not 'of' the island but a supplemental commentary upon it: Ariel's 'quality' could scarcely extend to a full symphony orchestra. Whereas it would seem that the musicians in the Jacobean theatres were hidden from the audience, either within the tiring-house or in the gallery over the stage,[26] in proscenium-arch theatres the orchestra pit makes an emphatic physical divide between audience and stage (even if, as in Tree's performance, the band was 'hidden beneath a mass of vegetables'[27]). Visually as well as aurally, this music clearly belongs to the world of the audience, rather than the onstage world of the play. In more recent times, as the pressure of economics has reduced the scale of theatre bands, the diminished musical forces can at least suggest that the music of the island is, at some level, of a scale which might be generated by the spirits whom Prospero commands.

Whatever the scale of the musical accompaniment, however, composers face the central problem of devising a sound-world appropriate to their (or their director's) vision of Prospero's island. This act of translation involves both the choosing of an appropriate musical language, and also the selection of particular instruments to create a convincing island soundscape. Until the 1950s the composer's palette was largely confined to the instruments of the conventional symphony orchestra, thus creating a sound-world familiar to the audience, though historically distant from the seventeenth-century characters on stage. Any 'strangeness' therefore needed to be generated through stylistic means. In more recent years there has been much more freedom to deploy unusual instrumental timbres to signify the alterity of Prospero's island, enforcing a kind of double alienation, both from the historical time of the play's composition and, potentially at least, from the familiar musical landscape of the modern audience. But in every case the cultural signification of particular instruments can be brought into play. In Shakespeare's time, for example, it was likely that the 'solemn music' for which the play calls on a number of occasions would be performed by recorders, conventionally associated with the otherworldly. For Poel's production in 1897, Arnold Dolmetsch arranged 'authentic' music, with Ariel playing a pipe and tabor.[28] The early music industry was then in its infancy and these sounds might well have seemed both antique and strange. They would certainly sort with Poel's project to strip away what he considered the excesses of nineteenth-century practice to return to an imagined seventeenth-century theatrical mode. For a modern audience, however, for whom the principal association of the recorder is with painful memories of primary school, some other alternative probably needs to be found.[29] In Stephen Oliver's score for the 1982 RSC performance Ariel played panpipes, then particularly fashionable for their slightly exotic coolness; Sean Davey's score for the 1993 performance made use of synthesized harp and glockenspiel sounds to surround the appearances of Ariel and other moments of magic in the play.

The semiotic codes of instrumental sounds are by no means fixed, and, particularly in more recent years, the advent of electronic resources has enabled directors and composers to suggest a sound that is clearly not produced by direct human performance. Most famously, Peter Brook's 1957 production employed a tape he himself assembled, described by one reviewer as 'like a combination of glockenspiel, thundersheet, Malayan nose-flute and discreetly tortured Sistine choirboy'.[30] This refusal of a conventional score—which provoked widely divergent responses amongst critics—was entirely deliberate on Brook's part. The alienness of the sounds suited his emphasis upon the darker potential of the play, and created a suitably strange soundscape. But it was also a product of his beliefs about the function of incidental music itself. In a newspaper article he wrote: 'It is no longer the ideal to go to an eminent composer ... and ask him to write a score to accompany a play. ... A good incidental score nowadays is more a matter of timbre and tone colour than of harmony or even of rhythm; it has to appeal to a mind which has at least one and three-quarter ears fully occupied with following the dramatic narrative; it is, in fact, quarter-ear music.'[31] Evidently for Brook the prime function of music is to contribute to the establishment of an overall directorial perspective on the play. In the process, however, his alien sounds left Ariel, the play's principal musical performer, in a difficult position. A provincial reviewer complained: 'A vague wash of sound will not do for Ariel's songs but it is all he gets for accompaniment, and against it he merely intones the words, like a vicar at matins.'[32] This unsympathetic comment registers the way in which Brook's adoption of music at the opposite extreme from the quasi-operatic settings of Sullivan or Sibelius brings to the fore the question of Ariel's function as musician in the play, and focuses attention on the particular effects of the translation of the text of a song lyric into performed music.

The two songs for Ariel by Robert Johnson which survive, and which were presumably used in early performances of *The Tempest*, are clearly designed to meet the abilities of the boy actor who sang them; they are tuneful and largely untouched by the fashion for declamatory song which was just taking hold contemporaneously in the court masque. It would be perfectly possible that the actor could have accompanied himself on the lute, with an offstage group of singers picking up the refrains which seem to Ferdinand's ears to appear above him. At the same time, the timbre of the unbroken boy's voice might seem appropriate for the songs of I.ii, 'Come unto these yellow sands' and 'Full fathom five', which each draws upon the conventional attribution to music of a suprahuman power to calm and order both the natural disturbance of the storm and the unquietness of Ferdinand's feelings. The first Ariel must have been at the very least a competent singer, capable also of playing the pipe and tabor which lure the conspirators offstage in III.ii, and he clearly functioned as the conduit through which Prospero puts the sounds of the island to his own purposes. In the subsequent stage history of the play Ariel has not necessarily been called upon to sustain these qualities. Indeed, the actor playing the part (female from the Restoration until 1930) has not always been required even to sing the songs *in propria persona*. In the series of Benson revivals at the turn of the century, for example, it seems to have been more important that the actresses playing Ariel be capable of sprightly movement than vocal competence—on several occasions another actress was called upon to do the singing. In Peter Hall's 1988 National Theatre production, Ariel mimed to a prerecorded tape on which the songs were sung by a countertenor voice.[33] But the crucial fact is that the kinds of songs Ariel sings, and the competence with which they are performed, have multiple consequences for the play in performance.

Though the songs (with the significant exception of the last, 'Where the bee sucks') are embedded in the action of the play, and each aimed specifically at a character or characters onstage, they yet inevitably, like all performed songs, stand somewhat outside the action and enforce a moment of stasis (precisely the effect that Brook's 'quarter-ear music' attempts to circumvent). They thus serve simultaneously a number of different functions. They are certainly to be taken as symptoms or examples of the 'sounds and sweet airs' with which the island is, according to

Caliban, full, and therefore the musical language they employ will assist in the characterization of the island itself in the minds of the audience in a fashion analogous to the function of 'incidental' music. At the same time they gesture towards the conventional Renaissance understanding of earthly music as representing a celestial harmony which has of itself the power to charm animate and inanimate nature alike. It is a particular problem in adopting an electronic or aggressively modernist score that it is likely to challenge an audience's sense of what such a symbolic harmony might be. As Philip Hope-Wallace observed of Brook's production, 'we do not necessarily want to "come unto these yellow sands" in the manner of Roger Quilter, but so much twangling is like a restless radio next door'.[34] Finally, they are precisely that which in important respects characterizes Ariel, and therefore play an important part both in establishing a particular view of his individual character, and at the same time in defining his relationship with Prospero and the other singers in the play—Stephano, Trinculo and Caliban.

This last is not insignificant. For though the bulk of the music on the island is Prospero's, or at least under his direction, the conspirators define themselves in part by the fact that theirs is the only music which Prospero does not dictate. This is the case both with Caliban's song of freedom, and with their attempt to sing a 'catch', whose musical style—a single tune repeated by three voices—enacts their conspiratorial concord. In the Sibelius score, however, Stephano and Caliban are given fully orchestrated 'numbers' for their songs, 'The master, the bos'un, the swabber and I' and 'No more dams I'll make for fish'. In all the other scores I have so far examined, there is a clear distinction between Ariel's songs, accompanied by instruments, and these others, which are both unaccompanied and set to melodies which suggest in their rhythmic emphasis and lack of melodic refinement the folk song or work song. This contrast—in musical terms also a hierarchy—clearly excludes the 'lower' characters from the island's musical resources, and therefore gives particular point to the moment when Ariel (playing, according to the original stage direction, the pipe and tabor, associated with the popular, not the courtly) transforms their co-operative 'catch', thereby translating their music into Prospero's controlling language. If there is a flattening of this hierarchy—either by the elevation of the conspirators to full musical status, or else, as in the Brook 1957 performance, by diminishing the distinctiveness of Ariel's musical vocabulary, then one connection of music to the play's thematic preoccupation with social class and social control is occluded.

But the style of Ariel's songs is important in other ways to our perception of the nature of the character. So, for example, the extended, quasi-operatic settings of Arne, Sullivan or Sibelius by their very amplitude 'frame' the songs as formal arias, and, in demanding highly competent performance, establish 'singer-liness' as a dominant aspect of Ariel's presence. An extreme example is that of Julia St George, the Ariel in Calvert's Manchester performance of 1864, who, 'when she found that Sullivan's music was to be used, pleaded with great earnestness that she might retain Dr Arne's settings of Ariel's songs ... She gained her point, and her singing of "Where the Bee Sucks" was the success of the evening ... not until she had sung it for the third time was the play allowed to proceed'.[35]

Even without such elaboration and such disturbance of the dramatic momentum of the play, however, performance remains central to Ariel's role. But, as Auden observes, the relationship between his performance and his 'character' is elusive. He writes: 'Ariel is neither a singer, that is to say, a human being whose vocal gifts provide him with a social function, nor a nonmusical person who in certain moods feels like singing. Ariel is song.'[36] Auden goes on to suggest that his singing 'cannot express any human feelings because he has none. The kind of voice he requires is exactly the kind that opera does not want, a voice which is as lacking in the personal and the erotic and as like an instrument as possible'.[37] Auden's comments set out some of the problems that confront the composer in supplying music for Ariel to sing, and the actor in finding a manner of performance consistent with an overall perspective upon the character, but they oversimplify the problems that attend any particular setting in a specific production, where Ariel is a physical presence rather than an abstraction.

So long as the emphasis in productions was on an Ariel whose lightness and swiftness of movement suggested that the character's 'true nature' was delight in service, there was little problem in giving uncomplicatedly open and cheerful settings to 'Come unto these yellow sands' and 'Where the bee sucks', with an admixture of melancholy appropriate to Ferdinand's position in 'Full fathom five'. But in recent years, as part of a generally 'darker' conception of the play, the relationship between Prospero and Ariel has been subjected to closer and more troubled scrutiny. As long ago as 1951, a reviewer commented upon 'Alan Badel's really imprisoned Ariel—no tricksy elf, with none of the "childlike simplicity" that Coleridge found in the part, but an elemental spirit robbed of freedom and even tortured by the loss'.[38] In a series of recent productions (perhaps as a reaction to, or variation of, emphasis on Caliban as the colonial subject), the 'imprisonment' of Ariel has been increasingly stressed. In Michael Bogdanov's aggressively anti-romantic production of the play for the English Shakespeare Company in 1992 (with a set dominated by concrete pipes and a burnt-out Mini), Olwyn Fouéré characterized the part as that of a conspicuously reluctant performer. At no point in the play until given freedom in Act V did she move at more than a snail's pace. Simon Russell Beale's projection of a severely restrained servant in Sam Mendes's 1993 RSC production was less insistently literal in its representation of subjection, at least until the culminating moment when, on being freed by Prospero, he stared him in the face and spat.[39] But once the decision has been made to focus on Ariel's discontent, then an acute problem is raised with the songs. Beale is, in fact, an accomplished singer, and for him Sean Davey provided songs which demonstrated his vocal control—both the first two songs began with long held notes over the insistent arpeggio figuration which bound all the 'magic' music together, and then moved on into agreeable, if fairly conventional, melodic lines. There was, therefore, a tension between the warmth that the approachable musical language itself projected, and the impassive obedience with which Ariel delivered himself of his musical duty. Any singer, whether professional performer or spontaneous amateur, must generally be assumed to take pleasure in the act of singing and to immerse themselves in the song.

It is, of course, possible to argue that, until 'Where the bee sucks', Ariel is singing under Prospero's direction, and if, as in Hall's production, the singer mimes to a tape, then the suggestion of a gap between the performer and the song can be created. But once Ariel sings, then not only will the audience inevitably judge the quality of the performance as performance, but the consequence must be that the character becomes involved in the pleasure of that performance. As one reviewer remarked of Beale's performance, 'only when he sings in a beautiful tenor does he seem to understand anything about human feeling'.[40]

Nancy Meckler's production with Shared Experience Theatre in 1996/7 approached the same problem in a different fashion. She also emphasized Ariel's confinement by encasing Rachel Sanders in a long-sleeved, restrictive tabard, which was symbolically removed at the moment of her freedom.[41] But though physically restrained, Ariel as musician was given unusual prominence. As Peter Salem, the composer, wrote in his programme notes, 'all the sound in this production is created "live" by Ariel, either vocally or by striking a percussive instrument. This acoustic sound ... is fed through a radio microphone to a bank of sound processing equipment controlled by a computer, creating complex transformations of the acoustic sound in real time'. He saw this as a way 'to more strongly present Ariel as a hugely creative force which Prospero exploits to realize his imagination and conjure up illusions on his island'. At an intellectual level this is an ingenious resolution of some of the problems. The electronically produced sound, as in Brook's production, underscored strangeness and a disembodied, nonhuman quality. That Ariel generated all the music at Prospero's command underlined the functionality of the music within the play, while at the same time rendering more complex the balance between Prospero and his servant. Prospero's dependence upon his tricksy spirit, the fact that he is harnessing a musical power that is not simply 'his', was fruitfully emphasized. Yet the electronic trickery which produced the sounds, and the fragmentary result of the computer processing, militated against a response to any of the individual musical moments as specifically musical structures. To put it simply, one did not, could not, come away humming the tunes.

This music was ingenious and 'effective', but remained 'quarter-ear music' in Brook's terms. It had a 'composer', but the composer's art was, as it were, deconstructed by the technology through which it was generated.

To an audience familiar with computer sampling and electronic musical production, the effect was less alienating than at the time of Brook's production, when such devices belonged virtually exclusively to a musical avant-garde.[42] This illustrates a fundamental issue: any music for a theatrical production inevitably locates itself within a specific musical language which sets up patterns of feeling and understanding that operate autonomously, while at the same time contributing to the total statement of a particular performance. Where the text belongs to a different historical period there are, as in decisions about costume or setting, many ways of exploiting the relationship between the presentness of the performance and the intractable pastness of the play.

One of the curiosities of the music in the performance history of *The Tempest* is the way in which, though the text has been rearranged with considerable freedom over the centuries, and production values have changed significantly, the music, until well into this century, frequently involved the repetition of old and familiar settings, particularly of the songs.[43] Arne's settings had a life of at least two centuries; Sullivan's music was still being used in early twentieth-century performances. Assembled scores, like those used by Benson and Beerbohm Tree, blithely blended eighteenth-century English, classical Viennese and romantic German elements with an apparent indifference to any historical specificity or coherence of musical language. This indifference might be excused because of the imprecision of music's signification. As Edward Said remarks, music has a 'nomadic ability to attach itself to, and become a part of, social formations, to vary its articulations and rhetoric depending on the occasion as well as the audience'.[44] As a medium of translation, then, music is both powerful and imprecise, its signification always potentially exceeding its moment of origin. Ariel's musical endeavours throughout the play are devoted to the translation of Prospero's project into action; yet at its end, he sings a song of pleasure, pure and self-absorbed. In just the same way the musical score is derived from the purposes of a specific production, yet has the capacity to float free from the restraints of the occasion and become a freestanding aesthetic object; no longer quite a translation in the sense of a striving for close equivalence, but an independent work.

Nonetheless, in the context of this essay, it is the attempt to fashion a musical language appropriate to a particular production which is central; and two examples conclude this essay: those of Stephen Oliver in 1982 and Jeremy Sams in 1988. In each case their contribution had a major effect upon the play as it was experienced by the audience, and each contributed to a distinct directorial vision.

Hytner's 1988 production, with John Wood as Prospero, was set on a bare stage, dominated by a huge tilted disc, and, in Stanley Wells's words, it presented the story as 'an intensely human action'.[45] It was not universally applauded, but those critics who were most positive praised it for its spareness. Michael Coveney, for example, liked its 'release from RSC antiquarianism',[46] and Michael Billington its 'ability to create a consistent world on stage without lapsing into scenic confectionery'.[47] Jeremy Sams's music, modernist in character, with angular vocal lines, dissonant harmonies and frequent use of synthesized sound, suited this emphasis. But a modernist musical language, even in a comparatively 'soft' version, carries with it a variety of problems. At the most basic level, the extreme vocal range posed practical problems for Duncan Bell's Ariel, never comfortable and often overstretched. His difficulties in presenting the music to the audience compounded the fact that the language of contemporary 'high-art' music has never, despite its long history, been widely accepted by the public at large. Their perception of it as essentially alien, strange and 'difficult', can, of course, be accommodated within a vision of *The Tempest*. In this production, for example, the menacing undertones of the burden to 'Come unto these yellow sands' was emphasized (and further underlined by the cold blue light in which the stage was at this point drenched). So too the banquet presented to the Lords in III.iii was accompanied by music which looked forward to the judgmental entrance of Ariel as harpy, an effect intensified by insistent, heavy rhythms and discordant synthesizer sounds under Gonzalo's speech: 'Faith, sir, you need not fear' (III.iii.43). At one level it effectively undercut and ironized Gonzalo's optimism, but at the same time it placed in question his earlier comment on the 'marvellous sweet music' of the 'strange shapes'. Setting the audience's perception of the sounds against their apparent reception on stage might not matter much in this scene, but the problem came to a head in the masque scene of IV.i. The earlier part of the masque was performed as a kind of *sprechengesang*, Iris and Ceres speaking rhythmically over an austere musical accompaniment. Only at 'Honour, riches, marriage blessing' did Juno burst into song, at which a vision of the sunburnt sicklemen 'appeared behind a gauze in a harvest field full of wheat and poppies lit by late summer sunshine'.[48]

This rendition of the masque was disliked by virtually all critics. As one reviewer put it, 'The rich and strange is briefly overtaken by the rich and kitsch.'[49] Jeremy Kingston observed disapprovingly that 'the poetry of the betrothal masque is not negligible and bears vitally on the issue; it is therefore foolish to obscure the language with harsh, plinky-plunk music'.[50] The masque is always a problem in modern performance. Where the Victorians seized with delight on the possibility of elaboration (and invoked the Jacobean court masque to vindicate their licence), in recent years it has frequently been severely pruned. The difficulty with which it confronts the director is essentially that its theatrical and symbolic vocabulary is so deeply rooted in the specific aesthetic of the early seventeenth century that it imposes the necessity of translation into different but equivalent terms if it is not to sit as an uncomfortably alien and undigested presence. In this production the sudden introduction of a new visual mode, together with the disjunction between the musical language and the pleasure Ferdinand and Miranda take in the spectacle simply emphasized the problem.

It is precisely this difficulty that Stephen Oliver's score for the 1982 RSC performance, with Derek Jacobi as Prospero, seemed designed to solve. Visually this production was eclectic in style. The set was dominated by the hulk of a ship—symbolic but clearly Jacobean. The costuming of the play ranged from a more or less Jacobethan dress for the mortal characters, through a Rastafarian Caliban, to a 'space-age' Ariel—Mark Rylance, a 'slim youth in a silver body-stocking covered with multicoloured veins'.[51] This visual eclecticism was exactly complemented by Stephen Oliver's score. After a setting of 'Come unto these yellow sands' whose dissonance accentuated the ambiguous nature of the welcome to Ferdinand, the musical score used the resources of pastiche with telling resonance. 'Full fathom five' was set over a ground bass which, for those able to pick up the aural clue, brought into play memories of Purcell's noble laments in *Dido and Aeneas*, aptly intensifying the sense of loss of which it speaks to Ferdinand. In contrast to the 1988 performance, the strange shapes carried in the banquet in III.iii to the accompaniment of a 'sarabande', signalling the link between this episode and the court masque, and amply justifying the Lords' comments on the attractiveness of the harmony. But it was in the decision to set the masque in Act IV as a through-composed mini-opera that Oliver's strategy was fully vindicated. The masque's performers were costumed in early seventeenth-century dress, and the musical allusions in the score were to a range of styles from Monteverdi to Bach. The whole built up to a rapturous trio for Juno, Ceres and Iris, which made the blessing of the couple into an emotional high point of the whole production. This sense of fulfilment continued as Ferdinand and Miranda joined in the dance of the nymphs and reapers to a jolly 6/4 tune over a drone bass. For at least one reviewer, this was 'the showpiece of this magical production'.[52] The dissolution of the masque was, then, particularly painful to the audience, and at the same time suited well with the production's highlighting of Prospero's 'internal struggle between omnipotence and humanity'.[53] Precisely by suggesting, and inviting the audience through the music to participate in, a vision of plenitude, the production was able to integrate the masque into its larger purposes.[54]

But Oliver's adoption of a brilliant pastiche for his music brought with it difficulties as well as pleasures. Pastiche always runs the risk of 'fakery', a kind of heritage-industry cosiness; at the same time its intertextual reference can lapse into a self-conscious knowingness. Whilst it seems to me that this particular score largely avoided these traps, the anxiety which attended the setting of Ariel's final song, 'Where the bee sucks', is not unrevealing. Between the production at Stratford and its revival in Newcastle the song was shifted from its position in the text to act as an interlude between Acts IV and V, and the wiry, spare duet between voice and bassoon which Rylance first sang was recomposed as a much more conventional and lushly scored aria. The song is dramatically problematic, wildly inappropriate to the re-robing of Prospero which it accompanies. And it was perhaps for this reason, in a production which had attempted to make Prospero's ambition to recover his dukedom central to his motivation, that Ariel did not assist Prospero in his robing as he sang. Here Ariel sings for himself, and whilst finding a language appropriate to that self-speaking is always a problem a composer must face, in this score it seemed that the delighted exploration of a range of musical vocabularies throughout the play left Oliver nowhere to go at the end. His problem was compounded by the directorial decision that Ariel should simply not be present, so that Prospero's farewell was delivered to a spirit who had already departed.

As Inga-Stina Ewbank reminds us, there is a fundamental link between theatrical production and the arts of translation:

> Translation, then, is only one form of re-writing, and needs to be thought about and studied as such. In cutting, suppressing, restructuring and adding, theatre directors and (we must admit) academic critics, each in his or her way and for his or her particular purpose, are translators/re-writers of Shakespeare.[55]

To her list of 'translators' we may add the theatre musician, who similarly affects and conditions our reception of the Shakespearean text in performance, and who is similarly bound to the task of discovering 'new and appropriate performance styles that illuminate the texts and yet ring true in a world almost totally transformed, both in and out of the theatre, since their composition'.[56] It is perhaps time that the contribution of composers to that process becomes more fully recognized and more fully integrated into the historical study of performance.

NOTES

I am grateful to the British Academy for a grant which made possible the research for this paper.

1. Dennis Kennedy, *Looking at Shakespeare: A Visual History of Twentieth-Century Performance* (Cambridge: Cambridge University Press, 1993), pp. 4, 5.
2. See, for example, Catherine M. Dunn, 'The Function of Music in Shakespeare's Romances', *Shakespeare Quarterly*, 20 (1969), 391–405; David Lindley, 'Music, Masque and Meaning in *The Tempest*', in *The Court Masque*, ed. David Lindley (Manchester: Manchester University Press, 1984), pp. 47–59; Robin Headlam Wells, 'Prospero, King James and the myth of the musician-king', in *Elizabethan Mythologies: Studies in Poetry, Drama and Music* (Cambridge: Cambridge University Press, 1994), pp. 63–80; Howell Chickering, 'Hearing Ariel's Songs', *Journal of Medieval and Renaissance Studies*, 24 (1994), 131–72.
3. David L. Hirst, in *The Tempest: Text and Performance* (London: Macmillan, 1984) makes no mention at all of any music or composer in the second part of his book, the survey of performances. Ralph Berry, 'Reflections on Recent *Tempests*', in *Shakespeare in Performance* (London: Macmillan, 1993), mentions music not at all, and though the relevant chapter in Roger Warren's *Staging Shakespeare's Late Plays* (Oxford: Clarendon Press, 1990), is entitled 'Rough Magic and Heavenly Music: *The Tempest*', only one musical moment is discussed, and he never mentions that the music for the Peter Hall 1988 performance on which he focuses was provided by the distinguished composer Harrison Birtwistle.
4. *A Shakespeare Music Catalogue*, 5 vols, eds Bryan N. S. Gooch and David Thatcher (Oxford: Clarendon Press, 1991), vol. 3.
5. Though Gary Schmidgall writes that 'the history of musical *Tempests* is a long, melancholy one, punctuated by bursts of unintended hilarity'. *Shakespeare and Opera* (New York and Oxford: Oxford University Press, 1990), p. 280. Julia Muller, in 'Music as Meaning in *The Tempest*', *The Shakespeare Year-Book*, 4 (1994), 163–77, discusses the music in some of the seventeenth- and eighteenth-century adaptations of the play.
6. The chapter 'Romeos, Juliets, and Music', in Peter Conrad, *To be continued: Four Stories and their Survival* (Oxford: Clarendon Press, 1995), interestingly pursues this kind of study.
7. Music was commissioned from Honegger for a performance projected in 1923, but it did not take place until 1929. The score was published in 1924, and two of Ariel's songs were issued in 1925.
8. Composed as part of a score for an Old Vic performance in 1962, they were issued as songs with piano accompaniment in 1964.
9. As Dennis Kennedy observes, 'We work with imperfect tools and

often without a clear blueprint. Considering the amount of information that is usually not known, the discipline at times seems closer to archaeology than to history' (*Looking at Shakespeare*, p. 16).

10. See John Stevens, 'Shakespeare and the Music of the Elizabethan Stage', in *Shakespeare in Music: A Collection of Essays*, ed. Phyllis Hartnoll (London: Macmillan, 1964), pp. 3–49.

11. The clearest evidence that performance in acts was envisaged is that at the end of Act IV Prospero exits, only to appear instantly at the beginning of Act V.

12. Sullivan composed his music in 1860–61 as his Opus 1, but it was first used as incidental music for a performance in Manchester in 1864.

13. For a performance in Copenhagen to a Danish text by Edvard Lembcke.

14. *A Shakespeare Music Catalogue* lists almost 200 pieces (including Tchaikovsky's *The Tempest*) which in varying ways draw on the play for their inspiration.

15. Quoted from *Blackwood's Magazine* in Mary M. Nilan, '*The Tempest* at the Turn of the Century: Cross-Currents in Production', *Shakespeare Survey*, 25 (1972), 123. Richard Dickins, in *Forty Years of Shakespeare on the English Stage and Other Papers* (London, 1909), p. 121, quotes a writer in *The Times* calling for a Shakespearean theatre with 'above all, no incidental music'.

16. References to the text of *The Tempest* are to the edition by Stephen Orgel (Oxford: Oxford University Press, 1987).

17. Music specifically performs this function in II.i.182, and composers have not infrequently taken this as a cue to provide music to lull Miranda in I.ii.185. There is, however, a crucial difference between the two scenes, in that Ariel is specifically the agent who provides the music which causes the Lords' drowsiness, and is not present on the earlier occasion.

18. It is not clear in which of the subsequent revivals of the production was some minimal staging of the opening scene restored, nor whether this same musical accompaniment was retained.

19. *The Birmingham Gazette*, 31 March 1934.

20. See the description in Dennis Kennedy, *Looking at Shakespeare*, pp. 304–06. Adrian Noble imitated this effect in the RSC 1998 performance.

21. J. C. Worsley in *The New Statesman*, 7 July 1951.

22. Peter Holland commented: 'It is ... I believe, quite simply a mistake to have Ariel visibly controlling the storm ... for there are few stage effects in Shakespeare quite as thrilling as the realization that the hyper-realism of the opening scene, so quickly and economically accomplished, is really only a trick, not of the company of actors but of the play's magician', *Shakespeare Survey*, 47 (1994), 203. But he was flying in the face of what has become something of a performance cliché (dating back at least to Tree's 1904 production).

23. W. H. Auden, *The Dyer's Hand* (London: Faber and Faber, 1963), p. 466.

24. Nottingham Playhouse and Theatr Clwyd Company, in association with the Hebbel Theater, Berlin, 1995/6.

25. See Peter Holland in *Shakespeare Survey*, 49 (1996), 249, for an excellent brief account of this production.

26. The musicians were hidden by curtains during the action of the play, but those curtains might be opened to reveal them playing during the musical interludes they supplied before the performance and in entr'actes, thus preserving a distinction between their functions within and outside the world of the play itself.

27. Nilan, '*The Tempest* at the Turn of the Century', p. 123.

28. Orgel's observation that Dolmetsch used 'only the pipe and tabor' (p. 73) is inaccurate. A small ensemble, of virginals and viols, played a variety of music from the period, the rest composed by Dolmetsch. The pipe was a tin whistle, with Ariel onstage seeming to play a mock-up of the original three-hole pipe. My source is: Theatre Museum, Poel Collection, Box E.

29. Though the 1992 English Shakespeare Company production did use a recorder for Ariel's luring of Stephano, Trinculo and Caliban in III.ii.122.

30. *The Observer*, 18 August 1957.

31. *The Sunday Times*, 22 September 1957.

32. *The Leamington Spa Courier*, 16 August 1957.

33. Birtwistle's adoption of the counter-tenor voice may have owed something to Britten's revolutionary choice of Alfred Deller as Oberon in his opera *A Midsummer Night's Dream* in 1960. Though now more readily accepted than in the past, the androgyne quality of the counter-tenor is still felt by most as 'odd', even 'unnatural'.

34. *The Guardian*, 15 August 1957. The 1963 RSC production, for which Peter Brook and Clifford Williams were jointly responsible, also used an electronic soundtrack, which prompted Eric Shorter in *The Telegraph* (3 April) to a similar observation: 'The music that creeps by Ferdinand is not so much marvellously sweet as plainly science-fictitious: sinister blob-blobbings and interstellar echoes.' Conversely, the anonymous reviewer in *The Times* wrote, 'It has often been observed that music in the theatre has an almost immoral power of disguising dramatic inadequacy; electronic music, with its potent ability to conjure up ominous and magical atmospheres, redoubles the power.'

35. Mrs Charles Calvert, *Sixty Eight Years on the Stage* (London: Mills and Boon, 1911), pp. 70, 73.

36. W. H. Auden, *The Dyer's Hand*, p. 524.

37. W. H. Auden, *The Dyer's Hand*, p. 525.

38. *The Manchester Guardian*, 1951.

39. This spit (the most controversial moment in the production), though highly praised by Peter Holland in *Shakespeare Survey*, 47 (1994), 204, as a 'superb invention', was generally much disliked and was cut before the end of the run.

40. Paul Taylor, *The Independent*, 13 August 1993.

41. Lyn Gardner in *The Guardian*, 1 February 1997, commented on 'the sudden shocking realisation that the white designer number Ariel has floated about in all evening is in fact a straitjacket'. (Whereas Paul Martin in *The Morning Star*, 7 February 1997, saw only 'a bizarre final transformation of Ariel from spirit to undisguisably corporeal mortal form', exactly missing Meckler's point.)

42. *The Stage*, 6 February 1997, commented approvingly on the way Ariel's 'breath creates the rolling sea, her songs fill the isle', and Carol Carver in *The Ipswich Evening Star*, 26 October 1996, spoke of the way Ariel's 'contributions of mystic sound like wind chimes and wooden rattles are excitingly mixed by an expert sound technician'.

43. Even as late as 1934 nostalgia remained powerful. A *Daily Mail* reviewer of the Stratford production by Bridges Adams commented: 'The music sounds too much like diluted Purcell to give much pleasure. If Purcell music alone were used we should have nothing but praise for a brilliant opening' (17 April 1934).

44. Edward Said, *Musical Elaborations* (London: Chatto and Windus, 1991), p. 70

45. *Shakespeare Survey*, 42 (1990), 148.

46. *The Financial Times*, 28 July 1988.

47. *The Guardian*, 29 July 1988.

48. Stanley Wells's summary, in *Shakespeare Survey*, 42 (1990), 147.

49. Kate Kellaway in *The Observer*, 30 July 1988.

50. *The Times*, 28 July 1988.

51. Nicholas Shrimpton in *Shakespeare Survey*, 36 (1983), 154. Rylance was accompanied by five similarly costumed spirits, memorably christened by Robert Cushman in *The Observer* 'Ariel and his Full Fathom Five'.

52. *The New Statesman*, 20 August 1982.

53. Michael Billington, *The Guardian*, 12 August 1982.

54. As Billington commented: 'with the help of some pastiche Monteverdi music by Stephen Oliver, the play's masque-like ingredients are knitted into the whole'. Not all reviewers agreed. Eric Shorter complained that 'the sustained pageants, the multiplied Ariel and the songs which veer from the light fantastic to the heavy operatic are inclined to take our minds off the magic of the writing' (*The Daily Telegraph*, 13 August 1982).

55. Inga-Stina Ewbank, 'Shakespeare Translation as Cultural Exchange', *Shakespeare Survey*, 48 (1995), 7.

56. Kennedy, *Looking at Shakespeare*, p. 15.

'... tinap ober we leck giant': African Celebrations of Shakespeare

MARTIN BANHAM and
ELDRED DUROSIMI JONES

Shakespeare reached Africa perhaps as soon as or sooner than his work reached the most distant parts of his own country. In 1607 there are reports of performances of *Hamlet* and *Richard II* by British sailors off the coast of Sierra Leone. This hardly raised the floodgates of performance, but in 1800 the 'African Theatre' in Cape Town opened with a performance of *Henry IV* (which Part is not clear), and the amateur entertainments of colonial officers, the educational priorities of missionary and colonial government schools, plus the professional companies imported to entertain settler communities, ensured that the plays of Shakespeare—played in English—had a significant presence in many parts of the continent. But Shakespeare has also been performed and explored through the medium of translation and adaptation in a range of African languages and cultures. A recent 'provisional' bibliography by Jane Wilkinson[1] offers Kiswahili Shakespeares from Kenya (*Mabruk/Macbeth*, 1970; *Mlariba/The Merchant of Venice*, 1971) and from Tanzania (*Hadithi za Kiingereza*/Tales from Shakespeare, 1867, new version 1940; *Hadithi Ingereza*/ stories from *The Taming of the Shrew*, *The Merchant of Venice*, *King Lear* and *Timon of Athens*, 1900; *Mfanyi biashara wa Venice-Venisi*/Lamb's version of *The Merchant of Venice*, 1939; Julius Nyerere's famous translation *Julius Caezar*, 1963, revised version *Juliasi Kaizari*, 1969, together with his *Mabepari was Venisi/The Merchant of Venice*, 1969; *Makbeth* by S. S. Mushi, 1968 and the same translator's *Tufani/The Tempest*, 1969). Elsewhere we can find numerous translations of Shakespeare into Amharic by the

Ethiopian playwright Tsegaye Gebre-Medhin, including *Othello*, which reportedly ran in Addis Ababa for up to three years;[2] the Congolese Sony Labou Tansi's adaptation of *Romeo and Juliet* (1990); productions of *Macbeth* at Sonar Senghor's Théâtre Daniel Sorano in Dakar (*c.*1965); from South Africa, Solomon Tashekisho Plaatje's Setswana language *Diphoshophosho/The Comedy of Errors* (1930) and *Dintshontsho Tsa Bo-Juliuse Kesara/Julius Caesar* (*c.*1931?); and the extremely commercial version of *Macbeth*, *Umabatha* by Welcome Msomi (1972).

Kole Omotoso[3] also reminds us of another fascinating connection between the continent of Africa and Shakespeare when he comments that the ancient Arab stories of Majnun and Layla 'form the inspiration … of Shakespeare's *Romeo and Juliet*'. Omotoso is drawing attention to the Arabic plays *Majnun Layla* and *Masra Kliyubatra* (which translates literally as 'The Fall of Cleopatra'),[4] 'written with the knowledge of Shakespeare's *Romeo and Juliet* and *Antony and Cleopatra*'[5] by the distinguished Egyptian playwright Ahmad Shawqi (d. 1932). Previously in Egypt, *Othello*, translated as *Utayl* by Khalil Mutran, had been performed by the important Jurj Abyad troupe. To all the above should be added the various 'versions' of Shakespeare popular with the university travelling theatres—particularly that of Ibadan—in the 1960s. But even by such a listing one suspects that we are only revealing a fraction of Shakespearean adaptation, translation and production in Africa.

It is interesting, at this point, to return briefly to Julius Nyerere's contributions. Nyerere, the distinguished first President of Tanzania and one of modern Africa's most respected leaders (and, in Plastow's words, 'a Shakespeare enthusiast'[6]), seems to have undertaken his translations initially as a celebration of the richness and beauty of the Swahili language. Plastow quotes the following comment: 'As a way of disarming detractors of Swahili who said it could not be the vehicle of science and high culture, and who were opposed to its adoption as a national language, President Nyerere translated Shakespeare's *Merchant of Venice* and *Julius Caesar* into Swahili … thus assisting the meteoric rise of literature in Swahili to its status as a national literature today.'[7] But also, as Alamin M. Mazrui[8] suggests—

specifically in relation to *Mabepari wa Venisi*, which Mazrui tells us translates literally as 'the bourgeoisie of Venice'—Nyerere 'may have been more ideologically inspired by his shift towards *Ujamaa*'.

Immediately, from the list above, we must record three specific omissions, namely the work of the Nigerian playwright Wale Ogunyemi, the Mauritian Dev Virahsawmy and the Sierra Leonian Thomas Decker, for it is the work of these three playwrights as they engage with Shakespeare which we now wish to illustrate in greater detail. Ogunyemi's *A'are Akogun* (1969) is a fascinating 'Nigerian tragedy of the supernatural, based on Shakespeare's *Macbeth*'. Dev Virahsawmy has translated *Macbeth*, *Julius Caesar* and *Much Ado About Nothing* into Mauritian French Creole as *Trazedji Makbess* (1996), *Zil Sezar* (1987), and *Ena Ta Senn Dan Vid* (1995) respectively, and written a version of *The Tempest* called *Toufann* (1991). Thomas Decker translated both *Julius Caesar* (of which he also subsequently created an 'adapted' version) and *As You Like It* (*Udat Di Kiap Fit*) into Krio.

Wale Ogunyemi is one of Nigeria's most established playwrights, his plays ranging from popular domestic comedies to reworkings of Yoruba myth and history. *A'are Akogun*[9] is a strikingly compacted version of *Macbeth* which depicts the Macbeths (A'are Akogun, the leader of the army, and his wife Olawumi) entirely bewitched and manipulated by the Wizard—and creature of many disguises—Osowole (Hecate?) and the three witches. The play is presented in both Yoruba and English, allowing the possibility, in production, of one or both language texts being used, and certainly proposing a dynamic interaction between the two. Rich areas of action are depicted in scenes of ritual, mime and 'choreographic dialogue' with the constant presence of Yoruba drumming. Basic parallels exist with Shakespeare's story. A'are Akogun is praised by the old king (the Oba) for his valour in battle and elevated to the rank of A'are-Ona Kakanfo, Chief Warrior. The Oba's son Daodu (Malcolm) and a fellow warrior Jagun (Banquo) witness A'are Akogun's elevation with some concern. No sooner has A'are Akogun acquired his new rank than, working through the vehicle of his wife, whom they take over in a ritual of possession, the witches plant the seeds of ambition, driving A'are Akogun to murder the Oba.

The text here, in a manner typical of Yoruba storytelling, utilizes both proverbial riddles and a powerful repetitive choric chant:

Olawumi: Ijo omode ba dari koruru
Laa ruku ee wale.
Olawumi: The day a child plays with death
Is the day his corpse is brought from the farm.
Awon Aje: Paa!
Witches: Kill him!
Olawumi: Idojude laa habun.
Olawumi: The tortoise is discovered face downward.
Awon Aje: Paa!
Witches: Kill him!
Olawumi: Ifaya lale la a hegbin.
Olawumi: The snail is found crawling on the ground.
Awon Aje: Paa!
Witches: Kill him! …
Olawumi: Paa!
Olawumi: Kill him!
Aje 1: Paa!
Witch 1: Kill him!
Aje 2: Paa!
Witch 2: Kill him!
Aje 3: Paa!
Witch 3: Kill him!
Gbogbo: Paa!!!!
All: Kill him!!!!

It rises to a violent crescendo which sends A'are Akogun on his murderous mission.

The stage directions relating to this scene bring us to one of the subtle parallels between the source play and *A'are Akogun* and is reproduced in full below:

As the chanting reaches a compelling pitch, Akogun is so affected that the only response possible for him is to climb the steps and kill the Oba. He resists this valiantly but his feet lead him to the first step. A superhuman effort, however, aids him in turning away from the spell. He dashes off. No sooner is he out of sight than he backs in again followed closely by the unmasked and therefore invisible wizard. Osowole is holding a large dagger dangerously near Akogun's throat and he is moving forward in measured strides. Akogun backs away in great haste but he slips and falls. He is forced to grab the dagger to prevent it slitting his throat. Osowole relinquishes the dagger immediately and retreats. Akogun is left staring witlessly at the dagger with the inevitable irresistible heartbeat chant still in his ears. He dashes blindly up the stairs into the Oba's bedchamber. Four beats pass and the heartbeat chant stops dead. All on stage are absolutely immobile and quiet until Akogun emerges from the bedchamber chuckling madly to himself. Olawumi stops him.

Olawumi: You must return the weapon to the bedchamber.

Akogun looks at the dagger. His hand goes limp at his side as he increases the silent mad mirth.

Olawumi: Give it to me.

She takes the dagger and enters the bedchamber as Akogun descends the steps awkwardly. He is met at ground level by the armed Osowole in a murderer's mask and cloak. Osowole steadies him. Olawumi returns with an oil-lamp in her right hand. Carefully placing herself in the centre of the upper level, she screams: 'Egbami o!'

From here the action moves swiftly, with A'are Akogun taking the throne, the Oba's son Daodu fleeing and being hunted by the 'murderer' Osowole. At this point Ogunyemi ingeniously and wittily offers a second parallel to a famous scene from *Macbeth*—the Porter's scene. The three witches settle down to a game of *ayo*. This is a game played by distributing hard seeds (or small stones) around receptacles in a wooden board with the intent of capturing the opponent's seeds. The game is played rapidly and the sound of the seeds being dropped into the holes on the board echoes, in this context, the knocking on the door of Macbeth's castle. In the following quotation we have omitted the Yoruba text which, as above, is printed before the English text:

Witch 1: knock, knock. Wait!
Witch 2: knock, knock, knock. Speak on.
The mounds on your chest
Are things of inheritance. *Laugh.* …
Witch 1: knock, knock.
Tell me, has any one seen a bird fly
And he crashes into a tree?
Witch 2: knock, knock, knock.
A bird never flies and crashes into a tree,
never!
Witch 1: knock, knock.
That never happens where we are—in hell,
But it happens daily in the world.
When a drunkard drinks his senses with wine
His path becomes darkened
He dies
Not knowing when he runs into his doom. …
Witch 2: knock, knock, knock.
When a drunkard is drunk
He has an urge for sex
He runs madly after women
And when the woman finally submits
He is too tired and breathes heavily like agalinti
[a lizard]. …
Witch 2: knock, knock, knock.
Where we are is hell
Hell is where we are
Witch 3: knock, knock, knock, knock.
We can do
We can undo
We change people's fate.
Witch 2: knock, knock.
We find satisfaction in human distress and
sufferings
We eat human livers with impunity.

Witch 1: knock, knock.
Play the game
And let me beat you at it.

Olawumi comes across the witches at their game '*holding her bloody right hand before her*' but the witches place an invisible barrier around themselves as they discard her now as useless. Akogun, his wife mad and destroyed, appeals to the gods to deliver him from his fate, taking courage in Osowole's prediction that he can only be killed 'during the total intervention of the moon between the earth and the sun'. The action moves swiftly to its close in a sequence of mime and dumbshow, always driven by the drumming:

> *Osowole, in the murderer's mask, re-enters with a bloody sword which he presents to Akogun, who nods dumbly. Behind him the court is assembling in the dim light. One figure keeps his back turned. A thin keening wail from the witches causes him to turn around. The assembled court stare back at him. A table and stools are brought in by the witches. Food is served by them. All sit; Jagun, the courtiers, the wives, the witches and the one whose face remains turned away from sight. They beckon slowly to Akogun. He approaches the table in a trance and sits. They eat slowly and before long the one whose back is turned stands and turns slowly round. Akogun, to his horror, sees it is Daodu whom he thought killed by the murderer. There is rapid change of light denoting an eclipse. Akogun turns away … Daodu and Jagun advance upon him. He turns back, grabs the bloody sword of the murderer and retreats until he, Daodu and Jagun begin fighting. The fight is in slow-motion to rapid drums … the witches and Osowole withdraw. Akogun fights valiantly and succeeds in wounding Jagun. In doing so, he is open to a sweeping cut from Daodu. He falls … Osowole (unmasked) with the witches come in bearing the body of Olawumi … They look down at him. He raises himself on one elbow and points backwards helplessly to them whom he is seeing for the first time as if to ask why they have done this to him. They are still. The drums and lights fade as the assembly cowers back from Osowole, the witches and their burden …*

Ogunyemi's version of *Macbeth* offers a confident translation of the play into Yoruba idiom and traditional performance form. It puts at the heart of the action the power of the supernatural in a cultural context where such forces retain a relevance in society's consciousness and myths. The dramatic structure is tight and fast moving, layering language, music and movement in a manner typical of Yoruba popular theatre. The engagement with Shakespeare's text is one that celebrates it but moves beyond translation into cultural re-creation. An audience familiar with *Macbeth* will see in *A'are Akogun* a stimulating complementary text and a potential director of Shakespeare's play might be well advised to draw from Ogunyemi in the staging and interpretation of the witches.

Dev Virahsawmy[10] is one of the contemporary Mauritian writers concerned to establish Creole as 'the most effective language for dramatic experiment'. He has described how the language was 'until recently considered unfit for anything but cheap comic sketches'[11] and the decision to translate Shakespeare into an indigenous language (as with Nyerere) and to write other serious dramas in Creole is, linguistically, making a substantial cultural and nationalistic point. Virahsawmy's versions sometimes stay creatively close to the original and on other occasions are deliberately loose and 're-creative'. Examples of the former include *Trazedji Makbess*, *Zil Sezar* and *Enn Ta Seen Dan Vid*. Below, for illustration, are brief excerpts from these plays. The first two are from the translations of *Macbeth* ('Is this a dagger which I see before me?') and *Julius Caesar* ('Friends, Romans, countrymen'):

Enn pwagnar? Koumsa djivan mo lizié?
So lamanss dan porté. Mo sey trap li.
Li fonn mé li ress djivan mo lizié
Vizion lamor, eski yo ekzisté?
Ousa ziss lekim limazinasion,
Lafimé mansonz lespri fatchigé?

Mo bann frèr, ban kamarad ekout mwa.
Mo'on vinn lanterman pa pou pass siro.
Djitor ki nou fèr viv apré lamor,

Nou djibien anteré ar nou lekor.
Santem destern Sezar.

The translation of *Much Ado About Nothing* has interestingly special problems to address in the deliberately fractured language of the clowns. Dogberry's rallying of the watch (III.iii) is rendered in rough translation as follows:

Dogberi: Can we mistrust them?
Verzess: Absolutely confident, absolutely certainly. Or else I'll suicide them.
Dogberi: This would be too good a reward if their self-respect has not been soiled because we give them the honour to watch over the house of a great man.
Verzess: Tell them what to do.
Dogberi: In your opinion who is the most likely to be convicted for organizing a good conspiracy?
Police 1: Basdeo Farata *[literally, 'fat and lazy']* or Isoop Lamok *['failure'].* They both failed at the C.P.E. *[Certificate of Primary Education]*
Dogberi: Come over here both of you. Do you see. You have to thank God. Even Ministers pass the C.P.E. But to fail the C.P.E. you have to be a genius.
Police 1: Thank you boss!
Dogberi: You shouldn't become big-headed. I am choosing you for this erotic mission because you are the most incompetent ones, the most extravagant, the biggest flirts.

In addition to employing malapropisms, Virahsawmy plays with the clowns' attempts to show off by speaking in, inevitably faulty, French. All three translations seek to maintain the rhythm, basic structure and spirit of the original, and Shakespeare's tale is told faithfully.

Virahsawmy can, however, have more anarchic fun with Shakespeare and create a contemporary version that allows him to explore his own priorities. As illustrated by *Toufann*, these include the fantastic in a contemporary setting and biological, social and cultural intercommunalism. *Toufann* is subtitled 'a fantastic story' which seems to relate not only to the original play but to the playwright's treatment of it. Even characters in the play are renamed to appear as if they have come to this late play of Shakespeare's from earlier works. Gonzalo has become Poloniouss, Miranda is Kordelia, Antonio is Yago, Alonso is Lerwa [King] Lir, Sebastian is Edmon. Aryel is 'a tall blond with blue eyes' who has been created as a robot by Prospero, Kalibann is the mixed-race offspring of a black slave mother and white pirate who abandoned her, and—far from Shakespeare's monster—a person of intelligence and dignity, and Ferdjinan resists Prospero's plan to have him marry Kordelia, preferring a companionship with Aryel. Aryel explains to Ferdjinan that the island is not a permanent place but a stage in life it is necessary to pass through, where people make their own decisions and come to terms with their own reality. When Ferdjinand hugs Areyl, he responds:

> *Areyl:* I am not programmed to express my feelings. All physical contact disrupts the stability of my chips. If you touch me I lose control.
> *Ferdinjand:* Lose control ... You should lose control ... Forget about protocol, forget convention.[12]

The Trinculo/Stephano characters are here represented as Kaspalto and Dammarro, a drunkard and a junkie who find on the island coconuts full of whisky and fields of cannabis. When at the end of the play they clownishly attempt a *coup* they are told that the story is over:

> *Kordelia:* Kaspalto and Dammarro. Listen to me carefully. You came onto the stage too late. Don't you see the story is over?
> *Dammarro:* But what about us? We will never become kings. Every Tom, Dick and Harry has the right to become king. But we, the children of the people, are brushed aside as if we don't even exist.

Areyl: Don't worry, I will have a word with the boss.
I'll ask him to write a new story where *you*
become kings.

At the climax of the play Kordelia tells Prospero of her wish to marry Kalibann. Prospero protests:

Prospero: Think about your destiny Kordelia. It is
written that you can become a great queen
who will rule over a powerful empire ...
Don't turn your back on what was written.
Kordelia: By whom?
Prospero: Destiny.
Kordelia: Destiny wrote destiny?
Prospero: What you are trying to do is impossible. You
cannot marry Kalibann.
Kordelia: Why?
Prospero: Do I have to spell it out? He ... he ...
he does not have royal blood.
Kordelia: I am happy enough that he has human blood ...
we are not interested in your politics. We want
to live a life based on our feelings.
Prospero: Feelings! ... but what about reality?
Kordelia: Reality, father? What reality? Since this
morning no one knows what is real, what is
imaginary anymore. Dream has become reality,
reality has become a dream ... art is matching
itself against life ... a new reality is already
born, father ... We have to accept it.

With the intervention of Lir, Prospero accepts the marriage of Kalibann and Kordelia and relinquishes his powers (represented by a high-tech control console!).

Prospero: Do you see this key? This is the key to switch
on or off all my machines, the very heart of my
power ... But I think it's time that I retired
too. If I throw this key into the sea my
magical powers will also disappear, so will my
island and I will become one of you here. And

that's what I'll do. *(He throws it overboard)*
My rule is over. The Kordelia/Kalibann rule has
just begun ... Children! Don't make the same
mistake that your parents did.

Virahsawmy does not pretend that *Toufann* is anything other than a 'fantasy' based on *The Tempest*, but in a magical and entertaining context the play reminds us, through the cross-referencing to other Shakespearean characters, of destructive and prejudiced relationships between fathers and sons, fathers and daughters, the 'legitimate' and the 'illegitimate', black and white, servants and masters, and proposes that the future of the island depends on the relaxation of rigid and historically created postures and the acceptance of a new world where the individual is important and not his/her language, colour or sexuality. Together with the deliberate exploration of the possibilities of Creole, the integrated language of the various cultures of Mauritius, the playwright is bringing Shakespeare into play to offer a political and social statement about the future of his country. Shakespeare's exotic island is explored allegorically in terms of contemporary Mauritius.

From the 1930s until his death, Thomas Decker[13] had been aware of the need to use (Sierra Leonean) Krio much more widely than it had been used before and he had sought to prove that it was capable of such wider usage. It was his conviction that Krio could be used to express almost anything that could be expressed in another language and he sought to prove it by making translations from the classics of English literature—the authorized version of the Bible and the works of Shakespeare. In his introduction to his *As You Like It* adaptation, *Udat Di Kiap Fit*, he wrote about his 1964 translation of *Julius Caesar*:

> In that exercise my aim was twofold: first, to make propaganda for the Krio language by proving that the most serious things can be written in it and, secondly, to make it possible for people who had not had the opportunity of reading Shakespeare at school, [to] taste of the excellence of this great writer by seeing one of his most popular plays staged in their own language.

Decker referred to his later *Udat Di Kiap Fit* as an adaptation rather than a word-for-word translation, but in fact he follows Shakespeare's text closely and represents almost every speech. He abbreviates and omits some lines but also gives himself the liberty of 'realizing' rather than translating and some of his realizations are noteworthy; for instance, he represents Shakespeare's line 'What prodigal fortune have I spent that I come to such penury?' as 'Wetin a du fo kam ton di prodigal son?' This is not a translation; it assumes knowledge of the story of the prodigal son and merely makes reference to it. He will often offer an excellent idiomatic Krio translation as in 'I pray thee, Rosalind, sweet my coz, be merry' where Decker has 'Du ya cozin Rozalin lus bodi'. 'Lus bodi' means 'loosen body', 'relax'.[14] He will retain English words where necessary, as in 'Di nu chif bin don banish di ol chif we na in yon broder' ('The old duke is banished by his younger brother, the new duke'). Another good example of Decker's adaptation is the song to Rosalind by Orlando:

> From the east to western Inde,
> No jewel is like Rosalind.
> Her worth, being mounted on the wind,
> Through all the world bears Rosalind.

Krio has no word for the generalized term 'jewel'. Decker solves the problem by substituting a jewel of extreme significance to Sierra Leone—the diamond:

> From Kailahun to Sulima,
> Non dayamon no fayn lek Rozalin.
> Briz don ker in fem olobot,
> Ol man no wol no Rozalin.

Decker changes the title of the play and the names of the characters, and makes the location, flora and fauna tropical and specifically Sierra Leonean, but his play is essentially faithful to Shakespeare. His *Julius Caesar* Decker describes as a translation 'almost word for word' though he later 'indulged in a bold adaptation [with] the main aim to amuse'. Like Virahsawmy in his version of 'Friends, Romans, countrymen', Decker makes a conspicuous effort to be as close as possible to the original. In fact we offer two versions, the first from the manuscript of the play, and the second from a slightly later published version. This serves to remind us that Krio is a language that—certainly in the 1960s—was in a state of growth and refinement (and of Decker's dedication to that process).

Paddy, dem, country, una all way day
Nar Rome. Una len me una yase, yar.
Are cam berr Caesar, are nor cam praise am.
Dem kin member bad way person kin do
Long tem after de person kin don die.
But plenty tem de good way person do
Kin berr wit im bone dem. Make e be so
Wit Caesar. Bra Brutus done tell una
Say Caesar na been man way pass mark.
If e talk true, nar bad bad ting dis yar.
En Caesar don get im bad pay for dat.
Are take permission from Bra Brutus dem.
For cam talk nar Bra Caesar in berrin
En Brutus nar honourable O!
Den order wan sef nar honourable. *[Manuscript version]*

Padi dem, khontri, una ohl wey day
Na Rom. Meyk una ohl kak una yeys.
A kam ber Siza, a noh kam preyz am.
Dem kin memba bad wey pohsin kin du
Lohng tem afta di pohsin kin dohn dai.
Boht plenti tem di gud wey pohsin du
Kin ber wit im bon dem. Meyk i bi so
Wit Siza. Bra Brutohs dohn tell una
Sey Siza na bin man wey want pas mak.
If i tohk true, na badbad ting dis ya.
En Siza dohn get im bad pey foh dat.
A tayk pamishohn frohm Bra Brutohs dem
Foh kam tohk na Bra Sizar im berin.
En Bra Brutohs na ohnareybul O!
Dem ohda wan sef na ohnareybul. *[Published version]*[15]

Following on Thomas Decker's example, Dele Charley made two even more adventurous cultural adaptations in Krio of Shakespeare's plays, *Macbeth* (*Macuba*) and *The Merchant of Venice* (*Wan Paun flesh*). Macbeth is a paramount chief surrounded by his traditional warriors and the accompaniment of African musical instruments, while Shylock becomes a Foulah trader, Foulahs being among the most successful African traders in Sierra Leone.

We have looked, in the wider context of Shakespearean translations and adaptations in Africa, at three playwrights bringing their various skills and interests to bear on specific texts. In each case we would propose that the engagement has not been merely academic, but purposeful, serious, deliberate—and often ingenious. Ogunyemi has shown the dynamic fusion that can exist between the universal meaning of a Shakespeare text and a specific and culturally sympathetic performance mode. Virahsawmy brings Shakespeare into the political and social debates in his own society and, with Decker, employs the status of Shakespeare to draw attention to the riches and potential of a new language. We may speculate as to why *Julius Caesar* seems such a favourite of African playwrights and audiences, but, in Thomas Decker's words, Shakespeare indeed 'tinap ober we leck giant': 'doth bestride the narrow world/ like a Colossus'.

NOTES

1. Contained in 'Forum', *Research in African Literatures*, 28:1 (Spring 1997), 241–43.
2. Jane Plastow, *African Theatre and Politics: The Evolution of Theatre in Ethiopia, Tanzania and Zimbabwe* (Amsterdam: Rodopi, 1996), p. 222.
3. Kole Omotoso, 'Arabic Drama in North Africa', in *Theatre in Africa*, eds Oyin Ogunba and Abiola Irele (Ibadan: Ibadan Univ. Press, 1978), pp. 140–41.
4. See 'Egypt' in *The Cambridge Guide to Theatre*, ed. Martin Banham, new edn (Cambridge: Cambridge University Press, 1995).
5. Omotoso, 'Arabic Drama in North Africa', pp. 140–41.
6. Plastow, *African Theatre and Politics*, p. 129.
7. Plastow, *African Theatre and Politics*, p. 88, quoted from *African Literatures in the 20th Century: A Guide*, ed. Leonard S. Klein, (New York: Ungar, 1986), p. 217.

8. Alamin M. Mazrui, 'Shakespeare in Africa: Between English and Swahili Literature', *Research in African Literatures*, 27:1 (Spring, 1996), 64–79. This is an important and informative source article, which we wish to acknowledge.

9. Published in *Nigeria Magazine*, 100, April 1969, 404–14.

10. *En Ta Senn Dan Vid* (1995) and *Trazedji Makbess* (1996) are published by LPT Edition, Port Louis. *Toufann* is published by Boukié Banané, which we believe to be the author's own imprint. *Zil Sezar* has not been published.

11. See 'Mauritius' in Banham, *The Cambridge Guide to Theatre*.

12. We are greatly indebted to Roshni Mooneeram of the University of Leeds for a translation of *Toufann* and other advice on the Virahsawmy texts. *The Diksyoner Kreol Angle* (Port Louis: LPT, 1985–93) is a helpful reference work.

13. We have drawn substantially from material on Thomas Decker which was first presented by Eldred D. Jones to the Krio Workshop, Freetown, January 1990. The quotations from Decker are from this source unless otherwise identified.

14. See *A Krio–English Dictionary*, compiled by Clifford N. Fyle and Eldred D. Jones (Oxford: Oxford University Press, 1980).

15. See *Sierra Leone Language Review* 4 (1965), 74. Quoted in Loreto Todd, *Modern Englishes: Pidgins and Creoles* (Oxford: Blackwell, 1984), p. 273. Todd also offers us another gem: R. Awa's Cameroon pidgin translation of 'To be or not to be': 'Foh bi foh dis graun oh foh no bi sehf—dat na ting wei i di bring plenti hambag.'

(Post)colonial Translations in V. S. Naipaul's *The Enigma of Arrival*

SHIRLEY CHEW

> To understand Conrad, then, it was necessary to begin to match his experience. It was also necessary to lose one's preconceptions of what the novel should do ...[1]

Joseph Conrad was the first modern writer V. S. Naipaul encountered at the age of ten; and Conrad, seaman turned author, was also someone who 'had been everywhere before me' and who 'sixty to seventy years ago meditated on my world' (*CD*, p. 210). Indeed, Conrad's vision of this world, as some critics have remarked,[2] is one which Naipaul seems bound to repeat in his own work: 'half-made societies ... where there was no goal, and where always "something inherent in the necessities of successful action ... carried with it the moral degradation of the idea"' (*CD*, p. 208). This essay sets out with the view that Naipaul's attitude towards Conrad and Conrad's 'world' is not unambivalent, as is demonstrable from the opening quotation and, more extensively, from the complex manner in which colonial societies and identity are revisioned in *The Enigma of Arrival*.[3] It analyses Naipaul's dismantling in the novel of the colonial fantasy of 'security', that is, the notion of 'a fixed world' comprising, on the one hand, the timeless perfection of England, and, on the other, the disorder of 'half-made societies that seemed doomed to remain half-made' (*CD*, p. 207). It argues that the dynamics of the novel are sustained upon Naipaul's constructions of himself as colonized subject, migrant, and postcolonial writer, a series of translations and self-translations in which 'cartographic anxiety', impinging upon conceptions of 'the-world-as-exhibition',[4] becomes transformed into new perspectives and, hence, new mappings of territory and identity.

My examples below of some of the ways in which Conrad 'meditated' on his world are taken from the late essay 'Geography and Some Explorers'.[5]

> I stand here confessed as a contemporary of the Great Lakes. Yes, I could have heard of their discovery in my cradle, and it was only right that, grown to a boy's estate, I should have in the later sixties done my first bit of map-drawing and paid my first homage to the prestige of their first explorers. It consisted in entering laboriously in pencil the outline of Tanganyika on my beloved old atlas, which, having been published in 1852, knew nothing, of course, of the Great Lakes. The heart of its Africa was white and big.
> (*GSE*, p. 14)

Two moments of 'discovery' are rekindled in the passage: the first sighting of Lake Tanganyika in 1857 by Richard Burton and John Speke, and Conrad's own beginning attempt at remaking the world. While the boy aimed at bringing his atlas up to date, his act of homage also served, in Conrad's progressivist reading of geography, to mark a culminating point in the history of exploration. As outlined in the essay, just as 'geography fabulist' (the medieval phase) was succeeded by 'geography militant' (the post-Columbus phase) and, finally, 'the geography triumphant of our day', so, within geography militant itself, the fortuitous exploits of sixteenth-century navigators, such as Vasco Núñez de Balboa, gave way from the middle of the eighteenth century to the scientific spirit and hard-won knowledge of explorers like James Cook and Richard Burton.

By linking from the start his fanciful mapmaking with the deeds of adventurous men, Conrad draws geographical discovery into the province of romance:[6] both have their origin in action, in particular the lonely endeavours of the heroic individual in distant places and times; both yearn to 'remake the world in the image of desire';[7] and both, in their moments of greatest intensity, are characterized by a perfection that carries with it its own dissolution. Thus, according to Conrad, already held within the 'geographically great moment' when Balboa first caught sight of the Pacific were the rapacious pursuits of El Dorado to come. In the next century, the navigational successes of Abel Tasman in the southern Pacific were to be tainted with his shady dealings as an employer of the Dutch East India Company. And in Conrad's own day, out of the celebrated journeys of white explorers to the Great Lakes and the Congo was to occur 'the vilest scramble for loot that ever disfigured the history of human conscience and geographical exploration' (*GSE*, p. 17).[8]

As is generally known, Conrad drifted out of the British merchant navy after his journey to the Congo and, with the publication of *Almayer's Folly* in 1895, settled on writing as a career. The change meant the end of 'stepping in the very footprints of geographical discovery' as a seafarer, and the beginning of another kind of tracking, as the teller of tales of travel and remote places and adventure. In the concluding paragraphs of 'Geography and Some Explorers', however, there occurs one of his attempts to interconnect these two strands of activity, by returning to that special occasion in 1888 when he sailed the barque, the *Otago*, from Sydney through the Torres Strait and across the Arafura Sea to Mauritius. To use this unconventional route in the first instance was to retrace the journeys of several great seamen—Torres who sailed through the archipelago with New Guinea on his right and Australia on his left without realizing the significance of his passage; Tasman who mistook the strait for a large bay; and finally, Cook, the first to chart with accuracy this region to the south of the East Indies. To write of his own journey more than two decades after the event was Conrad's bid to capture again that 'hallowed ground' (*GSE*, p. 21) with its ghosts of explorer-heroes, wrecks, and crumbling landmarks; and to reinvent himself as seaman, adventurer, even empire-builder.

Edward Said has pointed out that 'nearly all [Conrad's] work ... carries the unmistakable mark of the sensitive émigré's obsession with his own fate and with his hopeless attempts to make satisfying contact with new surroundings'.[9] In this elegy of exploration and discovery, England as 'home' is once more selectively reimagined and in terms of the seas Britain controlled at the height of its naval power. Another feature of Conrad's geographical representation here has also to be noted. Despite the collaborative part geography has played in European imperialism,[10] the essay, published in 1924, contains no references to recent crises such as the Great War, the repercussions of the War upon Britain's prestige within the Empire, the decline of sea power in the face of new technology and inventions; and despite Conrad's knowledge of this region, it overlooks entirely the presence within the 'hallowed ground' covered by the *Otago* of the Asian, Arab and African peoples whose trade and cultures have crisscrossed the Indian Ocean centuries before the arrival of European explorers. Conrad's nostalgia is all-consuming. As he meditates upon the ruins of a world once seemingly complete, geography is made to subserve wishful thinking, and romance exemplifies that '*general* attribute' of its kind which is, in Henry James's words,

> experience liberated, so to speak; experience disengaged, disembroiled, disencumbered, exempt from the conditions that we usually know to attach to it and, if we wish so to put the matter, drag upon it ...[11]

Earlier on, I referred to Naipaul's ambivalent attitude towards Conrad. In the statements appended to the opening of this essay, that ambivalence is registered in the two possible meanings of 'to match'. In part, Naipaul's aspiration is to equal Conrad's experience as a traveller and writer; in part, it is to outrival him. From Conrad, he learned how to use the novel for purposes other than the comedy of manners; in turn, he has had to seek ways of eluding the enticements of the form as a vehicle for romance.[12] Crucially the experimentations derive from a different conception of displacement so that to have 'come unstuck' from one's native land (with the overtones in that phrase of liberation as well as disaster),[13] or to be borne across from 'tradition, family and geography', is not, as with Conrad, to come up against 'crushing isolation and the world's indifference',[14] but to occupy as well the 'ambiguous', 'shifting' and 'not ... infertile territory' of 'a translated man'.[15] A Trinidadian Indian, Naipaul is produced on the one hand as colonized subject by Orientalist discourse and the 'improving' benefits of 'English Literature',[16] and, on the other, as outcaste Brahmin by Hindu orthodoxy;[17] an author who started to publish in the late 1950s,[18] a time of deepening unrest within the empire, one of the thorny problems to which he persistently returns in his work concerns the decolonizing and rewriting of history;[19] a migrant for whom 'home' extends across plural and 'simultaneous dimensions', he exemplifies the predicament of displaced persons in seeking ways of moving between different languages and cultures 'without being split by the difference'.[20] *The Enigma of Arrival* enacts what it means to be living always already in translation through Naipaul's revisioning of his relationship with Trinidad, his investigations into the cultural idea of England, undertaken from within the English landscape itself, and his redefinitions of himself as a writer 'by his writing discoveries'.

Described as 'a novel in five sections'—'Jack's Garden', 'The Journey', 'Ivy', 'Rooks', 'The Ceremony of Farewell'—at the heart of *The Enigma of Arrival* is an account of the ten years Naipaul spent in Wiltshire, living in a cottage in the grounds of an Edwardian manor close to Stonehenge. A professional setback in 1969 and a general sense of disillusionment led to a period of retreat, followed by psychological and physical healing. In its broad structure the narrative is a network of journeys traversed in time and space. Against a historical background of European voyages to the Americas, the Middle Passage, the movement of indentured labourers from India and China to the Caribbean, and Third World migrations to Britain in the 1950s, there are Naipaul's own travels to and from Trinidad and, mentioned in passing, to India and Africa; and more locally, there are his daily walks across the downs in Wiltshire. Two sections of the novel are examined in detail in the rest of this essay: 'The Journey', consisting of Naipaul's initial departure from Trinidad in 1950, his subsequent returns to the island, and his withdrawal back to England; and 'Jack's Garden', consisting of his explorations of a more rural kind.

Part of the glamour of the first air journey to New York to

board ship for England arises from Naipaul's sense that the long years of hard study are at last reaping their reward. Given his colonial and, hence, Eurocentric education, the knowledge he has acquired (whether on the subject of classical French drama or Soviet cinema or the great names of art and architecture) is by and large removed from the material realities of the distant cultures in question, and, more disablingly, from the realities of life in Trinidad. Indeed, in a number of telling statements, 'real', as defined by Naipaul, is what is found in books;[21] and this 'real' is also deeply 'romantic', being something he will find intact when he moves from the colonial periphery to the metropolitan centre, itself imagined as the perfect 'elsewhere'. At once 'real' and 'romantic', too, is Naipaul's claim that he is 'travelling to be a writer'. Couched in that suggestive phrase—which seems to regard travel as purposive as well as a condition of perpetual self-making—is the 'exiled posture' often associated with modernist literature.[22] It links him to writers, such as, on the one hand, Kipling, Forster, J. R. Ackerley, Somerset Maugham and Conrad, who knew and wrote about faraway places; and, on the other, Joyce, Lawrence, Nabokov, who through emigration came to adopt the city as their 'modern country of the arts';[23] acquired 'metropolitan material' (p. 124); and displayed 'a particular kind of writing personality', one which is, above everything else, 'immensely knowing' (p. 125).

But, as well as being a tremendous adventure, travel and the big cities unsettle Naipaul by drawing attention to his disadvantages—gauche islander, racial other, solitary exile. New York, with its sophisticated bookshops, cinemas and luxuries, cheats and humiliates him; while London, mixing in the postwar years monuments of imperial grandeur and unedifying signs of decline, baffles with its incoherence and widespread changes. With metropolitan cities spoilt for romance, no longer 'real' as in the books he read, Naipaul is driven for his subjects back to 'the worlds I contained within myself, the worlds I lived in' (p. 135). One of these 'worlds', as revealed in *The Mimic Men* (1967), will turn out to be his first residence in London—the Earl's Court boarding house with its racial mixture of lodgers. Others, such as the peasant India of his ancestors, he will in time discover. But the 'world' with which he begins, and which is to transform him from a sterile aesthete into a writer, is 'my island and my community and the ways of our colony' (p. 110).

Given that imperialism is 'an act of geographical violence through which virtually every space in the world is explored, charted, and finally brought under control',[24] it is possible to see in Naipaul's new surge of interest in Trinidad an example of 'the imagination of anti-imperialism' at work, that is, the conscious engagement of the native person with 'the local place, whose concrete geographical identity must thereafter be searched for and somehow restored'. Nevertheless the contrast between the confident notes in Naipaul's 'my island and my community and the ways of our colony' and the hesitation in Said's 'somehow' is indicative. It helps to account for the 'cartographic anxiety' which is sounded in 'The Journey' and elsewhere in *The Enigma of Arrival*; and which is generally symptomatic of the predicament of representation in the modern world:

> We ground things, now, on a moving earth. There is no longer any place of overview (mountaintop) from which to map human ways of life, no Archimedian point from which to represent the world. Mountains are in constant motion. So are islands: for one cannot occupy, unambiguously, a bounded cultural world ...[25]

As the plane taking him away from Trinidad in 1950 rises into the air, Naipaul catches sight of a landscape which, in its pattern and order—'like a landscape in a book, like the landscape of a real country' (p. 97)—contrasts sharply with its ragged appearance at ground level. Once cloven in two, that is, tethered to history and also freed for romance, Trinidad continues to transform itself in the course of Naipaul's brief visits in person over the next four decades and the more sustained revisitings of his imagination. The actual place holds few attractions for him. Epitomizing the 'smallness' of a colony and the tackiness of a tourist resort, it also stands accused of being 'unique in the West Indies ... in the absence of a history'.[26] At the same time, Trinidad inhabits his fiction with a larger-than-life quality: a tiny country, it has given him 'the world as a writer' (p. 140); a speck on the map, it is part of the old Spanish empire and the expansiveness of the Orinoco river, in short, part of global history and 'the antiquity of the earth' (p. 144). These images, garnered out of a 'perpetual itineracy',[27] in which each journey repeats and qualifies the one gone before, 'one response overlaying the other' (p. 136), evoke Trinidad's many-sidedness. Simultaneously they speak of Naipaul's plural subject positions. For, as he is at pains to reiterate, in that moment of takeoff in 1950, the man was separated from the writer while, in his relationship with Trinidad, he had become insider and outsider at once, 'shuttling in-between frontiers'.[28]

If identity at 'the local place' is fragmented and uncertain, how then can Naipaul hope to reclaim that self-possession conveyed in 'my island', 'my community', 'our colony'? The problem is figured forth in the vicissitudes of the work he was commissioned to write in the late 1960s on 'my own city, Port of Spain'. Searching for material in the archives, Naipaul was captivated by his discovery of a new dimension to Trinidadian history, a time, from the close of the sixteenth to the early nineteenth century, untouched as yet by 'colonial torpor' and impinging still upon pre-Columbus antiquity, a period astir with a sense of empires and revolutions in the making (p. 143). As events turned out, Naipaul's angle upon the past had little to say to contemporary history. With the Black Power movement taking to the streets of Trinidad, the book was already an anachronism when it appeared in 1969.

Returning nearly twenty years later to the problem of *The Loss of El Dorado*, Naipaul rewrites the problem, forging out of the act of self-translation new and creative links between the 'real' and the 'romantic', the world imagined and the world lived.

> ... to look for the aboriginal, pre-Columbus island, I had to ignore almost everything that leapt out at the eye ... The landscape of the past existed only in fragments. To see one such fragment I looked at the drying-up mangrove swamp—green thick leaves, black roots, black mud—outside Port of Spain, ignoring the rubbish-strewn highway and the bent and battered median rail and the burning rubbish dump and the dust-blown shack settlement beyond the highway and the shacks on the hills of the Northern

> Range. From the top of Laventille Hill, among the shacks, I could imagine myself at the beginning of things if I looked selectively down at the Gulf of Paria—grey, leaden, never blue—and the islets in the Gulf. (pp. 146–47)

By his admission—'I looked selectively'—Naipaul rules out the idea of antiquity as a natural and preserved space. Here it is part of a shifting representational landscape in which geography and romance are in contention as well as collusion. In this respect, the siting and subverting of Laventille Hill as, to borrow Clifford's phrase, a 'place of overview' is strategic. Far from being 'hallowed ground', there is exposed on all sides a fractured and chaotic terrain presided over by the agents of change—highway, median rail, rubbish dump. Furthermore, as the precise details of Naipaul's position make clear—'from the *top* of Laventille Hill, *among* the shacks' (my emphases)—the 'place of overview' is itself encumbered with the signs of temporality. But Laventille Hill is also the spot where, romance and its conserving power joining forces with geography, a way back to a vanished past can still be imagined, and antiquity can be reinscribed upon the landscape as Naipaul looks down at the Gulf of Paria, at 'the beginning of things'.

Less than enchanted with London in the 1950s, Naipaul set about displacing his romantic vision of England:

> So I grew to feel that the grandeur belonged to the past; that I had come to England at the wrong time; that I had come too late to find the England, the heart of empire, which (like a provincial, from a far corner of the empire) I had created in my fantasy. (p. 120)

With his move to Wiltshire in 1969, he begins once more to seek a reaffirmation of that imagined perfection, this time amid the ample spaces and remnants and ruins of the English countryside. Having commented on Naipaul's travels to and from the Caribbean, I wish to concentrate now on his journeys of a local kind: his daily walks in the course of ten years within a small area marked out by farms, the Edwardian estate in the grounds of which his cottage is situated, the ancient towns of Salisbury, Amesbury and Wilton, the surrounding downs and Stonehenge. In so doing, I shall take further my analysis of Naipaul's 'perpetual itineracy' and the way it bends the narrative back upon itself again and again until linearity is lost amid a rhizome-like wandering. I shall argue that the recognitions, which his search for a timeless England compels, are worked out as much at the level of form and language as of direct encounters with change as an inseparable part of the rural landscape.

As a narrative strategy, walking involves an outward movement into strange territory and a return to recover one's own ground. Its dynamics of repetition and difference are the means by which the landscape and its inhabitants are revealed as at once familiar and alien, and identified in terms of their continuing as well as shifting relationships to the self. Walking draws together a variety of discursive possibilities: on-the-spot observation, reverie, moral comment, gossip, and flights of imagination.[29] It is rooted in a particular aesthetic which already informs Naipaul's habit of reading the landscape, a habit he learns to question and subvert though not to shed.

Literature has given him, even while a schoolboy in Trinidad, a geography of England that embodies the idea of the nation's permanence and antiquity; a not unwilling participant in the fantasy, Naipaul tries continually to map his experiences of Wiltshire on to this imaginary space. He knows from his school lessons that the Avon here is not the one connected with Shakespeare, and Salisbury is home to the Cathedral. He finds that to reread *Sir Gawain and the Green Knight* is to enhance his pleasure in the drawing in of the year. He attaches special significance to Jack's geese recalling the reference made to the species in *King Lear*. He is familiar with the myths surrounding Stonehenge, and may even have read Thomas Warton's sonnet on the subject. Not impossibly the paths he follows daily were trodden by Wordsworth while stranded on Salisbury Plain. Present at a sheep-shearing, he likens the scene to something from Hardy. Coming across an old horse left to roam in a nearby field, he responds to it in words and sentiments that echo Larkin's poem 'At Grass'.

With the landscape conceived of as a 'purely literary region' (*CD*, p. 207), human beings are scrutinized for their representative significance. In the case of Jack, for example, Naipaul notes: 'I saw his life as genuine, rooted, fitting: man fitting the landscape. I saw him as a remnant of the past' (p. 19). In that repeated use of 'fitting', with its several senses of 'proper', 'propertied', 'an integral part of', 'deserving', Jack's social function and moral worth are underscored. In the repeated 'I saw', Naipaul's assiduous efforts at making the farm worker appropriate to romance are also highlighted. Thus, framed within a garden,

> where (though surrounded by ruins, reminders of vanished lives) he was more than content to live out his life and where, as in a version of a Book of Hours, he celebrated the seasons (p. 20)

Jack becomes emblematic of labour and fertility; and, with action 'stilled to gesture',[30] emblematic of time passing as well as timelessness. However, like some Calendar scenes of the fifteenth century, Naipaul's setting also looks 'beyond the confines of wall or wattle fence, beyond the fixed spring or summer of the paradise garden', towards more mutable landscapes.[31] One of these, discernible in the pervasive language of 'ruins' and 'vanished lives' and the elegiac movement of the prose, is late eighteenth- and early nineteenth-century pastoral. As illustrated in the passages below, in particular in the shared rhetorical figure of epanaphora, the Wordsworthian parallels are especially marked:

> the earth was hard,
> With weeds defaced and knots of withered grass:
> No ridges there appeared of clear black mould,
> No winter greenness; of her herbs and flowers
> It seemed the better part were gnawed away …
> ('The Ruined Cottage', ll. 414–19)[32]

> there was no controlling hand now. No cutting back and tying up, no weeding; nothing done in the greenhouse. No work on the vegetable plot: scattered growths of green

> there, stray roots and seeds. No turning over of the earth in the bedding-out plot below the old hawthorn tree. (p. 42)

In 'The Ruined Cottage', a scene of utter desolation from the poet's point of view is reclaimed through Armytage's account of Margaret's suffering, and transformed into a symbol of the enduring influence of human feelings and effort. Correspondingly when Jack falls ill and dies, and the garden he has tended with such effort and devotion starts to run wild, his authenticity as a figure of romance seems for a brief moment indisputable, in so exemplary a fashion has he lived out his life on his 'special land', and so close besides is the 'fit' between his 'common tale' and Margaret's.

The ironies of Naipaul's subject position within this 'purely literary region' are soon apparent. Commenting on the identification of England with the island in English cultural imagining, Gillian Beer draws attention to its exclusive as well as aggressive energies:

> Defensive, secure, compacted, even paradisal—a safe place; a safe place too from which to set out on predations and from which to launch the building of an empire.[33]

Not surprisingly, the literary tradition which has made the English landscape available to the colonial is also responsible for his invisibility within it; and after twenty years in England, Naipaul is troubled still by an inculcated sense of his alienness. For if Jack is to be construed as 'the remnant of an old peasantry', what role has Naipaul to play in his own version of the medieval romance? And if, like Armytage, Naipaul can also be said to love a 'way-wandering life', what moral authority can he assume as the interpreter of the scene? A narrator who is also an outsider, he comes up against a number of disadvantages. Walking, as Wordsworth's poet-narrators can attest to, entails seeing, knowing, naming. Naipaul, however, is unable to take possession of Wiltshire in this manner since, to begin with, either he has no names for the objects he encounters or he brings to bear upon his surroundings a knowledge that has little relation to the actual. Later, as he grows to know the area at first hand, walking and working his routes regularly (like Jack's father, he sticks to his 'runs'), he finds his 'purely literary region' broken into continually by signs of change and accident. With dairy farming in Wiltshire falling into the hands of big business in the 1970s[34] and becoming radically transformed, newfangled machinery, tractors, trucks, metal-walled barns are as much a part of the scene as old farmhouses and cottages; and with workers migrating to the region because of the developing industry, Naipaul's neighbours are, like himself, mostly strangers to the place. Far from being part of the old peasantry, Jack, too, is a newcomer, his semblance of rootedness being due as much to Naipaul's imaginative chronicling as to his own labour.

Seeing with 'a literary eye' (p. 22), Naipaul translates literature into landscape. Bearing in mind Gayatri Spivak's asseverations that 'translation is the most intimate act of reading'[35] and, at the same time, potentially the most violent, I contend that, troubled and directed by his feelings of 'out-of-placeness' (p. 19), Naipaul's moments of 'seeing' are in many instances acts of intervention, involving him persistently in the rereading and retranslation of the landscape and the literature which produces it.[36] Some of his strategies of (dis)engagement are to be found in the passage below, excerpted from his memorializing of Stonehenge (pp. 23–25).

Of the two viewing points for the monument, the one at the top of the wide grassy way, leading up from the bottom of the valley and over the downs, conduces to elevated feelings:

> And in spite of that crowd, and the highways, and the artillery ranges (with their fluorescent or semi-luminous targets), my sense of antiquity, my feeling for the age of the earth and the oldness of man's possession of it, was always with me. A vast sacred burial ground, bounded by the sky—of what activity those barrows and tumuli spoke, what numbers, what organization, what busyness in these now virtually empty downs! That sense of antiquity gave another scale to the activities around one. But at the same time—from this height, and with that wide view—there was a feeling of continuity. (p. 24)

The indebtedness to Wordsworthian conventions is clear. There is the toilsome trek across bleak distances before the prospect is attained. There is the ruin object, reinvented as the symbol of permanence, the past surviving into the present. There is Naipaul's construction of himself, the stranger who in his rambles daily inscribes his presence upon this portion of England. Needless to say, the linguistic and stylistic correspondences are a self-conscious exercise in translation and, as self-consciously, Naipaul directs our attention to this, whether it is through the outlandishness of his masquerades,

> I never ceased to imagine myself a man of those bygone times, climbing up to have this confirmation that all was well with the world (p. 23)

or the occasional slips in his ventriloquism,

> this [ideal] world ... came to me as a lucky find of the solitude in which on many afternoons I found myself. (p. 24)

Mild jests at his own expense as these textual impersonations are, they signal at the same time a subversive power at work here, since translation, like 'mimicry', repeats 'the forms of authority at the point at which it deauthorizes them'.[37] To reinforce my statement, I shall go back to the passage reproduced above in which, arriving at the 'crest of the way', Naipaul looks across and down upon Stonehenge. What should be the climax of a journey imbricated with borrowings from Wordsworth, is, as it stands, curiously thin, and for two reasons. First, missing from Naipaul's promontory description—'from this height and with that wide view'—is the mastery of the scene which characterizes the Romantic poet's envisioning of landscape.[38] As on Laventille Hill, Naipaul is once again looking selectively down at the place. Yet, despite his efforts to blot them out, accidentals, such as the tourists, intrude—'always someone in red, among the little figures' (p. 24); and despite his 'sense of antiquity', his reading of the 'eternal pile' comprises only the broadest imaginings: 'of what activity those barrows and tumuli spoke, what numbers, what organization, what busyness in these now virtually empty downs!'

Equally anomalous in the same passage is the absence of any

direct references to Wordsworth's poetic engagement with this region of England and its prehistory. Particularly, there is 'Salisbury Plain'. Composed in the late summer of 1793, the poem reflects Wordsworth's acute alienation when, having recently returned from France, he saw everywhere the signs of a nation intent on war, and neglectful of its duties and responsibilities at home. A mishap which left him wandering for two days on the Wiltshire downs gave him the objective correlatives for the conflict he experienced as a stranger in his own country: the bleak Plain, Stonehenge, and a tale of loss, privation and homelessness.[39] Commenting on the ruin as a figure in late eighteenth-century poetry and the role it has played within the aesthetic of the picturesque in assimilating culture to nature, and the 'country' as nation to the 'country' as rural ground, Anne Janowitz argues for Wordsworth's political radicalism in his approach to the 'eternal pile' in this poem.[40] Is England's ancient past, and likewise its present, a condition of barbarity or civility, tyranny or freedom? The answers Wordsworth comes up with are self-contradictory: Stonehenge is the visible sign of England's antiquity and it also calls in doubt the authority of that antiquity; the Plain, as encountered by the Traveller and the Female Vagrant, is 'this terrain most unlike the fruitful country of nature's benevolence' and it is also 'England most like itself';[41] the Druids are savages gathered at their 'sacrificial altar fed/ With living men' and also mystical beings who show

> To vast assemblies, while each breath of night
> Is hushed, the living fires that bright and slow
> Rounding th'aetherial field in order go. (ll. 191–93)

Naipaul's contemplation of Stonehenge necessitates a withholding of the dark message and vision of 'Salisbury Plain' and, for this, two explanations offer themselves. One is that there can be no room in his romance of England's timeless perfection for Wordsworth's extreme political views. The other, more complex, explanation relates to the problem of rewriting history and identity within the postcolonial context. To expand upon this, I shall turn now to a major influence behind Wordsworth, to Spenser.

Specifically the double image of the Druids recalls Book VI of

The Faerie Queene and its two visions of the pastoral world as 'salvage nation' and 'civility'.[42] Spenserean romance in this respect translates the classical Silvanus/Orcus myth and, as David Richards maintains in a skilfully elaborated argument,[43] simultaneously participates in the contemporary translations of the myth that were taking place in European ethnographic representations of the New World. Richards's example is the Le Moyne–De Bry illustrations of the Timucuas of Florida published in 1591 (Books I–III of *The Faerie Queene* appeared in 1590 and Books IV–VI in 1596). A similarly dualistic image of the noble and the cruel savage, wild and civil societies, in European accounts of the native Caribbean is probed in Peter Hulme's *Colonial Encounters*.[44] As Hulme remarks, Carib and Arawak is 'a division variously articulated ... from Columbus's first jottings in his log-book to the historical and anthropological works written today'. Some of these early documents, in Spanish and English, from the closing decades of the sixteenth century lie behind Naipaul's *The Loss of El Dorado* and its account, in the early part of the book, of the New World adventure of Antonio de Berrio and Sir Walter Raleigh in the years 1580–1618. A key source is Raleigh's *The Discovery of the Large, Rich and Beautiful Empire of Guiana* (1595) which depends heavily on Spanish knowledge of the area. In Naipaul's retelling of the quest—El Dorado, a kingdom in a cold high region in the jungle whose people, unlike the naked bow and arrow jungle Indians, were 'clothed, civilized, artistic' and whose temples were full of gold[45]—pastoral romance is displaced by a history of defeats and despoliations. The individual plights of Berrio and Raleigh apart, it points to the dispeopling and wasting of Trinidad in a long succession of raids, resettlements, and pacifications carried out upon the Amerindians. Fifty years after the island was appropriated by Berrio as the Spanish base for El Dorado in 1592, it was little more than 'a ghost province'.

The Loss of El Dorado, as noted earlier in this essay, occupies a special place in the story of Naipaul's journeys and discoveries as a writer. It means, in this instance, that the 'sense of antiquity' he brings to his contemplation of Stonehenge is inflected by the 'aboriginal, pre-Columbus island' (p. 146) which he 'dreamed about and created from the documents' (p. 149) as well as by the English literature he has read. To write his own version of 'this historical part of England', he has necessarily to 'empty' the narrative space of the manichaean tropes which produce the colonial and the native as savage/tame other. Traces of Wordsworth's anti-pastoral persist. Just as the red dress or coat in the distance will continue to draw attention to the sightseeing crowd, however selectively Naipaul looks upon the site, so the army barracks, artillery ranges and military aeroplanes repeatedly associated with the area are a reminder of the warmongering face of the English nation.[46] The stress, however, falls elsewhere. At the heart of Naipaul's revisioning of antiquity, 'activity', 'numbers', 'organization' and 'busyness', are the words and the means by which the past and 'these now virtually empty downs' are repeopled, and the 'eternal pile ... on Sarum's plain' is returned to human significance.

'Busyness' is of course the quality identified with Jack (p. 33), and also with Naipaul himself, as he works, 'slowly, day by day', or 'allowing [his] hand to run; starting at different points', or animated by 'the rhythm of creation and walk, Africa in the writing in the morning, Wiltshire in the hour-and-a-half or so after lunch' (pp. 154–56). Like Jack, too, Naipaul can be said to have reinvented, through his labour amid alien surroundings, 'his own world' (p. 87). Within the geographical and textual space of *The Enigma of Arrival*, two strains cross and recross in intricate ways: the first, elegiac, solipsistic, bound to a mythical England; the second, alert, outward looking, making new sense of a changing environment by conscientious observation and by bringing the place into juxtaposition with other worlds, other lives. Within this hybrid terrain it is the early lessons Naipaul learnt through the senses and feelings that prove the most useful. They show him the correspondences—at once unlikely and just—between snow drifts in Wiltshire and sand cliffs in Trinidad; between Jack's garden and the garden Naipaul's father tried to get started in a patch of cleared bush, and, beyond these, 'those lush aboriginal Indian "gardens" [Columbus] had seen in 1498 in the south of the island' (p. 142), visible symbols all of 'busyness'. At other times Wiltshire becomes merged with his fictional spaces so that the 'textures and shapes and patterns' of the valley are refigured in distant landscapes which, in their turn, are projected back upon the English countryside.

> It is normally supposed that something always gets lost in translation; I cling, obstinately, to the notion that something can also be gained.[47]

One of the gains Naipaul enlarges upon is the 'benign' landscape of Wiltshire and its gift to him—after the literary setbacks and the illness 'that did away with whatever remained of youthfulness in me' (p. 83)—of 'a second life' as a writer and a person. The experience of healing is registered in his changing interpretations of Giorgio de Chirico's painting, 'The Enigma of Arrival', first encountered in a paperback booklet in the manor cottage. Mainly on account of its title, which the artist had borrowed from Apollinaire, the work attracts Naipaul in 'an indirect, poetical way', tapping into embedded and tangled feelings that escape definition however variously and obsessively he tries to realize them in fictional form. In time, as well as fear and panic, the painting comes to suggest some of the positive aspects of his residence in Wiltshire:

> my journey, the writer's journey, the writer defined by his writing discoveries, his ways of seeing, rather than by his personal adventures, writer and man separating at the beginning of the journey and coming together again in a second life just before the end. (p. 309)

The shapely lines and cadences of the above statement, taken from the last and shortest section of the novel, 'The Ceremony of Farewell', conjure up the idea of a unified self, evolving from within its own contained space. Subsequently, back in Trinidad following the death of his younger sister, and attending the rituals performed a few days after the cremation, Naipaul is once again overtaken by a powerful sense of disorder and incoherence. First, there are the (mis)translations: a version of Trinidad's history that blurs its several colonial epochs; English renderings of Hindu philosophical concepts wherein 'reincarnation' is elided with 'afterlife' and 'karma' is literalized as 'our past lives [having] dictated the present'. Then there are the incongruities of the scene: earth rites carried out on the terazzo floor of a verandah; the shadowy romance of El Dorado transmuted into money from oil and natural gas and suburban houses, gardens, streets. Finally, there are the broken lines of personal and family history, indicated in the contrasting figures of the silk-clad pundit, a first cousin, and Naipaul himself; and, more obscurely, the deep-seated scars of the psyche:

> There was no question, in 1953, when my father died, of my returning home. My brother it was, then aged eight, who performed and witnessed the terrible final rites of cremation.[48] (p. 314)

Returning to England, Naipaul begins 'to write very fast about Jack and his garden', writing which is impelled by a sharpened consciousness that 'our sacred world has vanished' and only the idea of it remains, only the enigma 'infinitely active and inaccessible in the image',[49] to be carried across into words, and somehow restored.

NOTES

1. V. S. Naipaul, 'Conrad's Darkness', in *The Return of Eva Peron with The Killings in Trinidad* [1980] (Harmondsworth: Penguin Books, 1983), p. 208. Subsequent references, *CD* followed by page number(s), are to this edition and included in the text of this essay.
2. See, for example, Rob Nixon, *London Calling: V. S. Naipaul, Postcolonial Mandarin* (Oxford: Oxford University Press, 1992), pp. 88–108.
3. V. S. Naipaul, *The Enigma of Arrival* [1987] (Harmondsworth: Penguin Books, 1988). Subsequent page references are to this edition and included in the text of this essay.
4. For a discussion of the provenance of 'the world-as-exhibition' and 'cartographic anxiety', see Derek Gregory, *Geographical Imaginations* (Oxford: Blackwell, 1994), pp. 34–42, and pp. 70–77.
5. Joseph Conrad, 'Geography and Some Explorers', *Last Essays*, p. 14, in *Tales of Hearsay and Last Essays* (London: Dent, 1963). Subsequent

references, *GSE* followed by page number(s), will be to this edition and included in the text of this essay. Under the title, 'The Romance of Travel', Conrad's essay appeared in February 1924 as a general introduction to a serial work called 'Countries of the World', and was reprinted in March of the same year under its present title in *The National Geographic Magazine*.

6. For an account of how Conrad follows, and undermines at the same time, the prescriptions of romance, see Ian Watt, *Conrad in the Nineteenth Century* (London: Chatto & Windus, 1980), pp. 46–48.

7. Gillian Beer, *The Romance* (London: Methuen, 1970), p. 79.

8. Similarly, recalling his own arrival at the Stanley Falls in 1890, Conrad finds in that moment intimations of impending loss mixed in with his sense of fulfilment, 'Geography and Some Explorers', p. 17.

9. Edward Said, 'Reflections on Exile', *Granta*, 13 (1984), 165. Compare Watt's remark that while Conrad 'loved the residues of the past, of the sailing ship, of the age of Palmerston and the Pax Britannica', he did not take enthusiastically to other aspects of England, for example, the English themselves, and 'his residence remained faintly provisional' (*Conrad in the Nineteenth Century*, pp. 23–24).

10. See, for example, Brian Hudson, 'The New Geography and the New Imperialism: 1870–1918', *Antipode*, 9 (1977), 12–19: 'the study and teaching of the new geography at an advanced level was vigorously promoted at the time [from 1870] largely, if not mainly, to serve the interests of imperialism in its various aspects including territorial acquisition, economic exploitation, militarism and the practice of class and race domination' (p. 12).

11. Henry James, Preface to *The American*, New York Edition, vol. 2 (New York: Charles Scribner's Sons, 1907), p. xvii.

12. According to Naipaul, 'You have to write a different book from thirty years ago: you can't write the same book. Because you change, your knowledge of the world changes, and the forms have to change to meet the demands of the material you've accumulated. We can be burdened by dead forms.' See Aamer Hussein, 'Delivering the truth: An interview with V. S. Naipaul', *The Times Literary Supplement*, 2 September 1994, p. 3.

13. Salman Rushdie, *Shame* (London: Picador, 1983), p. 86. I have found his comments on migrancy in this novel, and in his essays in *Imaginary Homelands* (London: Granta Books, 1991), extremely useful.

14. Said, 'Reflections on Exile', p. 165.

15. Salman Rushdie, *Imaginary Homelands*, p. 15.

16. Tejaswini Niranjana, *Siting Translation: History, Post-Structuralism, and the Colonial Context* (Berkeley: University of California Press, 1992), pp. 1–35. See, in particular, her account of translations from Sanskrit by Indologists, such as William Jones (1746–84) and Friedrich Max Müller (1823–1900).

17. 'Travel to foreign lands was believed to incur grave impurity for

members of the upper classes, which, according to some authorities, could never be expunged', A. L. Basham, *The Wonder that was India: A survey of the history and culture of the Indian sub-continent before the coming of the Muslims*, 3rd revised edition (London: Sidgwick & Jackson, 1988), p. 231.

18. Naipaul's first novel *The Mystic Masseur* appeared in 1957, and was followed by other novels, collections of short stories, travel writing, autobiographical pieces, and essays. His most recent work, *A Way in the World*, was published in 1994.

19. See, for example, 'Jasmine', in *The Overcrowded Barracoon* [1972] (Harmonsworth: Penguin Books, 1976), pp. 24–31.

20. Said, 'Reflections on Exile', p. 172; and Eva Hoffman, *Lost in Translation: A Life in a New Language* [1989] (London: Minerva, 1995), p. 274.

21. See, for example, his response to the boarding house in Earl's Court with its dining room situated in the basement. This is not a style of architecture to be found in Trinidad but something he knows about from his reading. To come across such a building was tantamount to 'entering the world of a novel, a book; entering the real world'. *The Enigma of Arrival*, p. 119.

22. Malcolm Bradbury, 'The Cities of Modernism', in *Modernism 1890–1930*, eds Malcolm Bradbury and James McFarlane [1976] (Harmondsworth: Penguin Books, 1981), p. 100.

23. Malcolm Bradbury, 'The Cities of Modernism', p. 101.

24. Edward W. Said, 'Yeats and Decolonization', in Terry Eagleton, Fredric Jameson, and Edward W. Said, *Nationalism, Colonialism, and Literature* (Minneapolis: University of Minnesota Press, 1990), p. 77.

25. James Clifford, 'Introduction: Partial Truths', in *Writing Culture: The Poetics and Politics of Ethnography*, eds James Clifford and George E. Marcus (Berkeley and Los Angeles: University of California Press, 1986), p. 9.

26. V. S. Naipaul, *The Middle Passage* [1962] (Harmondsworth: Penguin Books, 1969), p. 58.

27. According to the Martinican and Francophone critic, Edouard Glissant, 'the Caribbean is a land of *enracinement* (rooting) and *errance* (wandering, drifting)', and the themes and dynamics of departure and return are as intrinsic to Caribbean literature as the echoic notes in the words 'retour' and 'detour'. See Robert Aldrich, 'From Francite to Creolite: French West Indian literature comes home', *Writing Across Worlds: Literature and Migration*, eds Russell King, John Connell and Paul White (London: Routledge, 1995), pp. 101–24.

28. Trinh Minh-ha, 'No Master Territories', in *The Post-colonial Studies Reader*, eds Bill Ashcroft, Gareth Griffiths and Helen Tiffin (London: Routledge, 1995), pp. 214–18.

29. These pedestrian and other kinds of journeying are integral to the

generic plurality of the work. As well as a novel, *The Enigma of Arrival* is professional biography, romance, travel writing, history, and literary criticism, that is, Naipaul's survey and appraisal of his own published works.

30. Derek Pearsall and Elizabeth Salter, *Landscape and Seasons of the Medieval World* (London: Paul Elek, 1973), p. 134. I am grateful to Catherine Batt for references to this and other works on the medieval Calendar tradition.

31. Pearsall and Salter, *Landscape and Seasons*, p. 157.

32. *William Wordsworth: Selected Poetry*, eds Stephen Gill and Duncan Wu, World's Classics (Oxford: Oxford University Press, 1997), pp. 11–12.

33. Gillian Beer, 'The island and the aeroplane: the case of Virginia Woolf', in *Nation and Narration*, ed. Homi Bhabha (London: Routledge, 1990), p. 269.

34. I am indebted to Roger Ewbank for clarification on this point.

35. Gayatri Chakravorty Spivak, 'The Politics of Translation', in *Outside in the Teaching Machine* (London: Routledge, 1993), p. 180.

36. See also Niranjana, *Siting Translation*, pp. 171–72.

37. Homi Bhabha, 'Of Mimicry and Man: the Ambivalence of Colonial Discourse', in *Modern Literary Theory*, eds Philip Rice and Patricia Waugh (London: Edward Arnold, 1989), pp. 234–41 (p. 240).

38. Wordsworth was, of course, working with eighteenth-century modes of prospect poetry (see, for example, 'Edgehill' by Richard Jago). The conventions of this poetry have also been appropriated by nineteenth-century travel writing. Naipaul's narrative here parodies what Mary Louise Pratt calls 'the monarch-of-all-I-survey genre', a typical example of which is Richard Burton's account of his first view of Lake Tanganyika in 1860. See Mary Louise Pratt, *Imperial Eyes: Travel Writing and Transculturation* (London: Routledge, 1992), pp. 201–08.

39. Stephen Gill, 'Introduction', in *The Salisbury Plain Poems of William Wordsworth*, ed. Stephen Gill (Ithaca, NY: Cornell University Press, 1973). Later and revised versions of 'Salisbury Plain' are: 'The Female Vagrant' (1798); 'Adventures on Salisbury Plain' (1799 or 1800); 'Guilt and Sorrow; or Incidents upon Salisbury Plain' (1842).

40. Anne Janowitz, *England's Ruins: Poetic Purpose and the National Landscape* (Oxford: Basil Blackwell, 1990), pp. 116–26. Paradoxically, the figure of decay, the ruin, became in late eighteenth- and nineteenth-century poetry the 'historical provenance for the conception of the British nation as immemorially ancient'.

41. Janowitz, *England's Ruins*, p. 96.

42. See Edmund Spenser, *The Faerie Queene*, Book VI Canto viii, stanzas 35–49; and Canto x, stanzas 22–24. Among recent critics who have argued for a politicized reading of Spenser's pastoral landscape, see Andrew Hadfield, *Edmund Spenser's Irish Experience: Wilde Fruit and Salvage Soyl*

(Oxford: Clarendon Press, 1997): 'The landscape of Book VI is not *necessarily* that of rural Ireland; the problem is that it could equally be an England unable to contain hostile forces and challenges to its civilized order, signifying a breakdown of the distinction between the two nations' (p. 174).

43. David Richards, *Masks of Difference: Cultural Representations in Literature, Anthropology and Art* (Cambridge: Cambridge University Press, 1994), pp. 37–56.

44. Peter Hulme, *Colonial Encounters: Europe and the Native Caribbean 1492–1797* [1986] (London: Routledge, 1992), pp. 45–87.

45. V. S. Naipaul, *The Loss of El Dorado: A History* (London: André Deutsch, 1969), pp. 10, 22, 27.

46. The Falklands war in 1982 was a colonial war, like the American War, the cause of so many of the Female Vagrant's sufferings,

47. Rushdie, *Imaginary Homelands*, p. 17.

48. Basham notes: 'From the earliest hymns of the Rg Veda sons were looked on as great blessings. At least one son was almost essential, to perform funeral rites for his father, and thus ensure his safe transit to the other world', *The Wonder that was India*, p. 160.

49. Johann Wilhelm von Goethe, *Nachlass*, quoted in Tzvetan Todorov, *Theories of the Symbol*, trans. Catherine Porter (Oxford: Blackwell, [1977] 1982), p. 205.

Sentimental Translation in Mackenzie and Sterne

DAVID FAIRER

The eighteenth-century sentimentalist was expected to be a skilled interpreter of nonverbal communication. Sensitive to the nuances of facial expression or physical gesture, the 'man of feeling' was an expert reader of physiognomy, a translator of signs who could turn a look into a sentence, the slightest movement into an assertion, a question, or an invitation:

> There is not a secret so aiding to the progress of sociality, as to get master of this *short hand*, and be quick in rendering the several turns of looks and limbs, with all their inflections and delineations, into plain words. For my own part, by long habitude, I do it so mechanically, that when I walk the streets of London, I go translating all the way.[1]

At especially sentimental moments Laurence Sterne's narrators translate a character's eloquent gestures for us, whether it is Yorick exchanging silent courtesies with the old French officer in the box at the *Opéra Comique* ('the French officer might as well have said it all aloud', p. 171), or the concupiscible Widow Wadman waiting for Uncle Toby to reveal where he received his war wound:

> —You shall see the very place, Madam; said my uncle Toby.
>
> Mrs Wadman blush'd—look'd towards the door—turn'd pale—blush'd slightly again—recovered her natural colour—blush'd worse than ever; which for the sake of the unlearned reader, I translate thus—
>
> *'L—d! I cannot look at it—*
> *What would the world say if I look'd at it?*

> *I should drop down, if I look'd at it—*
> *I wish I could look at it—*
> *There can be no sin in looking at it.*
> *—I will look at it.*'[2]

This kind of sentimental translation has been well analysed by John Mullan, who notes how sentimental narrative 'has to translate, has to make "plain words" mediate the natural articulacy of feeling', and in so doing establishes a sociable relationship between narrator and reader ('those who are to benefit by the habit and art of his translation').[3]

My concern in this essay is to look behind the difficulties of sentimental translation to what I take to be an underlying problem—one that remains crucial for eighteenth-century notions of Sensibility.[4] However we express the concept ('verbalizing the language of feeling' or 'mediating between gesture and word') it is clear that sentimental translation is dependent on a basic difficulty inherent in the notion of bodily expression itself: its reliance upon the ability to connect matter and idea. Somewhere inside Widow Wadman thought has been physicalized: her blushes are external signs of mental activity.

It is generally recognized that the heightened sensitivity to feeling which characterizes Sensibility was indebted to theories of the nervous system developed in the eighteenth century, in which the Cartesian dualism of mind and body was replaced by more organic concepts of human physiology.[5] This has led theorists of Sensibility, such as Walter Jackson Bate and G. J. Barker-Benfield, into stressing the continuity of mental and physical.[6] Where mid-eighteenth-century writers were alert to a difficulty, some materialist criticism of the late twentieth century tends to interpret sentimental mechanisms as unproblematic 'signs', and to move between 'inner' and 'outer' with metaphorical ease. Robert Markley's influential essay, for example, with its stress on Sensibility as social performance, reads sentimental gestures as the body's 'outward, demonstrable, material signs' of its supposed 'inner virtues'.[7] I want to suggest, however, that by removing the ontological barrier and bringing mind and body into the same equation, eighteenth-century physiologists were in fact posing the old problem in a more urgent form.[8] Far from instigating a mind–body continuum, they planted an enigma in the heart of the new Sensibility.

Even the most convinced early exponent of psychosomatic medicine, the Leyden Professor Jerome Gaub (1705–80), announced in his 1747 lecture on mind–body interaction: 'I confess openly and state plainly that I know and understand nothing of all these things, and moreover, I have no hope that man will ever be able to understand them.'[9] This did not deter others from ingenious conjecture. In the late 1740s Robert Whytt, Professor of Medicine at Edinburgh, developed his *sentient principle* ('an immaterial, undivided substance that could "feel" stimuli and necessarily directed the appropriate response'),[10] but he encountered insoluble problems in trying to fit this immaterial communicating principle to the reflex system of the nerves.[11] George Cheyne had already faced the difficulty in *The Natural Method of Cureing the Diseases of the Body, and the Disorders of the Mind Depending on the Body* (1742), which was posited on the assumption that 'Mind or Soul' has the capacity of initiating motions in the body:

> How it exerts these Powers on *divinely organiz'd* Matter, I do not here pretend to say; but I conceive it acts on the Organs by means of the *Mechanism* of the Brain and its *Nerves*, which are an Infinity of differently situated, complicated and stretch'd little *Filaments* or *Fibrils*, fill'd with a soft *milky* cellular Substance, (like a *Rush* with its *Pith*) contain'd in small *membranous* extremely *elastic* Sacks or *Tubuli*, all whose *elastic* and *energic* Virtue consists in the proper *Tension* or *Vibrations* of these Sacks or *membranous* Coats, spread over all the *Solids* of the Body, which being extremely *elastic* and springy, convey *harmonious* and divinely proportion'd *Vibrations*, *Undulations* and *Tremors*, excited outwardly by Objects to this *sentient* and *intelligent* Principle ...

After a further page of explication worthy of Walter Shandy, Cheyne breaks off almost in despair: 'This is the best *Idea* I can conceive ... others may explain the Matter better, if they can.'[12]

And others did try. David Hartley postulated an 'infinitesimal elementary Body to be intermediate between the Soul and gross Body',[13] and William Smith conceived of a physiological equivalent of Newtonian æther, a 'subtile medium, or animal æther, contained in the nerves', which, he claimed, acted as a 'connecting medium' between mind and matter:

> this intermediate material ... makes the cement between the human soul and body; and is the instrument or medium of all its actions and functions. But of this infinitely fine and elastic fluid, I am afraid none will be able to determine the specific nature.[14]

Physiological theories of a nervous system may have been organic in intention, but at their core was an intractable problem, well summarized by L. J. Rather:

> How then can conscious (or unconscious) disturbances of the mind possibly initiate functional or structural changes in the body? Is it not clearly illegitimate—and physically impossible—to introduce anything mental or psychic into the bodily machinery as an effective force no matter how small the quantum of force is taken to be?[15]

This was what David Hume considered the most mysterious principle 'in all nature'.[16] As we see from these extracts, the problem recognized by eighteenth-century physiologists was one of mediation, of establishing a link that evidently must exist (Widow Wadman palpably *blushed*). The crux was to locate the meeting-point of mind and matter.

This had earlier proved a difficulty with the epistemological mechanisms of John Locke's theory of perception. Locke can help us distinguish between a mental associative connectedness, made between ideas within a mind, and that mind's engagement with an object's more recalcitrant 'primary' qualities (it is these, particularly solidity, that impinge on the infant Tristram Shandy). By differentiating the qualities which subsist within an object from those 'secondary' ones which are registered subjectively in the mind, Locke creates contradictions from which George Berkeley tried to rescue him.[17] Locke's philosophy finds itself mediating between objective and subjective: 'secondary' qualities depend on both a 'power' within the external object and a receptive capacity within the perceiving mind, and Locke's concern is how to mediate between the two. At some point object and idea must touch (in the sense that one brings about the other) either literally or figuratively, depending on which term sets the agenda, that is, whether the 'touching' is at the level of substance or idea. If it is neither, then we return to the question of how this move from physical to mental, from object to subject, has been negotiated. How can a mind deduce the object from the idea, since the latter is all it knows?[18] This question is at the heart of the Lockean mystery, and it is also at the heart of the way meanings are elicited by Sensibility. The vocabulary of sentiment, with its forceful 'impressions' and its 'touching' moments, often plays with the tangibility of emotion.

It is misleading, however, to think of the new physiology as supplying continuities or elisions of mind and body where they had previously not existed. The organic theories of the mid-eighteenth century repeatedly draw attention to the fraught question of how to mediate between matter and thought, how to carry across meanings from one to the other (note Cheyne's extraordinary collection of italicized terms). In a similar way, I wish to argue, the literature of Sensibility is interested in those moments when the transfer between mind and matter is made. Whether they are moments of sexual excitement or spiritual intimacy, imbued with sensual magic or endowed with spiritual grace (ideally both together), they are treasured by the 'man of feeling', whose sensibility is guaranteed and enriched by his ability to make the sentimental translation. A *frisson* of physical arousal confirms that the transfer between mind and matter has been made.[19]

Crucial to the mechanism of Sensibility is the physical object. This tends to be an independent, sometimes recalcitrant, entity which is brought into the context of human emotion and given meanings that link the sensate to the material and work to bridge the gap between mind and matter. Indeed, when materialism and idealism encounter each other, a sentimental moment can be created. Dr Johnson, that determined enemy of Sensibility, thought that by kicking a stone he could refute 'Bishop

Berkeley's ingenious sophistry to prove the non-existence of matter'; but he succeeded only in making a sentimental gesture: Johnson's transfer of emotion and energy effectively established a connection between his annoyance, his blood pressure, his foot, and the rock. The contact between the sash window and Tristram Shandy's private parts, or the fragment of parapet and Uncle Toby's groin, are in similar terms sentimental moments. In sentimental scenarios objects are forever being encountered as meanings that impinge on the life of the subject. They do not satirize Sensibility by bringing it up against a material reality: the insistent physicality of objects is vital to create the mind–matter interface along which Sensibility works.[20]

To discern connections between object and subject is at once the aim and the fate of Sensibility. Emotions are transferred from or onto things, not merely through Lockean association of ideas but by physical means also, and by procedures that are often subtle, even witty, and which make the reading of a sentimental text a more complex activity than is generally allowed. Transference of meaning works on the interrelated principles of exchange, substitution, slippage, and proliferation, and it embraces both physical and linguistic events (indeed there are repeated interchanges between the two). It may be manifested as an *exchange* of snuff-boxes, of glances, or of words; as a *substitution* of names for things, objects for emotions, or vice versa; as *slippages* (physical or mental) that make containment, of meaning by words or of eggs by a basket, impossible; or, in *Tristram Shandy* particularly, as a *proliferation* of the seminal energies, in which meaning is tumultuously generated not only from every sentence on every page, but at the infinite points of connection between them. By opening up lines of communication between an external world of matter and an internal world of idea, sentimental translation releases meaning from whatever might attempt to contain or define it: meaning therefore becomes transferable, not inherent. Consequently the problem of mediation which is evident in the physiology of the mid-eighteenth century is also crucial for the literature of Sensibility. If Sensibility depends on the mediation of experience, then those great mediators, time, space and language, tend to become richly problematic in sentimental fiction: they refract, rather than simply convey, ideas.

The following discussion will focus on three sentimental novels which are particularly alert to the kinds of translation I have identified: Laurence Sterne's *Tristram Shandy* (1760–67) and *A Sentimental Journey* (1768), and Henry Mackenzie's *The Man of Feeling* (1771). In each of them a playful element of generic self-consciousness helps to highlight the particular mechanisms of Sensibility that are at work.

An instance of the subtle way in which transference can work in a sentimental text is provided by the opening of *The Man of Feeling*. The novel's first sentence interlinks space and time, abstract and concrete, mind and matter, movement and stasis, with the greatest economy:

> My dog had made a point on a piece of fallow-ground, and led the curate and me two or three hundred yards over that and some stubble adjoining, in a breathless state of expectation, on a burning first of September.[21]

The book's uncompromising opening phrase, a piece of hunting jargon, hesitates between literal and metaphorical: there is no debating with the point the dog has made, and the two gunmen hurry towards it, breathless equally through their expectation and their physical haste, as the text incrementally prolongs our own breath with its fastidious location of itself across a space and at a point in time. Just as the scene links fallow ground to stubble, what is waiting to be cultivated to what has just been harvested, the next sentence gives us an anticlimax that is soon to prove a climax—the point of their chase may have gone, but the point of the story is about to be discovered:

> It was a false point, and our labour was in vain: yet, to do Rover justice, (for he's an excellent dog, though I have lost his pedigree) the fault was none of his, the birds were gone; the curate shewed me the spot where they had lain basking, at the root of an old hedge. (p. 3)

Doing justice to Rover may seem hardly the point, but the tactics of Sensibility usually find the point, like the missing birds, simultaneously decisive and elusive, just as Rover's excellence is not quite independent of the lost pedigree. The dog has found the place where the birds lay, but too late. Yet both birds and pedigree have left their mark, and at this moment as the narrator stirs and looks about him, a human absence registers itself in similar terms:

> I discovered, for the first time, a venerable pile, to which the inclosure belonged. An air of melancholy hung about it. There was a languid stillness in the day, and a single crow, that perched on an old tree by the side of the gate, seemed to delight in the echo of its own croaking.
>
> I leaned on my gun and looked; but I had not breath enough to ask the curate a question. I observed carving on the bark of some of the trees: 'twas indeed the only mark of human art about the place, except that some branches appeared to have been lopped, to give a view of the cascade, which was formed by a little rill at some distance. (pp. 3–4)

The narrator finds he has entered a setting marked by human feelings. This was a landscape someone had loved and in which they had loved, a place where plants and emotions had been cultivated. Someone had valued the picturesque view and someone (else?) had carved on the trees. The bark and branches remain scored by these gestures. It is typical of sentimental procedures that what is adjacent is declared to 'belong', a word that like so much sentimental vocabulary permits a human nuance; and in stressing the old (the old hedge, the venerable pile, the old tree) the passage exploits Sensibility's fascination with things that store and mediate former experiences: old objects bear witness to a past that has gone yet might be recoverable through memory. Linked to this temporal connectedness is the way the passage uses the contrast between a 'melancholy' that hangs around and a 'delight' that merely perches—the crow's happy self-engrossment has a harsh effect in this scene, in contrast to the silence of the narrator who observes and reads it for us. His physical lack of breath stops him talking and makes him look more intently; no longer hurried, it is as though his breathing were now being suspended for a Wordsworthian 'spot of time'.

The transfers of meaning that are occurring in this passage form a rich pattern in which absence and disappointment make the mind alert and more open to experience ('There is no state where one is apter to pause and look round one, than after such a disappointment', p. 3). In sentimental texts, failure or frustration tend to be rechannelled, and meaning and value sought in a new direction; restriction in one context often leads to proliferation elsewhere. An inability to generate children will find a way out through breeding ideas and theories; disappointments in the physical world will encourage new expectations for the mental world. All the time the play of ideas is waiting to substitute one text for another, a subjective text for an objective one, a figurative for a literal, while insisting on a translatability between them.

The sacred vessel of the sentimentalist is therefore a text that embodies this transference by mediating the material and non-material. One such ideal is a text that has been physically abused and is waiting to find a sympathetic reader who is not merely receptive to the meanings it contains but is sensitized to those that are attached more tangentially, more imaginatively, to it. For the sentimentalist in every sense the immaterial is material (and in using that phrase we note how under the aegis of Sensibility critical language slips from literal to metaphorical[22]). The ideal sentimental text/object bears transferred human meanings as a surrogate undergoing suffering or humiliation, whether it is the manuscript in which La Fleur's butter is wrapped, or the wasting fragments of her father's autobiography found by Adeline in Ann Radcliffe's *The Romance of the Forest*.[23] As Mackenzie's narrator finds a new point of interest, he recovers just such a text in the fragmentary history of the man who once inhabited the landscape:

> 'I should be glad to see this medley', said I. 'You shall see it now', answered the curate, 'for I always take it along with me a-shooting'. 'How came it so torn?' ''Tis excellent wadding', said the curate.—This was a plea of expediency I was not in a condition to answer; for I had actually in my pocket great part of an edition of one of the German Illustrissimi, for the very same purpose. We exchanged

> books; and by that means (for the curate was a strenuous logician) we probably saved both. (p. 5)

In this little parable of use and value, the meaning of each text shifts in the process of exchange, from an immediate practical excellence to something less tangible but of greater moment; it moves from a physical purpose to one that engages the mind. Each is saved by this 'expediency', by its 'suitability to the circumstances and conditions of the case' (*OED*), but its meaning is translated from matter to spirit in the process, from one expedient to another. The sentimental exchange is conscious of such decisive subjectivities, where an object accrues value and meaning by engaging with an individual human mind. This is not simply a matter of locating subjective value, but of recognizing ways in which sentimental writing transfers meaning between object and subject.

The sentimental exchange is therefore focused on the *token*, an evidential sign that carries translatable meaning and mediates between thing and idea, such as a love-token or a token of respect. The concept in its symbolic aspect is age-old, but the eighteenth century moved the token into the area of individual experience and particular circumstance, focusing on the problematic element of mediation. In *A Sentimental Journey*, Yorick's exchange of snuffboxes with Father Lorenzo concludes a complex emotional tennis match, a contention 'so sweet and pleasurable … to the nerves' that it can only be resolved by a mutual giving and receiving that lifts the monk's box into the spiritual dimension:

> I guard this box, as I would the instrumental parts of my religion, to help my mind on to something better: in truth, I seldom go abroad without it; and oft and many a time have I called up by it the courteous spirit of its owner to regulate my own, in the justlings of the world. (pp. 100–01)

The genie can be released whenever needed—indeed Yorick scrupulously records how during the preceding ten minutes of intense silence the monk rubbed the horn box on the sleeve of his tunic, so that it 'acquired a little air of brightness by the friction' (p. 100), a detail that also plays on the politeness of their exchange (*politus* = 'polished'). During these moments of unspoken communion the box has meaning transferred to it by a similar touching process, and this helps Sterne make a nice distinction between what the box contains and what has become attached to it. In the act of translation the box has been recategorized as a mediating object, valuable not for what it contains (snuff) but for what it has assimilated during the touching sentimental encounter—in this case Father Lorenzo's spirit.

The intimacies of sentimental exchange can be ghostly, in that they release spirits or create objects haunted by an intangible presence. Figures of Sensibility act as mediums in this way, and an encounter between two polished performers, each with a well-honed ability to translate ideas, can remind us of that extreme collapse of subject into object, the *doppelgänger*. Yorick meets his in Monsieur Dessein, the Calais hotelier:

> I perceived that something darken'd the passage more than myself, as I stepp'd along it to my room; it was effectually Mons. Dessein, the master of the hotel, who had just return'd from vespers, and, with his hat under his arm, was most complaisantly following me, to put me in mind of my wants. (p. 87)

The delightful word 'effectually' hesitates between 'in fact' and 'in effect', as Yorick becomes conscious of Monsieur Dessein's ghostlike presence; the hotelier is a man with little investment in objectivity, one who takes complaisance to the extreme by becoming for his guest an accompanying consciousness, ready 'to put me in mind of my wants'. Dessein's skill is to open up a sympathetic supply line that he can exploit. Their negotiation over the Desobligeant, which Yorick is hoping to get cheap, causes them to outdo each other in the transfer of sentiment:

> —Now was I the master of this hotel, said I, laying the point of my fore-finger on Mons. Dessein's breast, I would inevitably make a point of getting rid of this unfortunate *Desobligeant*—it stands swinging reproaches at you every time you pass by it—
>
> *Mon Dieu!* said Mons. Dessein—I have no interest—
> Except the interest, said I, which men of a certain turn of

> mind take, Mons. Dessein, in their own sensations—I'm persuaded, to a man who feels for others as well as for himself, every rainy night, disguise it as you will, must cast a damp upon your spirits—You suffer, Mons. Dessein, as much as the machine— (p. 88)

Yorick's tactic involves shifting Monsieur Dessein's 'interest' (i.e. self-interest) towards a sympathetic interest in the fate of the machine, sensitizing him to its plight, working to transfer the rain from the carriage to his own spirits, to make him first feel the Desobligeant's reproaches, then substitute himself for it. In making him 'a man who feels for others as well as for himself' Yorick brings both interests together, suggesting that *A Sentimental Journey* is less an exposé of Sensibility's underlying selfishness than an analysis of the way egotism and altruism transfer meanings between themselves. Such mutuality provides Monsieur Dessein with his triumphant reply:

> *C'est bien vrai*, said he—But in this case I should only exchange one disquietude for another, and with loss: figure to yourself, my dear Sir, that in giving you a chaise which would fall to pieces before you had got half way to Paris—figure to yourself how much I should suffer ... (p. 88)

His loss in the exchange, he insists, would be in sentimental, not hard, currency. The hotelier plays Yorick's game by keeping his suffering poised between egotism and altruism: he is a man of the world, but a man of feeling too. Yorick has met his *alter ego*: 'The dose was made up exactly after my own prescription; so I could not help taking it.' In the last of a series of substitutions Yorick finally must be his own victim.

It is in the mechanisms of charitable giving that sentimental translation is most literal and visible; but this is never a one-way affair. Whether the tribute of feeling is paid in tears or coin, it becomes part of an emotional economy, what Yorick calls a 'sentimental commerce' (p. 78), which allows meaning to circulate in relation to questions of justice, value, motive and will. The giving of coin makes judgments of value especially problematic, as in the famous scene of Yorick's distribution of his sous to the beggars of Montreuil. But it is Mackenzie who offers the most distended and fraught moment of transfer at the climax of Harley's encounter with the beggar and his dog:

> Harley had drawn a shilling from his pocket; but virtue bade him consider on whom he was going to bestow it.—Virtue held back his arm:—but a milder form, a younger sister of virtue's, not so severe as virtue, nor so serious as pity, smiled upon him: His fingers lost their compression;—nor did virtue offer to catch the money as it fell. It had no sooner reached the ground than the watchful cur (a trick he had been taught) snapped it up; and, contrary to the most approved method of stewardship, delivered it immediately into the hands of his master.
>
> * * * * * (pp. 22–23)

The Fall that is comically enacted here is contextualized with almost Miltonic sensitivity. In his moment of critical choice Harley succumbs to female charm, his will is suspended, and his hand crucially slackens. In its downward trajectory from giver to receiver, the coin slips from innocence to experience ('a trick he had been taught') as the naïve Harley himself falls for the practised routine of the beggar, who is just for an instant transformed into a master exploiting his steward. But Harley is seen to have played his part in the charitable economy. The nuances are very lightly touched, but once again the moment of transfer marks a subtle shift of meaning as Harley's passions briefly engage with bigger forces. In Mackenzie's fragmentary text, however, a row of benign asterisks intervenes at this point to relieve the incident of its consequences—whatever they might have been.

In Sentimentalism's many playful re-enactments of the Fall, the instant of falling is transformed to a dropping, a spontaneous loss of control or the slipping free of a feeling which manages to evade judgment. *Tristram Shandy* is scattered with such moments of grace, from the unravelling of Nannette's hair during the dance ('The whole knot fell down', p. 650; VII, 43) to the erasure from the record of Uncle Toby's oath: 'The ACCUSING SPIRIT which flew up to heaven's chancery with the oath, blush'd as he gave it in;—and the RECORDING ANGEL as he wrote it down, dropp'd a tear upon the word, and blotted it out for ever' (p. 511;

VI, 8). Here the contest between the letter and the spirit is generously decided. Such droppings, like Trim's letting fall of his hat in response to Bobby's death, can tap the power of ritual to mediate between the outward form and the inward grace:

> —'Are we not here now;'—continued the corporal, 'and are we not'—(dropping his hat plumb upon the ground—and pausing, before he pronounced the word)—'gone! in a moment?' The descent of the hat was as if a heavy lump of clay had been kneaded into the crown of it.—Nothing could have expressed the sentiment of mortality, of which it was the type and fore-runner, like it,—his hand seemed to vanish from under it,—it fell dead,—the corporal's eye fix'd upon it, as upon a corps,—and *Susannah* burst into a flood of tears. (p. 432; V, 7)

Trim's ritual enacts the point of death, the cusp of flesh and spirit. With his intense ability to make the body express an inner truth, Corporal Trim continues his role in the book as a corporal mediator of the divine by 'falling instantly into the same attitude in which he read the sermon' (p. 431). The others congregate round him, their eyes focused on the kneaded clay, the bread-flesh, that has been dropped before them ('the whole kitchen crouded about the corporal'). The moment is Sensibility's equivalent of Holy Communion, 'the type and fore-runner' of 'the sentiment of mortality', with Trim playing the priest-magician ('his hand seemed to vanish from under it'). The echoing of 'corpse'–'corps'–'corporal' suggests the ghostly presence of that other *corporal*, the linen cloth used to enfold the consecrated elements at the end of the mass ('nor are we angels', remarks Tristram in this chapter, 'but men cloathed with bodies'). With the dropping of Trim's hat we glimpse a mystery that permits the body's 'commerce with the soul' in a moment of translation when the transfer of meaning between flesh and spirit attains a religious intensity. For the sentimentalist too 'there is special providence in the fall of a sparrow'.

In the dispositions of Sensibility other things are dropped because its vessels, human and nonhuman alike, are porous. An underlying principle of sentimental translation is that meaning cannot be contained, that it has a propensity to slip through whatever tries to grasp it, so that the line between literal and figurative, object and subject, substance and idea, matter and mind, cannot be held. In *Tristram Shandy*, a novel of the sieve, the cullender and the wicker basket, of fissures, crevices and slits, these slippages form a comic mode in which all acts of transfer, especially when a human mind is the medium, are fraught with difficulties. '[T]hou art a leaky vessel, *Susannah*,' says Walter Shandy, as he entrusts the vital name 'Trismegistus' to his maid, who must carry it through time and space into the birthing room: 'canst thou carry *Trismegistus* in thy head, the length of the gallery without scattering?' (p. 344; IV, 14). But as with so much experience in the novel the message is refracted by the medium, like a stick in water: ''tis *Tristram-gistus*' she says, and the word 'Tristram' emerges with its freight of malign meanings ready to blight the newborn life. In *Tristram Shandy*, the most diverting of books, diversion itself becomes a principle: in the act of transference all meanings are liable to deviate; no road is straight; no vehicle is reliable.

Just as the book's characters 'pass thro' a certain medium which so twists and refracts them from their true directions' (p. 24; I, 10), so the narrative is subject to fits and starts, to things that cross its way,[24] and both mind and matter are bent in the process. The meanings of Uncle Toby's world have been translated by such bendings: by the parabolic track of the cannonball, by the bowling green (a place where nothing runs straight), and above all by a mind with an insistent bias of its own. Meaning is pulled out of 'true' to find its own channels, and any attempt to cancel out these forces tends to be futile. Walter's determination to 'counterbalance' the evil of the bent nose with the 'magic bias' of a noble name results in yet another accident. Tristram becomes the victim of the removal of the lead counterbalance from the window sash, as he was earlier victimized by the lead weight inside the grandfather clock, whose winding mechanism worked on the counterbalancing principle.[25]

Throughout *Tristram Shandy* the mechanisms of sensation and thought are comically exposed. Emphasis is therefore deflected from the *what* to the *how*. Meanings are dependent rather than inherent, so that attention is regularly diverted from an object to the thing from which it hangs or upon which it turns, like the noisy hinge on the parlour door ('nothing was well hung in our family', p. 449; V, 17). In comparing the eye to a cannon, Tristram notes that 'it is not so much the eye or the cannon, in themselves, as it is the carriage of the eye—and the carriage of the cannon, by which both the one and the other are enabled to do so much execution' (p. 707; VIII, 25). The novel causes the points on which meaning hinges, hangs, or turns, to make themselves felt. Walter Shandy's all-encompassing theory of auxiliary verbs demonstrates how meanings can in this way be made to proliferate ('The whole entirely depends, added my father, in a low voice, upon the *auxiliary verbs*.'[26]).

The meanings with which this essay has been concerned are created in sentimental texts at those points where some kind of translation between body and mind takes place, and a person is 'touched' by an emotion—a word's benign figurativeness will allow it to conduct meaning across the gap. This happens with the 'spark' ignited in the electric moment of Tristram's dance with Nannette:

> *Viva la joia!* was in her lips—*Viva la joia!* was in her eyes. A transient spark of amity shot across the space betwixt us—She look'd amiable!—Why could I not live and end my days thus? (p. 651; VII, 43)

The moment of transfer is *transient* (Lat. *transeo–transire–transii–transitum*: 'to pass over or across'), a word whose full meaning here extends beyond the obvious 'momentary, fleeting' to evoke its well-documented philosophical use as 'an act of the mind going out of itself' (i.e. transient as opposed to immanent[27]). In becoming aware of the richness of meaning at this moment we can move beyond our modern sentimental response (transient—how sad![28]) to an alert and vital eighteenth-century sentiment which recognizes that a whole epistemology is in play here: as sentimental translators we are invited to bridge the gap between the immanent (the joy *in* her lips and eyes) and the transient ('shot *across* the space').[29]

Far from eliding experience into a mind–body continuum,

sentimental texts find the discontinuities exciting. The gap in Nannette's petticoat ('the duce take that slit!') reminds us of Barthes's erotics of reading at the point where the edges do not quite meet ('Is not the most erotic portion of a body *where the garment gapes?*').[30] The novels I have been discussing find excitement at those moments when the sentimental and the satiric almost touch: each, after all, depends not on elision but on intimate juxtaposition. The fissure across which irony plays can also be the gap across which sentimental translation makes its connections.

NOTES

1. Laurence Sterne, *A Sentimental Journey through France and Italy by Mr. Yorick*, ed. Gardner D. Stout, Jr. (Berkeley and Los Angeles: University of California Press, 1967), p. 171. All subsequent page references are to this edition and included in the text of the essay.
2. Sterne, *The Life and Opinions of Tristram Shandy, Gentleman*, eds Melvyn New *et al.*, The Florida Edition of the Works of Laurence Sterne, 3 vols (Gainesville: University Presses of Florida, 1978–84), p. 772 (Volume IX, Chapter 20). All subsequent page references are to this edition and included in the text of the essay.
3. John Mullan, *Sentiment and Sociability: The Language of Feeling in the Eighteenth Century* (Oxford: Clarendon Press, 1988), pp. 160, 159. The problematics of this kind of sentimental translation between the verbal and nonverbal forms part of Mullan's wider discussion of how eighteenth-century sentimental fiction negotiates between sociability and the private self.
4. I use the term 'Sensibility' (capitalized) in its wider sense for the movement of ideas from the 1740s onwards which interested itself in the mechanisms of human feelings, and which was influenced by the philosophical writings of Locke and Shaftesbury, as developed by Hutcheson, Hume, Hartley and Adam Smith. I use the adjective 'sentimental' here in the sense indicated by the title of Sterne's novel, as 'of the feelings', 'of Sensibility'. Jerome McGann's distinction ('sensibility emphasizes the mind in the body, sentimentality the body in the mind') developed in *The Poetics of Sensibility* (Oxford: Clarendon Press, 1996), pp. 7, 33, proves useful for his purposes, though not for mine.
5. For a full account see G. J. Barker-Benfield, *The Culture of*

Sensibility: Sex and Society in Eighteenth-Century Britain (Chicago and London: University of Chicago Press, 1992), pp. 1–36. Earlier discussions of interest include Louis Bredvold, *The Natural History of Sensibility* (Detroit: Wayne State University Press, 1962); and T. Brown, 'From Mechanism to Vitalism in Eighteenth-Century English Physiology', *Journal of Human Biology*, 7 (1974), 179–216. Two literary critics alert to the complexities of the mind/body dilemma are John A. Dussinger, 'Yorick and the "Eternal Fountain of our Feelings"' in *Psychology and Literature in the Eighteenth Century*, ed. Christopher Fox (New York: AMS Press, 1987), pp. 259–76, and Ann Jessie Van Sant, *Eighteenth-Century Sensibility and the Novel* (Cambridge: Cambridge University Press, 1993).

6. Walter Jackson Bate, *From Classic to Romantic* (1946), p. 130; Barker-Benfield, *The Culture of Sensibility*, pp. 1–4. Barker-Benfield discusses the nervous system as a materialist theory, taking his cue from criticisms of Sensibility's materialism which date from the 1780s and 90s. By that time the mechanistic views of Albrecht von Haller and others were winning the day. The materialist position taken by Julien Offray de La Mettrie in *L'histoire naturelle de l'âme* (1745) and *L'Homme machine* (1748) was anathema, particularly in Britain where physiology remained largely animist. See R. K. French, *Robert Whytt, the Soul, and Medicine* (London: The Wellcome Institute, 1969), pp. 68–70, 161–68.

7. Robert Markley, 'Sensibility as Performance: Shaftesbury, Sterne, and the Theatrics of Virtue', in *The New Eighteenth Century: Theory, Politics, English Literature*, eds Felicity Nussbaum and Laura Brown (New York and London: Methuen, 1987), pp. 210–30 (pp. 219–20).

8. In *The Passions of the Minde in Generall* (London, 1601, rev. 1621) Thomas Wright had raised the question of 'how an operation lodged in the soul or mind can alter the body and move its corporeal humors from place to place'. See L. J. Rather, *Mind and Body in Eighteenth Century Medicine. A Study Based on Jerome Gaub's De regimine mentis* (Berkeley and Los Angeles: University of California Press, 1965), pp. 7–9.

9. Rather, *Mind and Body*, p. 48.

10. Christopher Lawrence, 'The Nervous System and Society in the Scottish Enlightenment', in *Natural Order: Historical Studies of Scientific Culture*, eds Barry Barnes and Steven Shapin (Beverly Hills and London: Sage Publications, 1979), pp. 19–40 (p. 25). The inverted commas highlight the way *feel* oscillates between physical and mental receptiveness.

11. See French, *Robert Whytt*, pp. 149–160.

12. George Cheyne, *The Natural Method of Cureing the Diseases of the Body, and the Disorders of the Mind Depending on the Body* (London: Geo. Strahan, 1742), pp. 94–95.

13. David Hartley, *Observations on Man, his Frame, his Duty and Expectations* (London, 1749), vol. 1, p. 34.

14. William Smith, *A Dissertation upon the Nerves* (London, 1768), pp. 42, 44, 49 ('Of the Nature, Manner, and Consequences of the Dependance, Influence, and Connection of the Soul and Body').

15. Rather, *Mind and Body*, pp. 1–10 (p. 3). See also K. Figlio, 'Theories of Perception and the Physiology of Mind in the Late Eighteenth Century', *History of Science*, 13 (1975), 177–212.

16. Hume's 'mysterious' principle was voluntary motion of the human body, 'by which a supposed spiritual substance acquires such an influence over a material one, that the most refined thought is able to actuate the grossest matter' (*An Enquiry Concerning Human Understanding* (1777), Section VII, Part I).

17. John Locke, *An Essay Concerning Human Understanding* (1690), II, 8; George Berkeley, *The Principles of Human Knowledge* (1710), I, 9–10.

18. Berkeley remarked that 'an idea can be like nothing but an idea' (*Principles*, I, 8).

19. On the association of Sensibility and sexuality, see Jean H. Hagstrum, *Sex and Sensibility: Ideal and Erotic Love from Milton to Mozart* (Chicago and London: University of Chicago Press, 1980), pp. 247–59.

20. See *Boswell's Life of Johnson, etc.*, ed. George Birkbeck Hill, rev. L. F. Powell (Oxford: Clarendon Press, 1934–64), I, 471 (6 August 1763). Berkeleyan idealism (anti-sentimental in my terms because denying substance) easily brushes off Johnson's challenge: it is one idea kicking another.

21. Henry Mackenzie, *The Man of Feeling*, ed. Brian Vickers (London, Oxford, New York: Oxford University Press, 1967), p. 3. All subsequent page references are to this edition and included in the text of the essay.

22. Roy Porter has noted how during the mid-eighteenth century 'words traditionally anchored in tangible, physical and literal meanings were widening in range, taking on predominantly abstract and figurative usage' ('Against the Spleen', in *Laurence Sterne: Riddles and Mysteries*, ed. Valerie Grosvenor Myer (London and Totowa, NJ: Vision Press and Barnes & Noble, 1984), pp. 84–98; p. 88). Van Sant (pp. 8–14) examines how the terminology of Sensibility works between literal and metaphorical uses.

23. *A Sentimental Journey*, pp. 125–29; Ann Radcliffe, *The Romance of the Forest* (1791), ed. Chloe Chard (Oxford University Press: The World's Classics, 1986), pp. 127–41 (Chapters 9 and 10). Tristram treasures his uncle Toby's Plan of Bouchain which bears witness to one of Mrs Wadman's assaults: 'there is still remaining the marks of a snuffy finger and thumb' and 'vestigia of two punctures ... which are unquestionably the very holes, through which it has been pricked up in the sentry-box' (*Tristram Shandy*, p. 531; VIII, 17).

24. 'I have ever a strong propensity, said my father, to look into things which cross my way' (*Tristram Shandy*, p. 138; II, 15).

25. Tristram hopes that the writing of Uncle Toby's amours will prove a benign counterbalance for his own life: 'Oh *Tristram! Tristram!* can this but be once brought about—the credit, which will attend thee as an author, shall counterbalance the many evils which have befallen thee as a man' (p. 401; IV, 32).

26. *Tristram Shandy*, p. 484; V, 42. Yorick remarks that mastery of the French language depends on understanding the use of *tant pis* and *tant mieux*, 'being two of the great hinges in French conversation' (*A Sentimental Journey*, p. 122).

27. *OED* 'Transient', 2. 'You may observe a difference of actions, of which some are immanent, or indwelling in the doer ...: some again are transeunt, or passing from the doer upon that which is done' (Alexander Gill, *The Sacred Philosophie of the Holy Scripture*, 1635, I, 98); 'An act of the mind going out of itself, in other words, a transient act' (Sir William Hamilton, *Lectures on Metaphysics*, 1870, II.xxv.118).

28. This is not to deny that transience, in the sense of 'mutability', is a prominent theme in *Tristram Shandy*. For Everett Zimmerman the novel is in this sense 'a monument to transience' ('*Tristram Shandy* and Narrative Representation', *The Eighteenth Century: Theory and Interpretation*, 28 (1987), 127–47).

29. Locke took for granted what Isaiah Berlin has called 'the old metaphysical dogma ... that a quality must exist "in" a substance, like a pin in a pincushion'. The preposition *in*, he adds, 'has proved exceedingly treacherous in the history of philosophy' (*The Age of Enlightenment* (New York: Mentor Books, 1956), p. 145).

30. Roland Barthes, *The Pleasure of the Text*, trans. Richard Miller (London: Jonathan Cape, 1976), p. 9. I am indebted to Dr Jane Stabler of the Department of English, University of Dundee, for this reference and for her valuable comments on a draft of the essay.

Hazlitt's *Liber Amoris; or, the New Pygmalion* (1823): Conversations and the Statue

JOHN BARNARD

> Love might or might not provoke kindness, gratify vanity, and clear the skin, but it did not lead to happiness; there was always an inequality of feeling or intention present. Such was love's nature.
>
> (Julian Barnes, 'The Revival', *The New Yorker*)

The subtitle of Hazlitt's *Liber Amoris; or, the New Pygmalion*, published anonymously in 1823, promises a retelling of Ovid's Augustan myth of transformation set in Regency England, a translation from classical to modern times. Unlike Ovid's poetic invention of a distant mythological past, Hazlitt's prose version takes place in the quotidian world of London's lodging houses. However, early nineteenth-century London has no pagan Venus who can effect the metamorphosis required by Hazlitt's narrator. Obviously, like Mary Shelley's *Frankenstein; or, the Modern Prometheus* (1818), the subtitle is ironic, and questions the pertinence of classical mythology to the modern world. There is a discomfitingly negative relationship between the shapely narratives of the past and their twisted, confusing contemporary forms, and in both stories the subjects refuse to obey their master.

Hazlitt's text recounts the story of H—'s unrequited love for S. L., told for the most part in his words. Part I is mainly made up of scenes based on reconstructed conversations in H—'s lodgings, Part II of H—'s letters to C. P—, and Part III of letters to another young friend, J. S. K—. The whole text is preceded by an 'Advertisement' which claims the book is based on a manuscript by 'a native of North Britain', who recently died in the Netherlands 'of disappointment preying on a sickly frame and morbid mind'.[1] The Pygmalion parallel is implicit: H— likens S. L. to 'a graceful marble statue' (p. 12), and she is frequently described as marble or stone as well as being called an idol and likened to a picture.

In the economy of Ovid's *Metamorphoses*, human intervention in the Gods' affairs normally works to the humans' ultimate disadvantage: uniquely the Pygmalion episode is affirmative, uniting art and nature.[2] As Marina Warner says of the transformation:

> When [Pygmalion's statue] steps out of illusion into reality through her creator's desire, she fulfills the delusory promises of art itself, the nearest equivalent to generation in the single, uncoupled manner of the gods that man can reach.[3]

Later versions move away from the Ovidian original. Pygmalion created his statue, repulsed by the wantonness of the Propoetides, the first prostitutes (themselves punished by being turned to stone). Not surprisingly, Pygmalion is easily seen as a misogynist and narcissist: 'Pygmalion's love for Galatea is really a form of self-love or will-to-power.'[4] Hazlitt's New Pygmalion, H—, belongs here.

Hazlitt's *Liber Amoris* has been difficult to read from its first anonymous publication for both intrinsic and extrinsic reasons. On 9 June 1823, a month after the book was published, *John Bull* began a three-week attack, publishing the full version of the actual letter Hazlitt had written to Sarah Walker on 9 March 1822. The identification of *Liber Amoris*'s 'H—' and 'S. L.' as Hazlitt himself and Sarah Walker, the daughter of his lodging-house keeper at 9 Southampton Buildings,[5] meant that *Liber Amoris* was autobiography, morbid, unmanly, and a revelation of the immorality of the 'Cockney' school. Charles Lamb thought it should have been called 'The new Hogmalion'.[6] Hazlitt's book quickly became a non-book. After 1823 no publicly available edition was published until the one in 1893 with an introduction by Richard le Gallienne.[7] But even if Hazlitt's identity had not been so soon discovered, the text he published in 1823 made, and makes, uncomfortable reading, particularly for a late twentieth-century (male) reader.[8] It is at once charged with emotion (as was the biographical case) and remarkably literary. Consequently, there have been two main ways of reading *Liber Amoris*. It is either an embarrassing and damaging autobiographical revelation (the dominant reading) or a self-conscious fiction which ironizes its narrator, 'H—'.

Recent accounts of *Liber Amoris* have moved away decisively from an autobiographical reading. Robert Ready understands Hazlitt's 'tale of character' in the context of his thinking about the sympathetic imagination, but in a negative way: 'The book is Hazlitt's major demonstration of passion blocking the sympathetic perception of an existence apart from one's own.'[9] He also discusses the remarkable literary allusiveness of Hazlitt's work in considerable detail. In a wide-ranging essay, Marilyn Butler reads *Liber Amoris* as a 'satirical counter-portrait' to other English Romantic autobiographies, identifying De Quincey's *Confessions of an English Opium-Eater* (1821) as a proximate cause.[10] Hazlitt's protagonist is a victim of the Romantic ideology, placing aesthetics above ethics. For Gary Kelly the work is a 'quasi-novel' about 'Romantic expressivity', 'a text which must undermine itself in the cause of an ultimate realism of representation'.[11] Both Ready and Butler emphasize the self-conscious way in which Hazlitt actively edited, added to, and rearranged his actual correspondence (entirely omitting his brief journal kept in March 1823).[12]

The original readers of *Liber Amoris* were pointed firmly in the same direction by the 'Advertisement': 'It has been suggested to the friend, into whose hands the manuscript was entrusted, that many things (particularly in the *Conversations* in the first Part) either childish or redundant, might have been omitted ...' (p. [ii]). The writer of the 'Advertisement' recognizes the unmanliness of H—'s narrative, and separates himself from *Liber Amoris*'s narrative voice.

All three recent readings 'explain' *Liber Amoris*, if slightly differently, and place it as a literary work. However, their emphasis on its generic status is very hard to hold onto while actually reading this very seductive male text. And while it may be a critique of the Romantic solipsist author in general (Butler), its main concern is with 'Romantic love'. Nor, while we are reading the book, can the question of an autobiographical reading be ignored. H—, writing from Scotland to C. P—, concludes the first letter of Part II with a postscript:

> I have begun a book of our conversations (I mean mine and the statue's) which I call LIBER AMORIS. I was detained at Stamford and found myself dull, and could hit upon no other way of employing my time so agreeably. (pp. 52–53)

The now-dead H— begins (like Hazlitt in actuality) to write his *Liber Amoris* as he journeys to Scotland knowing that at the very least his relationship with S. L. is problematic. Part I, we are told, was written as an 'agreeable' pastime (though the reader is more likely to think that the 'writer' in H— was acting more from compulsion than choice). The remainder of the work comprises H—'s epistolary version of subsequent developments. From the beginning, then, H— dramatizes and fictionalizes his autobiographical account. The unsuccessful affair is fictionalized as it happens. Although we have to learn to see through H—, in order to do so we have to read his version of events, so that we begin by colluding with H—'s narration because we have no choice. The truthfulness or otherwise of his telling becomes an imperative issue for the reader, and the ghost of the author is conjured up. As Sean Burke has said, 'the essential problem posed by the author is that whilst authorial subjectivity is theoretically unassimilable, it cannot practically be circumvented'.[13]

The intertextual relationship with Ovid, but also that with the many other texts quoted or alluded to by H— (in particular Rousseau, Shakespeare and Keats), further complicate the reader's difficulties. H— does not always seem able to appreciate how the texts he cites or echoes relate to his own case—he lacks a sense of irony, even though he knows 'I am not mad, but my heart is so' (p. 84). H— persistently tries to transform S. L. into a womanly ideal drawn from literature and, at key points, from art, an ideal assumed to be held in common with the reader (and H—'s two correspondents).

Even if De Quincey's *Confessions* is an immediate cause of the *Liber Amoris*, providing both a satiric target and an example of commercially successful confessional writing, Hazlitt's project bears a curious relationship to the issue of Leigh Hunt's *The Indicator* for 10 May 1820. There he would have found Hunt's translation of and comments on Rousseau's *scène lyrique*, *Pygmalion* (written 1762, acted 1772), which is followed by Hunt's account of Alain Chartier's 'La Belle Dame Sans Mercy', and, finally, by the first (pseudonymous) printing of Keats's 'La Belle Dame'.[14] Hunt's treatment of this material has no trace of irony. Indeed, he criticizes Rousseau for not making the 'sentiment sufficiently prominent'.

Although Rousseau's Pygmalion calls upon Venus (who does not appear), it is a portrait of the artist as narcissist:

> Yes, dear and charming object—thou worthy masterpiece of my hands, of my heart, and of the Gods! It is thou, it is thou alone—I have given thee all my being—henceforth I will live but for thee.[15]

The important point is not that of influence (though in Rousseau's version, like Hazlitt's, the statue is 'stone' or 'marble' and not, as in Ovid, made of ivory, a material once living, unlike stone). Rather this issue of *The Indicator* is a demonstration of the psychopathology of Romantic love, beginning with the male-constructed ideal woman, moving to Hunt's attack on the 'modern systems' which 'divide women into two classes, those who have no charity, and those who have no restraint', before concluding with Keats's figure of woman as sexual temptress and seducer.[16] Hunt presents these contradictory and confused representations with no sense of contradiction or tension, or of the way in which all three views are entirely male engendered. The question to be asked of the *Liber Amoris* is whether that work, too, accepts the psychopathology uncritically.

One small pointer to the literariness of the *Liber Amoris* is the *mise en page* of the first edition. Each section of Part I, the 'Conversation', starts a new page, as do all the letters in Parts II and III, and H—'s authorial interpolations. A short rule marks the end of each letter or section. Part of the effect is to call attention to the book as aesthetic object, with its extensive use of white space and the engraved title page. The latter has a small oval mezzotint by Samuel William Reynolds[17] of the ambiguous 'Italian picture', which precipitates the first conversation. The most important effect is to separate H—'s interpolations from the letters.[18] The reader is meant to think of them as being in a different mode. Take one instance:

> WRITTEN ON A BLANK LEAF OF ENDYMION
>
> I want a hand to guide me, an eye to cheer me, a bosom to repose on; all which I shall never have, but shall stagger into my grave, old before my time, unloved and unlovely, unless S. L. keeps her faith with me.
>
> * * * * * * * * * * * * * * *
> * * * * * * * *
>
> —But by her dove's eyes and serpent-shape, I think she does not hate me; by her smooth forehead and her crested hair, I own I love her; by her soft looks and queen-like grace (which men might fall down and worship) I swear to live and die for her. (p. 45)

This is set out on its own page (like the immediately following 'A PROPOSAL OF LOVE' and all the other authorial interpolations). We are to imagine this as originally written by H— for his eyes only.

These two sentences, which move from self-pitying despair to an equally desperate catching at hope, are a useful entrance to H—'s characteristic style and use of allusion. They are, in one way, very well written, writerly. The language and sentiments mix clichés with literary echoes, and the first sentence is a self-quotation from Hazlitt's letter of advice to his son, written alongside *Liber Amoris.*[19] S. L.'s 'dove's eyes and serpent-shape' recall Christabel's dream in Coleridge's poem (ll. 548–54) while the combination of 'serpent-shape' and 'crested hair' are drawn from a memory of Keats's *Lamia* (i.47–67). Both echoes are ominous ones, unlike the choice of *Endymion* as the book in which to write out H—'s innermost thoughts. H—'s literary taste has an ironic relation to Hazlitt's own. Hazlitt's 'On Effeminacy of Character', written not much earlier, thought Keats's 'Poetic Romance' of young love fulfilled, showed 'exquisite fancy', and a 'very delightful description of the illusions of a youthful imagination', but concludes, 'All is soft and fleshy, without bone or muscle'.[20] So the writer who put *Liber Amoris* together casts a cold eye on H—'s obsession.

There are several other Keats-like passages. 'I will make a Goddess of her, and build a temple to her in my heart, and worship her on indestructible altars, and raise statues to her' (pp. 105–06) is a reprise of the central episode in the 'Ode to Psyche'. 'Thou art divine, my love, and canst make me either more or less than mortal' (p. 8) uses the same trope as Porphyro. S. L. transforms herself in H—'s perception like another Lamia:

> It was a fable. She started up in her own likeness, a serpent in place of a woman. She had fascinated, she had stung me, and had returned to her proper shape, gliding from me after inflicting the mortal wound, and instilling deadly poison into every pore; but her form lost none of its original brightness by the change of character, but was all glittering, beauteous, voluptuous grace. Seed of the serpent or of the woman, she was divine! I felt that she was a witch, and had bewitched me. (pp. 163–64)

These similarities may or may not be echoes: what is significant is that H— exactly shares Keats's uneasily divided view of woman,[21] whose active sexuality is life-threatening, and uses identical images, tropes and stereotypes. H—'s alternating idealization and demonization of S. L. taps into the ambiguous psychic responses to women's sexuality in bourgeois Regency England. These in their turn are a precursor of Victorian (and Decadent) attitudes. B. W. Procter either wholly shared this fissured view of woman or was reading through the lens of *Liber Amoris* when, years later, he described the real Sarah Walker as follows:

> Her face was round and small, and her eyes were motionless, glassy, and without any speculation (apparently) in them. Her

> movements in walking were very remarkable, for I never observed her to make a step. She went onwards in a sort of wavy, sinuous manner, like the movement of a snake. She was silent, or uttered monosyllables only, and was very demure … . The Germans would have extracted a romance from her, endowing her perhaps with some diabolic attribute.[22]

Life, here, is being read through literature.

Keats's poetry is an almost suppressed presence in *Liber Amoris*. Only the reference to *Endymion* admits him into the text explicitly. This is the more remarkable since *Liber Amoris* is replete with quotations. These include the Bible, Horace, Virgil, Tibullus, the *Arabian Nights*, Chaucer, Spenser, Shakespeare, Dekker, Middleton, Milton, Dryden, Gay, Cowper, Burns, Wordsworth, Scott, Byron, Lamb, Procter and Leigh Hunt. The most frequently cited writer is Shakespeare (at least twenty quotations). H—'s collage of quotations have two immediate functions in his text. First, they give expression to his idealizing of romantic love, locating it in a Western tradition reaching back to Medieval courtly love and from there back to Catullus and Tibullus. It is these texts which provide H— with a language of love. If *Liber Amoris* offers a critique of Romantic solipsism, it also invokes the long tradition of courtly and Platonic love in the West. The quotations frequently have an ironic relationship to the narrator's hopes, proleptically promising a bad end to his courtship of S. L. Thus 'A PROPOSAL OF LOVE/ (*Given to her in our early acquaintance*)' (p. 46) is taken from Troilus's speech describing Cressida's 'winnowed purity' in love (III.ii.154–65). There are ominous quotations from *King Lear, Hamlet* and *Macbeth*. One of the highlights of H—'s relationship with S. L. is taking her, with her mother, to a performance of *Romeo and Juliet*, and he hopes to take her to *Othello*. Of the three quotations from *Othello*, one involves a remarkable revision of Shakespeare. H—, encouraged by C. P—'s report on S. L.'s honesty, blames himself for not trusting her:

> … those words of yours applied to the dear saint—'To lip a chaste one and suppose her wanton'—were balm and rapture to me. I have *lipped* her, God knows how often, and oh! is it even possible that she is chaste. (p. 61)

Iago's actual words describe a very different scenario:

> O, 'tis the spite of hell, the fiend's arch-mock
> To lip a wanton in a secure couch,
> And to suppose her chaste! (IV.i.69–71)

Many of H—'s quotations point to S. L.'s impurity and betrayal, while at the same time expressing his idealizing 'love' within their long literary lineage.

The most important intervention in that lineage for Hazlitt, H—, and their contemporaries was Rousseau, and the few early positive reviews made the connection.[23] However, the constant quotations in *Liber Amoris,* and H—'s second-hand language, are precisely what Rousseau proscribed. Julie is told by St Preux that it is language from the heart, not from books, through which we learn love:

> Qu'apprendions nous de l'amour dans les livres? Ah, Julie notre coeur nous en dit plus qu'eux, et le langage imité des livres est bien froid pour quiconque est les passioné lui-même![24]

St Preux's dictum is an impossible one (as Hazlitt seems to have known).

H— twice refers to Rousseau in *Liber Amoris*, once to the *Confessions*, once to the *Nouvelle Héloïse*, and Hazlitt claimed that he, presumably like H—, 'spent two whole years in reading these two works; and (gentle reader, it was when we were young) in shedding tears over them'.[25] In this, Hazlitt is a typical reader of his period. The presence of Rousseau runs much deeper than the two direct references to him in the *Liber Amoris* suggest. The second reference occurs at the end of Part II when H— imagines taking S. L. as his wife to visit the continental settings of the *Nouvelle Héloïse* (p. 122), presumably having first familiarized her with Rousseau's writings. The first reference, in Letter IV, is more complicated. H— has earlier in the letter called her 'my heart's idol' and writes to C. P—:

> I don't believe that any woman was ever courted more passionately than she has been by me. As Rousseau said of

> Madame d'Houptot (forgive the allusion) my heart has found a tongue in speaking to her, and I have talked to her the divine language of love. Yet she says, she is insensible to it. (pp. 62–63)

This combination of literary archness ('forgive the allusion') and self-congratulation, focuses attention less on the 'insensible' S. L. than on H—'s literary and verbal adeptness. H— is referring to the conversation between Rousseau and Mme d'Houdetot in the garden 'bosquet' in the *Confessions* (II, ix):

> Ce fut dans ce bosquet qu'assis avec elle sur un banc de gason, sous un Acacia tout chargé de fleurs, je trouvai pour rendre les mouvemens de mon coeur, un langage vraiment digne d'eux. Ce fut la première et l'unique fois de ma vie; mais je fus sublime, si l'on peut nommer ainsi tout que l'amour le plus tendre et le plus ardent peut porter d'aimable et de séduisant dans un coeur d'homme.[26]

This scene in the *Confessions* resonated in Hazlitt's mind. The passage just quoted gives H— exactly the words he needs. A little earlier, Rousseau, who was writing the *Nouvelle Héloïse* at the same time, sees Mme d'Houdetot as his fictional character:

> … je vis ma Julie en Mad^{e} d'Houdetot, et bientot je ne vis plus que Mad^{e} d'Houdetot, mais revétue de toutes les perfections dont je venais d'orner l'idole de mon coeur.

H—'s 'idol' then has a clear source here, as do the references elsewhere in the *Liber Amoris* to poison: 'j'avolois à longs traits la coupe empoisonnée, dont ne je sentois encor que la douceur'.[27]

From one point of view H— needs his repertoire of previous literary texts to give him a language to speak his love, which of course means that his experience in early nineteenth-century London is defined within words and sentiments not his own. But Rousseau's situation and H—'s map on to one another very oddly. Rousseau, upwardly mobile socially, has fallen in love with an upper-class wife, the victim of an arranged marriage, who already has a lover, and who refuses Rousseau's advances (we are told), so proving her virtue. The *Nouvelle Héloïse* is a variant on this story. St Preux, the tutor, and his aristocratic pupil, Julie, do indeed fall; but the new Eloisa marries as her father wishes, and her husband Wolmar brings St Preux to live with them, knowing that Julie's virtue will ensure a 'pure' relationship. What Rousseau does is to establish a peculiarly aligned version of courtly love. Julie, who has fallen once with St Preux, is allowed her lover's presence, provided she is a good wife and mother to her husband, and keeps clear of any physical intimacy. As she dies, she confesses she still loves St Preux (a passage much admired by Hazlitt).[28] H—, however, is married with a son, and pursuing a lower-class girl whom he wants to believe virginal and pure (but fears is a coquette or worse). He also knows she has previously fallen in love, a love which could not be fulfilled because of class difference. The extraordinary contemporary appeal of Rousseau's two works lay precisely in the way they took the woman's part. In the *Confessions* and the *Nouvelle Héloïse*, self-restraint on the side of both men and women is precisely the point. The fact that Rousseau in the *Confessions* sees Mme d'Houdetot as his fictional Julie provides a dysfunctional link. H—'s sentimental training in Rousseau means that he can identify himself with Rousseau and St Preux but, unlike them, has no idea of S. L.'s feelings. Rousseau's 'effeminacy', which empowers his women characters (though at the risk, as Mary Wollstonecraft feared, of degrading 'woman by making her the slave of love'[29]), becomes in *Liber Amoris* an imprisoning male reading.

Liber Amoris is firmly in the male domain. H—'s sexual obsession with S. L. uses the texts of exclusively male writers to express his feelings. He is thereby locked into contemporary stereotypical attitudes (for example, those taken by Hunt in *The Indicator*). Throughout *Liber Amoris*, H—'s language is literary where S. L.'s stilted letters and colloquial speech (when she is allowed speech) are not. The largest part of H—'s account of his infatuation is given in letters to two middle-class male friends who share H—'s cultural and literary interests, as well as his strongly gendered attitude to women and sexuality. Clearly, H—'s writings are intended to give him control over his inchoate feelings, and to exorcise his obsessive passion. (Hazlitt's transformation of his actual correspondence into fiction requires the death of H—, an act simultaneously of self-murder and exorcism.) H—'s male narrative largely silences S. L., and the reader is forced to read in the first instance, at least, from H—'s viewpoint. H— has a very clear idea of what he thinks he wants. In 'The Picture', H— attempts to persuade S. L. that her beauty resembles that of the miniature copy of a head from a Renaissance Italian painting: 'See, Sarah, how beautiful it is! Ah! dear girl, these are the ideas I have cherished in my heart, and in my brain; and I have never found any thing to realize them on earth till I met with thee, my love!' (p. 3).

H—'s strenuous efforts to make S. L. fit his cherished 'ideas' throughout *Liber Amoris* are based on a perfect woman entirely constructed from artistic and literary prototypes, here, the paintings of Guido or Raphael. Significantly, there is disagreement about whether the picture represents a Madonna or a Magdalen. H— believes it 'more like Raphael's St Cecilia "with looks commercing with the skies"' (p. 3), a view imaged in Reynolds's title-page vignette, which shows the head and shoulders of a young woman, in Renaissance dress, gazing upwards, her full just-parted lips suggesting the sublimated eroticism of St Cecilia.[30] Characteristically, too, the allusion to 'Il Penseroso' subverts H—'s intended meaning. He can hardly want S. L. to enjoy the solitary pleasure of Melancholy. H—'s self-absorption not only allows him to override S. L.'s objection that the picture is of a fair woman while she is dark, but his language, with its affected use of 'thy' and 'thine' and phrases like 'obstinate protusion', and 'suppressed sensibility', is one not understood by S. L.—'Do not, I beg, talk in that manner ...' (p. 2), she replies.

H—'s project is clear. In Pygmalion fashion (more like Shaw's than Ovid's), he will bring out S. L.'s sensibility and educate her through continental travel. He has already given her books, and 'The Picture' episode is part flattery, part educational lesson. The unreality of H—'s vision of mutual happiness is only too clear in Letter VIII when he recalls, with wishful thinking, breakfasts in his lodgings 'when [S. L.] had been standing an hour by my side, my guardian-angel, my wife, my sister, my sweet friend, my Eve, my all; and had blest me with her seraph-kisses!' (p. 79). Yet almost immediately after this evocation of S. L. as all-women-in-one, he asks if C. P— can resolve his tormented uncertainty as to whether S. L. is a goddess or demon—'She is one or the other, that's certain; but I fear the worst' (p. 80).

Liber Amoris is a story of a man possessed by an idealizing vision of a woman who refuses to participate in his language games. Benjamin Constant's *Adolphe* (1816), similarly supposed to have been written by a now-dead author, and also about an obsessively destructive passion, places language at its centre. Adolphe's love for Ellénore begins when he feigns a love letter:

> Les combats que j'avais livrés longtemps à mon propre caractère, l'impatience que j'éprouvais de n'avoir pu le surmonter, mon incertitude sur le succès de ma tentative, jèterent dans ma lettre une agitation qui ressemblait fort à l'amour. Échauffé d'ailleurs que j'étais par mon propre style, je ressentais, en finissant d'écrire, un peu de la passion que j'avais cherché à exprimer avec toute la force possible.[31]

Ellénore knows the dangers of words, and allows Adolphe to continue seeing her, but bans the language of love:

> Elle ne consentit à me recevoir que rarement, au milieu d'une société nombreuse, avec l'engagement que ne lui parlerais d'amour.[32]

As Tzvetan Todorov says, she 'is on guard because she knows that to allow the language of love is to allow love itself'[33]—which is exactly what happens a little later:

> Elle me permit de lui peindre mon amour; elle se familiarisa par degrés avec ce langage: bientôt elle m'avoua qu'elle m'aimait. [34]

The words create the feelings they describe. As S. L. knows. When H— tells her that he feels as 'Adam must have done when his Eve was created for him', she replies that 'She had heard enough of that sort of conversation' (p. 160), one of many refusals to participate in H—'s language of love. Her silences and refusal to share H—'s verbal world are S. L.'s victory.[35] She (and her mother) know that H—'s obsession is self-created and that, for all his claims of 'tenderness', H—'s love is aggressively possessive:

> You sit and fancy things out of your own head, and then say them at my charge. There is not a word of truth in your suspicions. (p. 27)

If S. L.'s victory is through silence and refusal of H—'s 'courtship', *Liber Amoris* is his final revenge. Quite early in their relationship he offers a markedly truncated version of Shakespeare's promise of poetic immortality for his lover which will last 'So long as men can breathe or eyes can see' (Sonnet 18): '… my Infelice! You will live by that name, you rogue, fifty years after you are dead' (p. 10). At the end of *Liber Amoris*, H—, having persistently tried to write her into his text, tries to write her out:

> She is diminutive in stature, and her measured step and timid air do not suit these public airings. I am afraid she will soon grow common to my imagination, as well as worthless in herself. Her image seems fast 'going into the wastes of time', like a weed that the wave bears farther and farther from me. Alas! thou poor hapless weed, when I entirely lose sight of thee, and forever, no flower will ever bloom on earth to glad my heart again! (p. 192)

But even as H— tries to write her 'image' out, he remains 'in thrall'—and he still needs to express himself through a quotation from Shakespeare's *Sonnets*, and to call up Othello's lament for Desdemona: 'O thou weed,/ Who art so lovely fair …'[36] The modern Pygmalion ends on his own, self-imprisoned by the texts which have formed his language of love.

Since we, as readers, only have access to the story through H—'s texts, and also share his literary legacy, the pathos of his predicament, which is what the work elaborates, even celebrates, is impossible wholly to resist as we read. It is only through a rereading that the pathos can be held in place, allowing H—'s action to be seen as what it is, a sustained campaign of psychological harassment, which at its height leads her family to fear for S. L.'s life (pp. 114, 142), after which H— exposes her behaviour first to her father and then to her mother. The Pygmalion story transposed to early nineteenth-century London, and mediated through Rousseau, reveals its extreme coerciveness towards the female object of desire.[37]

NOTES

1. *Liber Amoris: or, the New Pygmalion 1823* [facsimile], ed. Jonathan Wordsworth (Oxford and New York: Woodstock Books, 1992), p. [i]. Subsequent page references are to this edition and included in the text of the essay. I am grateful for the advice and leads given by my colleagues Inga-Stina Ewbank, Paul Hammond, John McLeod, Gail Marshall and John Whale. Hermione Lee gave help and ideas at a critical stage.

2. See Leonard Barkan, *The Gods Made Flesh: Metamorphosis and the Pursuit of Paganism* (New Haven and London: Yale University Press, 1986), p. 75.

3. *Monuments and Maidens: The Allegory of the Female Form* [1985] (London: Pan Books, 1987), p. 228.

4. Nigel Leask, 'Shelley's "Magnetic Ladies": Romantic Mesmerism and the Politics of the Body', *Beyond Romanticism: New Approaches to Texts and Contexts 1780–1832*, eds Stephen Copley and John Whale (London and New York: Routledge, 1992), p. 72.

5. Stanley Jones, *Hazlitt: A Life* (Oxford: Clarendon Press, 1989), pp. 337–39, 341–42.

6. Recorded by Mary Cowden Clarke on the title page of the copy in the Novello-Clarke Collection, Brotherton Library, University of Leeds.

7. A facsimile for private circulation was printed in [1884?] with '1823' on the title page. 500 copies were privately printed in 1894, with 'additional matter now printed for the first time', again with an introduction by Richard le Gallienne. This printed Hazlitt's letters in something like their full form for the first time.

8. See Tom Paulin's recent description of *Liber Amoris* as 'this obsessive, dangerous side of the male Protestant imagination', which he thinks is characterized by a 'nihilistic, self-flagellating desperation, a having-it-all-ways irony, a masturbatory, taut flaccidity in [its] recycled clichés', *The Day-Star of Liberty: William Hazlitt's Radical Style* (London: Faber, 1998), p. 45.

9. 'The Logic of Passion: Hazlitt's *Liber Amoris*', *Studies in Romanticism*, 14 (1975), 41–57.

10. 'Hazlitt's *Liber Amoris* and Romantic Satire', *Yearbook of English Studies*, 14 (1984), 209–25. P. P. Howe had previously argued for the artistic control of the *Liber Amoris* in *The Complete Works of William Hazlitt*, ed. P. P. Howe (London and Toronto: J. M. Dent, 1930–34), ix, 263, and 'Hazlitt and *Liber Amoris*', *Fortnightly Review*, 105 (1916), 300–10.

11. *English Fiction of the Romantic Period 1789–1830* (London and New York: Longman, 1989), pp. 258–59.

12. The evidence is most fully recorded in *The Letters of William Hazlitt*, eds Herschel Moreland Sikes, Willard Hallam Bonner and Gerald Lahey (New York: New York University Press, 1978). The transcription of the 1823 journal is seriously inaccurate: see Stanley Jones, 'Hazlitt's Journal of 1823: Some Notes and Emendations', *The Library*, 5th series, 26 (1971), 325–36.

13. *The Death and Return of the Author: Criticism and Subjectivity in Barthes, Foucault and Derrida* (Edinburgh: Edinburgh University Press, 1992), p. 173.

14. See 'Keats's Belle Dame and the Sexual Politics of Leigh Hunt's *Indicator*', *Romanticism*, 1 (1995), 34–49.

15. *The Indicator*, 31, 10 May 1820, 246.

16. *The Indicator*, 31, 10 May 1820, 246.

17. W. Carew Hazlitt identifies the engraver as 'Mr Reynolds of Bayswater' (*Memoirs of William Hazlitt,* London (1867), ii, 66). *DNB* has an entry on Reynolds, who seems intended rather than his son of the same name.

18. Ronald Blythe's *William Hazlitt: Selected Writings* (Harmondsworth: Penguin, 1970) runs the texts together and, unaccountably, omits the 'Advertisement'.

19. *The Letters of William Hazlitt*, p. 235. The letter was published as 'On the Conduct of Life' in *Table Talk* (1821–22), but this passage was omitted.

20. *The Complete Works of William Hazlitt,* viii, 254–55.

21. The shared tropes occur most disconcertingly in Keats's letters to Fanny Brawne.

22. *An Autobiographical Fragment*, ed. Coventry Patmore (London: 1877), pp. 181–82. Bryan Waller Procter (1787–1874), minor poet, belonged to Leigh Hunt's circle, and was a friend of Hazlitt.

23. See *The Examiner,* 22, 11 May 1823, 27–29, and Stanley Jones, *Hazlitt: A Life*, p. 338.

24. *Oeuvres Complètes*, eds B. Gagnebin and M. Raymond (Paris: Gallimard, 1959–95), ii, 61. ('What do we learn about love from books? Ah, Julie our heart speaks more about it to us than they do, and language imitated from books is thoroughly cold for whoever is impassioned themselves.')

25. 'On the Character of Rousseau', *The Complete Works of William*

Hazlitt, iv, 91. First published in *The Examiner*, 14 April 1816, reprinted in *The Round Table* (1817).

26. *Confessions, Oeuvres Complètes*, i, 444. ('It was in that wood, sitting with her on a grass bank beneath an acacia in full flower, that I found a language really able to express the emotions of my heart. It was the first and only time in my life, but I was sublime if such a word can describe all the sympathy and seductive charm that the most tender and ardent love can breathe into the heart of a man' (trans. J. M. Cohen (Harmondsworth: Penguin, 1953), p. 414). The peculiar misspelling of 'Houdedot' as 'Houptot' is hard to explain.

27. *Confessions*, p. 440. ('I saw my Julie in Mme Houdedot, and soon I saw only Mme Houdedot, but embellished with all the perfections with which I had just embellished the idol of my heart': 'I swallowed the poisoned cup in long draughts, and at first only tasted the sweetness' (trans. Cohen, p. 410).)

28. 'On the Character of Rousseau', *The Complete Works of William Hazlitt*, iv, 91.

29. *A Vindication of the Rights of Woman* (Harmondsworth: Penguin, 1973), p. 190.

30. On the appeal of St Cecilia, who allied feminine sensuality with religious themes, for late eighteenth-century artists, see Marcia Poynton, *Strategies for Showing: Women, Possession and Representation in English Visual Culture 1665–1800* (Oxford: Oxford University Press, 1997), pp. 272–95. Reynolds's vignette is in the same iconographic tradition as Sir Joshua Reynolds's *St Cecilia* (Poynton, *Strategies for Showing*, Plate 62).

31. *Adolphe: anecdote trouvée dans les papiers d'un inconnu*, ed. Paul Delbouille (Paris: Société des Belles Lettres, 1977), p. 124. ('My long drawn out battle against my own character, the irritation I felt at not having been able to overcome it, and my doubts about my chances of success all combined to tinge my letter with an emotional colour scarcely distinguishable from love. And, indeed, warmed up as I was by my own rhetoric, by the time I had finished writing I really felt some of the passion I had been at such pains to express' (trans. Leonard Tancock (Harmondsworth: Penguin, 1964), p. 50). Constant's book first appeared in 1816 in London and Paris editions. An English translation was published the same year, and it was translated into German in 1817. There were reviews in English periodicals. It was perhaps an influence on *Liber Amoris*.

32. *Adolphe*, pp. 131–32. ('She … agreed to see me, but only occasionally and when many others were present, [and] stipulated that I should never talk of love' (trans. Tancock, p. 56).)

33. 'The Discovery of Love: *Les Liaisons dangereuses* and *Adolphe*', *Yale French Studies*, 45 (1970), 120.

34. *Adolphe*, p. 133. ('She let me talk of my love and soon grew

accustomed to such language. Before long she confessed that she loved me' (trans. Tancock, p. 58).)

35. On silence as a marker of agency, particularly among women, see Iain Chambers, 'Signs of Silence, Lines of Listening', in *The Post-Colonial Question*, eds Iain Chambers and Lidia Curti (London: Routledge, 1995), p. 51.

36. Sonnet 12; *Othello*, IV.ii.67–69.

37. For other versions of the Pygmalion story, see Jane Davidson Reid, *The Oxford Guide to Classical Mythology in the Arts, 1300–1990* (New York, Oxford: Oxford University Press, 1993), ii, 955–62. For a mordant retelling of Ovid's tale, see Ian McEwan's 'Dead As They Come' in *In Between the Sheets* (London: Cape, 1978), pp. 61–77. Melvyn Bragg's *A Time to Dance* (London: Hodder and Stoughton, 1990) is a retranslation of Hazlitt's *Liber Amoris* (crossed with *Lolita*) which, unusually, allows the woman to speak (through letters within the narrator's long letter to her, which makes up the enclosing narrative). Jonathan Bate's *Cure For Love* (London: Picador, 1998) is the most recent reworking of Hazlitt's text.

Translating Value: Marginal Observations on a Central Question

GEOFFREY HILL

It took rather longer than I care to admit before I was prepared to concede that Ruskin's 'intrinsic value' is itself a term without intrinsic value.[1] The phrase is at best a promissory note, at worst a semantic relic to ward off the evil eye of commodity. One would suspect that I was taken with, and by, the idea of a talismanic key; an idea which I then read into Ruskin's words in order to find there the confirmation that I desired. Eisegesis instead of exegesis. Put somewhat differently, questions of value are inseparable from matters of translation; and translation itself involves more than the matching up of equivalent verbal signs.

It would be less than honest not to acknowledge that there is a personal edge to my academic concern with the nature of the intrinsic. It is not always easy to maintain, on questions that press harshly upon the self, that disinterestedness of observation which many would understand—and justly—to be an essential prerequisite for any description of value, or indeed for any honest attempt to arrive at such a description. Among the requisites for true criticism, according to Hume, are a 'mind free from all *prejudice*', 'a delicate taste of wit or beauty', 'a due attention to the object';[2] but this admirable prescription, and an honest endeavour to put it into practice, were ineffective against Hume's own prejudicate opinion that Bunyan is inferior to Addison and that any attempt to claim otherwise would be 'absurd and ridiculous'.[3]

One cannot, however, argue *ex hypothesi* that such quaint prejudicates have been replaced, two and a half centuries later, by the self-evidently superior practices of what we are to call *science de la littérature*. Ricks is right to argue that an objectivity which elides 'personal values' to 'personal preferences' and which, having further equated the false compound with 'interest' and 'prejudice', proposes its elimination in the best interests of mental hygiene, is itself interested and prejudiced and 'implacably hostile to literature'.[4]

In saying that questions of value are inseparable from matters of translation, I do not propose to limit that suggestion to the problems of translating from, say, Pascal's French into late seventeenth-century or modern English. Translation, conventionally understood, presents in a sustainedly demanding form matters which require vigilance of all users of language. To make an assessment, in 1997, of the vocabulary of David Hume's two essays 'Of the Delicacy of Taste and Passion' (1741) and 'On the Standard of Taste' (1757) is to face issues arising from his use of the term 'delicacy' which scarcely differ in degree from those which relate to questions of how best, in 1688 or 1950, to render Pascal's '*esprit de finesse*'. I have particularly in mind a recent observation that 'the taste model, even in Hume's sensitive hands, must be too simple'.[5] There is a difficulty with 'Hume's sensitive hands' if I may so express it; I cannot hear the semantic pitch of the word 'sensitive', even while I recognize that this word is intended as a succinct equivalent to Hume's own range of sense in his repeated use of the word 'delicacy' and its cognates. 'Delicacy' and 'delicate' in Hume's essays mean different things at different moments and 'Hume's sensitive hands' relates to Hume's language (for example, 'Those finer emotions of the mind are of a very tender and delicate nature'[6]) about as closely as 'the Polite Wit', 'the refin'd wit', or 'the nimbly discerning mind' relate to '*esprit de finesse*'.[7]

I find particularly noteworthy in Hume's thinking—as represented by the two essays under discussion—his readiness to take contingency into account ('The good or ill accidents of life are very little at our disposal'[8]) and his ability to bring it into semantic play ('Philosophers have endeavored to render happiness entirely independent of every thing external. That degree of perfection is impossible to be *attained*'[9]). One is aware of the pressure of collective opinion upon individual judgment but aware also that an original cast of mind can be attained even when the subject of debate is, in several senses, the subjection of the particular to the general, the ideal to the actual:

> It is natural for us to seek a *Standard of Taste*; a rule by which the various sentiments of men may be reconciled; at least, a decision, afforded, confirming one sentiment, and condemning another.[10]

If this sentence simply declared that it is necessary, within the social milieu, to determine a literary *sensus communis* of value whereby prescription and proscription may be generally agreed, I would accept without reservation that 'the taste model, even in Hume's sensitive hands, must be too simple'. What we term Hume's sensitivity of grasp and touch is largely revealed in the care with which he shows that the model cannot be simple: 'It is natural for us' is placed so as to be slightly outside, or a shade obliquely on to, the prejudicates which it presents. The phrase attains a position with respect to the idea. Hobbes's depiction of beliefs 'wrought into' human nature by custom and laws requires that we give due attention to the pitch of 'wrought into'; the phrase itself, its self attained in context.[11] Demonstrative vocabulary is not exempt from the contingencies which affect that which is demonstrated. Hobbes sometimes appears to think otherwise, but he does not write like one who takes exemption for granted. The significance of Hume on Taste is that he sees it partly as 'wrought', a matter of prejudicates, and in part arrived at through a mental discipline, a self-knowledgeable understanding of how deeply prejudiced we are, even—or especially—in our common agreements. In this respect at least, Hume recalls Hobbes and anticipates Wordsworth's attack on prejudicates in the 'Preface' to *Lyrical Ballads* and the *Essay Supplementary to the Preface* of 1815.

Although Wordsworth esteemed Hume among the very worst of critics, beaten into lowest place only by Adam Smith,[12] his two major critical pieces comprehend the nature and power of contingent circumstance in a way that could well be thought to derive from Hume's two papers:

> It is supposed, that by the act of writing in verse an Author makes a formal engagement that he will gratify certain known habits of association, that he not only thus apprizes the Reader that certain classes of ideas and expressions will be found in his book, but that others will be carefully excluded.[13]

The point at issue with 'It is supposed' is whether it indicates the acceptance or the rejection of majority opinion. According to my reading, Wordsworth does more than neutrally take note of the supposition; he is not so much taking as giving notice that certain required literary dues and social *congées* will not be offered in and by his work. It is true that in general usage the grammatical pitch of 'It is supposed' can be variable; herein is its particular usefulness: in the way it evades precise translation from, or into, mood and intention. In the 'Preface' to *Lyrical Ballads* he is more discreet than in the *Essay Supplementary* of 1815 where he shows himself vulnerable to his own disappointment and anger: 'But the ignorance of those who have chosen to stand forth as my enemies ...'; 'opponents whom I internally despise', etc.[14] Even in the earlier essay, however, the angry scorn is intermittently vented: 'those who talk of Poetry as a matter of amusement and idle pleasure'.[15]

Wordsworth's vulnerability bears upon my own approach to questions and issues of value. My strong prejudice in his favour being particularly marked at such points, we must consider the possibility that I overestimate here through sympathy as I may undervalue elsewhere because of antipathy. One may say, adapting Hume, that such forms of reaction 'transport' the speaker 'beyond all bounds of prudence and discretion',[16] render the work valueless as an instrument of general social intelligence. Drawing on the same authority one might plead the opposite case as a vindication of Wordsworth. Where Hume's requirement for this species of integrity is that 'the perfection of the man, and the perfection of the sense of feeling, are found to be united',[17] the defence might enter the plea that, where the imperfection of the man is nakedly realized in the speech, integrity and value are affirmed. It could be added that 'naked', for Wordsworth, is a term with ethical weight. Even then one would not have strong cause for complaint if the plea were rejected on the grounds of mere sentiment. One would perhaps be on firmer ground in making clear the significance to one's own thinking of the term 'realized'. I mean by 'realized' basically what Hume means by 'to fix and ascertain',[18] but with semantic resonances that he might reject; and I illustrate my Humean definition from an author whose realizations were outside Hume's range of hearing, acute though that was across the spectrum of 'the common sentiments of human nature'.[19] Bunyan's question, which for Hume would have been intrinsically absurd and ridiculous, is: how do you teach yourself to distinguish the treacherous common sense of the reprobate from the faithful knowledge of the elect; the answer is, you work at it:

> Then [*Christian*] went to the outward door, that leads into the *Castle yard*, and with his Key opened the door also. After he went to the *Iron* Gate, for that must be opened too, but that Lock went *damnable* hard, yet the Key did open it ...[20]

Bunyan's ability is to make a passage of emblematic discourse suddenly become the mind's activity: 'but that Lock went *damnable* hard'. The word is caught at the precise moment of translation from imprecation to recognition.

It so happens that this particular, and in context exemplary, instance of recognition takes the form of a pun; and it is a fact that, as numerous commentators have noted, 'many meanings can have *one word*'[21] and that 'Donne is really the kind of being to whom the word *done* can be applied'.[22] But that which unites the pun with other types of semantic recognition is the common factor of attention (which, in its time, has been the 'diligence' which the first Lutheran and Calvinist translators of the Bible attributed—rightfully for the most part—to themselves and, in its time, has been the phrase *Sedem animae in extremis digitis habent* which commended itself to Robert Burton, 'their Soule, or *intellectus agens*, was placed in their fingers ends'[23]). Emerson is therefore well within my range of understanding when he observes that Coleridge excels 'in the fineness of distinctions he could indicate, touching his mark with a needle's point';[24] so also is Housman's praise of his great predecessor in the emendation of Latin texts: that 'when one has halted at some stubborn perplexity of reading or interpretation, ... [one] turns to Bentley and sees Bentley strike his finger on the place and say *thou ailest here, and here*.'[25]

If moral discourse required no further justification than force of sentiment, strength of commitment; if ethical premise had a happily uncomplicated relationship to language, and language to value, there would be scarcely anything of significance in Ruskin's massive *oeuvre* to which '*thou ailest here, and here*' would not apply as a most telling epigraph. The text implicit in his major writings, though, so far as I know, it is made explicit only once, is Deuteronomy 27:17. In a letter to the *Manchester City News* (April 1884), he charges the proposed railway through the Derbyshire dales with a planned destruction of the peasants' landmarks:

> A landmark only!—and Heaven bless the mark—what better should they be? and who is he, and what is his guilt, who removes his neighbour's landmark?[26]

The Deuteronomic 'land-marke' of 1611 is set against the later 'scenic' sense acceptable to 'the tripper from Manchester or Birmingham'[27] whom the proposed railway will make free of the Dales, effectively disenfranchising the time-hallowed liberties of the peasantry. 'Cursed *be* he that remooueth his neighbours land-marke: and all the people shall say, Amen.'[28] 'Amen', so uttered, would be, for the theological moralist, whether Jewish or Christian, the absolute, clinching, recognition and assertion of value. Inevitably, Ruskinian secular attestations of value are tinged with the sardonic and elegiac.

This letter appeared one month later than *The Storm Cloud of the Nineteenth Century*, a volume comprising two lectures delivered in February 1884. It is a book about a curse, a curse incurred when England, together with her industrial neighbours and rivals, 'blasphemed the name of God deliberately and openly'. The 'plague-wind' and the accompanying 'plague-cloud' are at once the miasma of vast industrial desecration and a divine retribution visited upon ill-gotten wealth. Nature itself is now poisonously, blightingly, implicated in the evil reversal of natural process brought about by human greed and ingratitude: the wind drives a smoke cloud that looks 'as if it were made of dead men's souls'.[29] There is an element of sombre punning here if one comprehends Ruskin's visionary sense of 'illth', the neologism he coined for *Unto this Last* (1860–62).[30]

When *Unto this Last* was reissued in the Everyman Library in 1907, Oliver Lodge observed in his introduction that 'Mr Ruskin is always very precise in his use of language; every word employed by him is employed with due thought given to its meaning and history and uttermost significance.'[31] It is true that Ruskin is always definite—I choose this word as standing indeterminately between 'precise' and 'emphatic'—but I would question Lodge's terms. 'Intrinsic value', as Ruskin uses it, is emphatic but not precise; though its power of emphasis is due in great part to its capacity to *suggest* precision. Ruskin devotes many pages throughout his collected writings to establishing a density of evidence to justify his neologism 'illth'; by contrast 'intrinsic value' is, I would have said, *not* rooted in its 'meaning and history and uttermost significance'. It is whatever we desire shall stand as the moral opposite of illth and collective national bad faith.

When Hobbes, on the dedication page of *Leviathan*, celebrates the 'inhaerent' virtue of the dead Godolphin and when, several hundred pages later, returns to mourn the extinction of that inherency, in a Civil War skirmish, by 'an undiscerned, and an undiscerning hand';[32] when Hume appeals to the 'durable admiration, which attends those works, that have survived all the caprices of mode and fashion, all the mistakes of ignorance and envy',[33] 'inhaerent' virtue and 'durable admiration' directly anticipate Ruskin's 'intrinsic value'. Hume is not saying that the value is conferred by the admiration, but that society will in the end be brought to recognize the value that has always been there. In Ruskin's words, 'Used or not, their own power is in them and that particular power is in nothing else,'[34] or 'Everything costs its own Cost, and one of our best virtues is a just desire to pay it.'[35]

The basis of 'intrinsic value' lies in seventeenth-century monetary debate, in which it carried several conflicting senses. The monetarists in turn had drawn their term out of the language of the despised Scholastics.[36] Any study of the early fiscal terminology will demonstrate the historical inaccuracy of taking Ruskin's adoption of it in any absolute sense. His own rhetorical mannerism, in the twelfth letter of *Fors Clavigera*, is its own caveat:

> And you will find that the essence of the mis-teaching, of your day, concerning wealth of any kind, is in this denial of intrinsic value. What Judas, in the present state of Demand and Supply, can get for the article he has to sell, in a given market, that is the value of his article:—Yet you do not find that Judas had joy of his bargain.[37]

This—and with sorrow I say it—is rant. R. W. Dixon's remark, in a letter to Hopkins, that Carlyle 'spoiled Ruskin's style for him'[38] does not go unsupported; and *Fors Clavigera: Letters to the Workmen and Labourers of Great Britain* (1871–84), contains more than one eloquent tribute to the writer he called 'master'.[39] His closest approach to what Lodge calls 'due thought given to [the] meaning and history' of intrinsic value is in the Thirty Seventh *Fors* (January 1874); and here he strikes me as being, intentionally or unintentionally, in the line of Locke's thinking on this subject in the *Second Treatise of Government*. Locke argues that, although two pieces of land may have 'the same natural, intrinsick Value', it is 'Husbandry', '*Labour ... which puts the greatest part of Value upon Land*, without which it would scarcely be worth any thing'.[40] Intrinsic value, when considered in terms of an improved and improving husbandry, is that which, left simply to itself, will remain unrealized. Is it, then, anything more than a formal figure given as the basis for a set of estimates? In the January 1874 *Fors*, Ruskin uses not dissimilar terms: 'I should best like a bit of marsh land of small value'; 'I will make the best of it that I can, at once, by wage-labour, under the best agricultural advice.'[41] I cannot see how these ideals are essentially different from Locke's estimates. It is in the moral approach that they differ. Locke's attitude to the labourers engaged in the schemes of improved husbandry was 'unusually harsh' even by the standards of that time.[42] Ruskin's views are paternalistically benevolent. But this exists in his social writings as an aura, rather than as a realization, of language; and 'intrinsic value', which appears to carry precise meaning, is part of that 'aura'.

Christopher Ricks has observed that 'the longing for something indispensable, for a *sine qua non*, is part of the long history of being misguided not only about literary studies but about literature itself'.[43] I do not myself see that a longing for something indispensable is *per se* misguided; though I concede the dangers and would accept that most attempts to embody the 'longing' create metaphysical wraiths. Ruskin's 'intrinsic value' is, in and of itself, such a wraith; but, according to my argument, it remains a term which points in the right direction, towards semantic realizations that have some substance.

The question for Wordsworth is: how to confer 'moral existence' on those 'who, according to the classical morality', as Trilling reminds us, 'should have no moral life at all'.[44] The answer is, again, that you work at it. There is language and there is character, of which intelligence is a part and what we call 'personality' a part; and each is subjected to a considerable range of contingent forces:

> There is a comfort in the strength of love;
> 'Twill make a thing endurable, which else
> Would break the heart:—Old Michael found it so.[45]

To some extent the strength and endurance that the poem records are composed of elements which can equally bring about weakness and torpor. The gift which ensures the right reading subsists in the strength and endurance of the language, which itself contains elements that could easily be left to drift into a significantly different, Humean, acceptance of 'good sense, that directs men in the ordinary occurrences of life'.[46] Since I do not believe that 'texts' write themselves, I am here considering a quality of Wordsworth's intelligence and personality. The particular qualities which he values in human nature correspond to language, 'a thing subject to endless fluctuations and arbitrary associations'.[47] I do not propose that Wordsworth 'masters' the arbitrariness: that is something which Hobbes achieves in his own rich, enigmatic, and arbitrary style which shuts out most of what Wordsworth desires to include. Wordsworth, as in the three lines here quoted from 'Michael', feels intelligently through language, with its endless fluctuations and arbitrary associations in such a way that in recording how 'love ... will make a thing endurable' he makes out of language an entity able to endure. I would conclude from this particular instance, not as a general rule, that language is love's correlate; and that Wordsworth is here translating ethos into activity, an exchange which had eluded Hume, though I suspect that he would claim this aspect of translation to be a quibble for which he did not choose to stoop aside.[48] Endurance is one of the great words which lie directly on the active/passive divide, subject to the fluctuations and arbitrariness that Wordsworth cites; and it is here, on the line, that, through language, value is to be realized, provided that the writer can 'touch ... his mark with a needle's point', 'strike his finger on the place'.

In the course of this discussion I several times employ the term 'pitch', which elsewhere I have distinguished from 'tone'.[49] I was first drawn to consider its appositeness to these questions when reading, many years ago, Stallworthy's observation that 'where words are concerned [Yeats] has almost perfect pitch'.[50] In an uncollected essay I subsequently glossed Stallworthy's observation with a couple of sentences which may perhaps be usefully repeated here:

> A poet who possesses such near-perfect pitch is able to sound out his own conceptual discursive intelligence ... [He] is hearing words in depth and is therefore hearing, or sounding, history and morality in depth.[51]

Subsequently I added to this sense of pitch ideas drawn from Hopkins's spiritual writings, for example, 'Nothing else in nature comes near this unspeakable stress of pitch, distinctiveness, and selving, this selfbeing of my own.'[52] Hopkins's editor enters the caveat that 'GMH ... does not distinguish sufficiently between his "*pitch*" (which seems to be Scotus's *gradus*) and Scotus's *haecceitas* [this-ness].'[53] Technically speaking (which, as I follow through the argument, is simultaneously ethically speaking) two matters principally concern me in my own study of Hopkins's writings: (1) how he achieves the 'this' (the finished poem) which can properly be said to be the correlative of his 'this-ness' of self-being; (2) how he understands and resolves the technical paradox implied by his use of the colloquial 'unspeakable'; it is evident that his poems do 'speak' the 'unspeakable' at a pitch that simultaneously represents intense formality and idiomatic immediacy.

One other word has more recently become of particular significance to me as indicating that instantaneous realization of the correlative within the contingent which is for me the 'something indispensable', the '*sine qua non*', of working justly in words; of working justice into and through and out of language. The word first struck me (that I think is the entirely apposite verb) when, a couple of years ago, I was rereading Burke's *Reflections on the Revolution in France*: 'A politician, to do great things, looks for a *power*, what our workmen call a *purchase*.'[54] The statement is itself an epitome of the close contraries within a seemingly uncomplicated utterance. Despite the *OED*'s entry which gives this as the earliest recorded use of sense III.15.*fig.* ('A "hold", "fulcrum", or position of advantage for accomplishing something; a means by which one's own power or influence is increased') I do not recognize a parity between, on the one hand, 'politician/*power*' and, on the other, 'workmen/*purchase*'. Burke has effected a takeover of the workman's term and the *OED* regularizes the *coup*. 'Politician/*power*' is expansive; 'workmen/*purchase*' contracts in to the particular and the contractual. The viciousness of Burke goes with the expansive; the good in him speaks through the contractual.

Hobbes, in *Leviathan* (1651), provides the *OED*'s earliest citation for the use of *purchase*, sense I.7.*fig.* ('Acquisition at the cost of something immaterial, as effort, suffering, or sacrifice'): 'Our Senses and Experience ... are the Talents, ... to be ... employed in the purchase of Justice, Peace, and true Religion.'[55] In the work of words, the immaterial (senses, experience, talents) must take a purchase on the material, i.e. language-as-medium. In theory and principle this is a factor that Ruskin effectively comprehends. I have in mind not only 'Everything costs its own Cost, and one of our best virtues is a just desire to pay it' but also several of his observations on the art of Turner. It was one of these that

Hopkins—among the greatest English workers of purchase—took purchase on. Ruskin had praised an apparent incongruity in Turner's 'Pass of Faido', the insertion of a distant coach-and-horses in an otherwise empty landscape of majestic desolation. Ruskin dismissed the objection of Taste and Sensibility—that the intrusion of the quotidian and commonplace destroyed the sense of the Sublime—with a sublime practicality of his own: 'The dream insisted particularly on the great fact of its having come by the road.'[56] That is to say that the *value* of the 'dream' is authenticated, validated, by the recognition of the difficulty with which purchase is obtained: you work at it, work it through. Hopkins's recognition of the particular quality, the quality of the particular, not only in Turner's purchase on significant detail but also in Ruskin's purchase on the method by which Turner separates true from false vision, enables him to grasp and articulate one of his own most searching realizations of instress: 'Not imposed outwards from the mind as for instance by melancholy or strong feeling':[57]

> I see
> The lost are like this, and their scourge to be
> As I am mine, their sweating selves; but worse.[58]

Here, the entire personal and doctrinal issue—the matter at debate is that of the proximity to damnation—requires a syntactical membrane as thin as a semi-colon; the semi-colon that separates the two final words 'but worse' from the preceding phrases. The speaker of the poem cries out from the midst of a purgatorial desolation so intense that it is hellish; but finally it is not hell. I know that the damned suffer, the speaker declares; but I know also that I am not damned. It is, in a sense, a doctrinal formality, a matter of status; there is a touch of forensic dryness in the placing of that semi-colon; a dryness which is as significant as the extremity of suffering. The semi-colon, here, is at once recognition, fact, and value.

To preclude a final misunderstanding which could vitiate, retroactively, the entire course of my argument, I will say here that the issues of language and value under discussion in this essay are not to be mistaken for that *ignis fatuus* known to the philosophers as 'value-rich vocabulary'.

NOTES

1. John Ruskin, *Unto this Last & Other Essays on Art and Political Economy* (London: Dent, 1907), pp. 203–04; *Fors Clavigera: Letters to the Workmen and Labourers of Great Britain* (Orpington: George Allen, 1871–87), 9 vols, I, xii, 23 (Dec. 1871).
2. David Hume, *Ethical Writings*, ed. A. MacIntyre (Notre Dame, Indiana: Univ. of Notre Dame Press, 1965), pp. 286, 284, 280.
3. Hume, *Ethical Writings*, p. 278.
4. Christopher Ricks, *Essays in Appreciation* (Oxford: Clarendon Press, 1996), p. 317.
5. James Griffin, *Value Judgement* (Oxford: OUP, 1996), p. 22.
6. Hume, *Ethical Writings*, p. 280.
7. *Monsieur Pascall's Thoughts, Meditations and Prayers*, done into English by Jos. Walker (London, 1688), pp. 235, 236; *Pascal's Pensées*, trans. H. F. Stewart (New York: Pantheon Books, 1950), pp. 494–95.
8. David Hume, *Essays Moral, Political, and Literary*, ed. E. F. Miller (Indianapolis: Liberty Fund, rev. ed., 1988), p. 5.
9. Hume, *Essays*, p. 5.
10. Hume, *Ethical Writings*, p. 277.
11. Thomas Hobbes, *Leviathan*, ed. C. B. Macpherson (Harmondsworth: Penguin, 1968), p. 180.
12. William Wordsworth, *Poems*, ed. J. O. Hayden (Harmondsworth: Penguin, 1977), 2 vols, II, 934.
13. *Wordsworth's Preface to 'Lyrical Ballads'*, ed. W. J. B. Owen (Copenhagen: Rosenkilde and Bagger, 1957), p. 114.
14. Wordsworth, *Poems*, II, 923, 924.
15. *Wordsworth's Preface*, p. 122.
16. Hume, *Essays*, p. 4.
17. Hume, *Ethical Writings*, p. 284.
18. Hume, *Ethical Writings*, p. 278.
19. Hume, *Ethical Writings*, p. 280.
20. John Bunyan, *The Pilgrim's Progress*, ed. N. H. Keeble (Oxford: Clarendon Press, 1984), pp. 96, 274–75.
21. Sigurd Burckhardt, 'The Poet as Fool and Priest', in *ELH*, 23 (1956), 287.
22. Walter J. Ong, SJ, *The Barbarian Within, and Other Fugitive Essays and Studies* (New York: Macmillan, 1962), p. 94.
23. Robert Burton, *The Anatomy of Melancholy*, eds T. C. Faulkner *et al.* (Oxford: Clarendon Press, 1989–94), 3 vols, I, 79.
24. *The Early Lectures of Ralph Waldo Emerson*, eds S. E. Whicher and R. E. Spiller (Cambridge, MA: Belknap Press, 1959–72), 3 vols, I, 378.
25. A. E. Housman, *Selected Prose*, ed. J. Carter (Cambridge: CUP, 1962), p. 27.

26. *The Works of John Ruskin*, eds E. T. Cook and A. Wedderburn (London: George Allen, 1903–12), 39 vols, XXXIV, 571.

27. *Works of John Ruskin*, XXXIV, 571.

28. *The Holy Bible: An Exact Reprint … of the Authorized Version … 1611* (Oxford: OUP, 1985).

29. John Ruskin, *The Storm Cloud of the Nineteenth Century: Two Lectures Delivered at the London Institution* (Orpington: George Allen, 1884), pp. 62, 45, 57, 60, 58, 48.

30. Ruskin, *Unto this Last*, pp. 171, 216.

31. Ruskin, *Unto this Last*, p. xi.

32. Hobbes, *Leviathan*, pp. 75, 718.

33. Hume, *Ethical Writings*, p. 280.

34. Ruskin, *Unto this Last*, p. 204.

35. *Letters of John Ruskin to Charles Eliot Norton* (Cambridge, MA: Houghton Mifflin, 1904), 2 vols, I, 243.

36. *Locke on Money*, ed. P. H. Kelley (Oxford: Clarendon Press, 1991), 2 vols, I, 87n2.

37. Ruskin, *Fors Clavigera*, I, xii, 23.

38. *The Correspondence of Gerard Manley Hopkins and Richard Watson Dixon*, ed. C. C. Abbott (London: OUP, 1935), pp. 51–52.

39. Ruskin, *Fors Clavigera*, IX [Index], 82–83: entries under CARLYLE.

40. John Locke, *Two Treatises of Government*, ed. P. Laslett (Cambridge: CUP, 1988), p. 298.

41. Ruskin, *Fors Clavigera*, IV, 8. Phrases quoted out of sequence.

42. Neal Wood, *John Locke and Agrarian Capitalism* (Berkeley: Univ. of California Press, 1984), pp. 106–07.

43. Ricks, *Essays in Appreciation*, p. 319.

44. Lionel Trilling, *A Gathering of Fugitives* (Boston: Beacon Press, 1956), p. 39.

45. *Wordsworth: Poetry & Prose*, ed. W. M. Merchant (London: Hart-Davis, 1969), p. 205.

46. Hume, *Ethical Writings*, p. 294.

47. Wordsworth, *Poems*, II, 947.

48. My allusion is to Johnson, on Shakespeare's quibbles. See his *Preface*, 1765.

49. 'Dividing Legacies' in *Agenda*, 34:2 (Summer, 1996), 9–28.

50. Jon Stallworthy, *Between the Lines* (Oxford: Clarendon Press, 1963), p. 6.

51. 'The Conscious Mind's Intelligible Structure' in *Agenda*, 9:4–10:1 (Autumn–Winter, 1971–72), 14–23.

52. *The Sermons and Devotional Writings of Gerard Manley Hopkins*, ed. C. Devlin, SJ (London: OUP, 1959), p. 123.

53. *Sermons and Devotional Writings of Gerard Manley Hopkins*, p. 293.

54. Edmund Burke, *Reflections On The Revolution in France*, ed. C. Cruise O'Brien (Harmondsworth: Penguin, 1986), p. 267.

55. Hobbes, *Leviathan*, p. 409.

56. Cited in *The Journals and Papers of Gerard Manley Hopkins*, eds H. House and G. Storey (London: OUP, 1959), pp. 413–14.

57. *Journals and Papers of Gerard Manley Hopkins*, p. 215.

58. Text as given in *Gerard Manley Hopkins*, ed. Catherine Phillips (Oxford: OUP, 1986), p. 166. *The Poetical Works of Gerard Manley Hopkins*, ed. Norman H. Mackenzie (Oxford: Clarendon Press, 1990), pp. 181–82, gives variorum readings. Mackenzie states (xliii) that 'some famous poems ... were in fact left without a finalized text', 'I wake and feel the fell of dark' was one of these. Mackenzie adds (449) that the 'bracketed' MS reading 'As I am mine, their sweating selves; but worse' was added 'perhaps to reduce any suggestion that [GMH] felt worse than the lost'. I cannot see that the 'suggestion', even if only tenuously present, could have been theologically tolerable to Hopkins, once he had noticed it. The grammar of his self-correction strikes me as being powerfully characteristic.

Browning's Old Florentine Painters: Italian Art and Mid-Victorian Poetry

KELVIN EVEREST

I

Browning's admirers have often, and rightly, celebrated the achievement of his dramatic monologues, 'Fra Lippo Lippi' and 'Andrea del Sarto', published in *Men and Women* in 1855. My interest in them here, however, is not primarily literary-critical, and I do not propose to offer sustained critical commentary on the poetry itself, although my discussion does move towards a closer attention to some detailed features of the poetry. I am mainly interested in some larger questions raised by Browning's interest in those particular painters, at that particular time in the middle of the nineteenth century. The questions are, briefly, to do with how we might seek to explain Browning's choice of those subjects: what sort of factors, that is to say, combine to make such choices *possible*? What is involved in the process of cultural translation by which one set of historically specific forms can provide the material for quite different and historically remote cultural conditions and thereby function as the vehicle of a new expression? Browning's monologues are subtle and powerful character studies, but I want to propose that they also offer broader meanings. These meanings are developed from new possibilities in the significance of Italian art, which are strikingly emergent in Victorian cultural commentary. I am interested to explain how Browning's painter poems can come to have more, and more unexpected, meanings than those to which the critical consensus has usually confined them. But the explanation does, admittedly, produce a curious and mixed effect, as contexts which must be understood to constitute necessary conditions for the existence of the poems themselves start to proliferate and ramify. What follows is simply an example of some intellectual and methodological difficulties which arise in the attempt to account for the chosen materials as well as the formal and intellectual properties of complex poems.

Of course, questions about the determining possibilities of aesthetic choice, understood in an historical way, quickly raise big issues. It can be easy to miss large-scale historical and political changes, such as the French Revolution or the revolutionary crises in 1848 in Western Europe even as they are happening. But even the central participants in that kind of big obvious change are obliged to choose for themselves a style, a set of models, by which to identify, for themselves and for others, the meanings of the events in which they are caught up, and which they think of themselves as helping to make happen. Marx put it famously in the *Eighteenth Brumaire of Louis Bonaparte*, a political analysis in curious struggle with the conventions of narrative and itself prompted by the crisis of 1848:

> Hegel remarks somewhere that all the great events and characters of world history occur, so to speak, twice. He forgot to add: the first time as tragedy, the second as farce ... Men make their own history, but not of their own free will; not under circumstances they themselves have chosen but under the given and inherited circumstances with which they are directly confronted. The tradition of the dead generations weighs like a nightmare on the minds of the living. And, just when they appear to be engaged in the revolutionary transformation of themselves and their material surroundings, in the creation of something which does not yet exist, precisely in such epochs of revolutionary crisis they timidly conjure up the spirits of the past to help them; they borrow their names, slogans and costumes so as to stage the new world-historical scene in this venerable disguise and borrowed language.

So the revolution of 1848 dresses itself up sometimes as the France of 1789, or sometimes the France of 1793–95, just as revolutionary France in the 1790s 'draped itself alternately as the Roman republic and the Roman empire'.[1] This rhetoric can sound a touch overconfident nowadays. We might be inclined to allow the subjects of history a more volitional and deliberated responsiveness to change. Nevertheless, it remains an arresting proposition that change does not, perhaps cannot, become meaningful until it is situated in some received account of history. And this can lead to stylistic choices which disconcertingly alter the existing meanings and resonances of the past as they are taken up in new cultural situations.

It is evidently true that historical and political change, no matter how dramatic and inescapable, is rarely registered directly and immediately at other levels of human activity. At its *own* level it is not easily registered 'directly and immediately'; it usually needs to be dressed up in some ostensibly recognizable form. And each form of activity as, for example, poetry or the visual arts, has an inner logic of development, a sense of itself and its active history and materials, that will set limits to the possibilities and the forms of change at any given moment. No matter how powerful the stimulus from external change, artists can only react and develop from within the traditions and established materials of their chosen art form.

Artists, especially, must make choices from among the whole vast range of existing cultural materials. The instance of Browning's painter poems, however, helps us to focus more sharply on the factors which govern the available range of relevant cultural materials which might be considered to serve a particular new cultural condition. When trying to understand the particular specific forms taken by cultural events, we need to have regard, not just to the elements which distinguish the debate itself, but also to the range of cultural forms available for appropriation. What governs the availability of cultural forms for a given epoch?

Browning was clearly not the only Victorian writer who turned to Italian Renaissance art in the search for terms in which to carry forward the great cultural debates of the mid-century. In Carlyle, and Ruskin, and in the work of the Pre-Raphaelites, there is a consistent deployment of a certain image of early

Renaissance Italy as a cultural model which is set polemically against the killing effects of Victorian capitalism. And because this appropriation has become so familiar, through the very polemic of these exemplars, it can seem to us now to be a natural choice deriving from the innate qualities of the cultural model itself. But this naturalization is deceptive. Victorian Gothic, in Ruskin's sense, is a Victorian creation, a function of a certain complex nineteenth-century rhetoric. Because it has become so familiar, the particularities bearing on the original choice of model have been obscured.

But why that vision of that Italy, at that time? To return to our original question: what factors made the choice possible? It might be possible to develop an answer which lays stress on the innate aesthetic qualities of the appropriated model. The historically determined retrospective obviousness of the choice might, as it were, turn out to be naturally grounded after all. Perhaps there is something intrinsically germane to the purposes and the tastes of Victorian intellectuals, in the constituent stylistic features and the surviving substance of early Italian Renaissance art and architecture. But it is at least equally plausible that the taste was itself produced and nourished by a set of historical circumstances. It is on that possibility, at least, that I want to concentrate.

II

Browning's friend Alfred Domett was one of many who emigrated from England to escape the financial depression of the early 1840s. Browning wrote to him in 1842 of how, in England,

> every thing goes flatly on, except the fierce political reality (as it begins to be)—our poems, & etc., are poor child's play ... There is much, everything, to <be> done in England just now.[2]

The 'fierce political reality' was to come to a European crisis by the end of the decade. The conditions of that crisis were however, and obviously enough, different in each country. In England, the conditions were those of industrial capitalism, and English intellectuals felt their human and cultural impact acutely. The 1840s was a decade lived out in the fear of an English Revolution of the working class, that spectre of the first sentence of Marx's *Communist Manifesto* (its arguments were given an English orientation because its authors identified England as the supreme 'despot' of the European economy).

Apart from one or two monologues, such as the 'Italian in England' published in *Dramatic Romances and Lyrics* in 1845 and written in the voice of an expatriate fighter in the cause of the Carbonari, Browning held himself aloof from explicit political commentary, and from the great critical debate over the 'Two Nations' which raged throughout the 1840s.[3] By 1848 he had, indeed, avoided any personal engagement with the great political crisis in Europe by settling, quietly, in quiet Florence. After his secret marriage to Elizabeth Barrett in 1846 the couple moved to Florence in 1847 and stayed there until 1861. The Brownings were actually in Paris on 2 December 1851, when they watched from a hotel window as Louis-Napoleon paraded down the Champs-Elysées after having killed off the Republic of 1848. Elizabeth quite approved of Louis-Napoleon as a 'man of the people', a man who might unify Italy, whereas Browning stored up dislike. But Browning remained publicly silent about the crisis of the mid-century, and his poems are mostly innocent of reference to public events. It is also difficult to understand any striking feature of his stylistic character as a poet in terms of response to such events. After the move to Florence, Browning's personal life and, with small exceptions, his poetry offer only trivial and contingent points of contact with the larger political experience of upheaval in the middle decades of the century. In 1851 Charles Kingsley wrote of this withdrawal in his essay on 'Mr and Mrs Browning':

> But we will complain no more: though, indeed, our complaints are really compliments; for had we not felt certain that Mr Browning was worthy of better things, we should have left the matter to clear itself, as all poems do pretty accurately in 'the righteous sieve of Time'. But there are fine ballads in the second volume, healthy and English,

> clear of all that Italianesque pedantry, that *crambe repetita* of olives and lizards, artists and monks, with which the English public, for its sins, has been spoon-fed for the last half-century, ever since Childe Harold, in a luckless hour, thought a warmer climate might make him a better man ... How can Mr Browning help England? By leaving henceforth 'the dead to bury their dead', in effete and enervating Italy, and casting all his rugged genial force into the questions and the struggles of that mother-country to whom, and not to Italy at all, he owes all his most valuable characteristics.[4]

Nevertheless, Browning's next volume of poems, *Men and Women* (1855), found him more than ever preoccupied with Italy and Italian things, although not at all preoccupied with its politics any more than with England's. The mild reformist rule of Grand Duke Leopoldo II, who had been installed in Florence in 1815 by the monarchist allies, was indeed chiefly attractive to the very many English and other expatriate settlers in the city for its genteelly cultured and untroubled political life. As we have seen, in 1848 Elizabeth Barrett Browning was in her poetry avowedly a partisan of the Risorgimento whereas Browning remained silent. In *Men and Women* he appeared in fact to develop his Italian interests in an antiquarian direction more remote than ever from the life of his native society.

It is, however, interesting that Browning's preoccupation with the early Italian Renaissance should coincide with similar interests, at around the same time, in the work of influential English intellectuals who most certainly were engaged in the cultural and political debates around the 'Two Nations' problem and the question of the significance and social effects of the Industrial Revolution. In the work of, for example, Ruskin and Carlyle and the Pre-Raphaelites there is definitely a close and important connection between the rejection of Victorian capitalism, and a preference for the social and cultural example of the late medieval Italian city-states. This circumstance suggests that there is a resonance in Browning's own Italian interests, deriving from similar historical conditions, which gives the painter monologues an at least implicit dimension of cultural commentary. Apart from the two dramatic monologues in the personae of Italian painters, *Men and Women* includes, for example, 'Old Pictures in Florence', a difficult poem drawing in detail on Browning's reading of Vasari's *Lives of the Painters* and indicating a marked taste for what were then coming to be known as the Italian 'primitives'. These primitives were the relatively obscure painters of the generations preceding that period which still, in the first half of the nineteenth century, was acknowledged to represent the pinnacle of achievement in European painting, the High Renaissance of Raphael and Michelangelo.

'Old Pictures in Florence' laments particularly the decay of the surviving fresco paintings of the early Renaissance:

> Wherever a fresco peels and drops,
>   Wherever an outline weakens and wanes
> Till the latest life in the painting stops,
>   Stands One whom each fainter pulse-tick pains!
> One, wishful each scrap should clutch its brick,
>   Each tinge not wholly escape the plaster,
> —A lion who dies of an ass's kick,
>   The wronged great soul of an ancient Master.
>
> For oh, this world and the wrong it does!
>   They are safe in heaven with their backs to it,
> The Michaels and Rafaels, you hum and buzz
>   Round the works of, you of the little wit!
> Do their eyes contract to the earth's old scope,
>   Now that they see God face to face,
> And have all attained to be poets, I hope?
>   'Tis their holiday now, in any case.
>
> Much they reck of your praise and you!
>   But the wronged great souls—can they be quit
> Of a world where all their work is to do,
>   Where you style them, you of the little wit,
> Old Master this and Early the other,
>   Not dreaming that Old and New are fellows,
> That a younger succeeds to an elder brother,
>   Da Vincis derive in good time from Dellos.

And here where your praise would yield returns
And a handsome word or two give help,
Here, after your kind, the mastiff girns
And the puppy pack of poodles yelp.
What, not a word for Stefano there
—Of brow once prominent and starry,
Called Nature's ape and the world's despair
For his peerless painting (see Vasari)?[5]

In this awkward poem, written as part of the contemporary campaign for the completion of Giotto's bell tower next to the Cathedral in Florence, Browning seeks to redress the then current relative valuations of painters from earlier and later periods of the Florentine Renaissance. In particular, the Masters of the earlier period, and above all Giotto, are acclaimed in the poem for representing a 'naturalistic' revolution against the idealization and technical perfection of masterpieces in the tradition of classical Greece. The poem celebrates this naturalism as an essentially democratic art, claiming the transcendent values of humanity for ordinary experience. The classical subjects and the masterpieces of their embodiment have served to oppress by the unmatchable character of their perfection. The rougher and less perfectly polished manner of the primitives better suits the realities of quotidian historical experience:

You would fain be kinglier, say than I am?
Even so, you will not sit like Theseus.
You'd fain be a model? the Son of Priam
Has yet the advantage in arms' and knees' use.
You're wroth—can you slay your snake like Apollo?
You're grieved—still Niobe's the grander!
You live—there's the Racers' frieze to follow—
You die—there's the dying Alexander.

So, testing your weakness by their strength,
Your meagre charms by their rounded beauty,
Measured by Art in your breadth and length,
You learn—to submit is the worsted's duty.
—When I say 'you' 'tis the common soul,
The collective, I mean—the race of Man

That receives life in parts to live in a whole,
And grow here according to God's own plan.

Growth came when, looking your last on them all,
You turned your eyes inwardly one fine day
And cried with a start—what if we so small
Are greater, ay, greater the while than they!
Are they perfect of lineament, perfect of stature?
In both, of such lower types are we
Precisely because of our wider nature;
For time, theirs—ours, for eternity.

This exclusive idealism in art, contrasted as it is with the fast-disappearing achievements of the primitives, is in fact associated by Browning with the technical perfection celebrated by Vasari in the work of Vasari's sixteenth-century contemporaries, Michelangelo, Raphael and Titian (and, by association at least, Andrea del Sarto). The democratic Humanism of the poem's argument thus implies a political dimension in the artistic preferences that are articulated and are consonant with other contemporary English revaluings of early Italian art in a context of cultural polemic.

III

Browning's 'Old Pictures in Florence' objects to the values of the received standard periodizing of Florentine art. This periodicity derived, for Browning's generation, from Vasari, whose *Lives of the Painters* (first published in 1550) was widely known among the Victorians in the influential English edition and translation of 1850 by Mrs Jonathan Foster. Vasari provides a developmental overview of Italian art which discerns three broad phases, ascending towards the supreme achievements of his own time. The first of these phases comprises the art of Cimabue, Giotto, Duccio, and other artists who were working in the late thirteenth and fourteenth centuries. The second phase covers the period from the early fifteenth to the early sixteenth century, including the work of Uccello, Masaccio, Brunelleschi, Piero della

Francesca, Botticelli and Filippo Lippi. The heights are then finally arrived at with the major artists of the sixteenth century, notably Leonardo, Correggio, Raphael, Michelangelo; and Andrea del Sarto. The whole thrust of Browning's paired painter poems is effectively to tilt the axis of this set of valuations, and to relocate the high point of importance and achievement in Italian art away from Vasari's peak and towards the earlier periods. His choice of Lippo Lippi and Andrea del Sarto as specific exemplars presumably derives from the various artistic and thematic possibilities inherent in the biographical contrasts presented in the two lives.

This reorientation in artistic taste is associated with a critique of Victorian social experience, quite ubiquitously in the work of Browning's English contemporaries. It is useful, in trying to explain such a widespread and distinctive appropriation of such a specific cultural form, to consider the Preface to Luigi Lanzi's *History of Painting in Italy*, which after its appearance in Italian in 1795 became (especially in Thomas Roscoe's translation of 1828) an immensely influential handbook among English cultural commentators. Lanzi stresses the fundamental necessity for the art historian to conceive of the discipline's object of knowledge in periodized terms for, without this sense of progressive linearity, the materials under consideration lose coherence in a welter of undifferentiated information:

> The history of painting has a strong analogy to literary, to civil, and to sacred history; it too requires the aid of certain beacons, some particular distinction in regard to places, times or events, to divide it into epochs, and mark its successive stages. Deprive it of these, and it degenerates, like other history, into a chaos of names more calculated to load the memory than to inform the understanding.

Lanzi's argument insists upon the historical, the diachronic axis in analysis. If we attempt to conceive of art history in structural or systemic terms, then the underlying developmental and progressive character of the material will be obscured:

> We cannot ... adopt the method of the naturalist, who having arranged the vegetable kingdom, in classes more or

> less numerous, according to the systems of Tournefort or of Linnaeus, can easily reduce a plant, wherever it may happen to grow, to a particular class, adding a name and description, at once precise, characteristic, and permanent. In a complete history it is necessary to distinguish each style from every other; nor do I know any more eligible method than by composing a separate history of each school.[6]

And yet the very impact on Victorian cultural commentators of shifts in Lanzi's own discipline, the history of Italian art, suggests the opposite. In practice the periodizing of history tends to appropriate to the needs of the present an essentially synchronic model of history, in which periods are defined and acquire their distinctive values and meanings by their oppositional relation to other designated periods. Browning's 'antiquarian' interest in early Florentine painting is, as we have already noted, a particular instance of a larger movement towards a higher valuation of the Italian primitives in the early decades of the nineteenth century. It is very difficult to disentangle the various complex causes and effects of the rising taste for trecento and quattrocento painting. What is, however, certain is that subtle shifts in the received valuations of English art historians produce the materials for a social-cultural, and indeed a religious, debate in the 1840s of great ferocity. This debate takes up the altered internal relations within a periodized conception of Italian art, and uses them to give form to fundamental conflicts in the interpretation of industrial capitalism and the effects of the division of labour.

It may be that qualities in the cultural forms so taken up, which is to say, for example, aesthetic qualities understood as 'objective' or 'innate' properties of the art and architecture of the early Florentine Renaissance, may partly explain why they are used as they are in subsequent cultural debate. But these qualities can be no more than a *pressure*, not a sufficient condition in the explanation of the new meanings they come to have. It is just as helpful to think of the appropriation of newly active cultural forms as providing what might be described as an 'empty' cultural form, which is freshly available to cultural polemic as a result of complex historical and cultural determinations, and at the same time not already laden with values which are active in the receiving cultural context. Thus an image of the early Italian Renaissance finds itself deployed in a certain polemical fashion at least partly because it was available at the right moment.

IV

The effort to explain shifts of taste, such as the changing attitudes to early Italian art in the early Victorian period, returns us to other and wider issues. One very wide and relevant issue is the effect on the art market in Western Europe of the Napoleonic wars. Baron Vivant-Denon, for example, acted as Napoleon's adviser on 'acquisitions' for the Imperial project of the Musée Napoléon in the Louvre throughout the period of Napoleon's dominance in Europe. In this role he oversaw what was effectively a systematic programme of 'cultural annexation' involving large-scale movement of the major works of the High Renaissance in Italy and their relocation and centralization in the great centrepiece gallery of the new imperial order. There was at the same time a massive release onto the market of a few very large and important private collections, principally composed of further great paintings in the then received taste, which saturated the market in that taste, and thus drove dealers to a speculative manipulation of the art market by an active development of interest in hitherto less admired, and less collectable, earlier paintings and artefacts. The extraordinary collection of the Duke of Orleans, for example, was sold in 1792 as part of the Duke's deeply misguided project to succeed Louis as King of France. Most of this collection found its way to London in the 1790s, where it duly made a momentous impact on Hazlitt and his generation. Another great collection released on to the market around this time was that of Cardinal Fesch, Napoleon's uncle.

The dealers were motivated to seek new commercial possibilities by the abundance of 'slack' capital in the fortunes of the new English trade barons, whose *arriviste* pretensions, joined with the persisting appetite for prestigious cultural acquisition of those with plenty of 'old' money, created the perfect conditions in which to promote a new taste for early paintings. A fresh supply of such paintings was partly kept up by the punitive taxation imposed on noble families of the occupied states by the French administration. Thus many long-unconsidered and virtually forgotten paintings in private hands were at once a necessary resort for their impoverished owners and a newly transferable asset in the burgeoning market. This complex of political, social and cultural developments itself coincided with a whole range of further collateral developments, sometimes related, sometimes not, which combined sharply to increase the value of early Italian art, and also to increase the stock of specialized and general knowledge of the material. Charles Eastlake, for example, brought a new influence to bear as Secretary to the National Gallery from 1843 to 1847, when he introduced to the new fashions in artistic taste a professional art historian's thoroughness in exploring the development of painting; but this was just one instance of the general tendency for commentary and scholarship to follow the demands of trends generated at quite deep levels of historical change. By the 1840s the taste for primitives was expounded in many works directed at the tourist and purchaser interests of newly monied art buyers in need of advice. Some of these works themselves served diverse interests. Carlo Lasinio's *Pictures and Frescoes of the Campo Santo in Pisa*, so immensely influential on the Pre-Raphaelites, was aimed in the spirit of the Risorgimento at a nationalist audience who sought re-education in the cultural heritage of pre-occupation Italy (there is a similar dimension in Lanzi's work, which serves the Risorgimento by looking back beyond the chauvinistically Florentine perspective of Vasari). A different influence in the later 1840s flowed from Lord Lindsay's *Sketches of the History of Christian Art* (1847), which brought something like a professional historical perspective to bear, and gave an enlarged sense of origins and social context in studies of the early Renaissance. This volume was reviewed by Ruskin, who himself had become deeply involved in early Italian painters after his trip to Lucca, Pisa, Florence and Venice in 1845, a journey which produced the new judgements of the second volume of *Modern Painters* (1846). Ruskin, Lord Lindsay and Samuel Rogers combined in 1847 to found the Arundel Society, which published a series of chromo-lithographic reproductions of newly rediscovered primitives or semi-primitives, at the rate of six each year. The series included such masters as Fra Angelico and Masaccio, and also Lippo Lippi. Even the Prince Consort, Albert, had strong and well-known interests in Italian art in the 1840s, reflected in his chairmanship of the Royal Commission in 1843 to decide on the mural paintings to decorate the Houses of Parliament. There was an accusation that the Prince's strong and distinctive tastes were really an excuse to justify the purchase by the nation of the large art collection of a relative of the Prince, Prince Oettingen-Wallerstein, in 1848.

All of these examples simply offer detailed instances of a gathering and increasingly widespread effort of historical retrieval and cultural commentary relating to the primitives. This effort then helps to bring into being the cultural conditions which make possible the central articulations of a new meaning, for the Victorians, of the early Renaissance in Italy. Ruskin is, of course, absolutely central to the shift of focus which this trend in aesthetic fashion comes to serve in the great Victorian debates about the effects of industrial capitalism on the quality of human experience. This debate needs no detailed rehearsal here. It is inaugurated at least as early as 1807, and the striking account of industrialized Birmingham in Southey's *Letters from England*. It runs thereafter as a characterizing theme of English literary social criticism, through Carlyle and Arnold, Lawrence and Leavis, and right up to still active and serious debate about the social meaning of literature, and the proper degree of social and political engagement for literary criticism. In the characteristically Victorian inflection which concerns us here, Italian trecento and quattrocento art and architecture are proposed as the historical model most appropriate to stand in opposition to the conditions and effects of labour in the nineteenth-century English experience. Ruskin's *Seven Lamps of Architecture* (1849), and above all 'The Nature of Gothic', published in the second volume of *The Stones of Venice* (1853), offer the key and defining articulations of this deployment of the historical model.

The image typified in Ruskin has two aspects. Trecento and quattrocento art is understood as the production of a civilization where individual labour is expressive and socially integrated.

Furthermore, this artistic achievement is conceived as the product of the triumph of civilization over barbarism; which triumph is represented as having subsequently declined into the decadence of the late sixteenth and seventeenth centuries. Here too was a politically charged image, one that Michelet, for example, could call up to give an historical identity to the progressive forces newly and temporarily defeated in the debacles of 1848 and 1851.

V

This complex and deep-rooted set of contexts operates powerfully in Browning's choice of the two painters which form the subjects of his famous dramatic monologues. The sense of creative vitality which pervades 'Fra Lippo Lippi', contrasted as it so beautifully is with the faded silver-grey tones of Andrea del Sarto's subtle but profound failures, offers an implicit comparative judgement on epochs in the history of Florentine art. But this judgement is also charged with a contemporary resonance which invests art-historical commentary with a social and political dimension. Browning's Lippo Lippi, in an opposition to the technically accomplished but lifeless human case of Andrea del Sarto, stands for an insurgent natural humanism in the face of outmoded constraints on the spirit; but he can stand also for the alienated Victorian poet-intellectual, whose own relation to his immediately preceding literary tradition is thus implicitly sketched in the Renaissance painter's personal dilemma and, indeed, in the aesthetic articulated in the poem.

In each of the paired monologues, the desired woman (or, as it is in Lippi's case, women) is a type of the muse, and presents an understated image of each painter's differently compromised ambitions to realize his talent in achieved great paintings. Thus Lippo's celebratedly enthusiastic promiscuity becomes a kind of historical testimony to his vital engagement with the human sources of his art (this is picked up in Browning's treatment from what was anyway very much Lippi's Victorian image in, for example, Lanzi and Mrs Jameson). His poem is set at the hour before dawn, and in spring, and these *aubade*-like attributes fit well with his historical positioning and significance. His condition embodies a general project to find in human realities the source of transcendent archetypes. The spiritual abstractions of the medieval Christianity which is Lippi's employer must be grounded, for him, in a keen responsiveness to the earthly and to the actualities of colour and outline. These commitments, of course, make for serious contradictions in Lippi's life, and it is part of his energy that he looks to defy these contradictions, at least to a considerable extent. His art is the expression of a humanist spirit struggling free from the historical conditions which have made it possible, and Browning's dramatization is at once an historical analysis and a complex image of his condition as alienated and expatriate Victorian poet. Just as Lippi seeks a resolution of his contradictions in affirming the emphatically human basis of an art serving spiritual ends, so Browning embodies an articulation of his own historical condition in his representation of the Italian painter.

Andrea del Sarto's monologue is autumnal, its hour twilight. In his work, as he understands too well, an arid technical perfection has drained the human reality of its spiritual dimension. Browning works out the theme mainly through the brilliant dramatization of Andrea's cruelly dead marriage, which biographical circumstance was central in the received account of Andrea's life deriving from Vasari. We should recall that the 'actual' substance of the historical del Sarto's life and work, and what the Victorians knew of that and how they interpreted it are not at issue. Indeed, Browning builds what is now agreed to be a serious factual error into 'Fra Lippo Lippi' by representing Masaccio as a pupil of Lippi's. Browning's poems offer an image of their subjects substantially shaped not by the content of the historical source but by the meanings and values discovered in and projected onto the historical image in Browning's contemporary culture. Browning's Andrea is trapped, emotionally and artistically, by an obsessional and almost explicitly self-conscious distorted perception of an illusory perfection of appearance. In the poem this is concentrated in biographical terms on his promiscuous wife, who stands implicitly for the spiritless technical accomplishment of his art, to which the painter is similarly in thrall. This image of Browning's is, within the articulations of our own present-day art-historical understanding, demonstrably false; or to put it another way, it is essentially a function of Browning's Victorian situation. The figure of Lippi, too, is plainly distorted in Browning's representation, relative to our own contemporary understanding. The passage towards the end of 'Fra Lippo Lippi' in which the painter undertakes to produce a picture for the nuns of S. Ambrogio, as an act of penance, is not historically reliable, and Browning is also wrong to discover a self-portrait in the painting by Lippi.[7]

But Browning is not finally concerned to identify himself with Lippi, even if the cultural resonance of the poem depends on a perception of the possibilities for similitude in the cases of the Florentine painter and the Victorian poet. The dramatic nature of the monologue implies a critical distance in Browning's perspective. Lippi images Browning in his naturalistic overgoing of the impulse to a spiritualizing of experience. But Browning's superior artistic freedom, his freer embrace of the natural and the secular, are signalled in the qualifications entered in the poem concerning Lippi's artistic integrity (ultimately compromised by the exigencies of his economic dependency on the Church and by the hypocrisy of his way of life). He backs down in the end from the bold affirmations of his aesthetic, and invites the watch who have apprehended him to excuse his loose tongue because he has been drinking.

Browning's poem is characteristic of its historical moment in using Italian materials as a vehicle for English cultural debate. 'Fra Lippo Lippi' is about an English poet in the mid-nineteenth century, a poet whose own artistic practice, embodied in the rhetoric of the poem itself, can welcome the dawn which Lippi himself, in the end, cannot face:

> Your hand, sir, and good bye: no lights, no lights!
> The street's hushed, and I know my own way back—
> Don't fear me! There's the grey beginning. Zooks! (ll. 390–92)

This dawn defines the limitations of Lippi's own artistic achievement and, contrastively, points up Browning's artistic boldness in distinguishing the confident and forward-looking character of his own role in the development of the English poetic tradition—he is ready for the new day. The poem is undoubtedly a powerful character study, but it also looks beyond that dimension of its achievement to encompass the whole complex and various Victorian rhetoric of the early Renaissance.

NOTES

1. Karl Marx, *The Eighteenth Brumaire of Louis Bonaparte* (1852; 2nd edition 1869), in *Surveys From Exile*, ed. David Fernbach (Harmondsworth: Penguin, 1973), pp. 146–47.
2. To Alfred Domett, 13 July 1842: *The Brownings' Correspondence*, eds Philip Kelley and Ronald Hudson, 13 vols published to date (Winfield, Kansas: Wedgestone Press, 1984–), vi, 33.
3. See Disraeli's *Sybil* (1845).
4. Unsigned article in *Fraser's Magazine*, xlviii (1851), 170–82; quoted in *Browning: The Critical Heritage*, eds Boyd Litzinger and Donald Smalley (London: Routledge, 1970), pp. 147–48.
5. All quotations from Browning's poetry are from *Robert Browning; The Poems*, ed. John Pettigrew, supplemented and completed by Thomas J. Collins, 2 vols (Harmondsworth: Penguin, 1981).
6. Luigi Lanzi, *History of Painting in Italy* (1795), trans. Thomas Roscoe (1828), new revised edition, 3 vols (London: Bohn's Library, 1847), i, 13, 15.
7. The painting is described in 'Fra Lippo Lippi', ll. 357–77; the supposed self-portrait, now known to be a representation of Canon Maringhi, who commissioned the painting in 1441, is described in ll. 359–68.

Thackeray and the 'Old Masters'

LEONÉE ORMOND

Among the great Victorian novelists, Thackeray could probably best be described as a natural connoisseur of the fine arts. George Eliot and Hardy acquired considerable expertise in matters of art, but both set out with a deliberate intention to learn the subject which was very different from Thackeray's comfortable familiarity. This may help to explain why Hardy's novels make more direct reference to painters and their works than do those of Thackeray, although an equally plausible explanation could be found in the later date at which Hardy was writing. After the onset of the Aesthetic movement, reference to the work of the Old Masters, usually for purposes of comparison, became a frequent literary device.

In introducing his knowledge of the fine arts into his novels, Thackeray was conscious that certain painterly techniques could be translated directly into fiction. In Chapter 44 of *The Virginians*, for example, he adapts the tradition of the *conversazione* group portrait to give an ironic prologue to Harry Warrington's first meeting with the Castlewood family after he has lost his money. Life becomes a form of art, says the narrator. If we enter a household during a row, there is time for a rearrangement before the guest reaches the drawing room, and finds everybody there engaged just as they should be, reading, arranging flowers or warmly greeting those whose arrival they have been cursing a few seconds before. For a writer as concerned as Thackeray with the gap between appearance and reality, the ideals of beauty and style which are found in great works of art provided a kind of shorthand for the endless folly which his novels dissect. One art form provides a parallel for another, but a parallel which is neither rigid nor overprecise.

Thackeray was emphatically a pre-Aesthetic writer. Had he lived to see the Aesthetes his satirical response would have been devastating. This is not, however, to label him a 'philistine'. Indeed, his feeling for the eighteenth century played a part in stimulating one of the most important movements in aesthetic taste, the Queen Anne revival.

Thackeray's love of the arts was lifelong. A gift for rapid sketching declared itself in boyhood, and he dreamed of a career as a painter. At eighteen he travelled to Paris and familiarized himself with the collections of the Louvre and the Royal Library. A year later, having left Cambridge without a degree, he spent eight months in Germany, where he may have taken the opportunity to visit the Picture Gallery at Dresden. He returned to Paris in 1832, joined a life school and made a number of copies of Old Master paintings, including two portraits by Titian, a portrait of Charles VII (then attributed to Leonardo) and two Dutch seventeenth-century works, an interior by Pieter de Hooch and *The Concert: Singing and Playing the Lute* by Gerard Terborch. These copies, he told Edward Fitzgerald, were 'all of them very bad'.[1]

Thackeray slowly abandoned his ambition to become a painter, but he continued to draw and to illustrate his own work, keeping his critical eye in by writing reviews of the Royal Academy, various watercolour exhibitions and sometimes of the Paris Salon. Contributions on art and artists appeared in several journals including *Pictorial Times*, *Fraser's Magazine* and *The Morning Chronicle*. He continued to visit Paris regularly for the rest of his life, and other journeys took him to European collections of Old Masters in Germany, Belgium, Holland, Italy and Austria. In 1852, when he was in his forties, he had a moment of regret: 'I have been trudging to pictures all day and am come home quite tired of 'em but still whenever I see them I want to give up everything and shut myself up for 2 years and turn painter. This feeling was uncommonly strong at Munich.'[2] Some of these journeys, but by no means all, are recorded in published essays, others in letters, and his last visit to Italy, made with his daughters in the winter of 1853–54, is best documented in *The Newcomes*.

The Louvre collection in Paris has remained very much as Thackeray saw it, but the National Gallery in London was far smaller than the gallery which we know today. Like the Dulwich Picture Gallery, which had opened to the public ten years earlier in 1814, the National Gallery was strong in seventeenth-century works: by the French landscapists, including Claude Lorrain and Nicolas Poussin, by the Spaniard Bartolomé Murillo and by the Bolognese School (the Carraccis, Domenichino, Guido Reni and Guercino). Another powerful holding in both galleries was in the English eighteenth-century Masters: Thomas Gainsborough, Sir Joshua Reynolds and George Romney. A few Italian Renaissance masterpieces had been acquired for the National Gallery, including Sebastiano del Piombo's *Raising of Lazarus* and Titian's *Bacchus and Ariadne*.

Not surprisingly, the majority of Thackeray's fictional references to the Old Masters come in his *künstlerroman*, *The Newcomes*,[3] which began publication in 1853. With some sense of nostalgia and self-indulgence, Thackeray allowed his own experiences to colour his descriptions of Clive Newcome responding to pictures in the Louvre, the National Gallery and the Vatican picture collection. These passages, written in the form of letters, allowed the novelist to express Clive's personality, with his rapid (and somewhat superficial) enthusiasms. Clive is nearly nineteen when he travels to Paris with his father, recovering from the fatigue of completing a pretentious (and unsuccessful) history painting. He therefore arrives at the Louvre at the same age and at much the same date as Thackeray himself. There is little reason to doubt that this passage is largely autobiographical. Chapter 22 plays a part in the overall narrative of *The Newcomes* through the introduction of Mme de Florac, the former love of Colonel Newcome, but its real function is to allow Thackeray to talk about his early visits to the Louvre, and (incidentally) to the National Gallery.

Clive's first reaction on entering the Louvre is to fall in love with one of the museum's most famous works, the Venus de Milo. Venus temporarily effaces the charms of his 'Diana', Ethel Newcome. A few years before writing *The Newcomes* Thackeray had rated the Venus de Milo 'the grandest figure of figures. The wave of lines of the figure wherever seen fills my senses with pleasure ... I have been sitting thinking of it these 10 minutes in a delightful sensuous rumination'.[4] This was praise indeed, since Thackeray dismissed with scorn the majority of famous classical statues, including the Laocoön and the Dying Gladiator. The 'simpering' Venus de' Medici in Florence, he thought a 'humbug'.[5] 'You tell me that the Venus de' Medici is beautiful … Can't I judge for myself? … She is pretty, but she has no expression.'[6]

Moving to the Louvre's Old Masters, Clive enthuses about the 'portraits of Titian' (two of which Thackeray had himself copied), and the 'swells by Van Dyck … I'm sure he must have been as fine a gentleman as any he painted!' (Ch. 22). The reference to male portraits, like the elegant *Charles I in Hunting Dress* and the double likeness of Rupert of the Rhine and his brother, suggests the thrust of Clive's appreciation. Given the remarks which he has just made about 'snobs' at Boulogne and 'ruffian' revolutionaries, it is not surprising (for all his praise of Carlyle) to find him ranking Van Dyck's gentlemanliness almost as highly as his painting.

Affection, or even patriotism, inspires Clive to tell Arthur Pendennis that, for all the 'half a mile of pictures at the Louvre', 'there are a score under the old pepper-boxes in Trafalgar Square as fine as the best here'. These twenty, to Clive's mind, include Sebastiano's *Raising of Lazarus*, Titian's *Bacchus and Ariadne* and Clive's favourite Raphael, *St Catherine of Alexandria*, purchased in 1839. This was a work whose acquisition in 1839 Thackeray had greeted with enthusiasm, telling his readers to spend half an hour in the National Gallery: 'where, before the "Bacchus and Ariadne", you may see what the magic of colour is; before "Christ and Lazarus" what is majestic, solemn, grace and awful beauty; and before the new "Saint Catherine" what is the real divinity of art'. Modern painters were all 'very nice men; but what are you to the men of old?'[7]

These three paintings remain the acknowledged masterpieces of the National Gallery. As a satirist and iconoclast, Thackeray often made a point of avoiding conventional responses to works of art; but here at least his taste was entirely that of his own time.

Thackeray's enduring liking for Raphael's *Saint Catherine* contrasts sharply with his other early responses to Raphael. For the Victorians, as for the generations before them, Raphael was the greatest of painters, a supreme, and even divinely inspired, master. In the writing of the young Thackeray, disparaging remarks about Raphael reflect a prevailing personal iconoclasm. In a letter to Edward Fitzgerald of 1835, he even announced that he preferred John Flaxman's drawings to Raphael's and commented that the Raphaels in the Louvre 'do not strike me more than they did before'. 'I have seen those rough Lodges of Raphaele, & still do not believe', he told Fitzgerald, impiously employing the Christian symbolism so often associated with Raphael.[8] Fitzgerald replied at length, proclaiming his own belief in Raphael's supremacy.

One of the most popular Raphaels in the Louvre was a work painted in 1507 when Raphael was twenty-four, the age at which Thackeray wrote in such disparaging terms to Fitzgerald. This was the *Virgin, Child and St John*, known as *La Belle Jardinière*, an ingenious and tender synthesis of a mother with two children (fig. 1). It struck no sympathetic note in Thackeray, however, and he declared war on the whole genus in an article on 'The French School of Painting' of 1839: 'I hate those simpering Madonnas. I declare that the "Jardinière" is a puking smirking miss, with nothing heavenly about her.'[9]

Thackeray's response to *La Belle Jardinière* is particularly revealing in a novelist so often attacked for endorsing a sentimental image of an adoring mother, most notably with Amelia Sedley in *Vanity Fair*. His approach to the Raphael work, admittedly that of a young man, tends to suggest the opposite, that Thackeray, in his late twenties at least, was hostile to what he saw as sentimental motherhood.

Another remark in the 'French School of Painting' was aimed at the later Raphael, not the painter of *La Belle Jardinière* but the lacklustre *Saint Elizabeth*, which is also in the Louvre. Four years before the formation of the Pre-Raphaelite Brotherhood, whose credo reflected disillusionment with Raphael's late works and those of his followers, Thackeray was declaring: 'I say, that when Raphael painted this picture [*Saint Elizabeth* in the Louvre] two years before his death, the spirit of painting had gone from out of him; he was no longer inspired; *it was time that he should die*!!'[10]

The same point was made in *Of Men and Pictures* of 1841, with Thackeray telling his readers that he had been 'severely reprehended' for saying that 'Raphael at thirty had lost that delightful innocence and purity which rendered the works of Raphael of twenty so divine.'[11] Thackeray was himself thirty, and the joke would not have been lost on him. He goes on, however, to remark that it was 'the very quaintnesses and imperfections of manner observable in his [Raphael's] early works' which made them 'so singularly pleasing to me'.[12] At a time when Thackeray was scornfully condemning what he called the Catholic (largely German Nazarene) art of the nineteenth century, which was much influenced by these qualities in Raphael's early style, this is a little puzzling. Clearly, however, Thackeray himself saw no contradiction.

Thackeray's penchant for dethroning the icons of taste, and the later works of Raphael in particular, is once more in the ascendant in Chapter 35 of *The Newcomes*. It is when Clive Newcome reaches Rome that he begins to 'utter heresies', as Thackeray himself had probably done when he first visited the city in 1844. After telling his correspondent of his difficulties with Roman Catholic ceremonies, Clive turns to one of the most widely acknowledged masterpieces, Raphael's last work, *The Transfiguration*, in the Vatican Gallery (fig. 2). Here Christ rises in bright light, with Moses and Elias beside him, while some of the disciples begin to awake and others, gesticulating dramatically, gaze upwards. To the right are the family and friends of an epileptic child. Without the presence of Christ, his followers have been unable to heal him. Clive considers that the 'scream of that devil-possessed boy' with his violently raised arm 'jars the whole music of the composition'. Such 'grotesque and terrible' actions do not, he believes, belong in a painting by Raphael.

Although Clive praises Raphael's 'loving spirit' and 'noble mind', he dislikes large Raphael paintings like *The Transfiguration* and what he calls the 'set harangues' (Ch. 35), presumably the frescoes in the Vatican Stanzi like *The School of Athens* and *The Disputation on the Sacrament*. Clive favours the painter of women and children, Browning's 'Rafael of the dear Madonnas',[13] or the Raphael of those small fragments which Clive prefers to 'large and pretentious' gallery pieces: '[you] come upon a gray paper, or a little fresco, bearing his mark—and over all the brawl and the throng you recognize his sweet presence' (Ch. 35).

In 1840, more than a decade before he wrote *The Newcomes*, Thackeray had seen an exhibition of Raphael's drawings which profoundly impressed him, and it is probably this experience which conditioned Clive's comment about works on 'gray paper':

> These were little faint scraps, mostly from the artist's pencil—small groups, unfinished single figures, just indicated; but the divine elements of beauty were as strong in them as in the grandest pieces: and there were many little sketches, not half an inch high, which charmed and affected one like the violet did Wordsworth; and left one in that unspeakable, complacent, grateful condition, which, as I have been endeavouring to state, is the highest aim of the art.[14]

The reference to Wordsworth is telling, recalling the Romantic preference for the inspired fragment over the more laboured finished work, a preference for small works being a marked characteristic of Thackeray's own judgements as an art critic: 'A man's sketches and his pictures should never be exhibited together; the sketches invariably kill the pictures; are far more vigorous, masterly, and effective.'[15]

Like Dickens, Thackeray believed that a painting, and particularly one with a religious subject, should speak to the spectator simply and directly. Looking at a *Crucifixion* by the French eighteenth-century painter Eustace Le Sueur in Paris in 1840, Thackeray found it badly coloured but 'earnest, tender, simple, holy ... There is more beauty, and less affectation, about this picture than you will find in the performance of many Italian masters, with high-sounding names (out with it, and say RAPHAEL at once)'.[16] The pursuit of simplicity made some artists problematic for Thackeray, including not only Raphael, but, even more strikingly, Rubens. Thackeray was deeply impressed by Rubens's technique, but disturbed by the fleshy qualities of his painting: 'I would as soon ask Alexandre Dumas for a sermon,' he said in 1860.[17] Both Raphael and Rubens were, Thackeray felt, often too painterly to express heartfelt emotion.

An excess of emotion presented Thackeray with another problem. In Chapter 35 of *The Newcomes*, Clive contemplates Michelangelo's *Last Judgement* in the Sistine Chapel:

> Michael Angelo's great wall ... What an awful achievement! Fancy the state of mind of the man who worked it—as alone, day after day, he devised and drew those dreadful figures! Suppose in the days of the Olympian dynasty, the subdued Titan rebels had been set to ornament a palace for Jove, they would have brought in some such tremendous work: or suppose Michael descended to the Shades, and brought up this picture out of the halls of Limbo. I like a thousand and a thousand times better to think of Raphael's loving spirit. As he looked at women and children, his beautiful face must have shone like sunshine; his kind hand must have caressed the sweet figures as he formed them. If I protest against the 'Transfiguration', and refuse to worship at that altar before which so many generations have knelt, there are hundreds of others at which I salute thankfully.
>
> (Ch. 35)

What Clive says here probably reflects the novelist's own view. Thackeray, like many tourists of his time, had seen a copy of *The Last Judgement* before going to Rome. His admiration for Michelangelo's statues, especially *Moses*, was unbounded, but he felt *The Last Judgement* to be shocking, 'astonishing'. Examining 'even a single figure of it' produced a sensation amounting 'almost to pain'.[18] However, when asked for his 'top ten' paintings by an American journalist in 1852, Thackeray included *The Last Judgement* among them, not, presumably, because it gave him pleasure, but because of the sublimity of the pain which it stimulated. Thackeray frequently applies the word 'sublime' to Michelangelo's works, and for him, as for Edmund Burke, the sublime included feelings which were deeply disturbing as well as pleasurable. Clive is not a 'Michael Angelo or a Beethoven' (Ch. 39) and Thackeray evidently felt him to be a dangerous model for a nineteenth-century artist. Elsewhere he notes that, for children, or a poor man (and perhaps for the majority of his readers), simple pleasures, something 'less vast' than the sublimities of Michelangelo, are the best recipe.[19] Thackeray's own pseudonym, 'Michaelangelo Titmarsh', represents an intention to deflate his own credentials in the face of an overwhelming, but totally undomestic, genius.

Clive's response to the darkness and gloom of Michelangelo's *Last Judgement* was not an unusual one. Dickens, who first saw it in 1845, a year after Thackeray, was unable to 'discern ... any general idea, or one pervading thought, in harmony with the stupendous subject'.[20] Dickens, unlike Clive Newcome, warmly praises *The Transfiguration* as 'Raphael's Masterpiece', although it is perhaps significant that even Thackeray placed it in his 'top ten' list. What is striking about Clive's/Thackeray's extended commentary on the rival claims of Raphael and Michelangelo is the expression of dislike for discordant, 'grotesque' and 'terrible' elements like the raised arm of the boy in Raphael's painting.

Earlier in *The Newcomes* a similar anxiety is expressed about the red coat of the horseman in *Departure for a Ride*, a painting in the Louvre by the seventeenth-century Dutch painter Aelbrecht Cuyp. This patch of red in an otherwise quiet landscape worries 'the well-known portrait painter, Alfred Smee, Esq., R.A.' for whom 'the red was a positive blot upon the whole picture' (Ch. 17). Smee is not a character whose views we can take entirely seriously. He makes these remarks while saying that the small area of red ribbon on Colonel Newcome's coat gives him a rare opportunity 'just to warm up' the intended portrait. This is all part of a bid to get the Colonel to sit to him. Smee's hypocrisy in complaining about the dangers of painting red is revealed when Sir Brian Newcome sits to him: 'in a flaring deputy-lieutenant's uniform' and Smee goes on to entreat 'all military men whom he met to sit to him in scarlet'. What *is* clear is that Thackeray had looked hard at the Cuyp painting, and had probably himself argued out the case for and against the red coat, a case which could be applied to literature as much as to the fine arts. How far does a startling element complete or jar a composition? Cuyp was very popular with the early Victorians and Thackeray himself often refers to him as a standard of excellence when judging contemporary landscape painting. Probably Thackeray approved the red coat, but one cannot be sure.

Thackeray's treatment of female characters is one of the most hotly debated issues in criticism of his fiction, many critics having detected an essential ambiguity here. Thackeray's remarks about paintings and statues which represent women, even allowing for the different times at which they were written and the varying audiences he was addressing in letters, articles and novels, betray some of his most inconsistent and revealing attitudes towards art. 'Simpering' and 'sweet' are key words in his repertoire. To be sweet is to approximate to an ideal, but painted or sculpted women who simper have been created synthetically, without true emotion.

A striking example of Thackeray's strategy of using his art and historical interests to underline his concern with the position of women comes in Chapters 28 to 30 of *The Newcomes*, a part of the novel which is mockingly described as the 'Congress of Baden'. In Hogarthian style, Thackeray describes the life of the town of Baden Baden, part spa, part fashionable resort.

Clive Newcome and his fellow painter J. J. Ridley, arrive in Baden on their journey to Rome. J. J., characteristically, settles into painting a 'little village maiden of seven years old', a work later bought by a bishop from the next year's Royal Academy exhibition (Ch. 30). Clive meanwhile joins the social throng, although without overwhelming enthusiasm. Thackeray's attention is directed to the theme of the marriage market which is to offer up Lady Clara Pulleyn to Barnes Newcome and (so it appears) Ethel Newcome (for whom Clive cherishes an immature love) to Lord Kew. The narrator asks the reader:

> Have you taken your children to the National Gallery in London, and shown them the 'Marriage a la Mode' [by Hogarth]? Was the artist exceeding the privilege of his calling in painting the catastrophe in which those guilty people all suffer? (Ch. 31)

Ethel Newcome becomes the pivotal figure in this account of corruption. We know that Lady Clara, whose parents need to sell her to the highest bidder, will collapse under pressure, but what will become of Ethel? The situation is presented in pictorial terms, through the eyes of three interested parties, Clive, J. J. and Ethel herself. For Clive, seeing Ethel with Lord Kew among the Baden crowds, the pictorial image comes, not from Hogarth, but from classical legend. He perceives the women as 'heroines' of 'discreditable' stories, Calypso with Ulysses, Ariadne with Theseus and Bacchus, Medea with Jason and Creusa. (Thackeray's intense dislike of French neoclassical painting may well play a part in his choice of comparison here.) By contrast, J. J. parallels Ethel to an English heroine, 'the Lady amid the rout of Comus' (Ch. 31).

Thackeray skilfully translates his experiences as a reviewer at the Old Watercolour Society exhibitions into a flashback scene between Ethel and her grandmother, the dowager Lady Kew. Ethel has a view of herself which is entirely modern when the two women stop before a painting by William Henry Hunt, an artist whom Thackeray admired, and to whom he always dedicated a section of his annual review. The subject is 'a friendless young girl cowering in a doorway, evidently without home or shelter' (Ch. 28). Ethel reacts scornfully to the contrast between her formidable grandmother, who is pushing her into a loveless match, and the pathetic subject of the Hunt watercolour. In real life, Lady Kew, with her rigid ideas of caste, would have had no sympathy at all, but, through the medium of art, such an 'excellent judge' can enjoy the excellence of the 'pathetic', the 'plaintive beauty' of the child in the watercolour.

The 'friendless young girl' has been sold, as J. J.'s 'strawberry girl' will be, and Ethel is intelligent enough to perceive the parallel:

> we young ladies in the world, when we are exhibiting, ought to have little green tickets pinned on our backs, with 'Sold' written on them; it would prevent trouble and any future haggling, you know. Then, at the end of the season, the owner would come to carry us home. (Ch. 28)

She even steals a green 'sold' ticket, and mocks her grandmother by wearing it on her 'white muslin frock' that evening. On the surface, Ethel could hardly be less like a 'friendless young girl', but, as an unmarried woman, Ethel, for all her character and spirit, counts for little more than the feeble Lady Clara.

From his account of men who regard women as commodities to be bought, Thackeray largely excepts his hero, Clive. Even Clive's innocence is, however, under strain. At the end of Chapter 29, he witnesses the despair of Jack Belsize at his enforced separation from Lady Clara: 'a sure presentiment told him [Clive] that his own happy holiday was to come to an end' (Ch. 30). Clive decides to leave Baden at once, recognizing that he, like Jack Belsize, will not be found acceptable as a husband. Thackeray chooses to represent the idealism of Clive's feeling for Ethel through a series of comparisons to four famous statues and old master paintings, drawn from a number of European collections, and all of them favourites of Thackeray himself. Each work is carefully selected to reflect on an aspect of Clive's response to Ethel, with 'her form, her glorious colour of rich carnation and dazzling white, her queenly grace when quiescent and in motion' (Ch. 30).

> As he looked at a great picture or statue, as the 'Venus' of Milo, calm and deep, unfathomably beautiful as the sea from which she sprung; as he looked at the rushing 'Aurora' of the Rospigliosi, or the 'Assumption' of Titian, more bright and glorious than sunshine, or that divine 'Madonna and Divine Infant' of Dresden, whose sweet faces must have shone upon Raphael out of Heaven: Clive's heart sang hymns as it were, before these gracious altars; and somewhat as he worshipped these masterpieces of his art, he admired the beauty of Ethel. (Ch. 30)

None of these images is even remotely 'sweet' or 'simpering', but Clive is nevertheless idealizing Ethel here. Earlier in the novel he knew that the sensuous Venus de Milo did not supply an accurate metaphor for their relationship, but here he even associates Ethel with the inspired and celestial madonnas from Titian's *Assumption of the Virgin* in Venice or Raphael's *Sistine Madonna* in Dresden. Clive's other parallel, with the 'rushing "Aurora"' of Guido Reni, is closer to his experience of Ethel. Aurora sits in her chariot, queenly and determined, surrounded by suppliants and controlling fiery horses with one hand. This painting, in the Casino of the Palazzo Rospigliosi (now Pallavicini-Rospigliosi), was one of the leading tourist sights of nineteenth-century Rome (fig. 3). Aurora was also one of the few iconic works of the time to project a strong female image. Privately, Thackeray rejected another, the *Cumaean Sibyl* by Domenichino, as 'a great clumsy woman affected ogling, and in a great turban'.[21] He was probably reflecting changing tastes (the declining reputation of the Bolognese painters) but this was possibly a straightforward reaction to a female face which, not being sweet, had little appeal.

Two of the three paintings to which Clive compares Ethel, the Titian *Assumption* and the *Sistine Madonna*, were listed in Thackeray's 'top ten', together with two other images of transcendent womanhood, Murillo's *Immaculate Conception* (the Soult version then in the Louvre and now in the Prado, Madrid), and the so-called *Notte* by Correggio, *The Adoration of the Shepherds* in Dresden. These four religious works would have fallen within a category defined by the Victorians as 'High Art', the expression used for certain Old Masters and (less frequently) for modern painters whose noble subjects and elevated style rendered them wholly admirable. This was a concept of which Thackeray, always on the lookout for pretension, was very wary. He wrote humorously of the need for the second-rate which mere 'earthy' mortals feel when faced with the sublime but unattainable qualities of a Raphael or a Milton,[22] summing up his objection to sublimity with characteristic irreverence: 'I say that Shakespeare or Raphael never invented anything that on a hot day at half-past five o' clock is equal to Ay and oysters.'[23] Similar provisos appear throughout his art criticism, as if by poking fun at famous works of art he could avoid becoming sententious. Though he might mask it in this way, his natural response to such works was often one of keen aesthetic pleasure. As he grew older, Thackeray increasingly employed Raphael's name as one synonymous with greatness, but he never entirely gave up lampooning the painter and his followers for the 'simpering beauties of some of the Virgins of the Raphael school'.[24]

Thackeray himself was only too familiar with the assumed

distinction between 'high' and 'low' art since reviews of his own novels frequently revolved around this very issue. Thackeray was associated with realism and frequently compared to Dutch painters like Teniers or Adriaen Ostade or, even more frequently, to William Hogarth. When, comparatively late in life, Thackeray lectured on Hogarth, he recognized the often repeated parallel between his own work and that of the eighteenth-century painter. Appropriately, Thackeray begins by approaching Hogarth as a fellow creator of narrative, commenting, as he often did, that Hogarth's storytelling techniques are simple and moralistic, lacking the sophistication necessary for a novel. Much as he may have admired Hogarth's qualities as an artist, he was anxious to distance himself as a storyteller. In his account of *Marriage à la Mode*, Thackeray dwells with most pleasure on Hogarth's telling use of detail, and the way in which, within a static format, characters reveal themselves. The Earl 'sits in gold lace and velvet ... His coronet is everywhere: on his footstool, on which reposes one gouty toe turned out; on the sconces and looking-glasses; on the dogs; on his lordship's very crutches; on his great chair of state and the great baldaquin behind him'. In the meantime his son 'is admiring his countenance in the glass, while his bride is twiddling her marriage ring on her pocket-handkerchief'.[25]

An obvious delight in the application of such realistic and human touches is also clear in Thackeray's account of the Dutch seventeenth-century paintings which he saw in the Rijksmuseum in Amsterdam and the Mauritshuis in The Hague during a holiday with his daughters in 1860. He had been in Belgium in 1840 and 1843 and the two articles which he wrote about these journeys, 'Little Travels and Road-Side Sketches' of 1843 and 'A Roundabout Journey: Notes of a Week's Holiday' of 1860 include some of the most extended criticism of Old Master paintings which Thackeray ever wrote, although, surprisingly perhaps, almost none of this material appeared in his fiction.

In the Mauritshuis, Thackeray saw a painting which he placed on his 'top ten' list of 1852, Rembrandt's *Anatomy Lesson*. Eight years later, when listing only four favourite works to carry off like Napoleon, Thackeray again included the Rembrandt (together with another work from the same gallery, Paul Potter's

Young Bull). In the Rembrandt, 'Some of the heads are as sweetly and lightly painted as Gainsborough … not plastered, but painted with a free, liquid brush.'[26] He spent longer, however, looking at a painting by an artist whom he acknowledged as inferior to Rembrandt, *The Banquet of the Civil Guard* by Bartholemew van der Helst in the Rijksmuseum, which was, for Thackeray, 'one of the great pictures of the world'[27] (fig. 4). This large, and emphatically masculine, group portrait shows the civic Guard at a sumptuous banquet, dressed in their full regalia. For an account of it Thackeray facetiously quotes the long statement in the Rijksmuseum catalogue, but then goes on to record some of his personal observations, noting that the sitters are individually characterized and that hands are as well painted as faces:

> None of your slim Vandyck elegancies, which have done duty at the cuffs of so many doublets; but each man with a hand for himself, as with a face for himself. I blushed for the coarseness of one of the chiefs of his great company, that fellow behind WILLIAM THE DRUMMER, splendidly attired, sitting full in the face of the public; and holding a pork-bone in his hand. Suppose the *Saturday Review* critic were to come suddenly on this picture! Ah! what a shock it would give that noble nature! Why is that knuckle of pork not painted out? at any rate, why is not a little fringe of lace painted round it? or a cut pink paper? or couldn't a smelling-bottle be painted in instead, with a crest and a gold top, or a cambric pocket-handkerchief, in lieu of the horrid pig, with a pink coronet in the corner? or suppose you covered the man's hand (which is very coarse and strong), and gave him the decency of a kid glove? But a piece of pork in a naked hand? O nerves and eau de Cologne, hide it, hide it![28]

This is 'low art' indeed and Thackeray's remarks about simple realism, represented here by the unconcealed pork-bone, suggest a wider interpretation of the painting, one which emerges more directly in the following paragraph when Thackeray pays tribute to the self-portrait of Jan Steen: 'He is a glorious composer. His humour is as frank as Fielding's … I think the composition in some of Jan's pictures amounts to the sublime, and look at them with the same delight and admiration which I have felt before works of the very highest style.'[29] A good many scenes of Dutch seventeenth-century life, including those of Steen, would (like the novels of Fielding) have offended Victorian proprieties. By calling them 'sublime', Thackeray is challenging the distinction between high and low art. At his best, the compositions of Steen seem to Thackeray to be of the 'very highest style'. This is a point which Thackeray had made twenty years before when, coupling Hogarth and Fielding, he suggested a parallel between the 'coarse pictures' of both men:

> The world does not tolerate now such satire as that of Hogarth and Fielding, and the world no doubt is right in a great part of its squeamishness; for it is good to pretend to the virtue of chastity even though we do not possess it ... Fielding's men and Hogarth's are Dickens' and Cruikshank's, drawn with ten times more skill and force, only the latter humourists dare not talk of what the elder discussed honestly.[30]

Thackeray's own position on this issue is by no means unclouded. Judith Fisher argues that his upbringing made him particularly squeamish about explicit sexuality and that he slides round, mindful of his audience's lack of sophistication.[31] Whatever the truth of this, it was not open to Thackeray to indulge in the 'coarse' satire of Hogarth or Jan Steen in his published work, although in private male company (around the *Punch* table, for example) he felt free to do so. He chose instead to press insistently upon the ever-present gap between pretension and actual practice and behaviour. A rumbustious opportunity to refer to painters and paintings comes through his satire of upper-class hypocrisy. He found a perfect vehicle for such satire in a series of mocking descriptions of family portrait galleries.

In his novels, Thackeray points up the contrast between the painted image and the truth by reference to such well-known portraitists as Van Dyck, Thomas Hudson, Sir Peter Lely, Sir Joshua Reynolds and Sir Thomas Lawrence. In *The Newcomes* the monotony of a country house collection is summed up in a single

Fig. 1: Raphael, *La Belle Jardinière* from a print of 1809.

Fig. 2: Raphael, *The Transfiguration* from a print of 1815.

Fig. 3: Guido Reni, *Aurora* from a print of 1785.

Fig. 4: Bartholemew van der Helst, *The Banquet of the Civil Guard* from a print of 1648.

sentence. Following on from a description of the staterooms and the furnishings comes 'the admirable likeness of the late Marquis by Sir Thomas; of his father by Sir Joshua, and so on' (Ch. 11). Thackeray uses this device in *Vanity Fair*, deepening it through the cruel contrast between posed youth and decrepit age:

> Bareacres Castle was theirs, too, with all its costly pictures, furniture, and articles of vertu—the magnificent Vandykes; the noble Reynolds pictures; the Lawrence portraits, tawdry and beautiful, and, thirty years ago, deemed as precious as works of real genius; the matchless Dancing Nymph of Canova, for which Lady Bareacres had sate in her youth—Lady Bareacres splendid then, and radiant in wealth, rank, and beauty—a toothless, bald, old woman now—a mere rag of a former robe of state. Her lord, painted at the same time by Lawrence, as waving his sabre in front of Bareacres Castle, and clothed in his uniform as Colonel of the Thistlewood Yeomanry, was a withered, old, lean man in a greatcoat and a Brutus wig. (Ch. 49)

Thackeray's feeling for the eighteenth century, an unfashionable era in his day, gave him a natural interest in the art of the period. From the portraits of Sir Joshua Reynolds, as Thackeray gratefully acknowledged in his 'George III' lecture, the women and men of the age still looked out at him. Barry Lyndon, his wife and son Bryan are painted by Reynolds in the guise of Hector parting from Andromache and Astyanax. The parallel has a touch of the absurd, but the implications turn out to be more profound. Bryan, like Astyanax, is to die young, to be thrown from his horse where Astyanax is thrown down from the walls of Troy. Reynolds frequently posed his sitters in classical or allegorical roles, but the fall of Troy would have been far too dark a theme for an eighteenth-century family portrait. Thackeray does more here than attempt historical accuracy through a precise use of detail.

Thackeray is not alone in invoking the elegance of the Georgian world by reference to Reynolds, but he is unusual in alluding to the French artists of the period. They were generally in low repute because of their immoral subject matter and their association with a corrupt court heading towards revolution. Thackeray would have known of the great collection of rococo paintings gathered together by Frederick the Great. Barry Lyndon is simply following the example of his former master by hanging paintings by François Boucher and Carle van Loo in the principal bedrooms of Hackton Castle:

> in which the Cupids and Venuses were painted in a manner so natural that I recollect the old wizened Countess of Frumpington pinning over the curtains of her bed, and sending her daughter, Lady Blanche Whalebone, to sleep with her waiting-woman, rather than allow her to lie in a chamber hung all over with looking-glasses, after the exact fashion of the Queen's closet at Versailles. (Ch. 17)

Thackeray gives this reference a further twist. It was not the Countess of Frumpington who affected prudery, but the women of Thackeray's own day. Of Thackeray's contemporaries, only Disraeli (whom he savagely attacked in *Codlingsby*) was worldly enough to introduce the rococo into his novels without prudish comment. It was only after Thackeray had died that Walter Pater, among others, rediscovered Antoine Watteau and rescued his reputation.

It could be argued that Barry Lyndon, an eighteenth-century adventurer, is simply following the fashion of a dissolute age by buying van Loo and Boucher, but this is not how the passage is meant to be read. Thackeray was genuinely in advance of his own time. In 'On the French School of Painting', published in 1839, five years before *Barry Lyndon*, Thackeray writes with delight of Watteau's *Embarkation for Cytherea* in the Louvre: 'a rare piece of fantastical brightness and gaiety'.[32] It is as though Thackeray were trying to convince himself that he should not approve of the painting as he writes of the dandies 'ever smirking' and standing in attitudes, the women with their fans, and the cupids, 'bubbling up in clusters as out of a champagne-bottle, and melting away in air. There is, to be sure, a hidden analogy between liquors and pictures: the eye is deliciously tickled by these frisky Watteaus, and yields itself up to a light, smiling, gentleman-like intoxication'.[33]

In spite of himself, Thackeray never succeeded in condemning Watteau or the other masters of the rococo style. His own collection at Palace Green included a portrait by van Loo, a scene with cupids sporting by Boucher and a *Concert Champêtre* by Watteau. As a true connoisseur, Thackeray condemned pastiches of Boucher and Watteau, like those in Rosey Newcome's parlour with its 'frightful Boucher and Lancret shepherdesses' leering over the portières (Ch. 63), but there can be little doubt of his admiration for the real thing.

In all his writing about the Old Masters, whether in fiction or nonfiction, Thackeray pays little attention to the painterly qualities of their work. The sensuality of a painter like Rubens seems almost too much for him, and he resists his seductive qualities. Nevertheless, his approach to paintings was not restricted to consideration of their subject matter and morality. Even though he sometimes fought against it, his aesthetic response to works of art was very alert and immediate. Nothing illustrates the difficulty of establishing a set of standpoints for Thackeray's view of the Old Masters more clearly than his approach to the rococo. The ideas which he presented to his middle-class readers were not synonymous with his own, for he could not resist drawing parallels with intoxication and surrender when discussing the pictures of Watteau. Here was a man for whom fine paintings, like fine wines, were dangerous but ultimately too entrancing to resist.

NOTES

Unless otherwise stated, references to Thackeray's nonfictional writings are to the Biographical Edition (London: Smith, Elder, & Co., 1898–99).

1. *Letters and Private Papers of W. M. Thackeray*, ed. G. N. Ray (London: OUP, 1945–46), I, 276.
2. *Letters*, III, 60.
3. *The Newcomes*, World Classics (Oxford: OUP, 1995). All subsequent chapter references are to this edition and included in the text of the essay.

4. *Letters*, II, 503–04.
5. V, 45; II, 187.
6. XII, 397.
7. XIII, 280.
8. *Letters*, I, 288 and 286.
9. V, 57.
10. V, 57.
11. XIII, 370.
12. XIII, 370–71.
13. See Browning, 'One Word More', in *Men and Women and Other Poems* (London: Dent, 1993).
14. *Letters*, XIII, 328.
15. XIII, 355.
16. V, 56–7.
17. 'A Roundabout Journey', *Cornhill*, II (1860), 628.
18. *Letters*, V, 46.
19. Thackeray, *Stray Papers*, ed. L. Melville (London: Hutchinson, 1901), p. 211.
20. *Pictures from Italy*, ed. D. Paroissien (London: Deutsch, 1973), p. 195.
21. *Letters*, III, 340.
22, V, 56.
23. *Stray Papers*, p. 178.
24. *Letters*, XIII, 355.
25. VII, 559–60.
26. 'A Roundabout Journey', p. 637.
27. 'A Roundabout Journey', p. 637.
28. 'A Roundabout Journey', pp. 638–39.
29. 'A Roundabout Journey', p. 639.
30. *Stray Papers*, pp. 104–5.
31. Judith L. Fisher, 'Thackeray and the Visual Arts', *Victorian Studies*, XXVI (1982), 65–82.
32. *Letters*, V, 55.
33. V, 55.

William Morris and Translations of Iceland

ANDREW WAWN

On 7 September 1871, a middle-aged Englishman stood on the railway station in Edinburgh. He was short, fat, red-faced, bull-necked, bush-bearded and 'quite bewildered'.[1] He had been away from Britain for the whole summer; everything now looked very strange and he hardly knew where to buy a ticket for. He had been to Iceland and enjoyed it. The last words of his journal account of that visit leave us in no doubt about this: 'Iceland is a marvellous, beautiful and solemn place ... where I had been in fact very happy.' He was still happy enough when he arrived home to write out two short poems about Iceland which he had newly composed. He sent copies[2] to Jón Sigurðsson, one of the two Icelanders who had stood with him on the railway station, having sailed with him all the way from Iceland. Jón had long been a major philological figure amongst the Copenhagen-based Icelanders; and by this time he was known as *forseti* (president) as a mark of his hugely influential role over three decades as a parliamentarian, diplomat and lobbyist, as Iceland inched towards a restoration of the national independence which it had surrendered to the Norwegian king in the middle of the thirteenth century.[3] The idea was for Jón to have the poems translated into Icelandic and published in *Ný Félagsrit*, the Icelandic literary journal of which he was editor.

Jón received and read both poems, and then wrote to Eiríkur Magnússon, the other Icelander who had been with the portly Englishman in Edinburgh—and Iceland. Jón told Eiríkur that he did not much like the poems: the poet 'regards our mother Iceland as rather pale and haggard, dismal and sad'.[4] He would have much preferred heroic songs celebrating Iceland's saga-age glories, rather than gloomy lyrics by brooding Englishmen. Out of courtesy he chose to have just one of the poems translated, by Steingrímur Thorsteinsson, a major late nineteenth-century Icelandic poet also based in Copenhagen. This one poem was selected because it seemed marginally less lugubrious than the other, which was unceremoniously rejected.[5]

The bulky and bearded English poet was, of course, William Morris and the two poems which he sent to Jón Sigurðsson were eventually published in England twenty years later—one was called 'Iceland First Seen' and the other 'Gunnar's Howe above the House at Lithend'.[6] 'Í landsýn við Ísland' was duly published in *Ný Félagsrit* in 1872,[7] long before British readers set eyes on the English version, in Morris's 1891 collection *Poems by the Way*;[8] but Icelandic readers never saw a translation of the allegedly pallid 'Gunnar's Howe'—that was the one which 'we won't bother with'.

'Gunnar's Howe' has bothered few Morris scholars since its first publication,[9] despite the subtle evidence it offers of the celebrated Victorian saga translator's imaginative engagement with medieval Iceland in general, and the epic *Brennu-Njáls saga* in particular. This essay seeks to examine not only 'Gunnar's Howe', but also a forgotten tribute to Morris written at the time of his death by a leading late nineteenth-century Icelandic poet. I want to suggest that Jón Sigurðsson may have misjudged Morris's poem; far from being a melancholy response to Iceland, 'Gunnar's Howe' can be seen (for all its surface greyness) as a glowing tribute to the land of lava and lyme grass. Iceland had made William Morris 'very happy' at a time when the relationship between his wife Janey and Dante Gabriel Rossetti at Kelmscott Manor[10] continued to offer him every reason to be gloomy, and this happiness shines through the poem. I then wish to comment on Matthías Jochumsson's poetic obituary of Morris. Though written in 1896, 'Vilhjálmur Morris' was not published until 1923; it has, to the best of my knowledge, never been commented on by Morris scholars. The poem voices Icelandic pride at the attention devoted to its medieval literary culture by one of Victorian Britain's greatest Icelandophiles. During his life,

Morris was a tireless translator of and enthusiast for Icelandic sagas and Eddic myth and legend;[11] in death he finds himself translated and mythologized, paraded and celebrated in Matthías's poem alongside the great figures of Edda and saga whom he did so much to promote within the English-speaking world, and with whose turbulent lives he so closely identified. Taken together, then, 'Gunnar's Howe' and 'Vilhjálmur Morris' allow us to reflect on what might be termed Morris's translation of Iceland, and Iceland's translation of Morris.

William Morris's priority when he arrived in Iceland was to visit the southern sagasteads associated with the greatest of all the Icelandic family sagas, *Brennu-Njáls saga*, or 'The Story of Burnt Njal', as it was known to Victorian readers of Sir George Dasent's pioneering and field-commanding 1861 English translation. Morris viewed the prospect with a pilgrim's excitement, and by his subsequent writings he signalled arrestingly that *Brennu-Njáls saga*, sites such as Gunnarshaugr (Gunnar's Howe), and Icelandic culture in general were worthy objects of serious philosophical reflection and artistic creativity for literate and sentient Victorians. His knowledge of *Brennu-Njáls saga*, derived as much from the Icelandic original as from Dasent's *Burnt Njal*, enabled him to animate every desolate location he visited; and led him to demand this same visionary capacity in others. Whilst still on the outward voyage, peering impatiently through the mist, Morris relates every feature of the emerging Icelandic coastline to the saga: he glimpses Svínafell 'under which Flosi the Burner lived', whilst the Vestmannaeyjar lie 'just opposite to Njal's house at Bergthorsknoll'.[12] Journeying on horseback to the actual sites, everyone 'at the height of ... excitement',[13] it does not take long for Morris's teeming imagination to translate a mound by the house at Bergþórshváll into the site of Njáll's house;[14] the next day (21 July) he finds the hollow where Flosi and the hundred burners hid before the final attack on Njáll and his family (there was now room for only a dozen men, notes Morris,[15] but is assured by the local farmer that the river has eroded the space once available for the other seven dozen); the pond where Kári doused his burning clothes proves to be little more than a patch of marshy ground overgrown with rushes, but there were signs that a brook had once flowed from there; more excitingly, the farmer tells the travellers that he had come across a bed of ashes when digging the foundations of a new parlour. Moving inland, Morris reaches Gunnar's homestead at Hlíðarendi[16]—the Lithe, as he, like Dasent, calls it. Time and (quite literally) tide have 'sadly wasted and diminished' meadows which had once been 'Gunnar's great wealth';[17] but Morris is still able to observe the traditional site of Gunnar's hall, the hollow where Sámr the hound howled his last loyal message of warning, and 'Gunnar's Howe' itself, the subject of his poem.

The saga events which underpin the poem are simple enough: Gunnar Hámundarson, the great but luckless farmer-chieftain, is murdered by vengeful foes who surround his farmhouse at the end of a long narrative sequence spanning the first half of the saga, during which he and his friend Njáll Þorgeirsson find it ever harder to contain the social disruptions generated by a witches' brew of rank misfortune, motiveless malignity, and interfamilial strife. Gunnar defends himself heroically before dying in front of his hard-hearted wife and loyal mother; he is buried in a cairn on the hillside. There are soon tales that the dead Gunnar can be heard singing cheerfully in his grave. We can follow the moment in Dasent's translation:

> Now this token happened at Lithend, that the neat-herd and the serving-maid were driving cattle by Gunnar's cairn. They thought that he was merry, and that he was singing inside the cairn. They went home and told Rannveig, Gunnar's mother, of this token ... Now those two, Skarphedinn and Hogni, were out of doors one evening by Gunnar's cairn on the south side. The moon and stars were shining clear and bright, but every now and then the clouds drove over them. Then all at once they thought they saw the cairn standing open, and lo! Gunnar had turned himself in the cairn and looked at the moon. They thought they saw four lights burning in the cairn, and none of them threw a shadow. They saw that Gunnar was merry, and he wore a joyful face. He sang a song, and so loud, that it might have been heard though they had been further off.

'He that lavished rings in largesse,
When the fights' red rain-drops fell,
Bright of face, with heart-strings hardy,
Hogni's father met his fate;
Then his brow with helmet shrouding,
Bearing battle-shield, he spake,
"I will die the prop of battle,
Sooner die than yield an inch,
Yes, sooner die than yield an inch".'

After that the cairn was shut up again.

'Wouldst thou believe these tokens if Njal or I told them to thee?' says Skarphedinn.

'I would believe them,' he says, 'if Njal told them, for it is said that he never lies.'

'Such tokens as these mean much,' says Skarphedinn, 'when he shows himself to us, he who would sooner die than yield to his foes; and see how he has taught us what we ought to do.'

'I shall be able to bring nothing to pass,' says Hogni, 'unless thou wilt stand by me.'

'Now,' says Skarphedinn, 'will I bear in mind how Gunnar behaved after the slaying of your kinsman Sigmund; now I will yield you such help as I may. My father gave his word to Gunnar to do that whenever thou or thy mother had need of it.'

After that they go home to Lithend.[18]

Dasent's better informed readers, of whom William Morris was certainly one, would have known that any old northern hero smiling in the face of death, before or after it occurred, was guaranteed entry into Valhöll (Valhalla). Thomas Bartholinus's *Antiquitatum Danicarum de Causis Contemptæ a Danis adhuc Gentilibus Mortis* (1689) is a compendium of instances of the phenomenon, and found a fascinated eighteenth-century European readership; and Gunnar's last stand and afterlife found an honoured place in the volume.[19] His was the ultimate invincible spirit—the distillation of clear-sighted heroic valour in life; coolly defiant at the point of death; good humoured in his grave thereafter. It was a medieval subject, anthologized by a humanist, and just waiting for a romantic poet to do it justice.

William Morris was not, in fact, the first English writer to sense the scene's poetic potential. Richard Hole's 'The Tomb of Gunnar', published in the *Gentleman's Magazine* in 1789, announces itself as 'a free translation, or rather imitation [from] ... an old Gothic romance', with Bartholinus's volume as the direct source.[20] Hole had neither read the saga nor visited the region. There was no readily accessible edition of the saga for a late eighteenth-century British reader; Hole could not have read the Icelandic of the 1772 first edition;[21] and no Latin translation of *Njála* appeared until Jón Jónsson's Copenhagen version of 1809.[22] As for visiting the *Njála* sagasteads, this was out of the question—no-one visited sagasteads in 1789. There had, in fact, been a British expedition to Iceland that very year, led by John Thomas Stanley, a young Edinburgh-educated scientist. Yet for all the young Stanley's own lifelong fascination with old northern myth and legend,[23] during his Iceland travels he had eyes only for the unfathomable mechanics of the hot springs at Geysir—then regarded as one of the wonders of the natural world. The *Njála* country was within comfortable riding distance for Stanley and his young colleagues—but it would never have occurred to them to seek out the haunts of a saga about which they knew little or nothing. Thus Hole's necessarily armchair engagement with the old north finds him taking the narrative skeleton of the *Njáls saga* scene from Bartholinus, deriving the mood music from Thomas Percy's canonical *Five Pieces of Runic Poetry* (1763), and from Thomas Gray's hugely influential 'The Descent of Odin' and 'The Fatal Sisters' (1768), and adding the familiar poetic paraphernalia of the late eighteenth-century British sanguinary sublime—the gloom of night, the spectral presences, the banquet for the beasts and birds of battle. The sylvan shepherd and his Augustan sheep soon retreat in horror from the scene:

> 'What mean those aweful sounds that rise
> From the tomb where Gunnar lies?'
> Exclaims the shepherd in affright;
> As by the moon's uncertain light,

Athwart the solitary plain,
He homeward drives his fleecy train.

Sarhedine and Hogner (the nearest that the poet comes to the unfamiliar saga names of Skarpheðinn and Högni) are made of sterner stuff, however. With Hole now into his stride, the glutinous noun phrases flow like lava, and a crisp and cloudy late summer evening in Iceland re-emerges as a dank and vaporous British autumnal night—the intrepid heroes head for the tomb 'While darkly-rolling vapours hide/ In their dun veil night's glittering pride.' The 'fearless' pair are suddenly confronted with the ghostly Gunnar, clad in his battle-gear and in high good humour. Picked out by the moonlight and with a smile playing across his 'aweful brows', the hero speaks in suitably Bartholinean tones:

'Unmanly flight the brave despise;
Conquest of death's the warrior's prize;
The strife of spears disdain to shun,
Nor blast the fame by Gunnar won!'

The saga goes on to reflect on whether the vision is to be believed; Högni's self-doubt is voiced, as is Skarpheðinn's loyal support. No such thoughts find a place in Hole's robust reimagining of the scene—Gunnar's call to arms and vengeance is immediate:

'Grasp the sword, and gird the mail!
Scorning alike to yield or fly,
Resolve to conquer, or to die!
A banquet for the wolf prepare,
And glut the ravenous birds of air!'

By such means a late eighteenth-century poet translates the (as yet) unfamiliar world of the Icelandic family saga into the (then) fashionable sensibility of Eddic poetry.[24]

Morris's response to this same saga scene in 'Gunnar's Howe' could hardly be more different. There was much Augustan grime to remove from the canvas, but every encouragement to do so in mid-Victorian Britain.[25] George Dasent's translation was one of the great books to emerge from the Victorian rediscovery of the European middle ages;[26] and steamship technology and the consequent development of what passed for a north Atlantic tourist industry now made the prospect of travel to Iceland a good deal less daunting. Morris devoured Dasent's translation; he also read the saga in Icelandic with his faithful grammatical guide Eiríkur Magnússon; and then he journeyed to Iceland, and visited the site traditionally thought to be Gunnar's tomb. The high priority he attached to this visit is hardly surprising: 'I don't know anything more consoling or grander in all literature (to use a beastly French word) than Gunnar's singing in his house under the moon and the drifting clouds.'[27] Morris's 1871 Iceland journal records his first visit:

> we come at last on a big mound rising up from the hollow, and this is Gunnar's Howe: it is most dramatically situated to remind one of the beautiful passage in the Njála where Gunnar sings in his tomb: the sweet grassy flowery valley with a few big grey stones about it has a steep bank above, which hides the higher hilltop; but down the hill the slope is shallow, and about midways of it is the howe; from the top of which you can see looking to the right and left along the Lithe, and up into the valley of Thorsmark.[28]

It was to that 'terrible' valley that they were to journey the following morning. But for now they lay around Gunnar's howe, climbed further up the slope, and then not long before midnight they returned to gaze again at the mound, with the moon no more than a 'little thin crescent', incapable of casting any light on the saga hero, should he have obligingly reappeared to greet his guests.

In seeking to give poetic expression to his own responses to this site of saga pilgrimage, Morris would have needed no reminding that literary times and philological tastes had changed since Hole's day. Firstly, night thoughts no longer quickened sensitive pulses, though adjectival gothicism—the 'aw(e)ful', the 'terrible', the 'hideous', the 'dreadful'—finds a surprisingly vigorous new lease of life in Morris's journals.[29] Secondly, an invigorating philological awareness was now abroad—thus 'literature' was now 'a beastly French word'. In the manuscript copy which Morris sent to Jón Sigurðsson the poem's title is simply 'Gunnar's Howe'—neither poet nor recipient needed any titular indication of the scene's location. By the time of its 1891 first publication, the title ('Gunnar's Howe above the House at Lithend') has been adjusted to nod in the direction of Dasent's translation (in which Hlíðarendi became 'Lithend'); but Dasent's fondness for the Gaelic-derived 'cairn' was not shared by Morris—he much preferred 'Howe' (from OI *haugr*), thereby signalling and celebrating the closeness of the English and Icelandic languages. Morris may have known—his great admirer W. G. Collingwood (who painted the site during his 1897 saga-steads tour)[30] certainly did—that amongst the many *-howe* place names in the English Lake District was 'Gunner's Howe'.[31]

In Morris's private annotation to his Icelandic journals (which were originally prepared for Lady Georgiana Burne-Jones,[32] and not published until 1911) he shows just how important such attention to philological detail could be. His account of Gunnar's howe prompts him to add a translation of the relevant lines from the saga. Though he frequently refers to Dasent's translation in his Icelandic journals, for actual quotation Morris prefers to trust himself:

> Skarphedin and Hogni were abroad one evening by Gunnar's howe, on the south side thereof: the moonshine was bright but whiles the clouds drew over: them seemed the howe opened and Gunnar turned in the howe, and lay meeting the moon; and they thought they saw four lights burning in the howe, and no shadow cast from any: they saw that Gunnar was merry, and exceeding glad of countenance: and he sang a song so high that they had heard of it even had they been farther off.[33]

A glance at Dasent's version of the same passage (quoted above) reveals the extent to which Morris is very much his own philological man. He is sometimes more accurate,[34] rarely gilding the Icelandic lily for the sake of lyricism or immediacy. He allows himself no Dasentian liberties—the Icelandic text has no 'stars'; nothing was shining 'clear'; the repose of 'drew' for *dró fyrir* seems more appropriate—and more accurate—than the busyness of 'drove', and the drama of Dasent's 'all at once' has no textual authority. On the other hand, Morris's eagerness to swim against the tide of colloquial expectation, his insistence on the closely cognate nature of the two languages, could lead to unwonted eccentricity—Dasent's pragmatic 'every now and then' for *stundum* re-emerges as the aggressively archaistic 'whiles'; the impersonal Icelandic *þeim sýndisk* might be better served by Dasent's 'they thought they saw' than by Morris's 'them seemed', more a transliteration than a translation; and what is a reader who knows no Icelandic to make of Morris's '[Gunnar] lay meeting the moon'? With other elements the contest is more even: 'exceeding glad of countenance' sounds distractingly biblical as a rendering of *með gleðimóti miklu*, yet Morris would have had little patience with Dasent's 'wore a joyful face', with its 'beastly' French loan word and its failure to signal the intensifying *miklu*. It may be fair to conclude that at every point Dasent, a pragmatic proselytizing Icelandicist, has a discernible readership in mind;[35] for Morris translation was more a private philological reverie. Certainly Dasent's translation was still winning new readers for the saga as an Everyman paperback in the 1970s, whereas the Morris/Eiríkur Magnússon translations, which preached opaquely to the converted, have long been unavailable.[36]

The first person narrator of Morris's 'Gunnar's Howe' is thus addressing a very different audience from Richard Hole's omniscient third person figure—and a markedly different tone is soon established:

> Ye who have come o'er the sea to behold this grey minster
> of lands,
> Whose floor is the tomb of time past, and whose walls by
> the toil of dead hands
> Show pictures amidst of the ruin of deeds that have over-
> past death,
> Stay by this tomb in a tomb to ask of who lieth beneath.[37]

The language is carefully archaized—'Ye', 'o'er', 'behold', 'lieth'—but the present tense suggests immediacy and even urgency. We may take it that Morris is addressing modern travellers, with the plurality suggested by 'ye' rather than 'thou'. The tone suggests a solemnity in tune with the respect and awe that such travellers ought to be feeling as they move through the sagasteads. The imagery in the first verse is, we may assume, exactly that which Jón Sigurðsson had found unsympathetic. Iceland is a 'tomb' (three instances), it is linked with 'death' and 'dead hands' and 'ruin', and, recalling 'gráleit', it is 'grey'. Jón seems to have misunderstood Morris's sense of that adjective, for it was his favourite when describing Iceland. It occurs four times in this poem, twice in 'Iceland First Seen', it is ever present in 'The Lovers of Gudrun' in *The Earthly Paradise*, and in *Sigurd the Volsung*, and it can be found over a hundred times in his Iceland journals, in describing lava, moss, streams, clouds, cliffs, plain, sky, seas, and slopes. But 'grey' was not a dull colour for Morris. It was important for his view of Iceland and, at much the same time, it was important for his work with fabric design. In 1875, whilst hard at work on *Sigurd the Volsung*, Morris wrote to Thomas Wardle his Staffordshire-based colour technologist, and it is clear that achieving the 'required shade' in 'the battle about the "Grey"' was causing them a good deal of trouble, and that Morris would not be satisfied until a solution was found.[38] It was, after all, only against a correctly dyed dark grey background that the rich foreground colours of curtain or carpet could show up properly. So it is in the Iceland journals. We find no 'monotony of grey' there,[39] but rather 'grey', 'dark grey', 'not very dark grey', 'dark … and dreadful grey', 'lightish grey', 'dark ashen grey', 'light green and grey', 'greyer than grey', 'light grey-blue', 'yellowish grey', 'ragged grey', 'inky grey', 'woeful grey', 'spotted grey', 'dark grey bordered with white', 'heavy grey', 'cold-grey', light grey becoming 'greyer and greyer', and many other shades. When he returns home to England, it is on a 'soft warm grey morning', sailing on a 'calm and grey sea', that he spots the 'long grey line of Scottish coast'. Awaiting him back in Oxfordshire was the light grey stone of his old college and of the newly rented Kelmscott Manor. Writing to Georgiana Burne-Jones from Verona in 1878 we find Morris confessing to feelings of boredom with the local buildings: 'even in these magnificent and wonderful towns I long rather for the heap of grey stones with a grey roof that we call a house north-away'.[40] Grey, then, was a fundamental colour for William Morris—solemn, dramatic, everchanging; and in the Iceland journals it is the essential background against which the stunning primary colours of Iceland flicker across page after page like northern lights. Small wonder, when Morris can find so much colour amidst the greys of a modern Icelandic landscape, that he has no trouble in finding the appropriate shade of grey for his old northern sagasteads, for their interior decorations, and even for the eyes of the heroes and heroines in his narrative poems.

Morris's 'Gunnar's Howe' landscape is not just 'grey'—it is a 'grey minster of lands'. Morris knew all about grey minsters from his familiarity with Oxford college chapels, London abbeys, European cathedrals and, not least, the many churches all over England for which his firm had supplied stained glass windows and other fittings during the prosperous 1860s.[41] The dedicated Victorian travellers and tourists whom Morris addresses in the poem—those whose over-familiarity with the sultry south of Europe[42] tempted them to turn to the 'costes colde' of the north—expected to visit minsters. If Iceland's ecclesiastical architecture fell short in this respect, the silk purse of a cathedral could be created out of the sow's ear of a rural church by deft pencil and brush work (as the *Illustrated London News* artist showed in Reykjavík in the summer of 1874),[43] or cathedrals could simply be imagined. Morris's Iceland journals sometimes view rockscapes with the eye of an ecclesiastical architect: 'ruined minster looking rocks';[44] one mountain 'like a huge church with a transept',[45] and another 'just the shape of Castle St Angelo in Rome'.[46] In the poem the travellers are invited to view the lava-strewn ground of Iceland as a minster floor; its pictured walls can be imagined, thanks to the 'toil of dead hands' (saga writers) who tell of (ruined) deeds whose fame lived on for Victorian enthusiasts through saga translations. Morris's copy of the poem sent to Jón Sigurðsson shows that he is thinking of sagas—for 'deeds' in the 1891 printed text, the manuscript reads 'great tales'. Gunnar's 'Howe' is, thus, a small tomb within the great minster of the Icelandic land and landscape. It is a tomb within a tomb; a place of awe and mystery and history and romance and beauty and solemnity; it is not at all 'haggard, dismal and sad'.

At the heart of the poem is Morris's fascination with the idea of the spirit of Iceland's heroic past living on in the straitened circumstances of Iceland's nineteenth-century present. It was a past which Morris rarely sought to recall with scholarly objectivity; his demands on it were insistent and revealingly personal. He wanted to 'have a part/ In that great sorrow of thy children dead';[47] he wanted the great outlaw Grettir as a 'friend to me life's void to fill';[48] and, ever the unfulfilled lover, he wanted Iceland, as mother, sister and lover 'all in one', to 'wrap me in the grief of long ago'.[49] He was eager for his fellow English travellers, whether on horseback in Iceland, or in library armchair back in Britain, to 'have a part' in the tale of Gunnar and Njáll. The heroes of the sagas were long dead; as were the sagamen who recorded their heroics so memorably; so, too, were the generations of scribes who copied the saga manuscripts. Dead, too, were those Eddic heroes whose deeds begat the tales told at banquets and woven into the tapestries at Hjardaholt ('The Lovers of Gudrun'), and Lymdale[50] (*Sigurd the Volsung*). Yet, through the 'toil' of forgotten hands, whether those of minstrel on harp, weaver on loom, scribe on vellum, or (in Morris's own lifetime, as never before) translator and poet on paper, the past could be substantially repossessed by the present. In 'Iceland First Seen', the continuity and survival of that lonely volcanic outcrop is celebrated 'amid waning of realms and of riches and death of things worshipped and sure'.[51] The personified Iceland voices the explanation—'I abide here the spouse of a God, and I made and I make and endure'. If 'making', in either the medieval sense of poetic creativity, or in its later less specialized meanings, could help to fill the silences of 'life's void', then the workaholic Morris, 'the Thor of the Library' (in Eiríkur Magnússon's phrase) had nothing to fear. He could ensure the survival and transmission of old northern literary culture single-handedly.

As the poem develops, Morris's anxiety (insistence even) that all should share his own fervent engagement with that saga-age culture is soon emphasized:

Ah! the world changeth too soon, that ye stand there with
unbated breath,
As I name him that Gunnar of old, who erst in the
haymaking tide
Felt all the land fragrant and fresh, as amidst of the edges
he died.
Too swiftly fame fadeth away, if ye tremble not lest once
again
The grey mound should open and show him glad-eyed
without grudging or pain.
Little labour methinks to behold him but the tale-teller
laboured in vain.

For all its gothic filigree Richard Hole's poem had followed the saga's narrative line doggedly; whereas with his reference to Gunnar falling 'in the haymaking tide', Morris here touches the events of the saga for the only time. The tone seems feverish and impatient. What happens if someone comes to Iceland and fails to feel the spell of Gunnar when visiting Hliðárendi. It could happen. By the 1870s people visited Iceland for many reasons—sport fishing, commercial fishing, geology, buying Icelandic horses to work down the coal mines in Britain, buying Icelandic sheep, investigating the possibility of producing and exporting sulphur for gunpowder—and some went simply because by the 1870s Iceland became, for the nineteenth-century trendy traveller, what the lower slopes of the Himalayan mountains have become a century later for the mobile-phoned merchant banker.[52]

Morris went to Iceland at a time when the northbound traveller had never had it so good. Creature comforts abounded. Travel book advertisements confirm that, amongst the quayside merchants ministering to the Iceland traveller at Leith, it was the age of ladies' inflatable baths, specially prepared food hampers, and odour-free leggings and overalls 'specially adapted for Travellers in Iceland'; the steamship service (£8 return, first class) boasted 'superior accommodation' in well-ventilated staterooms; and, awaiting the weary traveller in Reykjavík, was its oldest established hotel, 'thoroughly renovated and enlarged', with 'new commodious dining room', and (even better news) a 'billiard and smoking room have just been added'.[53]

Morris's poetically expressed fear of the insensate traveller, obsessed with odour-free leggings, and deaf to the sound of sagas, was well founded: witness the leaden-souled response of Anthony Trollope's fellow travellers to the elegiac lyricism of Gunnar's famous description of his Hlíðarendi homestead with its 'bleikir akrar og slegin tún' (in Dasent's translation, 'the corn-fields are white to harvest, and the home mead is mown').[54] This scene, which has moistened the eyes of Icelandophiles for a hundred years and more, is cited solely as proof of the existence of corn in medieval Iceland.[55] Such breezy heedlessness could lead to cultural oblivion, as Morris reminds us in a memorable passage in *Sigurd the Volsung* in which Regin tells the youthful Sigurd how he had taught mankind to reap, sow, sail, sing and weave—only to find, within a generation, that these gifts were now attributed to the gods Frey, Thor, Bragi and Freyja.[56]

In 'Gunnar's Howe' it seems unthinkable, or at least intolerable, to Morris that the ancient 'tale-teller laboured in vain'; yet he was himself to discover just how fragile could be the 'thin thread of insight and imagination'[57] which linked saga past to Victorian present. Sometimes restoring the thread required much labour. In 1873 he visited the 'Howe' again; the bright evening of 1871 had given way to a wet and 'melancholy' morning two years later. He himself seems to have found it 'some labour' to achieve the longed-for sense of bated breath: 'it was not until I got back from the howe and wandered by myself about the said site of Gunnar's hall and looked out thence over the great grey plain that I could answer to the echoes of the beautiful story—but then at all events I did not fail.'[58] In 'Gunnar's Howe' the 'thin thread' is still strong and taut, with strong philological support. In the second stanza *tide*, *edges* and *methinks* echo Old Icelandic forms: the conscientious Victorian reader would have discovered that *tíð* is glossed in the 1874 Richard Cleasby–Guðbrandur Vigfússon *Icelandic–English Dictionary* (the ultimate scholarly resource for the Victorian translator of Iceland) as 'tide, time', and *egg* as 'an edge'; and, unlike many other Victorian visitors to Hlíðarendi, Morris knew well that 'methinks' lay comfortably along the grain of the Icelandic impersonal form *þykkir mér*.

By the poem's third stanza, talk of tombs has given way to a celebration of the defeat of death by the power of Gunnar's song, recorded in a saga by a 'man unremembered', and passed down the ages so as to bridge 'all the days that have been', or at least nine hundred years' worth of them:

> Little labour for ears that may hearken to hear his death-
> conquering song,
> Till the heart swells to think of the gladness undying that
> overcame wrong.
> O young is the world yet, meseemeth, and the hope of it
> flourishing green,
> When the words of a man unremembered so bridge all the
> days that have been.
> As we look round about on the land that these nine
> hundred years he hath seen.

Here is just the life-affirming optimism that Jón Sigurðsson missed, but which Morris seemed always to be able to find in Iceland. His Hlíðarendi experience was about life, about 'gladness *un*dying', about 'youth', about 'hope', about Gunnar *singing* after his death, and about the noble saga of Gunnar and Njáll, told in the words of a long-forgotten sagaman, yet still alive in the minds of true travellers and pilgrims nine hundred years later. If the sagaman's fragile witness could sound so loud generations later, after damp, decay, fire, loss, theft, and relocation had wrought their random havoc on written records, then the world was indeed still young, and hope still green (the only other colour to be found in the poem), and the human heart could properly 'swell' with pleasure. So it is that the last verse returns from broad humanitarian musings to the dusk of the summer evening of 21 July 1871 which, Morris recalls in the poem, never quite grows dark and which finds nature bustling with activity:

> Dusk is abroad on the grass of this valley amidst of the hill:
> Dusk that shall never be dark till the dawn hard on
> midnight shall fill
> The trench under Eyiafell's snow, and the grey plain the sea
> meeteth grey.
> White, high aloft hangs the moon that no dark night shall
> brighten ere day,

For here day and night toileth the summer lest deedless his
time pass away.

The three stages of an Icelandic summer circle of the sun are here linked by alliteration. Dusk dissolves first into dawn and then day, which eventually drifts into dusk. Night is banished before dark has a real chance to take hold; no intervention of the moon is required. Just as there are no sharp divisions between day and night, so the demarcation line between land and sea is unclear from a distance. The one runs into the other which runs into the one again. All the time the sense is of process and continuity, and the final line highlights the energy, progress, vitality, activity—the making and enduring—of a summer season not wishing to leave without having *done* something. The poem began with ancient 'deeds' preserved through the words of a saga; in July 1871 new deeds were being done in Iceland, and two new poems were forming in the mind of a sagastead pilgrim. Gunnar sang of doing brave deeds irrespective of death—and, for Morris, those brave deeds still spoke their message through the subsequent good desktop heroism of saga writer, scribe, editor, and a great English translator. In writing 'Gunnar's Howe' Morris, like those before him, was 'making' in order that the saga and its heroic vision might 'endure'.

Indeed, though Morris was not to know it, his own death was to bring him an heroic new life, linked to the noble Gunnar of Hlíðarendi. Gunnar, together with Njáll and many another worthy of Edda and saga, can be found paying tribute to Morris, the English 'skald', in a remarkable but neglected poetic obituary. Morris's celebrity in Iceland as a champion of their old literature led to several generous tributes being published in Iceland at the time of his death. Matthías Jochumsson's poem 'Vilhjálmur Morris' represents an additional laudatory voice, uncommented upon by Morris scholars, and an almost forgotten work even in Iceland.[59] Matthías Jochumsson knew Morris long before his death. Visiting London in 1874 he asks Eiríkur Magnússon to 'greet on my behalf the great troll, the living, lion-strong, Welsh Volsung'.[60] By 1876 Morris could lay even stronger claim to the soubriquet 'Welsh Volsung', for he had followed up his 1869 translation (in collaboration with Eiríkur Magnússon) of

Völsunga saga with his vast poetic paraphrase *Sigurd the Volsung*. It seems entirely fitting, therefore, that Matthías should have portrayed Morris as the mighty dragon-slaying Sigurðr, with his victim Fáfnir presented as a monstrous personification of the inequalities of wealth which held London in thrall at the time of the poet's death. The 1996 Morris centenary may have concentrated on Morris's domestic griefs, and the ambiguities—for some the glaring hypocrisies—underpinning Morris's distinctive blend of private capitalism and public socialism. For Matthías Jochumsson in 1896 the picture was much less complicated: Morris was a hero, an *Íslandsvinur* (friend of Iceland), and a doughty champion of the poor in Britain. If his death was a source of grief, his life was cause for celebration, and the creation of new myth.

Written in traditional *fornyrðislag* metre, and drawing heavily on a richly allusive reservoir of Eddic vocabulary, 'Vilhjálmur Morris' begins by reminding the reader that Morris fell in love with the idea of the north from an early age—he drank from the sacred vessels of Icelandic poetry when still a 'mjólkurbarn' (literally, a milk child); and claims that Iceland ('Snælands dóttir') never set eyes on a greater poetic genius ('snjallari snilling'). A parade of revered medieval Icelandic historians and saga heroes, each of whose words and works was known well to Morris, then express their tributes. Ari Þorgilsson[61] rejoices that Icelandic history now has an authoritative voice in England; Egill Skallagrímsson[62] says that his old adversary King Aðalsteinn of England[63] valued no warrior more than Iceland treasures William Morris; Snorri Sturluson[64] and Sæmundr fróði[65] salute the English hero; and, lastly, a group of saga worthies appears, each from a work (*Laxdæla saga*, *Gunnlaugs saga ormstungu* and *Brennu-Njáls saga*) which Morris had either promoted in Britain by translation or paraphrase, or for which he had a special fondness:

Mæltu orðheill	Good report they gave
ítrum gesti	the glorious guest—
einn ok sérhverr	each and all
afreksmanna:	of the action men:
Gunnar ok Gestr,	Gunnar and Gestur,

Gizur ok Hjalti,	Gizur and Hjalti,
Einar ok Kjartan,	Einar and Kjartan,
Ormstunga, Njáll.[66]	Wormtongue and Njáll.[67]

Morris's doctor claimed that Morris died 'of simply being William Morris, and having done more work than most ten men'.[68] Matthías Jochumsson mythologizes the moment, by drawing parallels with Morris's Sigurd. He thus enables Morris to participate in the Völsung legends which he had devoured as a young reader, and which he had served so loyally as translator and poet. There were, indeed, parallels between the way the workers left the 'plough alone in the furrow' to watch Sigurd's triumphant return to the Niblung court[69] and the similar levels of curiosity exhibited by nineteenth-century Icelanders at the progress of the English skald around their country. Yet Matthías prefers to equate Morris's tireless work amidst the wearisome world of metropolitan revolutionary socialism, with Sigurd's attack on Fáfnir:

Liggr linni	Lies the serpent
um Lundúnaborg;	round London;
þá vitum meinvætt	know we that fearsome creature,
mesta í heimi,	foulest in the world,
eys hrælogum	sprays with destructive fire
á hremmdar dróttir	the fettered folk,
gandr þúsundrað	the monster of a billion
granabyrða.	burdens of Grani.[70]

Morris's path lay not to the greyness of Gnítaheiði but rather to the drafty and dispiriting committee rooms of Farringdon Road—but, unlike Sigurd, his all-conquering hero, he did not live to ride home in triumph with the hoard of gold:

róð svá Vafurlogann	[he] rushed thus into the flames
vann á Jörmungandi:[71]	flayed the mighty monster:
Dundi vítt í veröld	Resounded wide in the world
vorri. *Þar féll Morris.—*	Of us all. *There fell Morris.*

But the Englishman's own brand of heroic sacrifice will, Matthías hopes, earn him lasting fame in modern Iceland:

Hátt í lofi lifi
listfagr ástvin Braga,[72]
—maðr kenni þat manni!—
Morris á foldu Snorra!

May high in praise live
Bragi's art-rich hero,
—may man teach this to man—
Morris in Snorri's land.

Matthías's wish has certainly been granted, even if (ironically) his own poem has played little part in the process. Morris's life and works certainly excited much interest in 'Snorri's land' during the 1996 Morris centenary celebrations. We may claim at least this for Matthías's neglected tribute—it is there that the great translator of Iceland finally finds himself translated by Iceland; it is there that the myth-maker is mythologized; and there that the loyal skald becomes a skaldic kenning. How Morris would have relished the completion of this fine philological circle.

NOTES

In this essay I adopt Icelandic spelling for Icelandic names and texts, for example, Njáll. Morris, like Dasent before him, modernized and Anglicized these spellings, for example, 'The Saga of Burnt-Njal'.

1. William Morris, *Icelandic Journals* (Fontwell, Sussex: Centaur, 1969), p. 185. The volume is a facsimile of the first edition of the *Journals* in *The Collected Works of William Morris*, ed. May Morris, 24 vols (London: Longmans and Green, 1910–15), VIII.
2. MS Lbs. [Landsbókasafn Íslands] JS 143.
3. See Páll Eggert Ólason, *Jón Sigurðsson*, 5 vols (Reykjavík: Hið íslenzka þjóðvinafélag, 1929–33), passim.
4. 'þykir móðir vor heldur gráleit og gelgjuleg, dauf og döpur': quoted in Finnbogi Guðmundsson, 'Um þjóðlegan metnað Jóns Sigurssonar', *Andvari* (1971), 134–35.
5. 'I think that poem about Gunnarshólmi is even more [gloomy] in nature, and I think we won't bother with it' (kvæðið um Gunnarshólma er þó enn meira í þá stefnu, og ég held við reynum ekki við það).
6. The title of the poem in the holograph manuscript copy (see note 2) sent to Jón Sigurðsson is simply 'Gunnar's Howe'.
7. *Ný Felagsrit* 29 (1872), 187–89.
8. 'Iceland First Seen' in *Poems by the Way* (London: F. S. Ellis, 1891): see *Collected Works*, IX, 125.

9. The most knowledgeable discussion of Morris's Iceland-related poetry remains Ruth C. Ellison, '"The Undying Glory of Dreams": William Morris and "The Northland of Old"', in *Victorian Poetry*, ed. Malcolm Bradbury, Stratford upon Avon Studies, 15 (London: Edward Arnold, 1972), pp. 139–75.

10. Most recently discussed in Fiona MacCarthy, *William Morris* (London: Faber, 1994), pp. 251–59, 319–23 and passim.

11. The fruits of his joint labours with Eiríkur Magnússon are to be found in the six volumes of translations published in the Saga Library (London: Bernard Quaritch, 1891–1905), and in *Three Northern Love Stories* (London: Ellis and White, 1875). An insightful recent discussion of Morris the saga translator can be found in Gary Aho's introduction to the William Morris Library series reprint of *Three Northern Love Stories*, Second Series, 11 (Bristol: Thoemmes, 1996).

12. Morris, *Icelandic Journals*, p. 21. Early in his voyage, when sailing near the Shetland Isles, Morris seeks to identify the place where Kári Solmundarson undertakes the saga's final act of vengeful violence (p. 10).

13. *Icelandic Journals*, p. 40.

14. *Icelandic Journals*, p. 43.

15. *Icelandic Journals*, p. 45.

16. The name means 'slope or mountain end'. *OED lith* sb.2 reminds us of the parallel Old English form, and its presence in post-medieval English place-names and dialect.

17. *Icelandic Journals*, p. 47.

18. George Webbe Dasent, *The Story of Burnt Njal, or Life in Iceland at the End of the Tenth Century* (Edinburgh: Edmonston and Douglas, 1861), vol. 1, pp. 249–51; *Brennu-Njáls saga*, ed. Einar Ólafur Sveinsson, Íslenzk fornrit XII (1954), ch. 78.

19. Thomas Bartholinus, *De Antiquitatum Danicarum* (Copenhagen: J. P. Bockenhoffer, 1689), pp. 279–81 (ii.2).

20. *Gentleman's Magazine* 59/4 (1789), 937.

21. Ólafur Olavius [Ólafsson], ed., *Sagan af Niáli Þórgeirssyni og sonum hans* (Copenhagen: J. R. Thiele, 1772).

22. *Nials-saga. Historia Niali et filiorum, Latina reddita, cum adjecta chronologia, variis textus Islandici lectionibus, earumque crisi, nec non glossario et indice rerum ac locarum.*

23. On Stanley and Iceland, see Andrew Wawn, 'John Thomas Stanley and Iceland: the Sense and Sensibility of an Eighteenth-Century Explorer', *Scandinavian Studies*, 53 (1981), 52–76.

24. More generally, see Margaret Omberg, *Scandinavian Themes in English Poetry 1760–1800*, Studia Anglistica Upsaliensia, 29 (Uppsala: Uppsala University, 1976).

25. On Victorian cultivation of the old north, see Andrew Wawn, 'The

Cult of "Stalwart Frith-thjof" in Victorian Britain', in Wawn, ed., *Northern Antiquity: The Post-Medieval Reception of Edda and Saga* (Enfield Lock: Hisarlik Press, 1994), pp. 211–54; and 'George Stephens, Cheapinghaven, and Old Northern Antiquity', *Studies in Medievalism*, 7 (1995), 63–104.

26. Andrew Wawn, 'The assistance of Icelanders to George Webbe Dasent', *Landsbókasafn Íslands, Árbók 1989*, nýr flokkur, 14 (1991), 73–92.

27. *The Collected Letters of William Morris*, ed. Norman Kelvin, 4 vols (Princeton: Princeton University Press, 1984–96), I, 344.

28. *Icelandic Journals*, pp. 48–49; for his second visit, see p. 207.

29. See, for example, the country looked 'strange and awful' (*Iceland Journals*, p. 28) and the mountains 'very awful and mysterious' (p. 154), the 'terrible gorges' (p. 41) and 'this terrible though beautiful valley' (p. 150), and the 'dreadful lonely place' (p. 113), the 'dreadful upper valley' (p. 114) and the 'dreadful looking rift' (p. 170).

30. W. G. Collingwood and Jón Stefánsson, *A Pilgrimage to the Saga-Steads of Iceland* (Ulverston: W. Holmes, 1899), p. 29. The haunting pictorial record created by Collingwood's numerous water colours has been made available in *Fegurð Íslands og fornir sögustaðir*, eds Haraldur Hannesson *et al.* (Reykjavík: Örn og Örlygur, 1991).

31. Thomas Ellwood, *The Landnama Book of Iceland as it illustrates the Dialect, Place Names, Folk Lore, and Antiquities of Cumberland, Westmorland, and North Lancashire* (Kendal: T. Wilson, 1894), p. 58.

32. MacCarthy, *William Morris*, p. 281.

33. *Icelandic Journals*, p. 49. The equivalent Icelandic text is in *Brennu-Njáls saga*, Íslenzk Fornrit, XII, pp. 192–93.

34. Only sometimes—*ópinn* is an adjective, and not the past participle which Morris appears to take it as.

35. I have learnt much about Dasent's approach to translation in discussions with Professor Robert Cook of the University of Iceland.

36. Though see above, note 11.

37. I quote from *Collected Works*, IX, 179.

38. Kelvin, *Letters*, I, 267–68.

39. MacCarthy, *William Morris*, p. 283.

40. Kelvin, *Letters*, I, 487.

41. See Charles Harvey and Jon Press, *William Morris: Design and Enterprise in Victorian Britain* (Manchester: Manchester University Press, 1990), a revelatory study of Morris the vigorous capitalist.

42. See John Pemble, *The Mediterranean Passion: Victorians and Edwardians in the South* (Oxford: Oxford University Press, 1987).

43. *Illustrated London News*, 29 August 1874; front page, and p. 206; 5 September 1874, p. 216; 12 September 1874, pp. 253, 256–57, 274; 19 September 1874, p. 271. The occasion for this extensive coverage was the visit to Iceland of the Danish King, to commemorate the thousandth anniversary of the arrival of the first settler.

44. *Icelandic Journals*, p. 151.

45. *Icelandic Journals*, p. 37.

46. *Icelandic Journals*, p. 131.

47. 'To the Muse of the North' in *Collected Works*, IX, 116.

48. *Collected Works*, VII, xxxvi. Morris and Eiríkur Magnússon had translated *Grettis saga Ásmundarsonar* as *The Saga of Grettir the Outlaw* (London: F. S. Ellis, 1869).

49. 'To the Muse of the North' in *Collected Works*, IX, 116.

50. *The Story of Sigurd the Volsung and the Fall of the Niblungs* (London: Ellis and White, 1877), p. 173; the wall hangings of the Niblung hall (p. 217) have images of Viking vessels, the Valkyrie, Mímir's fountain, and Miðgarðsormr.

51. *Collected Works*, IX, 126.

52. See Gary Aho, '"Með Ísland á heilanum": Íslandsbækur breskra ferðalanga 1772 til 1897', *Skírnir* 167 (1993), 205–58. Much less well informed, but infinitely more politically correct is Pamela Bracken Wiens, 'Fire and Ice: Clashing visions of Iceland in the Travel Narratives of Morris and Burton', *Journal of the William Morris Society* 11/4 (1996), 12–18.

53. Detail from the advertisements in W. G. Lock, *Guide to Iceland; A Useful Handbook for Travellers and Sportsmen* (Charlton: W. G. Lock, 1882).

54. Íslenzk Fornrit, xii, 182; Dasent, *Burnt Njal*, p. 236.

55. Anthony Trollope, 'Iceland', *Fortnightly Review*, ns, 30 (1878), 175–90.

56. *Sigurd the Volsung*, p. 111.

57. *Icelandic Journals*, p. 168.

58. *Icelandic Journals*, p. 207.

59. Written in 1896, the poem was first published in *Eimreiðin* 29 (1923), 257–61, together with a prose tribute by Matthías. The text had been discovered by the poet's son. The text cited in the present article derives from *Matthías Jochumsson: Ljóðmæli,* ed. Árni Kristjánsson, 2 vols (Reykjavík: Õsafoldarprentsmiðja, 1956–58), I, 557–71.

60. 'heilsaðu þeim mikla jötni, þeim lifanda, ljóneflda, welska Völsungi'; quoted in *Bréf Matthíasar Jochumssonar*, ed. Steingrímur Matthíasson (Akureyri: Menningarsjóður, 1935), p. 126.

61. Ari þorgilsson (1067–1148), Icelandic historian.

62. Egill Skallagrímsson, eponymous hero of *Egils saga Skallagrímssonar*.

63. Aðalsteinn reigned 924–39; his many dealings with Egill are described in *Egils saga*.

64. Snorri Sturluson (1178–1241), author of *Heimskringla* which Morris and Eiríkur Magnússon translated.

65. Sæmundr Sigfússon (1056–1133), historian.

66. Gestr Oddleifsson and Kjartan Ólafsson from *Laxdæla saga* and hence 'The Lovers of Gudrun' (1869); Gunnlaugr 'Worm-tongue' from

Gunnlaugs saga ormstungu (one of the *Three Northern Love Stories*, 1875), and from *Burnt Njal* Gizurr, Hjallti Skeggjason and Einar Eyjólfsson (prominent figures in the judicial processes of the saga) and, of course, Gunnar of Hlíðarendi and Njáll Þorgeirsson.

67. My translations from the poem are relatively free; I attempt, wherever sense allows, to signal something of the spikily alliterative nature of the original. I am much indebted to Hallfreður Örn Eiríksson and Gísli Sigurðsson of the Stofnun Árna Magnússonar á Íslandi for guiding my reading of Matthías Jochumsson's poem.

68. MacCarthy, *William Morris*, p. vii.

69. *Sigurd the Volsung*, p. 226.

70. A characteristic Icelandic kenning, meaning 'gold'; in Icelandic sources, Grani was Sigurðr's horse; its 'burdens' refers to the gold which it carried home after Fáfnir's defeat.

71. An Eddic compound (see *Völuspá* v. 50) used for the *midgarðsormr* (World serpent), here used for Fáfnir.

72. Bragi was the Old Norse god of poetry.

Aestheticism in Translation: Henry James, Walter Pater, and Theodor Adorno

RICHARD SALMON

> Truth still lives in fiction, and from the copy the original will be restored
>
> Friedrich Schiller (tr. Thomas Carlyle)

Schiller's celebrated defence of the redemptive social value of art as autonomous aesthetic illusion (*Täuschung*, translated as 'fiction' by Carlyle)[1] offers a suggestive proleptic commentary on the close relationship between late nineteenth-century aestheticism and a certain logic of translatability. Whilst this defence alludes to a familiar mimetic conception of the relationship between art and life—between the 'copy' and its 'original'—it also enacts a striking defamiliarization of this paradigm by claiming for aesthetic illusion a truth which is lacking from its ostensibly reflected source. Art, Schiller would seem to say, offers a truth which is lacking from truth; only within the translated form of the copy is the language of the original preserved. Aesthetic illusion thus acquires autonomy from objects in reality not so as to abandon mimesis (not for art to become wholly separate from life), but, rather, in order to redeem it. The value of art for social critique resides precisely in its function as a repository for those hypothetically mimetic truth-claims (however 'illusory', in a negative sense, their embodiment) which can no longer be located within existing socio-historical conditions.

In aestheticist writings of the late nineteenth century, similar questions concerning the translation and/or transposition of 'art' and 'life', 'original' and 'copy', and 'truth' and 'illusion' are raised with even greater insistency than is apparent in Schiller, which is not to say that identical solutions are proposed to them. Oscar Wilde's calculated inversion of the mimetic dependency of art upon nature in 'The Decay of Lying' (1889) ('Life holds the mirror up to Art, and either reproduces some strange type imagined by painter or sculptor, or realises in fact what has been dreamed in fiction')[2] is only the most well-known and seemingly unambiguous assertion of the transpositionality of normative relations between binary oppositions often associated with aestheticism. Indeed, through its sustained and self-conscious interrogation of the boundaries between art and life, aestheticism might well be defined as an aesthetic of transpositionality *par excellence*; one in which the activity of moving across or between opposing positions within a single textual, discursive, or cultural domain is most intensively foregrounded. These transpositional practices, though, extend beyond the mere inversion of binary oppositions or even the attempted subversion of notions of authenticity/originality which are perhaps most readily evoked by the name of Wilde. In this essay, I intend to focus upon a somewhat different, more complex, aspect of the transpositional logic of aestheticism, one which is centrally figured in Henry James's 'translation' of Walter Pater's aesthetic theory into the fictive form of Gabriel Nash, one of the characters in his novel of 1890, *The Tragic Muse*. Within this text, James is simultaneously engaged in several different types of transposition, not only of aesthetic theory into the medium of fiction, but also of one aesthetic and generic form of fiction into another, and, perhaps most importantly, in relation to the thematic concerns of the novel, of aesthetics into politics. In respect of the latter, *The Tragic Muse* enables us to address a question which is crucial to any reassessment of the politics of literary aestheticism: namely, the extent to which its cultivation of autonomous aesthetic illusion (in a Schillerian sense) is capable of crossing over into indirect forms of political protest or social critique.

As Jonathan Loesberg has observed, it is nowadays customary amongst politically-minded critics to use the word 'aestheticism' as little more than a generalized term of opprobrium, 'a vague synonym for imagining a realm of art entirely separate from social or historical effect'.[3] Yet no adequate response to this summary dismissal of aestheticism can avoid the genuinely difficult questions posed by the nature of its relationship to political commitment, as Loesberg himself risks doing by his premature conflation of the two.[4] The effect of immediately identifying aestheticism with a radical politics would be to jettison the claim to aesthetic autonomy which is constitutive of the former. By contrast, I wish to contend that the category of aesthetic autonomy remains of central importance to any critical retrieval of the radical political content of aestheticism. In order to develop this contention further, the first section of this essay turns to the aesthetic theory of Theodor Adorno, and, more particularly, to Adorno's dialectical analysis of the antagonistic relationship between autonomous and politically-committed art contained in his essay 'Commitment' (1962).[5] Whilst Adorno could not be described as an advocate of historical (i.e. late nineteenth-century) aestheticism, his own commitment to autonomous art referring explicitly to a critical genealogy of modernism, his theory of aesthetic autonomy does, as I hope to demonstrate, usefully reopen a debate on the transposed politics of aestheticism.

At the centre of Adorno's concern in 'Commitment', then, is an assessment of the competing claims of autonomous and politically-committed art. Yet whilst he is often inaccurately viewed as a straightforward proponent of the former claim, in this essay Adorno proceeds by mediating the two sides of the antinomy:

> Committed art, necessarily detached as art from reality, cancels the distance between the two. 'Art for art's sake' denies by its absolute claims that ineradicable connection with reality which is the polemical *a priori* of the attempt to make art autonomous from the real.[6]

For Adorno, then, the real significance of the opposition between autonomy and commitment cannot be grasped from one side or the other, but only from the perspective of a divided totality. On the one hand, art cannot disavow its ontological status as (merely) art simply by willing itself closer to empirical reality; on the other hand, art cannot be construed as an absolute negation of empirical reality without, at the same time, concealing the empirical grounds for its negativity. With regard to the latter of these two equally misguided claims, Adorno makes it clear, here and elsewhere in his writings, that '[w]orks of art that react against empirical reality obey the forces of that reality ... There is no material content, no formal category of artistic creation, however mysteriously transmitted and itself unaware of the process, which did not originate in the empirical reality from which it breaks free'.[7] Hence, the very endeavour of art to achieve autonomy—its endeavour to become 'art for art's sake'—must be viewed as a *determinate negation* of heteronomous socio-historical conditions. As J. M. Bernstein has convincingly argued, Adorno's defence of autonomous art is always conditional upon the paradoxical recognition that 'art's autonomy ... is enforced, that is, that art contain[s] a heteronomous moment, that its autonomy is for the sake of heteronomy'.[8] Yet, by the same token, art most effectively demonstrates this necessary connection with empirical reality only by protesting against it. If autonomous art is to reflect critically upon the heteronomous element within itself, this protest can be neither removed from its ground in reality, nor immediately resolved back into it.

Adorno's analysis of the antinomy of art and empirical reality would suggest, therefore, that there is a distinction to be made between two differing claims to aesthetic autonomy: firstly, an absolute (or affirmative) denial of art's grounding in empirical social experience, and, secondly, a determinate (and thus critical) negation of the same. By invoking the slogan of 'art for art's sake' it is clear that Adorno wishes to identify a bad form of aestheticism, as much as he would also insist on the need to preserve the conceptual claim to autonomy inscribed within it. Once the principle of 'art for art's sake' is turned into the positive content of the art-work, it lapses into an empty 'theodicy', which is evidently Adorno's own judgement on historical aestheticism *per se*.[9] Indeed, to adopt this principle as a 'message' which the work directly affirms would be to repeat the same error with which Adorno convicts committed art: 'The notion of a "message" in art, even when politically radical, already contains an accommodation to the world.'[10] On this account, one might argue that the more art insistently declares its autonomy from heteronomous socio-historical conditions, the more shamefully it is implicated within them.

Yet despite Adorno's tendency to construe aestheticism itself as an uncritical affirmation of aesthetic autonomy, his own critical theory of autonomous art does not, it seems to me, provide any criteria upon which to prohibit *a priori* its application to texts which belong, historically at least, to the moment of 'art for art's sake'. Although, in his later *Aesthetic Theory* (1970), the aporetic situation confronted by modernist art is sometimes perceived as a direct consequence of the preceding historical failure of aestheticism, neither historical nor conceptual boundaries between the two artistic movements are precisely demarcated.[11] Moreover, it should also be acknowledged that references to aestheticism within Adorno's *oeuvre* are by no means uniformly dismissive. In a celebrated riposte to Walter Benjamin's 'The Work of Art in the Age of Mechanical Reproduction', for example, Adorno argues that 'the centre of the autonomous work of art does not itself belong on the side of myth ... but is inherently dialectical': hence '*l'art pour l'art* is just as much in need of a defence' as the mass-produced art to which it is opposed in Benjamin's essay.[12]

Adorno's willingness to defend the normative value of aestheticism, even within the historical form which he so often criticized, may be seen even more clearly in his essay on the correspondence of Stefan George and Hugo von Hofmannsthal published in *Prisms* (1967).[13] Although this essay does not contain one of Adorno's most programmatic or cohesive statements on the question of autonomous art, it does offer a specific commentary on late nineteenth-century aestheticism, and, more particularly, a suggestive account of its political import for materialist criticism. As in his more general references to 'art for art's sake', the central thrust of the essay is directed against orthodox Marxist objections to the bourgeois category of aesthetic autonomy, and thus aims to counter the reduction of this category to mere ideology. In the context of the *fin de siècle*,

Adorno notes, the accusation that aestheticism represents a reactionary 'flight from reality' usually involves an invidious contrast with the 'progressive' form of naturalism.[14] Yet even if such an interpretation of aestheticism were warranted (which, in the case of George and Hofmannsthal, Adorno disputes), this in itself would at least preclude the opposing, equally ideological, desire to reproduce empirical reality in its immediate forms of appearance. It is this latter tendency which Adorno ascribes to realism in general. Despite the overtly critical content to be found within many realist texts, Adorno argues that a straightforwardly mimetic response to social experience remains essentially affirmative of that experience: 'to insist on the rendering of social reality in its immediacy is to adopt the empirical bias of the bourgeoisie which is supposed to be the object of criticism.'[15] The very form of the 'progressive' realist text, in other words, reproduces the illusion of immediacy which its critical content claims to dispel, and, for this reason, 'realism' may be convicted of being unreal. Conversely, in its apparent 'flight from reality', aestheticism attempts to preserve art's estrangement from this illusory immediacy of social experience. In more familiar terms, one might paraphrase Adorno as saying that aestheticism maintains a critical distance between art and life, but only so as the former can continue to reflect on the latter by way of negation. It is in this sense that the artistic productions of George and Hofmannsthal can be construed as sites of transposed political cognition, exemplifying, albeit within a different historical moment, Adorno's assertion, made towards the end of 'Commitment', that '[t]his is not a time for political art, but politics has migrated into autonomous art, and nowhere more so than where it seems to be politically dead.'[16] In Adorno's view, it is only by working from within the enforced (heteronomous) autonomy of art from politics in late capitalist culture that art can re-acquire the political voice which it has been denied. Only a fiction which has become estranged from empirical social reality can provide the means of regaining access to its lost 'original'.

It is tempting perhaps, at this juncture, to declare forthwith that James's *The Tragic Muse* is one such example of a fiction in which 'politics has migrated into autonomous art … nowhere more so than where it seems to be politically dead', and, thus, to proceed upon a straightforward 'translation' of Adorno's theory into James's practice. Approaching James's novel from the perspective of Adorno's theory of autonomous art, however, generates as many questions as it offers solutions, and it is not my intention to suggest an easy coalescence of the two. *The Tragic Muse* is, of course, a novel which is very directly concerned with the subject of aesthetic autonomy and with the freedom of art and artists, but this is precisely what might lead one to question its own formal autonomy as a work of fiction. The very fact that James deals so directly with the theme of art's autonomy from the world of politics might perhaps be taken as an indication of the affirmative mode of aestheticism against which Adorno warns. In his later Preface to *The Tragic Muse*, James, indeed, reinforces this impression by stating that he had long aimed to provide 'some dramatic picture of the "artist-life" and of the difficult terms on which it is at best secured and enjoyed'; the novel thus representing the culmination of his desire 'to "do something about art"—art, that is, as a human complication and a social stumbling-block'.[17] The self-conscious use of quotation marks in this passage is suggestive of James's allocation of the theme of 'art' to an imagined fund of mimetic resources. Art, that is to say, becomes one of a number of possible subjects for the novelist, with perhaps a due ironic recognition of the mechanical nature of this procedure. By this account, *The Tragic Muse* would appear to have been conceived rather in the spirit of the literary naturalist's attempted topography of the total division of social labour[18]—a mapping within which the sphere of the 'aesthetic' is examined from a transcendent authorial perspective—than through an unfolding of its immanent experience. Not only does this reading of the Preface correspond accurately to the loosely discursive quality of the novel itself, but it also fits in, retrospectively, with the trajectory of James's literary career. In some respects, *The Tragic Muse* may indeed be read as the last in the series of lengthy realist/naturalist novels which he wrote during the 1880s.[19]

In this particular instance, though, James's broadly realist narrative framework sits rather uneasily alongside the content of the novel's aesthetic debate. According to Adorno, realism may be viewed as a mode of social discourse, which, by virtue of its apparent proximity to empirical experience, always implicitly affirms the possibility of narrating that experience in communicable form. By contrast, the critical value of aestheticism, he writes in his essay on George and Hofmannsthal, lies in its cultivation of an 'aesthetic affectation' which is 'asocial' in character, and hence resistant to the communicative norms of bourgeois culture: 'Aesthetic fictions speak the true monologue, which communicative speech merely conceals.'[20] From an Adornian perspective, then, James's declaration of intention in his Preface to *The Tragic Muse* heralds an unlikely, even contradictory, admixture of 'aesthetic' and 'realist' elements. By proposing to '"do something about art"—art, that is, as a human complication and a social stumbling-block', James implies, contrary to Adorno, that it *is* possible to narrate the monologic sphere of aesthetic autonomy within an empirical social context. The novel itself may be read as an ample demonstration of this authorial ambition: through the intertwined narratives of Nick Dormer and Miriam Rooth, James documents the artist's struggle to achieve autonomy as a social fact, however unsuccessful the struggle may turn out to be. At the same time, James, I would suggest, is aware of the tension which exists between his realist narrative of the social process of attaining artistic autonomy and the immanent realization of autonomy itself. This tension is crystallized in the 'Preface' when he writes of the difficulty of representing Nick's success as an artist:

> Any presentation of the artist *in triumph* must be flat in proportion as it really sticks to its subject ... For, to put the matter in an image, all we then—in his triumph—see of the charm-compeller is the back he turns to us as he bends over his work. 'His' triumph, decently, is but the triumph of what he produces, and that is another affair. (p. 13)

According to this testimony, James's realist narrative reaches an epistemological impasse when forced to narrate the very circumstance towards which it aspires. The novel cannot represent the artist 'in triumph' because to do so would be to violate the nature of that triumph, which lies in the objective autonomy of artistic production, rather than in the subjective freedom of the artist. Hence, the social discourse of realism is tacitly conceived as an essentially heteronomous form, one that is incapable of penetrating or reproducing the interior world of aesthetic experience. All that remains possible for the realist novelist is to register a negative image of the artist as biographical subject: 'the back he turns to us as he bends over his work'.

This, however, is not to suggest that James's use of realism simply gives way before the ineffable. Rather, it is precisely by representing the artist's struggle to achieve autonomy within the context of existing social conditions that *The Tragic Muse* works towards a redefinition of aestheticism itself. What, in Adorno's terms, would appear to be James's contradictory transposition of aestheticist content into social realist form may also be seen as part of his attempt to scrutinize the idealism of Paterian aestheticism. At the centre of this critical project is James's exploration of the meaning of autonomy as freedom, a theme which resonates throughout the novel. Almost all of the central characters in *The Tragic Muse* can, indeed, be taken to embody variations on this theme. It is true not only of the representatives of 'art', but also of those figures ranged on the apparently opposing side of politics or the social 'world', that their primary concern is with establishing the autonomy of the individual self against the outside pressure of social relations. Whilst this concern is most clearly exemplified by Nick's ambition to achieve independence as a painter, and most explicitly theorized by the aesthete Gabriel Nash, it is also adumbrated in the more unlikely forms of Julia Dallow and Peter Sherringham. We learn, for example, that Julia's desire for Nick is driven by an 'affection that isolates and simplifies its object', as opposed to one 'that seeks communications and contact for it' (p. 103). Thus, far from representing an absolute antithesis to the pursuit of artistic autonomy, as her schematic function in the novel would appear to prescribe, Julia herself is implicated in a desire to escape from socially-constructed identity which is directly avowed elsewhere. Julia's stance towards Nick is, in fact, one of a piece with Peter's attitude towards Miriam, with Nick's relationship with Gabriel, and with Gabriel's general theory of conduct. What is striking about the pattern set in all of these relationships is the manner in which each subject endeavours to render his/her object autonomous by stripping it of all extraneous social 'contact'. By revealing this unstated affinity between Julia's political ambition of detaching Nick from Gabriel's aesthetic influence and Gabriel's aesthetic design of detaching both himself and Nick from all forms of political control, James not only undermines the stability of his binary opposition between 'art' and 'the world' (p. 1), but also begins to problematize the notion of autonomy itself.

Evidently, Julia's desire to 'isolate' and 'simplify' the object of her affection is to be read as a manipulative, which is to say heteronomous, use of the claim to autonomy. In this guise, the autonomy of the object serves merely as a pretext for its absorption by the subject, as becomes even more evident in Peter Sherringham's pretence of giving Miriam her 'independence' by 'disconnect[ing] and isolat[ing]' her from an embarrassing theatrical milieu (p. 144). Yet more importantly, in the context of this essay, James's ironization of this manipulative strategy also implicates the ostensibly liberating aestheticism expounded by Gabriel Nash. From his first appearance in the novel, Gabriel functions as a barometer by which the autonomy of the other characters—but, principally, that of Nick—can be measured. While Nick's path towards the 'independent life' of painting is notoriously circuitous (p. 67), Gabriel's posture of complete indifference to all extraneous social conditions emerges fully-fledged; hence, as Nick remarks, '[h]e doesn't shade off into other people; he is as neat as an outline cut out of paper with scissors' (p. 63). As an advocate of radical self-determination, Gabriel is intransigent in his refusal to be defined and delimited by any form of social communication. Not only does he reject the worldly professionalism represented by Julia and Peter, but, more significantly, as Jonathan Freedman has noted, he resists the professional ethos which Miriam and Nick apply to the practice of art,[21] even dismissing the activity of writing as a mere 'convenience' for 'others' (p. 35). In a clear (if slightly unfair) reference to Pater, Gabriel's cultivation of aesthetic sensation can only be communicated in a private 'terminology'.[22]

It is this Paterian model of radical subjective autonomy, I would argue, which is implicitly contested by James in the course of the narrative. Although Gabriel is clearly seen to exercise a positive influence in stimulating Nick's desire for artistic freedom, his influence is also potentially damaging insofar as it allows no possibility for freedom to be objectified in works of art. Nick's insistence upon the importance of 'doing'—of strenuous artistic production—thus leads to his eventual rejection of Gabriel's doctrine of 'being'—his cultivation of a purely subjective aesthetic experience. It is worth noting, however, that the culminating moment of this process occurs only after Nick has attained a 'new consciousness of freedom' in his vocation as an artist (p. 394); only after he has succeeded in extricating himself from inherited social and political obligations, in other words, does Nick come to recognize the unavoidability of social relations. Thus, for Nick, individual freedom is defined not by an abstract refusal of social identity, as in Gabriel's model of aestheticism, but rather through a recognition of the individual's complicity with society, which emerges precisely at the moment of his resistance to it. In what amounts to the central epiphany of *The Tragic Muse*, Nick realizes that '[e]verybody with whom one had relations had other relations too, and even indifference was a mixture and detachment a compromise' (p. 394). This perception of the unavoidability of 'compromise' need not be taken as heralding Nick's eventual reabsorption by the philistine world of bourgeois society, though nor is this possibility excluded from narratorial conjecture at the end of the novel. Instead, it may be viewed as a more complex stage in the dialectic of aesthetic freedom which unfolds through the course of the novel. Although such a dialectical process cannot be congealed into anything as static as an authorial mouthpiece, it seems clear, nonetheless, that Nick's consciousness of complicity within a network of social relations represents an advance beyond Gabriel's solipsistic declaration of subjective autonomy. Such a consciousness is defensible not only in the provisional finality of epiphanic perception but as a process which must be endured in each of its contradictory moments. Nick's agonizing experience of self-division, which impels his rapid oscillation between artistic and political commitments, is, of course, an embarrassment in the face of Gabriel's serene consistency: 'I don't know *what* I am', he confesses at one point in the novel (p. 122). Further to this, we are told that Nick 'paid the heavy price of the man of imagination; he was capable of far excursions of the spirit, disloyalties to habit and even to faith, he was open to rare communications' (p. 281). But, for James, the rare capacity of remaining open to 'communications' does not imply that the subject is simply coerced into submission by a brutally heteronomous social order, as Gabriel would suggest. Rather, it must be read positively as a capacity of heightened receptivity to the otherness of others, befitting the Jamesian ideal of the 'man of imagination'. At the moment when the narrator offers this characterization of Nick's consciousness, we see him swayed from his artistic commitments by admiration for Julia's sacrifice of *her* personal self-interest.

In developing this contrast between the respective social and aesthetic positions occupied by Nick and Gabriel, James, it can be shown, mounts his most explicit critique of Paterian aestheticism. It is, of course, by no means unusual to read Gabriel as a figure of the contemporary aesthete, but though various critics have attempted to identify James's 'source' for this figure, it is surprising that so few have recognized the specificity of James's translation of Paterian theory into the text of *The Tragic Muse*.[23] This act of translation can be seen most clearly through James's negotiation of the duality of 'being' and 'doing' formulated by Pater in his 1874 essay on Wordsworth (an essay reprinted in *Appreciations* in 1889, the year in which James began work on *The Tragic Muse*). In this essay, Pater presents Wordsworth's poetry as an example of the inherent critical value of an aesthetic stance of 'impassioned contemplation'.[24] By adopting such a stance as an 'end-in-itself', Wordsworth, according to Pater, resists the prevailing instrumental habits of thought, under which aesthetic experience is reduced to a subservient means to moral or political expression. Hence, 'Wordsworth's poetry, like all great art and poetry, is a continual protest' against the 'predominance of machinery in our existence' (p. 61). In this view, art is capable of acquiring a critical 'function' only when it has dispensed with the thought of its possible functionality: only when the means of artistic expression have been liberated from the need to serve ulterior ends (and thus permitted to exist as ends in themselves) can art be construed as a genuine 'protest' against existing societal imperatives.

Rather like Adorno, and contrary to popular critical opinion, then, Pater offers an explicitly politicized defence of the value of autonomous art: one that is predicated, however, upon the maintenance of art's autonomy from 'politics'. Moreover, in Pater's discussion, the autonomy of aesthetic experience is ontologized in such a manner that it must refuse any entanglement with the exigencies of practice:

> That the end of life is not action but contemplation—*being* as distinct from *doing*—a certain disposition of the mind: is, in some shape or other, the principle of all the higher morality. In poetry, in art, if you enter into their true spirit at all, you touch this principle, in a measure: these, by their very sterility, are a type of beholding for the mere joy of beholding. To treat life in the spirit of art, is to make life a thing in which means and ends are identified: to encourage such treatment, the true moral significance of art and poetry. (p. 62)

Here, Pater's definition of aesthetic experience as a mode of 'being' may be seen as a way of conceptualizing its absolute liberation from all manifestations of means–ends rationality. Conversely, with the term 'doing', he designates not only practical activity in the ordinary sense, but also, more specifically, the extraneous function which art is obliged to perform within a repressive utilitarian culture. It is in this context that Pater views aesthetic contemplation, paradoxically, as the highest form of ethical conduct: the 'true moral significance of art' lies in its capacity to attain freedom from the constraints of mere didacticism.

But if, in this sense, Pater is clearly a proponent of the

autonomy of aesthetic experience, it is also important to recognize the way in which his aestheticism simultaneously elides the boundary between 'art' and 'life', transposing each into the terms of the other. In the essay on Wordsworth, as elsewhere in his writings, Pater does not confine aesthetic experience to a specialized realm of artistic production or consumption, but expands it into a general theory of conduct.[25] His injunction to 'treat life in the spirit of art' represents not only an obvious attempt to aestheticize 'life', but, concomitantly, to de-differentiate the category of the aesthetic from its enforced autonomy within modern (post-Kantian) cultural experience.[26] To this extent, Paterian aestheticism projects a utopian desire for the reintegration of art into everyday life, which, ironically, is closer to Peter Bürger's interpretation of twentieth-century avant-gardism than to his largely negative comments on nineteenth-century aestheticism.[27] If, in Bürger's celebrated account, the twentieth-century avant-garde attempted to erode the boundary between art and praxis by demystifying the institutionalized aura of art, then Pater, it might be argued, tried to achieve a similar goal from the opposite perspective: rather than abolishing the autonomy of aesthetic experience, he takes it as the very model for a general cultural renovation. It is for this reason that Pater's well-known advocacy of 'art for art's sake' does not simply consecrate a uniquely privileged realm of value, centred upon the art-work itself. As Wolfgang Iser has correctly observed, Pater's use of this phrase differs from that of Gautier, for instance, by envisaging art (or, more precisely, aesthetic sensation) not as a pure negation of empirical reality, but, rather, as the means by which reality can be perceptually transfigured.[28]

Yet, from a Jamesian perspective, Pater's projected de-differentiation of the aesthetic—his desire to translate art into life—would seem to incur a severe penalty. In order to avoid the danger of art being reduced to a mere epiphenomenon of instrumental thought, Pater risks abandoning the objective autonomy of the art-work itself. As 'being' rather than 'doing', art and aesthetic experience may perhaps succeed in escaping from the means–ends logic of economic (commodity) production. Yet, in the process, Pater essentially subjectivizes the claim to aesthetic autonomy, preserving it, primarily, inside the consciousness of the subject who 'treats life in the spirit of art'. In *The Tragic Muse*, by contrast, James would appear to suggest that it is only through an acceptance of the objectification of aesthetic experience, and of the corresponding sublation of the empirical subjectivity of the artist, that a true autonomy can be reached. This process of objectification is necessary for otherwise art could only be autonomous in conditions of subjective freedom; conditions which, as *The Tragic Muse* demonstrates, are always contingent and rarely attained. But, for James (as for Adorno), objectification also means that art is forced to purchase its autonomy at the cost of admitting its unavoidable entanglement with the heteronomous imperative of production.

Returning to James's fictional reworking of Paterian terminology, then, we can see how *The Tragic Muse* not only inverts Pater's assertion of the primacy of 'being' over 'doing', but also recognizes the difficulties inherent on both sides of this duality. The position which Gabriel occupies in the novel remains an important one since it allows James to examine the very real constraints imposed upon art by the burgeoning consumer culture of the late nineteenth century. As Freedman has observed, it is Gabriel who most clearly recognizes the danger of Miriam's commodification as a theatrical spectacle, as well as sensing the possibility that Nick will be reabsorbed into 'society' by way of the bourgeois art market.[29] Yet to assume, with Gabriel, that all artistic production is irredeemably degraded by its commodification is, in the first instance, to neglect the constitutively ambivalent status of art within bourgeois society. For commodification, as various critics have observed, is not merely an external imposition upon the autonomy of the art-work, but is, as well, immanently related to the foundation of the claim to aesthetic autonomy itself. It is, in fact, only with the historical development of the capitalist system of market exchange that art acquires a functional freedom which reflects the autonomy of the commodity form in general: hence, W. F. Haug's reminder that '[a]lthough the work of art according to our spontaneous assumption is something that is opposed to commerce, we owe it to commerce.'[30]

In accordance with this socio-historical insight, *The Tragic Muse* can also be seen to argue that, whilst the work of art cannot be exempted from its status as a commodity, neither can it be completely exhausted by it. Despite the inauspicious material conditions in which both Miriam and Nick are forced to produce, their work evidently retains at least some elements of objective freedom. In response to Gabriel's dismissive view of Miriam's profession, for instance, Peter Sherringham objects that 'you see her too much as a humbug and too little as a real producer ... she loves the thing for itself' (p. 352). Whereas, in Gabriel's Paterian outlook, 'doing' cannot be anything other than extraneous to a serious cultivation of the 'thing for itself', Miriam's devotion to the practice of her art reveals an autonomy which is inseparable from the process of material production. Although Miriam's art is similar, in some respects, to Gabriel's equally performative 'art of life', the difference between them lies in the actress's capacity to alienate her self within concrete dramatic representations (p. 34). Under the tutelage of Mlle Carré, she learns how to mediate a strong subjectivity through the objective requirements of artistic technique. In the case of Nick's career, we are presented with an even more striking, though arguably less successful, fictive example of what James, in his 'Preface' to *The Golden Bowl*, termed the 'religion of doing'.[31] It is Nick who most forcibly articulates James's critique of Paterian aestheticism through his insistence that '[a]rt was *doing*—it came back to that—which politics in most cases weren't' (p. 393). To be sure, the resolute productivism of this stance is not one that the text can unequivocally endorse. There are moments in the novel when Nick's solution to his vocational dilemma seems, ironically, to affirm a quintessential bourgeois imperative: the blindness of his decision to 'produce' registering the very system of external coercion from which he has endeavoured to escape. It is for this reason that 'being' cannot simply be replaced by 'doing', as Michael Anesko appears to propose, without losing the dialectical tension of James's text.[32]

Jamesian aestheticism does, however, differ from Pater's more celebrated version by virtue of its insistence on the primacy of objective over subjective autonomy, and thus it entails a more pragmatic or 'realistic' accommodation to the material conditions of artistic production. Similarly, one might argue, as I suggested earlier, that *The Tragic Muse* frames its debate upon aestheticism within the form of a realist novel. Yet James's realistic aestheticism (if such an oxymoron be allowed) is not merely an uneasy compromise between antagonistic forms and positions. It may also be viewed as a necessary response to the same 'irresoluble contradiction' which Adorno locates at the heart of the modern category of the aesthetic. As an object of 'purposefulness without purpose' (to use Kant's paradoxical formulation), art, Adorno recognizes, is implicated in the instrumental rationality which it simultaneously disavows:

> The contradiction between what is and what is made, is the vital element of art and circumscribes its law of development, but it is also art's shame: by following, however indirectly, the existing pattern of material production and 'making' its objects, art as akin to production cannot escape the question 'what for?' which it aims to negate.[33]

Despite all of his polemics against realism as a literary form, then, Adorno's theory of autonomous art arrives at a position which is not dissimilar to James's in its acknowledgement of art as a paradigm of material production. Like James, Adorno refuses either simply to affirm or to abandon the desire for autonomy which aims to negate the question of 'what [art is] for'; unlike Pater, they both of them suggest that art is compelled to encompass 'being' *and* 'doing'.

Earlier in this essay I suggested that aestheticism, through its characteristic manipulation of normative cultural and epistemological boundaries, might well be defined as an aesthetic of transpositionality, but it remains to be stated, finally, how James's encounter with Paterian aestheticism exemplifies or modifies this claim. On one level, of course, James's 'quotation' of Pater's essay on Wordsworth within the fictional discourse of *The Tragic Muse* could itself be read as an instance of intertextual literary translation; one which immediately disproves the existence of hermetically-sealed boundaries between texts. On another level, James's handling of the conflict between artistic autonomy and political commitment within the same novel can be seen to question and transpose polarized terms of opposition, not least through its culminating realization of the necessary interrelationship between the individual self and society. Nick Dormer's ostensible movement away from politics and towards art might, thus, be defended against the accusation of mere escapism by means of the Adornian argument that autonomous art, by virtue of its capacity to recognize its complicity with social experience in the act of protesting against it, carries with it a critical charge that is absent from the officially-recognized sphere of politics. Yet the transposition of politics into art that is witnessed explicitly within Adorno's theory and, putatively, within James's fiction must also be distinguished from the attempt to reintegrate art into life which is espoused by Pater (and by Walter Benjamin in dialogue with Adorno). The transpositional logic of Paterian aestheticism leads to a radical dissolution of the boundaries between aesthetic experience and empirical reality, and thus threatens to erode the autonomy of art in the very name of extending it. Art is translatable into life, but at the apparent risk, for James, of relaxing the tension between 'original' and 'copy' upon which the dynamic of translation still depends.

NOTES

This essay is dedicated to Inga-Stina Ewbank, who first encouraged me to work on James as a postgraduate student ten years ago.

1. See Friedrich Schiller, *On the Aesthetic Education of Man. In a Series of Letters*, ed. and trans. Elizabeth M. Wilkinson and L. A. Willoughby (Oxford: Clarendon Press, 1967), p. 56. For Carlyle's translation, see his *Life of Friedrich Schiller* (London: Chapman and Hall, 1893), p. 156.
2. Oscar Wilde, 'The Decay of Lying' in *Complete Works of Oscar Wilde* (Glasgow: HarperCollins, 1994), p. 1085.
3. Jonathan Loesberg, *Aestheticism and Deconstruction: Pater, Derrida, and de Man* (Princeton: Princeton University Press, 1991), p. 1.
4. Loesberg, *Aestheticism and Deconstruction*, pp. 4–9, 143.
5. See Theodor Adorno, 'Commitment', trans. Francis McDonagh in

Ernst Bloch, *et al.*, *Aesthetics and Politics* (London and New York: Verso, 1980), pp. 177–95.

6. Adorno, 'Commitment', p. 178.

7. Adorno, 'Commitment', p. 190. For a different inflection on this argument, see Theodor W. Adorno, *Aesthetic Theory*, trans. Robert Hullot-Kentor (London: Athlone Press, 1997), pp. 225–27.

8. J. M. Bernstein, *The Fate of Art: Aesthetic Alienation from Kant to Derrida and Adorno* (Cambridge: Polity Press, 1992), p. 196.

9. See Adorno, 'Commitment', pp. 193–94.

10. Adorno, 'Commitment', p. 193.

11. See Adorno, *Aesthetic Theory*, pp. 237, 270–71, 321.

12. Theodor Adorno, 'Letters to Walter Benjamin' in *Aesthetics and Politics*, pp. 121–22.

13. See Theodor W. Adorno, 'The George–Hofmannsthal Correspondence 1891–1906' in *Prisms*, trans. Samuel and Shierry Weber (Cambridge, MA: The MIT Press, repr. 1994), pp. 189–226.

14. Adorno, 'The George–Hofmannsthal Correspondence', p. 218.

15. Adorno, 'The George–Hofmannsthal Correspondence', p. 217.

16. Adorno, 'Commitment', p. 194.

17. Henry James, *The Tragic Muse*, ed. with an introduction by Philip Horne (Harmondsworth: Penguin, 1995), p. 1. All subsequent page references are to this edition and included in the text of the essay.

18. For this interpretation of the naturalist project, see Fredric Jameson, *The Political Unconscious: Narrative as a Socially Symbolic Act* (London and New York: Routledge, 1983), p. 190.

19. The novel bears marked similarities, for example, to both *The Bostonians* (1886) and *The Princess Casamassima* (1887): in general terms, each of these texts deals thematically with contemporary 'social' issues, while formally each deploys an obtrusively external narrative voice.

20. Adorno, 'The George–Hofmannsthal Correspondence', pp. 224–25.

21. See Jonathan Freedman, *Professions of Taste: Henry James, British Aestheticism, and Commodity Culture* (Stanford, CA: Stanford University Press, 1990), pp. 185–86.

22. In his 'Preface' to *The Renaissance*, for instance, Pater emphasizes the radically private nature of aesthetic experience, but stops short of denying all possibility of its communication. See Walter Pater, *The Renaissance: Studies in Art and Poetry*, ed. Adam Philips (Oxford and New York: Oxford University Press, 1986), p. xxx.

23. For a discussion (and critique) of critical attempts to identify the 'source' for Gabriel, which does recognize his resemblance to Pater, see D. J. Gordon and John Stokes, 'The Reference of *The Tragic Muse*' in *The Air of Reality: New Essays on Henry James*, ed. John Goode (London: Methuen, 1972), pp. 147–54. Freedman also notes Gabriel's espousal of Paterian

doctrine, but prefers to position him as a Wildean figure: see *Professions of Taste*, pp. 183–92.

24. See Walter Pater, 'Wordsworth' in *Appreciations With an Essay on Style* (Evanston: Northwestern University Press, 1987), p. 60. All subsequent page references are to this edition and included in the text of the essay.

25. For a further example of this tendency in Pater's thought, see his 'Preface' to *The Renaissance*, pp. xxix–xxx.

26. For a consideration of the category of the aesthetic in terms of the differentiation of mental faculties imposed by Kantian philosophy and its subsequent impact on modern culture, see Wolfgang Fritz Haug, 'Towards the Dialectics of the Aesthetic' in *Commodity Aesthetics, Ideology and Culture* (New York and Bagnolet: International General, 1987), pp. 131–43.

27. See Peter Bürger, *Theory of the Avant-Garde*, trans. Michael Shaw (Minneapolis: University of Minnesota Press, 1984), pp. 27–54.

28. See Wolfgang Iser, *Walter Pater: The Aesthetic Moment*, tr. David Henry Wilson (Cambridge: Cambridge University Press, 1987), pp. 31–32.

29. See Freedman, *Professions of Taste*, pp. 187–90.

30. Haug, 'Towards the Dialectics of the Aesthetic', p. 136. For a similar observation on the historical relationship between the category of aesthetic autonomy and the commodity form, see Terry Eagleton, *The Ideology of the Aesthetic* (Oxford: Blackwell, repr. 1995), p. 9.

31. See Henry James, *Literary Criticism: French Writers, Other European Writers, The Prefaces to the New York Edition* (New York: Library of America, 1984), p. 1340.

32. See Michael Anesko, *'Friction with the Market': Henry James and the Profession of Authorship* (New York and Oxford: Oxford University Press, 1986), pp. 137–38.

33. Theodor Adorno, *Minima Moralia: Reflections from Damaged Life*, trans. E. F. N. Jephcott (London: Verso, 1978), p. 226.

Helena Faucit: Shakespeare's Victorian Heroine

GAIL MARSHALL

Any artistic production inevitably involves an act of translation, a transference of a form, commodity, or idea across a boundary, be that boundary one of time, space, language, or cultural medium. Shakespeare and his works are among the most durable and flexible of translated media, and seem unlikely to be easily exhausted. Particularly interesting are the ways in which 'Shakespeare' operates both as an enabling medium and as an object who is himself translated. Within the economy of translation, the facilitating medium is a common point of reference, a shared experience which first makes conceivable the possibility and desirability of that exchange that is the end result of an act of cultural translation or transmission. That medium is far from being a necessarily passive part of the translation and, indeed, may itself be transformed, or at least refigured, by the generosity and expansiveness which characterize acts of the best form of cultural transmission. Shakespeare's work has become a form of common currency which facilitates exchanges of theatrical and cultural practice, and which is itself made anew in that act. Such is his status that he can enable the initial act of recognition, or will to recognize, upon the acceptance of which a translation vitally depends.

Two recent examples of the absorption of a Shakespearean reference into popular culture demonstrate how the playwright's fame may carry the life of the Victorian performer forward into a new century, and crucially into new media. The film, *In the Bleak Midwinter* (1995), one of Kenneth Branagh's numerous homages to Shakespeare, included an all-too-brief recognition of Ellen Terry and Henry Irving's 1888 production of *Macbeth* at the

Lyceum Theatre. John Sessions' camp theatrical character appears dressed as Ellen Terry, in a costume and wig inspired by John Singer Sargent's portrait of Terry in that role.[1] Richard Briers impersonates Irving's Macbeth. Thus, through the recognition engineered by Branagh, one who would himself carry on their tradition of popularizing Shakespeare, two of the most important performers of Shakespeare in the nineteenth century live on into the twentieth.

Similarly, in her novel *Wise Children* (1991), Angela Carter represents Terry's story through the familiar medium of Shakespearean references. In telling the story of Estella Hazard, Nora and Dora Chance's grandmother, Carter draws on some of the most popular aspects of Terry's story, and in particular on her work in Shakespeare. Estella was best-known as a Shakespearean actress, as was Terry, and, in her, Carter epitomizes the mischief and irrepressibility that were Terry's trademarks. Her contemporaries record of Estella that 'A star danced and she was born',[2] the same Shakespearean tag Terry adopted for herself. Following that initial invocation of Terry, whose lectures on Shakespeare also provide one of the novel's epigraphs,[3] Carter employs the Terry-figure as a focus for the memories of a variety of well-known legends about female performers, such as Nellie Melba, and Sarah Bernhardt, whose female Hamlet is copied by Estella. Even for those readers unaware of Terry's story and work, the references to Shakespeare provide a vocabulary through which she and her impact can be told and effectively translated for an audience removed in time, place, and theatrical experience, from Terry's own period.

In both of these instances, Shakespeare provides a medium which is familiar and authoritative enough to establish an initiating link between contemporary audience and past performer. In the words of Anna Jameson in 1832, 'the great name of SHAKSPEARE [sic]' invokes 'a bond of sympathy among all who speak his language'.[4] However, Jameson's Shakespeare was not the same figure as that to which we might appeal today. He was then revered rather as a writer and poet than as a dramatist. His work was rarely seen uncut on the early nineteenth-century stage and, when seen at all, was liable to prove disappointing. As

Hazlitt notes, 'the reader of the plays of Shakespear [sic] is almost always disappointed in seeing them acted; and, for our own part, we should never go to see them acted, if we could help it'.[5] Jameson's Shakespeare is one created out of her conversations with the actress Fanny Kemble (who had not, however, acted all of the parts discussed by Jameson), and out of her own reading, rather than out of her theatre-going.

The nineteenth century, and particularly the Victorian period, was, however, the period which established the foundations for the kind of theatrical authority which we accord to Shakespeare today. Part of that authority derives from the kind of psychological verisimilitude with which Anna Jameson credits Shakespeare. Writing in 1832, Jameson was one of the earliest nineteenth-century women to comment substantially on Shakespeare and his depiction of women, and was instrumental in establishing Shakespeare's authority on that subject. She uses Shakespeare's women 'to illustrate the various modifications of which the female character is susceptible, with their causes and results' (p. 7). It is not Jameson's explicit intention to offer up Shakespeare's women as exemplary paradigms, but rather to seek to offer, through a study of them, an assessment of what it is possible for women to achieve, and to support her contention:

> [that] the condition of women in society, as at present constituted, is false in itself, and injurious to them,—that the education of women, as at present conducted, is founded in mistaken principles, and tends to increase fearfully the sum of misery and error in both sexes. (pp. 7–8)

Much of Jameson's introduction, which is written in the form of a dialogue between 'Alda', the voice of the author, and her male opponent, 'Medon', is taken up with her justification for using examples from Shakespeare, rather than from history, for her analysis of the actual and potential situations of women. In Shakespeare, Jameson finds 'complete individuals, whose hearts and souls are laid open before us: all may behold, and all judge for themselves' (pp. 21–22). Jameson accords to Shakespeare unrivalled authority on the subject of 'the feminine character' in its many variations:

> I wished to illustrate the manner in which the affections would naturally display themselves in women—whether combined with high intellect, regulated by reflection, and elevated by imagination, or existing with perverted dispositions, or purified by the moral sentiments. I found all these in Shakspeare [sic]. (p. 55)

Jameson is clearly concerned to establish a 'special relationship' between Shakespeare and Victorian women. It was one that endured for the rest of the century, the benefits of which proved entirely mutual. In Shakespeare, Victorian women found a champion, and actresses a means of occupying the stage free from the suspicions of immorality usually attending the female performer. In them, Shakespeare was translated from page to stage, from the Renaissance to the nineteenth century. The rest of this essay will demonstrate the complementarity of this relationship, and the multiple processes of mutual translation involved in it; and it will draw in particular on the example of Helena Faucit, later Lady Theodore Martin, one of the most prominent of Victorian actresses, and one who was pre-eminent in her Shakespearean roles. In looking both at Faucit's *On Some of Shakespeare's Female Characters* (1887) and at her husband's biography of her, I will show how Faucit creates herself, and is seen, as a Shakespearean heroine, but one who is thus also a most exemplary Victorian woman. In the carefully constructed narratives of Faucit's life, the terms 'Victorian' and 'Shakespearean' are synonymous; they translate each other in Faucit's lexicon of idealized femininity.

Faucit's *On Some of Shakespeare's Female Characters* ostensibly purports to be an attempt 'to express in simplest language what I feel deeply about these exquisite creations of Shakespeare's genius'.[6] Having had 'the great advantage of throwing [her] own nature into theirs' (p. viii), Faucit positions herself simply as a mediating agent placed between the 'sister-women' of her time (p. viii) and Shakespeare; and suggests that her primary interest in doing so lies in enhancing the love and understanding of the former for the playwright. She writes, in a way which shares the enthusiasm and commitment, if not the aggrandizing fervour of Jameson, that

> My best reward would be, that my sister-women should give me, in return, the happiness of thinking that I have helped them, if ever so little, to appreciate more deeply, and to love with a love akin to my own, these sweet and noble representatives of our sex, and have led them to acknowledge with myself the infinite debt we owe to the poet who could portray, as no other poet has so fully done, under the most varied forms, all that gives to woman her brightest charm, her most beneficent influence. (pp. viii–ix)

In the letters which follow, her primary means of achieving this end is to position herself as one essentially formed by Shakespeare, and thus as exemplifying the benefits he can confer on Victorian women. In allying herself so closely with Shakespeare's women, Faucit of course confers upon herself their idealized status.

The process of Faucit's construction as a Shakespearean heroine begins while she is still at school. During what appears to have been at times a lonely childhood, Faucit writes that her books 'filled my young heart and mind with what fascinated me most—the gorgeous, the wonderful, the grand, the heroic, the self-denying, the self-devoting' (p. 5). Within her reading, which included *The Arabian Nights*, *Pilgrim's Progress*, and *Paradise Lost*, Shakespeare was the greatest influence. 'Thus', she recollects, 'I had lived again and again through the whole childhood and lives of many of Shakespeare's heroines long before it was my happy privilege to impersonate them and make them, in my fashion, my own' (p. 6). By her own account then, Faucit is in some measure parented by Shakespeare, his visions of femininity shaping her own from an early age.[7] She recollects that the particular heroines of her youth were those 'who were put most sorely to the proof ... Juliet, Desdemona, Cordelia, Imogen'. She notes in explanation, 'Pathos, heroism, trial, suffering—in these my imagination revelled' (p. 231).

It is thus that Faucit strikes the keynote of her relationship with Shakespeare: not so much in the particular characteristics of the heroines she selects, but in the way in which she describes how that relationship is facilitated, that is, through the imagination, and through as close an identification as possible with

Shakespeare's women. As Faucit writes at the end of her letter on Ophelia, 'I tried to give not only [Shakespeare's] words, but, by a sympathetic interpretation, his deeper meaning—a meaning to be apprehended only by that sympathy which arises in, and is the imagination of, the heart' (p. 20). Faucit does not share Jameson's fascination with the sheer variety of Shakespeare's heroines, but is attracted rather by the ways in which they seem to her to be able to articulate either her own predicament, or her youthful sense of a feminine ideal. In Faucit's usage, and in that of her later critics and reviewers, the term imagination is used to signal not an intellectual effort of affiliation with the unfamiliar, but rather a form of instinctive identification with what is already either known or desired.

This approach generates an appreciation of Shakespeare's women which is based on the possibility of their proximity to Faucit's own character and situation as a Victorian. She writes of them as 'my heroines—for they were mine, a part of me' (p. 49). As a strategy designed to generate popularity and warm regard, it could hardly fail. Theodore Martin suggests that Faucit succeeded because she 'put in living form before her audiences the types of noble womanly nature as they had been revealed by our best dramatic poets, and especially by Shakespeare' (p. 166), and that she 'was in herself a "Shakespeare-Lady" to many in her social life, as well as upon the stage' (p. 105). There is something essential in this relationship, something mutually life-conferring which is based on, and facilitated by, both the reverence in which Shakespeare and his female characters were held and by the particular form of theatrical aesthetic that Faucit was adopting. Her very choice of characters to write about is significant in signalling the approach she took to Shakespeare, and the ways in which she set about writing her own story alongside her tribute to the playwright. Ophelia, Portia, Desdemona, Juliet, Imogen, Rosalind, and Beatrice are, without exception, in Faucit's hands, rendered exemplary women who are capable of rousing an audience to that height of moral appreciation which was the end of Faucit's art. Her art had to be a potent influence for good in her audience, and Shakespeare provided the best means of achieving that end: 'but for her', as Martin observed, '[audiences] would never have known the impulses of elevating thought and feeling, which a woman of a lofty nature can arouse, by the living commentary of voice and look and movement, in the impersonation of ideal characters upon the stage' (p. 231). Faucit is thus elevated by enabling newly idealized versions of Shakespeare's women to be staged.

Faucit's own conception of her function is indicated in a characteristically fulsome tribute to the recipient of one of her letters, John Ruskin. In the opening comments of her letter on Beatrice, she writes of how Ruskin had used Shakespeare's heroines 'to illustrate the part women have played, and are meant to play, in bringing sweetness and comfort, and help and moral strength, into man's troubled and perplexing life' (p. 291). These words are, of course, more appropriate to Ruskin's project in texts such as *Sesame and Lilies* (1867) than they could possibly be to Shakespeare's Beatrice, whose function is, as Anna Jameson noted, that of a 'character of the intellect' rather than of the emotions. Faucit goes on to compare Beatrice unfavourably with Rosalind: 'Her character is not to me so engaging. We might hope to meet in life something to remind us of Beatrice; but in our dreams of fair women Rosalind stands out alone' (p. 292). The opposition between the women of life and of dreams, between the real and the ideal, is a distinction fundamental to Faucit's theatrical aesthetic, and to an understanding of her success. Her insistence upon striving towards a feminine ideal, combined with her imaginative identification with Shakespeare's heroines, created a figure who became a member of the court circle and a great favourite of Queen Victoria,[8] but who was also associated with the stage without once attracting to herself any hint of scandal. She wrote to the Bishop of Manchester in 1878, when she had retired from the stage but was still giving semi-public readings of Shakespeare:

> I have ever found my art a most purifying and ennobling one, and the aim of all my life has been to educate and elevate myself up to it. To live in the contemplation of high thoughts, clothed, as in Shakespeare, in the loftiest language, 'to show virtue her own feature, scorn her own

> image', self-sacrificing heroism its own reward, how can this be lowering to a well-regulated mind?
>
> (quoted in Martin, p. 350)

Shakespeare thus becomes both the inspiration and the most appropriate vehicle for Faucit's moral aspirations, the voice which most fully tells of her (and perhaps all Victorian women's) proximity to an ideal which his heroines embody.

There might seem, initially, to be a potential contradiction in Faucit's own espousing of a self-professed ideal status in her extensive writing on Shakespeare's women, and in her own approximation to their outstanding virtues, of which modesty is an important component. However, Faucit avoids this problem by insisting upon the 'naturalness' of what she is doing, the lack of an artificial layer of consciousness between herself and her characters. Faucit reports the advice of an older actor, a Mr Elton, that she must stop thinking of herself and her shortcomings, lest she 'should spoil [her] style, the charm of which was [her] self-forgetfulness and power of identifying [herself] with the character [she] was acting' (p. 51). This self-forgetful identification is the keynote of Faucit's performances, and that which enables her to be found most natural when she is identifying most successfully with those characters who were especially favoured by her Victorian audiences.

The rhetoric of the natural is inevitably an ideologically significant one, telling more perhaps of expectations satisfied than of what is actually to be seen in a performance, and it dominates those critical responses to Faucit which are painstakingly recorded by her biographer and husband. Martin often invoked his wife's 'natural' acting in order to counter the popularity, and what he saw as the highly-trained acting style and moral improprieties of the French stage. He describes how the 'natural' actor will first approach a part with the two elements of patience and conscience which enable interpretation, and ensure that 'no personal considerations' can interfere with the actor's interpretation of 'the author's purpose'. He goes on, 'It is only when so prepared, that the actor will be free [...], without losing his hold of nature, [to] surround with a halo of ideality what will otherwise not rise above the level of the commonplace. Truth to nature is the basis of all good acting' (p. 337).

The location of the natural, the means of its discrimination, is often seen to reside in the wisdom and authority of Shakespeare. Martin describes Faucit as being 'true both to Shakespeare and nature' (p. 276), in such a way as to collapse the gap between the two. Faucit herself writes in her diary, 'How ever fresh and new, like nature herself, are these exquisite women of Shakespeare!' (5 October 1869; quoted in Martin, p. 302), and in her study notes of Portia that she seemed to the actress to be 'a perfect piece of Nature's handiwork' (pp. 25–26). This conjunction then of the specially favoured actress, the playwright, and nature, seems to have been almost impervious to criticism. Even the famously dissenting voice of G. H. Lewes appears not to have been able to maintain his hostility to Faucit for long.[9]

The benefits to Faucit of her part in this relationship are evident and indisputable. Despite appearing in the works of other highly reputable playwrights, such as Browning and Bulwer Lytton, it was as a Shakespearean actress that she was principally known for the entirety of her long career, which stretched from 1836 to her benefit performance of Rosalind in Manchester in 1879. It was arguably also the status of Shakespeare, and what Faucit had made of him, that enabled her to carry on acting after her marriage in 1851, a circumstance which, though not exceptional, was certainly unusual outside the dynastic theatrical families of the nineteenth century, such as the Terrys. Following her official retirement, Faucit continued to impersonate Shakespeare's heroines in readings at her, and her friends', homes, events at which she was often assisted by Henry Irving. Faucit's readings, sometimes given to as many as eighty people, elide further still the possibility of a gap between Faucit and the heroines who had become her own during the century. Their location in a space which becomes both domestic and public serves only to highlight the mutual identification of the actress, the Victorian wife, and Shakespeare.[10]

The benefits to Shakespeare and to his plays of this relationship are evident in critics' recognition of the ways in which Faucit bases her interpretation of her parts on her direct study of

Shakespeare's texts, rather than on her understanding of a corrupted stage tradition (thus perpetuating the concern of her erstwhile mentor, William Macready, to dramatize as far as possible Shakespeare's words). Martin writes that Faucit 'took her inspiration direct from the text of the poet' (p. 40), and that in the case of Rosalind, her depiction was of 'the Rosalind whom Shakespeare drew', rather than the character of 'hoydenish vivacity' (p. 65) to whom audiences were more accustomed. In contrast to Hazlitt, the Victorian critic George Fletcher maintained that it was only on the stage that 'current misconceptions regarding Shakespeare' could be rectified, and only by such an artist as Faucit.[11] To this end, he hopes that Helena Faucit may find 'in our metropolis, a stage and a manager equally capable and willing with herself, to return to Shakespeare, to nature, and to everlasting truth' (p. 198).

The possibilities of 'authenticity' and respect for the text that such an approach might seem to offer were, however, themselves always to be mediated through the possibilities acceptable to a Victorian audience. Shakespeare was congenial insofar as he might seem to enamour audiences of Faucit's palatable version of femininity. It is perhaps no surprise that Faucit's two most popular parts were Rosalind and Juliet. Of the former she writes that 'in impersonating [her] I was able to give full expression to what was best in myself as well as in my art' (p. 238). She reserves her closest identification for the part of Juliet, which, she writes, 'seems inwoven with my life' (p. 85). The limitations of both Faucit and her audiences may be seen in their responses to two of Faucit's most frequently acted Shakespearean roles, those of Rosalind and Lady Macbeth. In this final part of my essay, I want to look at how Faucit went about representing these two characters, and negotiating the expectations established by her predecessors. In what follows, we will see the way in which Faucit operated as a 'translator' of Shakespeare for the nineteenth-century legitimate theatre, and how far she was guilty, in that act of translation, of collapsing her parts into an homogenizing aesthetic.

In many respects, of course, these two roles seem diametrically opposed. Rosalind is, as Faucit notes, 'evermore tattling', whereas Lady Macbeth is 'ominously terse' (quoted in Martin, pp. 319, 161); the former, in Faucit's hands, became an idealized heroine, in her words, 'dear and fascinating', full of 'grace and dignity' (pp. 238, 239), whom she always delighted in acting, whereas of the latter she writes that 'To the last time of my performing the character I retained my dread of it' (p. 233). Audiences often juxtaposed the two parts to demonstrate how varied seemed to them Faucit's gifts of representation. Martin quotes a letter from Dorothea Baird Smith which records that she and her sister had never 'seen anything so overwhelming in its terrific majesty and pathos as the Lady Macbeth. The Rosalind and Juliet were all of the perfect loveliness we remembered them, but the Lady Macbeth leaves me without words to express the deep sense of awful grandeur, pity, and terror with which it impressed me' (pp. 357–58). In similar vein, Jane Lushington writes to thank Faucit for 'one of the greatest pleasures I have ever had. The graceful sweetness of Rosalind—dear Rosalind—made me really love her so ... and Lady Macbeth has left me awed and trembling with an almost painful pleasure that I can not put into words' (p. 358).

Both letters are responding to a reading given by Faucit in 1879, when the planned rendition of parts of *Romeo and Juliet* and *As You Like It* was supplemented, at the audience's request, by the sleepwalking scene from *Macbeth*. In some respects, the two parts seem almost to produce each other in the minds of her audiences, and indeed in Faucit's own writings. Not surprisingly perhaps, she does not give a whole letter over to Lady Macbeth, but the fullest account of that role appears as a preliminary to her letter on Rosalind.[12] The connection between the two characters seems to be closer than a simple opposition would suggest. The more one reads of responses to both Rosalind and Lady Macbeth, the more one notices the extent to which there is a continuity in critical language and in the paradigms extracted from Faucit's appearances.

In some measure, the lasting success of Faucit's influence on perceptions of *As You Like It* seems to be that she has gone some way to erasing from critics' and audiences' minds the earlier tradition of playing Rosalind as a boisterous, hoydenish figure. As Charles H. Shattuck suggests, it was Faucit who definitively effected Rosalind's transition from a merrily comic breeches part to a type of exemplary femininity.[13] The opportunities in the role which made it attractive to the popular burlesque actress Madam Vestris were explicitly repudiated by Faucit who, as Imogen, had quarrelled with Macready over his expectation that she would wear revealing tights when she had to appear as a young boy (p. 162). In her hands, according to Martin, Rosalind became a new part, as her audiences realized: 'she showed them a Rosalind—Shakespeare's very own—which all their reading had never led them even to surmise ... she *discovered* Rosalind' (p. 126). The Rosalind who was 'so dear to [Faucit's] imagination' becomes, in a female friend's words, 'so pure, so innocent, so earnest, so noble!' (p. 248).

Such responses are generated by Faucit's reading of the role as one in which Rosalind's femininity is inescapably present to the audience, even when she is dressed as Ganymede. She held it to be necessary that she should 'preserve a refinement of tone and manner suitable to a woman of Rosalind's high station and cultured intellect' (p. 264). The woman is never forgotten in the guise of the boy, and that, not in order that greater comic effects might be enjoyed, but rather that the essence of her femininity might be seen to permeate even the rustic boy's disguise. In many ways this makes for a somewhat serious reading of the play, and one which emphasizes the differences of masculinity and femininity rather than their liminality. Juliet Dusinberre suggests that, in Arden, 'Theatrical disguise robs courtship of the artificial exaggeration of masculine and feminine difference sustained in the skirmishes between Phoebe and Silvius,'[14] but such a reading was not available to the spectators of Faucit's Rosalind. Her 'exuberance of sportive raillery' is not celebrated for its own sake, but for the emotion 'palpitating at the speaker's heart' (Faucit, p. 273) which is strong enough to shine through even Ganymede's boyish zest. Recent critics have seen, in the metatheatricality of a disguised Rosalind performing Rosalind, a demonstration of the 'constructed nature' of the feminine rather than its innateness.[15] Faucit's performance insists rather upon the ineluctability of her femininity.[16]

The same function is performed by Faucit's Lady Macbeth in

whom critics seemed relieved to find an essential femininity which went some way to explaining, if not quite to justifying, her part in her husband's crimes. In Faucit, audiences felt again that they had found 'the true Lady Macbeth', a 'natural character, a generous woman, depraved by her very self-devotion to the ambitious purpose of a merely selfish man', a character who had been produced by Faucit's 'own womanly instinct thoughtfully working upon the lucid indications of the poet' (George Fletcher, quoted in Martin, p. 228). Womanliness is the keynote of Faucit's appearance, and it is especially felt in the banquet and sleepwalking scenes, where her displays of wifely tenderness, and of chilling remorse and despair, may be seen to best effect. Fletcher suggests that recent critical readings of the part accord with Faucit's understanding of it, but that it takes a woman of her kind to exemplify, and definitively to establish, a new reading, unhampered by the 'traditional perversions' of the stage. A later critic compared Faucit's rendering of the role with that of 'Mrs Siddons's massive person and sculptured genius', and finds in comparison that Faucit's was an 'essentially human, and even womanly representation of Lady Macbeth' (quoted in Martin, p. 312). The complexities of Shakespeare's part are scarcely discernible in the satisfaction with which the critics welcome Faucit's simply feminine, even rather pitiable and pathetic, Lady Macbeth.

The Victorian critics, as so many critics both before and since, are concerned to emphasize that they have found the true Shakespeare, that something of the dramatist's essence has been uniquely revealed to their enlightened perceptions. Helena Faucit was crucial in effecting this privileged relationship with Shakespeare, the primary vehicle of which was her femininity. It is this aspect of her work and reputation which forges the link between Victorian audiences and Shakespeare. An early review of Faucit writes of her nature as being 'not so much that of a woman, as that of WOMAN. She infuses, so to speak, the *personality* of the feminine character into every delineation' (quoted in Martin, p. 161). Again, it is this femininity which becomes the medium which enables Shakespeare's translation into an important Victorian playwright, and contributes considerably to Shakespeare's official confirmation at the end of the nineteenth century as England's national poet, complete with his own Memorial Theatre in Stratford. Faucit played the leading role in the production of *Much Ado About Nothing* with which the theatre opened in 1879. Thus, far from always being the vehicle of an actress's memory and repute, the playwright may sometimes be beholden to his translators for his own standing, even for his survival in the theatre.

The transaction between Faucit and Shakespeare ensured, for her, financial security, a professional life which appears to have been genuinely sustaining and fulfilling, the adoration of generations of theatregoers, and an entrance into spheres of society not usually visited by theatre professionals. Her 1844 Rosalind in Edinburgh was even the means of her securing a husband, for it was that role that caused Theodore Martin to fall in love with her. More importantly, however, Shakespeare in his turn effected a crucial translation for Faucit. His plays enabled the synonymity, in her and in responses to her, of the artist and the woman. As Martin, ever her greatest champion writes, 'The artist reacted on the woman and the woman on the artist' (p. 405). Only in Shakespeare could such a symbiosis be envisaged at that time, and arguably only in the Shakespeare of Helena Faucit. In a reversal of one of her benefits to him, the playwright's final gift to his Victorian interpreter is to enable her to translate her acting from the domain of the stage to the more durable realms of the page. Drawing on that unimpeachable authority which she herself had done so much to confer, Faucit writes in *On Some of Shakespeare's Female Characters* not only of Shakespeare's heroines, but of the whole plays, of other aspects of her career, of her private life, and of her social standing. Through Shakespeare, she claims for herself considerable authority as a commentator on the stage and, crucially, is enabled, whilst in some measure camouflaging her story behind her comments on Shakespeare's women, to give her own reading of her performances. She thus make claims for her autonomy, independence, and critical self-awareness as an artist, which might otherwise have been overlooked.

Adopting the social and theatrical rhetoric of the day, Faucit and her critics often note her capacity for losing herself in her part, for achieving a complete identification with her role, and thus seeming to relinquish agency to the playwright whose words she speaks. However, the relationship between actress and author was far from the simple, one-way transaction such a rhetoric envisages. Faucit also finds herself through Shakespeare, as woman, artist, and author. On her funeral monument, Martin had inscribed Leontes's description of Hermione: 'The sweet'st companion, that e'er man/ Bred his hopes out of'. However, far from being the simple monument of inspiring and passive femininity that this quotation would make of her, Faucit in her turn bred her hopes out of, and found their satisfaction in, Shakespeare's women. In speaking their language, she found her own.

NOTES

1. The portrait, which is in the National Portrait Gallery, is itself of course a form of translation, and one which is particularly resonant for the Victorian actress who would otherwise scarcely be able to transcend the moment of her onstage presence. In an age before mechanical reproduction of the work of the theatre, the portrait was a crucial means of transmitting the performer's physical impact. This particular portrait also involved the translation of Terry's purpose in interpreting this controversial part, an interpretation which, by her own testimony, was not one which was fully realizable on the late-Victorian stage of the culturally prominent Lyceum theatre. In the painting, Terry is poised at the moment (unacted upon the stage) when Lady Macbeth raises a crown above her own head, and it suggests, as Ellen Terry writes in *The Story of My Life* (London: Hutchinson, 1908, p. 306), 'all that I should have liked to be able to convey in my acting as Lady Macbeth'.

2. Angela Carter, *Wise Children* (London: Chatto & Windus, 1991), p. 12.

3. The epigraph records Terry's observation: 'How many times Shakespeare draws fathers and daughters, never mothers and daughters.'

4. Mrs [Anna] Jameson, 'Preface' to *Characteristics of Women, Moral, Poetical, and Historical*, 2 vols (London: Saunders and Otley, 1832), p. ix. Subsequent page references are to this edition and included in the text of the

essay. Jameson's work went through seven editions in the nineteenth century, changing its title in 1896 to the more accurate *Shakespeare's Heroines*.

5. William Hazlitt, *A View of the English Stage; or, A Series of Dramatic Criticisms* (1818); quoted in Stanley Wells, 'Shakespeare in Hazlitt's Theatre Criticism', *Shakespeare Survey*, 35 (1982), 47. I am grateful to John Barnard for drawing this aspect of Hazlitt's writing to my attention.

6. Helena Faucit, Lady Martin, *On Some of Shakespeare's Female Characters* (Edinburgh and London: Blackwood, 1887), p. viii. Subsequent page references are to this editon and included in the text of the essay. Faucit's work is made up of eight essays, originally published for private circulation as letters to a number of friends, including Geraldine Jewsbury, John Ruskin, and Robert Browning. The letters also appeared as articles in *Blackwood's Magazine* in the early 1880s.

7. Faucit makes no mention of her parents in her writings, though Theodore Martin explains that both were professional actors, and had separated when Faucit was young. Faucit thus replaces a genealogy of the professional theatre, common to actresses at the time, with one which has a more exalted literary basis. See Sir Theodore Martin, *Helena Faucit (Lady Martin)* (Edinburgh and London: Blackwood, 1900), pp. 1–3. Subsequent page references are to this edition and included in the text of the essay.

8. Faucit's entrée into Court life was initially effected by her husband who was the first biographer of the Prince Consort. However, after her first visit to the Queen at Osborne in 1868, Faucit seems to have generated a genuine affection in Queen Victoria. She and her husband were even honoured with a royal visit to their country home when the Queen visited Wales in 1889. Faucit spent much of her time in reading to the Queen and in helping the Royal children with amateur dramatics.

9. G. H. Lewes wrote a poor review of Faucit's Rosalind in March 1865, to which the Martins apparently reacted badly. In a letter to his eldest son, Lewes writes, 'The Martins, as I feared, are disgusted with my notice of Rosalind [in the *Pall Mall Gazette*]. She is so accustomed to be smeared with fulsome undiscriminating praise that criticism is an offence' (letter of 25 March 1865; quoted in Gordon S. Haight, ed., *The George Eliot Letters*, 9 vols (New Haven and London: Yale University Press, 1954–78), IV, 186). Possibly anticipating their displeasure, Eliot herself wrote a very warm letter to Faucit about the same performance. However, the two couples did not remain estranged for long, as there was a genuine warmth between them, perhaps because Faucit was one of the earliest married women to visit Eliot.

10. The same boundary-blurring aspect marks the convention of the construction of her book in the form of letters to her friends.

11. George Fletcher, *Studies of Shakespeare* (London: Longman, 1847), p. 237.

12. In *On Some of Shakespeare's Heroines*, Faucit gives a brief appendix on Lady Macbeth (pp. 344–47), but most of it is taken up with a letter on the subject of her Lady Macbeth by Dr William Stokes of Dublin.

13. Charles H. Shattuck, *Mr Macready Produces 'As You Like It'; A Prompt-Book Study* (Urbana, Illinois: Beta Phi Mu, 1962), n. p.

14. Juliet Dusinberre, *Shakespeare and the Nature of Women*, second edn (Basingstoke: Macmillan, 1996), p. 250.

15. See Jean Howard, 'Crossdressing, The Theatre, and Gender Struggle in Early Modern England', *Shakespeare Quarterly*, 38 (1988), 418–40 (p. 435).

16. This goes some way to explaining the difficulties Faucit had in giving the epilogue of *As You like It*, which explicitly acknowledges the boy-player originally responsible for acting Rosalind.

'More a Russian than a Dane': the Usefulness of *Hamlet* in Russia

PETER HOLLAND

In April 1879, Anton Chekhov, then aged 19, wrote to his youngest brother, Mikhail Pavlovich Chekhov, recommending some reading:

> Take a look at the following books: *Don Quixote* (complete, in all seven or eight parts). It's a fine work by Cervantes, who is placed on just about the level of Shakespeare. I recommend Turgenev's 'Hamlet and Don Quixote' to our brothers if they haven't read it already. As for you, you wouldn't understand it.[1]

Turgenev's essay had originally been given as a lecture in 1860, the year of Chekhov's birth. My own essay is designed to be an extended gloss on Chekhov's letter. But it is also intended as a gloss on Oswald LeWinter's comment at the end of his introduction to the most conveniently available translation of Turgenev's piece into English (in his fine collection of essays called *Shakespeare in Europe*): 'Turgenev's essay is concerned less with Shakespeare and Cervantes than with the implications for society of their characters.'[2] The 'less ... than' form of the sentence is provocative: less with the texts, play and novel, as literary constructs, than with the social implications abstracted or derived from them by Turgenev.

I shall be substantially concerned with charting the history of those social implications, of the implication and embedding of *Hamlet* into Russian social and political history, the embedding of the text into a social meaning. I shall be outlining the history of Russian *Hamlet* translations and the social contexts for

Turgenev which gave *Hamlet* a specific cultural meaning, and then with the ways in which Chekhov's negotiations with *Hamlet*, the shadowing of some of his work by *Hamlet*, are themselves the outcome of that specific interconnection, a series of links defined and limited by Turgenev's perception of the play and circumscription of the play's field of meaning into an argument for social change. It will lead, finally, to a further stage of seeing how the play has functioned recently in productions in Eastern Europe, in the countries of the former Soviet bloc, the Warsaw Pact, in the last few years.

My concern throughout will be with the particular ways in which *Hamlet* penetrates Russian culture. While the history of texts is necessarily historically and geographically defined, there is a performative history to a text's function in a culture. The Russian construction of *Hamlet* is neither Shakespeare's nor our own; instead the play, as it acquires significance across the history of its appropriation, performs a particular function in Russia, a function which is more social and political than aesthetic.[3] That function is fragmentary and referential, deriving from an accumulative cultural meaning which may have only tangential links to the original play, and as much from assumptions about the play as from any sustained reading of it. My concern traces the afterlife of *Hamlet* in Russia through a study of the ways in which the text is put to use, made to earn its right to exist in a different culture.

The alterity of a text, its otherness within a particular cultural frame, can be seen most directly in the creation of translations. The translations themselves become historical statements, their own specific cultural meanings differently made available through allusions to them, for translations themselves can exist within a text. Let me underline this by looking at a specific problem of translation within a text, of the absorption of translation by a culture within the social and historical definition of particular translations.

In Act 1 of Chekhov's *The Seagull*, just before Treplev's play is about to start, the audience is getting restless. His mother, Arkadina, an actress, sees Treplev coming out from behind the makeshift stage and, when he asks her to be patient, starts putting on an impromptu performance of her own:

'O Hamlet, speak no more:
Thou turn'st mine eyes into my very soul;
And there I see such black and grained spots
As will not leave their tinct.'

Arkadina's quotation, in Russian, from Shakespeare gives Treplev his cue; he has clearly played Hamlet to his mother's Gertrude before and we can see, of course, that there are a number of ways in which this act of quotation is both a reflection of the performative relationship between them and a very specific allusion to Treplev's problems with his mother's relationship with Trigorin. But what does Treplev say? The two most commonly available modern translations into English have him saying the same thing, for there is apparently no space here for the translator's skills:

'Nay, but to live
In the rank sweat of an enseamed bed,
Stew'd in corruption, honeying and making love
Over the nasty sty—'[4]

Treplev, that is, carries on the quotation from Shakespeare's *Hamlet*, from the closet scene, using the gap Gertrude/Arkadina has accidentally opened up, to deliver one of the most vicious descriptions of sexual activity available.

But that is not quite what Treplev actually says. He certainly quotes from *Hamlet* but Chekhov used a particular translation, the translation by Nikolai Polevoy which is far from accurate in representing the Shakespeare text. A retranslation of Polevoy's version would read 'And why did you give yourself to vice and seek love in the abyss of vice?'[5] There is no nasty sty, no rank sweat, no stewing in corruption but instead a rather bland moral statement, sharply put but not unpleasant in its linguistic register, not likely to cause offence. Chekhov, from the array of translations that might have been available to him, chose here to quote from the only edition to soften Hamlet's lines.[6] To understand fully the quotation from *Hamlet* at this point in *The Seagull*, then, we would need to chart the history of translations, to see whether Arkadina, as a provincial actress, might have been more used to performing Polevoy rather than other versions or whether the restrained, censored style of Polevoy carries other implications. Chekhov, of course, might well not have known that Polevoy's translation changed the text so markedly and have used this translation simply because he had a copy conveniently on his shelves, the edition of Polevoy's translation with an introduction by Chekhov's friend A. S. Suvorin in which Suvorin apologized for the inaccuracies of Polevoy's version while praising it as 'perfectly suited to the stage' since it was the version used in a famous production starring Mochalov.[7] The apparently direct translation of *Hamlet* is itself culturally implicated. It is already embedded in the discourse of *Hamlet* in Russia.

Russian versions of *Hamlet* began in 1748 with the publication of an adaptation by Alexander Petrovich Sumarokov, first performed in 1750.[8] Sumarokov, probably the first major Russian dramatist, worked not from the English text but from the French version by Pierre Antoine de La Place, published in the second volume of his *Théâtre Anglais* (1746). This indirection is itself significant, a consequence of the appropriation of French culture by the Russian aristocracy. In this version there is no ghost or gravediggers, nothing to interfere with a classical orthodoxy of conventional Francophile tragedy. Gertrude has already repented of her involvement in the murder of old Hamlet and Claudius has plans to kill her, as well as Hamlet, so that he can marry Ophelia—Polonius is firmly implicated in the original murder here. Hamlet, meanwhile, has plans to kill Polonius, as well as Claudius, which puts Ophelia into an awkward position from early on in the play. She has to plead with Hamlet for her father's life just as Polonius is about to kill her. But it also focuses the drama on a debate in Hamlet between his duty to revenge and his love for Ophelia. Hamlet turns into a hero straight from Corneille and the moral quandary replaces any more substantial—or Shakespearean—issue. At the end, Hamlet kills Claudius offstage, Polonius commits suicide, also offstage, and Hamlet and Ophelia leave the stage, both alive, to get married and reign happily ever after.

If Sumarokov's play seems far away from Shakespeare's, then that is exactly what Sumarokov wished. When accused that his play was derived from Shakespeare *via* La Place, he responded that the critic 'is greatly mistaken' and argued that 'My *Hamlet* ... except for the monologue at the end of the third act and the praying of Claudius, hardly resembles the tragedy of Shakespeare.'[9] Shakespeare's name does not appear anywhere in the 1748 edition of Sumarokov's play. The play is never marked as Shakespeare's, its authorship invisible because culturally insignificant.

After 1762, Sumarokov's play disappeared from the stage, primarily because of awkward parallels between the plot of *Hamlet* and the political situation. The murder of Tsar Peter III by a group of conspirators including Grigori Orlov led to the crowning of the Tsar's widow, Catherine II, whose lover was Orlov.[10] The Tsarevich, later Tsar Paul I, was thus rather too recognizably a Hamlet with Catherine II as a Gertrude now on the throne and with Orlov as Claudius. The play, that is, becomes useless theatrically and politically dangerous, precisely because of the precision of its potential interconnection with the audience's perception of power politics.

A later translation by S. Viskovatov, published in St Petersburg in 1811, was, like Sumarokov's, adapted from a French source by Jean-François Ducis, but heavily infused with a graveyard gloom as if Hamlet had read *Night Thoughts*. His Hamlet roams graveyards at midnight and contemplates revenge while sitting on a tomb.[11] More significant was the verse translation by Mikhail Vronchenko, published in 1828, a version that prided itself on being accurately translated line by line and, where possible, word for word. Vronchenko's aim of accuracy was a consequence of his recognition of the 'almost inexpressible beauties' of Shakespeare.[12] By this point Shakespeare's name and aesthetic value was achieving considerable cultural importance. But Vronchenko's stilted style was essentially unactable; as Pushkin commented, 'an iron weight hangs on every one of Vronchenko's lines.'[13]

Though he cut the text by a quarter and simplified Shakespeare's imagery wherever possible, Nikolai Polevoy's translation, the one Chekhov used in *The Seagull*, was the first reasonably accurate one used in Russian theatre. It was premiered in Moscow in January 1837 and was hugely successful, not least because of the brilliance of Mochalov as Hamlet. Polevoy attended many of the rehearsals and had published his own writing on Shakespeare and numerous translated essays on the plays in his periodical *The Moscow Telegraph*.[14]

Polevoy's emphasis in the translation was on a weak Hamlet, a man continually complaining of his own failure, a failure of will when confronted with a moral obligation, a duty. Anything that might tend to create a more heroic, less vacillating Hamlet, was carefully excised: there is, for example, no fight with the pirates in the course of his journey to England. The sense, strongly marked in the translation, of an individual's powerlessness in the confrontation with a strong but inert state machine, something that we might think of as particularly appropriate to later radical and oppositional readings of the play under the Soviet state, was in itself a political emphasis perfectly appropriate for the Russia of the early nineteenth century. Polevoy added and adjusted to increase this emphasis on Hamlet's sense of his own failure: 'Oh Hamlet, Hamlet!' says his hero, 'Disgrace and shame on you.' But it also began an emphasis on the generalizability, the applicability of the character to a broader social malaise. The most famous line of the translation, a line much quoted, is 'Afraid, I am afraid for man!', a line added to Hamlet's 'Look here upon this picture, and on this' in the closet scene.[15] As Polevoy himself stated, '[Hamlet's] sufferings are understandable to us: they found a painful response in our soul'—note that quintessentially Russian use of the word 'soul'—'we weep with Hamlet and we weep for ourselves.'[16] The empathetic response to the character is redirected towards the empathizers. As the great Russian literary critic of the period, Belinsky, who saw Mochalov's performance at eight of the ten performances in its first run, commented in a famous essay on the production and particularly on Mochalov's performance, 'Hamlet, do you understand the meaning of this word? It is great and deep: it is the life of man, it is man, it is you, it is I, it is each of us.'[17]

What plainly lies behind Polevoy's translation is the single greatest determinant on European Romantic views of the play, the account by Goethe in *Wilhelm Meister's Apprenticeship* (1796). His image of Wilhelm Meister and of Hamlet was of individuals fated and unable to control that fate. Hamlet becomes, in Goethe's formulation, essentially weak but explicably and excusably so. The failure to carry out his duty is a consequence both of a failure of will and a moral weakness but also the impossibility of achieving that obligation that is imposed on him. Goethe's Hamlet is essentially passive in response to his situation. The key lines in the play for Goethe were 'The time is out of joint. O cursed spite/ That ever I was born to set it right.' 'To me, it is clear', he wrote, 'that Shakespeare sought to depict a great deed laid upon a soul unequal to the performance of it.' Goethe's argument depends on a strongly argued belief in the essential nobility and goodness of Hamlet, in his sensitivity and intelligence, his emotional responsiveness and perception, but always coupled with a consequential unworldliness. As he summarized it:

> A beautiful, pure, noble, and most moral nature, without the strength of nerve which makes the hero, sinks beneath a burden which it can neither bear nor throw off; every duty is holy to him,—this is too hard. The impossible is required of him,—not the impossible in itself, but the impossible to him. How he winds, turns, agonizes, advances, and recoils, ever reminded, ever reminding himself, and at last almost loses his purpose from his thoughts, without ever again recovering his peace of mind.[18]

Goethe's reading had, in Germany, specific cultural implications: as Manfred Pfister comments, '*Hamlet* in Germany has not been a play like any other, but a screen on which to project the changing constructions of German national identity.'[19] When Furness dedicated his New Variorum edition of *Hamlet* 'to the "German Shakespeare Society" of Weimar, representative of a people whose recent history has proved once for all that "Germany is *Not* Hamlet"',[20] he was responding to Ferdinand Freiligrath's attack on German thought and its refusal to issue in revolutionary action in a poem of 1844 which opens 'Yes, Germany is Hamlet!'[21]

What Freiligrath was attacking was what came to be known as Hamletism. Goethe's image of Hamlet in *Wilhelm Meister* is a consequence, a working-through to its logical limits of an individualist view of Hamlet. Hamlet's dissociation from the world of Elsinore was the enabling device that allowed for a transposition from the social world of interaction, defined as a political and social context for activity, into a private sphere. This private and disengaged Hamlet, endlessly considering and analysing, creates a mode of thought and sensibility in which what are perceived as the character's strengths are precisely those that define and circumscribe the impossibility of engagement. The 'beautiful, pure, noble, and most moral nature' that Goethe outlined derived the value of those qualities, seen entirely as positive, from their disengagement. If the world is soiling, then the value placed on the retreat into the mind is inevitably high. Hamletism, the intellectual justification for this retreat, can be traced through most of Western Europe as a phenomenon, a validation of asociality, of the right of the sensitive soul, young and emphatically male, to claim the inability of social action as a justification for lethargic dissociation.

In Russia, the attack on Hamletism began early. Belinsky soon turned against Polevoy's translation, attacking it for its melodramatic romanticism and attacking Shakespeare for the uselessness of his drama in dealing with contemporary Russian society since the reality of contemporary Russia could not be represented 'in the spirit and form of Shakespearean drama'.[22] As Belinsky and his successors sought to demand that literature make a deliberate and definable social intervention, that it be seen to foreground its political position in relation to contemporary social life, so they necessarily found in Hamletism an epitome of everything they despaired of. As Hamlet the character could be seen as separable from his play, as the individual could be seen occupying a space disjunct from the community, so Hamletism was seen as a retreat into the self from the pressures of social action and civic responsibility. Since Hamlet was seen as embodying a sphere of literary activity premised on a high value being placed on that disjunction, *Hamlet* became modelled as the site of struggle, the text which needed to be argued over and reviewed for its embodiment of that social irresponsibility.

In the writings of Chernyshevsky, a follower of Belinsky,

Hamletism became enmeshed with the definition of a crucial group of Russians, dubbed the 'superfluous men' or 'alienated men'. In Isaiah Berlin's definition, a superfluous man is a member of this 'tiny minority of educated and morally sensitive men, who, unable to find a place in his native land, and driven in upon himself, is liable to escape either into fantasies or illusions, or into cynicism or despair, ending, more often than not, in self-destruction or surrender'.[23] Hamlet, precisely because of Shakespeare's profound representation of early modern subjectivity, had come to represent all that was unacceptable to those advocating social concern. Hamlet, for Chernyshevsky, was a typical representative of the class that owned serfs and therefore his situation displayed its 'falseness or unnaturalness', simply because serf-owning was morally wrong.[24]

Turgenev's lecture, 'Hamlet and Don Quixote' emerged out of this view and I must summarize Turgenev's argument.

In order to produce a balanced revaluing of Hamlet, Turgenev chose an unlikely opposite in Cervantes' character, chosen because, as he states in the first lines of the essay, 'The first edition of Shakespeare's tragedy *Hamlet* and the first part of Cervantes' *Don Quixote* appeared in the same year at the very beginning of the 17th century' (p. 166). The two types, embodying for Turgenev 'two opposite fundamental peculiarities of man's nature', contain all people: 'nearly every one of us resembles either Don Quixote or Hamlet' (p. 166). Turgenev's view that 'in our day ... the Hamlets have become far more numerous than the Don Quixotes' (p. 166) is precisely an indication of Russia's ineffectuality when it came to bringing about social change.

Turgenev's search for definition of the opposites necessitated an immediate rethinking of Don Quixote, no longer a ridiculous figure but an embodiment of

> faith in something eternal, immutable; faith in the truth, in short, existing *outside* of the individual, which cannot easily be attained by him, but which is attainable only by constant devotion and the power of self-abnegation. (p. 167)

Against this ideal of idealism, Turgenev placed his definition of Hamlet:

> Now what does Hamlet represent?
>
> Analysis, first of all, and egotism, and therefore incredulity ... But this I, in which he does not believe, is dear to Hamlet ... because he finds nothing in the whole universe to which he can cling with all his heart ... He is conscious of his weakness; but even this self-consciousness is power; from it comes his irony, in contrast with the enthusiasm of Don Quixote ... he knows not what he wants nor why he lives, yet is attached to life. (p. 168)

As the description of Hamlet develops, Turgenev balances this damning attack with a recognition of Hamlet's pain:

> I will not be too severe with Hamlet. He suffers, and his sufferings are more painful and galling than those of Don Quixote. The latter is pummelled by rough shepherds and convicts whom he has liberated; Hamlet inflicts his own wounds—teases himself. In his hands, too, is a lance—the two-edged lance of self-analysis. (p. 169)

More significantly, that understanding of Hamlet's self-laceration is set in tension with the undeniable attractions of the character: 'Hamlet's appearance, on the contrary, is attractive ... Everybody flatters himself on passing for a Hamlet. None would like to acquire the appellation of "Don Quixote"' (p. 169). But the attractiveness is set, in turn, against the possibility of sympathy and the near-impossibility of love:

> To love him is almost impossible; only people like Horatio become attached to Hamlet ... Everyone sympathizes with Hamlet, and the reason is obvious: nearly everyone finds in Hamlet his own traits; but to love him is, I repeat, impossible, because he does not love anyone. (p. 170)

While Turgenev recognizes the comedy of Don Quixote, he reads through and under the comedy. The attack on the windmills is stupid, it is thoughtless, it is undertaken without consideration but, Turgenev argues,

> The man who sets out to sacrifice himself with careful forethought and consideration of all the consequences—balancing all the probabilities of his acts proving beneficial—is hardly capable of self-sacrifice. Nothing of this kind can happen to Hamlet ... I suppose that, were truth itself to appear incarnate before his eyes, Hamlet would still have misgivings as to whether it really was the truth. (p. 170)

As the indictment proceeds, various crucial statements enunciate implicitly the values that Turgenev seeks and which Hamlet is found, item by item, to lack entirely:

> The Hamlets are really useless to the people; they give it nothing, they cannot lead it anywhere, since they themselves are bound for nowhere ... Moreover, the Hamlets detest the masses. How can a man who does not respect himself respect anyone or anything else? ... And much more than birth alone goes to make Hamlet an aristocrat. (pp. 172–73)

The assault is savage, making Hamlet diabolic:

> Hamlet embodies the doctrine of negation, the same doctrine which another great poet [i.e. Goethe] has divested of everything human and presented in the form of Mephistopheles. (p. 174)

Hamlet, then, comes to represent an aristocracy that is self-serving and self-interested. As Turgenev suggests towards the climax of his argument, 'the Hamlets are an expression of the fundamental centripetal force of nature, in accordance with which every living thing considers itself the centre of creation and looks down upon everything else as existing for its sake' (p. 176). Don Quixote's centrifugal devotion and self-sacrifice, set against Hamlet's self-regard and self-interest, are transposed in the argument into an analogy with movement which is itself political: Hamlet and Don Quixote become 'two forces of inertia and motion, of conservatism and progress' (p. 176).

The infertile, non-creative Hamlet is then the nexus of a

definition of an aristocracy that claims its superiority as a justification for patronizing social disregard. The isolation which Hamlets claim for themselves out of their assumption of superiority is thus the source of their failure to leave a trace: 'they are lonely, and therefore barren' (p. 173). Turgenev is not a democrat or egalitarian. There is nothing here that suggests a social revolution in which the aristocracy will be lined up against the wall. Instead he is demanding a form of social responsibility across classes: it is precisely what Chekhov is attacking in *The Cherry Orchard* when he allows Anya's excited account of her mother's extravagances in restaurants ('We'll sit down to dinner in a station restaurant, and she orders the most expensive item on the menu. Then she tips all the waiters a ruble each.'[25]) to resonate against Varya's inability to feed the workers on the estate out of what is left of the family money after Ranevskaya has been overspending in Paris. Turgenev's vision, though fundamentally conservative about social structures, is a remarkable critique of the self-indulgence of an essentially aristocratic basis of a core tradition of tragedy. The people, substantially excluded from the self-centred world of tragic action, have, for him, claims on those noble souls who are too busy exploring their own minds and 'have ta'en too little care of this'. The demand to do what Hamlet and Hamletism conspicuously fails to do is a recognition of the claim that Lear in the storm comes to realize, the demands that the 'poor naked wretches' can and should make of those with power.

As, towards the end of the lecture, Turgenev manoeuvres away from the simplified binary structure that underpins his argument, he provides a redefinition of the relationship between the archetypes and the social—and hence between the literary and the social—through a limitation of the applicability of genre:

> [By] a wise dispensation of Nature, there are neither thorough Hamlets nor complete Don Quixotes ... just as the principle of analysis is carried in Hamlet to tragedy, so the element of enthusiasm runs in Don Quixote to comedy; but in life, the purely comic and purely tragic are seldom encountered. (pp. 180–81)

The impurity of social life when measured against the absolutism of literary genre prevents the absolutism of the characters. People tend towards one manifestation or the other, mixing them, not adopting them exclusively. There is, in this, both a comforting denial of the absolute but also a radical denial of the strategies literature uses to establish its models. Tragedy is seen not only as useless but also as untrue: the choice of Hamlet as the central expression of tragedy is bound up with the recognition that Hamlet is an extrapolation, not a representation, an extreme that can only be related back to social behaviour through recognition of the limits of applicability.

Hamlet, character and play, then, comes to stand for the limits of tragedy in relation to social existence and the desired model of political engagement. Hamlet's social uselessness is, for Turgenev, socially useful, a means of charting what social responsibility should be by identifying its opposite. In this model, tragedy, for which *Hamlet* stands as the representative example, is self-indulgent, replacing the demands of society with the sensitivity of the self-interested.

There is, in this, a remarkable subversion of the excuse that the pro-Hamlet faction advance: the determinism of fate. Turgenev's argument denies the determinism of tragedy, seeing in its construction of a necessity only a means of avoiding social responsibility. Hamlet, far from being accurate in his understanding of the world as fatalist, is seen as providing himself with an alibi for his own failure, an alibi that is consoling in its ascription of failure to powers beyond the individual, unseen and unbeatable forces.

In an important letter about his play *Ivanov*, Chekhov tried to explain the difference between his central character and the normal response of the Russian intelligentsia:

> The producer thinks Ivanov an odd-man-out [superfluous man] *à la* Turgenev ... If Ivanov emerges as a villain or odd-man-out ... the play clearly hasn't come off and there can be no question of staging it ... The man's hardly left school when he's already bitten off more than he can chew—thrown himself into education, the peasant problem, scientific farming, ... making speeches, writing to ministers,

> fighting evil, applauding virtue … Physically tired and bored, he can't understand what's happening to him … When narrow, unreliable people get in a mess like this, they usually put it all down to their environment or join the ranks of Hamlets and … superfluous men, and that comforts them. But Ivanov is a very straight person. He tells the doctor and the audience quite frankly that he can't make himself out, keeps saying he doesn't understand.[26]

What Chekhov defines here as the evasive comfort of being Hamlet, offered as an adequate explanation for giving up on society, is explored throughout Turgenev's writing both before and after 'Hamlet and Don Quixote'. It is there in novels like *Rudin* and *On the Eve*, in short stories like 'The Diary of a Superfluous Man' and in plays like *A Month in the Country*. It is there perhaps most directly of all in the brilliant short story 'A Hamlet of the Shchigrovsky District' written in 1849 and included in the collection *Sketches from a Hunter's Album*.

The narrator, staying at the house of a wealthy landowner, heads to bed and falls into conversation with another house guest with whom he is sharing a room. The other figure is never described, never seen, only heard, endlessly listened to. The voice, compulsively talking about his own life history, goes on through the night until shut up by the complaints of another guest in the next room. He becomes simply a voice, narrating his life, defining his sense of his own abilities and failure to realize them, a voice constructing himself as tragic hero in a dull and uninteresting world that he sees as unable to appreciate his talents but which, self-deprecatingly, he does not blame for ignoring him. The nameless voice fashions his view of himself, indulging unstoppably in the creation of himself as a figure determined to find his life subject to the slings and arrows of outrageous fortune. In the end, before finally going to sleep, the narrator starts to ask the man his name:

> 'No, for God's sake,' he interrupted me, 'don't ask me or anyone else for my name. Let me remain for you an unknown person, a Vasily Vasilyevych who has been crippled by fate … But if you earnestly want to give me

> some kind of title, then call me ... call me Hamlet of the Shchigrovsky District. There are many such Hamlets in every district, but perhaps you haven't come across any others.[27]

The bitter comedy of the story's style, the mockery of the would-be Hamlet, contains within it a character who sees himself as a participant in a tragedy, dogged by his own sense of being a 'superfluous man'. But the context for the tale redefines both the pretension to tragedy and the enveloping of the character by narratorial comedy. The first publication of *Sketches from a Hunter's Album* in 1852 resulted in Turgenev's arrest and exile to his estate. The volume's depiction of the oppression of the serfs, the 'dead souls' of Russian society, was unacceptable to the authorities and the stories played a direct part in the movement that led in 1861 to the emancipation of the serfs, the event which for Firs in Chekhov's *The Cherry Orchard* marked the irrevocable change in Russian society, the beginning of the troubles. Turgenev was justifiably proud of the part his writings played in the emancipation movement.

The Hamlet of the Shchigrovsky District is then doubly tragic: a figure in the tragedy he writes himself into but also part of a larger tragedy, the tragedy of the ineffectuality and social irresponsibility of the Russian intelligentsia, the tragedy of failing to connect with their community. The indulgent literariness of one form of tragedy, the construction of tragedy as a solely literary form, is framed and diminished by its revaluation within a larger social tragedy of a society comfortably choosing to see itself as unable to do anything about its appalling problems.

Turgenev's essay on Hamlet and Don Quixote was widely disseminated. In 1876, for instance, three years before Chekhov's letter about it, the essay was included in a Russian schools edition of *Hamlet* in Polevoy's translation, together with two essays by Belinsky, published in St Petersburg (1876). Turgenev and Belinsky now represented a critical tradition appropriate to accompany the Shakespeare text for student use. When Chekhov came to recommend the Turgenev essay to his brothers they would have no difficulty finding it.

Chekhov's own exploration of *Hamlet* extends through the

whole of his work, his continual negotiation with tragedy recurrently defined through a negotiation with *Hamlet* and Hamletism, with the parameters for his response strongly defined by Turgenev's essay. At his comic best, Chekhov places Hamlet within the voice of a self-indulgent, neurasthenic response to the tedium of the capital in the little story 'In Moscow' (1891):

> I am a Moscow Hamlet. Yes. In Moscow I visit the houses, the theatres, the restaurants, and the editors' offices, and everywhere I say exactly the same thing: 'God, what boredom! What oppressive boredom!' And they answer me sympathetically, 'yes, truly, terribly boring.'[28]

By the end of the story, the sense of failure leads to the complete recognition of what might have been and, typically, of the lack of external justification for that lack of accomplishment:

> I could have learned and known everything; ... I might have studied and loved European culture, commerce, trade, village economy, literature, music, painting, architecture, hygiene; I might have built a good pavement in Moscow, traded with China and Persia, diminished the death-rate, combated ignorance, corruption, and all the abominations that hinder us so when we try to live. I might have been reserved, courteous, cheerful, kind-hearted; I might have rejoiced over every success of others, since, however small, every success is already a step towards happiness and truth.
>
> Yes, so I might! So I might! But I am a foul rag, trash, sour fruit; I am a Moscow Hamlet ...
>
> I toss about under my bed-cover, from side to side, am unable to sleep, and always keep wondering why I am so bored, and until morning there sound in my ears the words: 'Take a piece of telephone wire, and hang yourself to the nearest telegraph-pole! There is nothing but that left for you!' (pp. 322–23)

The story, in effect, transposes Turgenev's 'Hamlet of Shchigrovsky District' from country to city. In the course of the journey the type has been redefined, his provincialism becoming the world-weary urbanity of metropolitan man. But he is still whining and complaining. In 1882, Chekhov reviewed a production of *Hamlet* at the Pushkin Theatre in Moscow. He did not like what he saw: Hamlet, he complained, is represented as a whiner, though 'Hamlet was incapable of whining ... Hamlet was a man of indecision, but he was never a coward.'[29]

It is that tension between whining cowardice and indecision that defines the use of *Hamlet* within *The Seagull*.[30] For Konstantin Treplev, the would-be Hamlet of *The Seagull*, is unquestionably a whiner. Hence when Gielgud set out in 1925 to play Treplev as 'a very romantic character, a sort of miniature Hamlet' he found that it simply did not work.[31] Treplev has pretensions to be a Hamlet, he sees his mother as Gertrude, her lover, Trigorin, as his Claudius. Nina becomes, in this pattern, Treplev's Ophelia. The usefulness of *Hamlet* here is as a structural underpinning for the play, a suggestion of what the play might be and hence, precisely and carefully, what it is not. The *Hamlet* structure and the repeated *Hamlet* references are placed by Chekhov within two differing forms of control: on the one hand, there is the structure of self-dramatization, Treplev's desire to play out *Hamlet*, to cast the others (who are often very willing to participate in this transposition) into the play that would justify and magnify his situation. To be Hamlet is more consoling, an external literary high-cultural form that turns the comparative triviality of the problems Treplev is negotiating into the material of weighty tragedy. Hamlet becomes Treplev's aspiration to make his own life into tragedy. Treplev's quotations from *Hamlet* then become part of his own fully aware invocation of Shakespeare analogous to the language of the 'Moscow Hamlet'.

But set against this internal analogy, created by the characters and summoned up by their intentional allusions, comes a second form of *Hamlet*-reference. Treplev may be a devoted believer in the cult of Hamletism but he is also placed by Chekhov within a structure of action that continually evokes the analogy only to deny it. It is there, for instance, in the play-within-a-play which Treplev creates, a play displaced from its structural position in *Hamlet* and made into a representation of artistic desire misformed, incomplete. It is, above all, there in the play's exploration of Nina, the Ophelia who refuses to play as cast.

From the start the analogy with Ophelia is carefully drawn: Nina's mother is dead and her father resists her association with Treplev/Hamlet. More threateningly, she is from the start linked to water: she lives over the lake and her surname, Zarechny, suggests 'across the water'. It is as if the possibility of death by drowning is hanging over her. The threat is of capitulation to the pattern, the abdication of will in the submission to a structure of tragedy which seems inevitable and unavoidably implicit within the play's form. Even the madness which is so painfully a presence for Nina in the last act of the play seems both a consequence of the dreadful experiences she has undergone and a further sign of her determinist alignment with Ophelia.

But, close though she is to madness, tempting though it is for her to commit suicide, Nina refuses the role, refuses to follow through her implication into the destiny of being Ophelia. The model is conjured up only to be altered; the passivity of following the pattern, of taking the analogy as destiny and thereby abdicating individual decision, cannot be accepted by Nina. It allows Nina to leave the play with an openness of ending, of her ending, that denies the Shakespearean form. Nina, in effect, walks out on the tragedy, denying the conventionality and fatalism of tragic closure. In *The Seagull* it is Hamlet, not Ophelia, who dies and the ambiguities of Ophelia's death, suicide or not, are turned into the clear self-slaughter of Treplev.

Treplev finally casts himself, therefore, as a bad Hamlet, a whining coward of a Hamlet, the kind of reading of the role Chekhov had castigated earlier. He does what the Moscow Hamlet cannot be imagined as bringing himself to do but it does not turn him into a Hamlet worthy of admiration. Treplev's suicide only confirms the emptiness of the Hamlet Turgenev had outlined.

Treplev was the third and last of Chekhov's extensive dramatic negotiations with *Hamlet* and Hamletism, following *Ivanov* and the central character of Chekhov's first full-length play, *Platonov*, the man of whom one character says, overexplicitly, 'You all think he's like Hamlet.'[32] For these characters and others in the plays in which they are placed as quasi-heroes, the usefulness of *Hamlet* lies in the audiences' construction of a difference from and a resistance to being Hamlet. The response to the world defined in conventional, classical tragedy, embodied in the potential of being Hamlet, is an evasion, a denial.

At exactly the time at which Chekhov was writing *The Cherry Orchard*, Tolstoy reached the culmination of his response to Shakespeare, and particularly to *King Lear* with his 1903 essay, *On Shakespeare and On Drama*.[33] Tolstoy's loathing for Shakespeare extended to *Hamlet* as well, a response as much consequential on Turgenev as Chekhov's had been. As he wrote to Strachov in 1896, 'What coarse, immoral, mean, and senseless work *Hamlet* is ... [Shakespeare] was so occupied with effects that he didn't take the trouble to give the main character any character.'[34] The extension of the search for the definition of the character of Hamlet becomes, in Tolstoy's demolition of the play, a characterlessness onto which an unthinking intelligentsia had projected its approval.

Tolstoy's most sustained account of Shakespeare was generated by his wish to write a preface to Ernest Crosby's essay on 'Shakespeare's Attitude towards the Working Classes'.[35] Crosby's account of Shakespeare as a reactionary, deeply and unequivocally contemptuous of the workers, prompted Tolstoy. For Tolstoy, the subject of Shakespeare's plays 'is the lowest, most vulgar view of life, which regards the external elevation of the lords of the world as a genuine distinction, despises the crowd, i.e., the working classes—repudiates not only all religious, but also all humanitarian, strivings directed to the betterment of the existing order'.[36] The attack on *Hamlet* and Hamletism now becomes entirely explicit: Shakespeare's moral values, aristocratic and antiproletarian, disqualify his characters and his plays from praise.

Tolstoy's political rejection of Shakespeare was impossible in Soviet Russia. In the Soviet state the negotiation between the wish to value *Hamlet* as a classic of world literature, in spite of Tolstoy, and the wish to make it conformable with Soviet ideology, was tortuous. Its meaning is conspicuously marked by the politics of two productions of *Hamlet*, both rehearsed in 1989 as the Soviet state was collapsing.

Hamlet's usefulness as a means through which it was possible to comment indirectly on the oppressive state was current throughout Eastern Europe. *Hamlet* was, after all, a play which was banned from productions in Soviet Russia under Stalin, a ban which halted the rehearsals of a production (using a new translation by Boris Pasternak) being directed by the co-founder of the Moscow Art Theatre, Nemirovich-Danchenko. The play was always seen as potentially dangerous, signified by the custom, after the ban was lifted, for the line 'There's something rotten in the state of Denmark' to be applauded by the audience, not because of their knowledge of the current state of Danish politics but straightforwardly as an allusion to the Soviet state. Nikolai Okhlopkov, who directed the play at the Mayakovsky Theatre in Moscow in 1954, saw the play as an account of oppression in which the key concept was that 'For Hamlet, the world is a prison', made visible on stage by a front drop of a massive iron grille, suggesting prison bars through which, at Laertes's return, the people could be seen trying to break into the palace. As Okhlopkov declared, 'Here, even to exist is to suffer oppression',[37] a declaration that can only be seen as a comment on the state within which the production was rehearsed, not the state within which the play's fiction is set.

Productions throughout Eastern Europe under Soviet control always sought to define themselves in relation to the official line on the play as a drama of the intellectual as proto-revolutionary hero, Hamlet as the figure chosen by history to reform the entire social world. Hence a 1964 production in Bulgaria made the play into an attack on the continuation of the 'cult of personality' after its supposed abolition in 1956. Or, at its most extreme, a Romanian production in the mid-1970s used Hamlet to show the nightmare of Ceaucescu's regime by turning everyone into Hamlet's enemy so that the ghost was only a trick, set up by Horatio, a member of the secret world of Claudius's court of spies, deliberately aiming to lead his 'friend' into a trap, Hamlet here becoming terrifyingly isolated in a state where treachery and plotting, spying and reporting were ubiquitous.

In 1989 Heiner Müller, the German dramatist, was rehearsing a production of *Hamlet* at the Deutsche Theater in East Berlin.

At the time when the Berlin Wall was coming down and the East German state was collapsing, Müller turned immediately to *Hamlet*. As he said at the time,

> What could right now be a topical play in the GDR? The only thing that came to my mind was *Hamlet*. A play that deals with crises in the state, with two epochs and with the fissure between them. This fissure is straddled by an intellectual, who is no longer certain how to behave and what to do: the old things don't work any more, but the new ways aren't to his taste.[38]

Hamlet becomes insistently and necessarily topical, the tragedy of the intellectual in times of social change.

In the same year, 1989, Andrzej Wajda, the Polish film and theatre director, directed his fourth production of *Hamlet* for the Stary Theatre in Cracow.[39] His first had been in 1960 and had emphasized the Polish context, making Hamlet an intellectual who used his intelligence to cut through the façades of state power to come to an accurate understanding of the nature of the political state. Hamlet's intellect, in this 1960 production, was his only resource against state tyranny, a tyranny which was not altered by the end of the play: Wajda showed a Fortinbras just as ruthless as Claudius. By 1989, in the context of the collapse of the Eastern bloc, Wajda's view of the play had changed enormously. The politics of this production were defined by the production's resolute refusal to be political, a deliberate rejection of the play's Soviet significance. Instead the play was performed with an overriding emphasis on its metatheatricality. The set viewed the action from backstage, from the dressing-rooms and the wings, with a fragment of the 'real' stage glimpsed upstage. The play was performed as a text conscious of its own performance, not least by the casting of a female actor, Teresa Buzisz-Krzyzanowska, as Hamlet.

For all its dazzling theatrical brilliance, Wajda's *Hamlet* seems to have circumscribed the function of *Hamlet* to a metatheatricality, the theatre feeding off itself. The timeless, universal *Hamlet*, the *Hamlet* of classical theatre, becomes uselessly untimely, a failure of engagement, a willingness to be Turgenev's

Hamlet rather than his Don Quixote. In defining tragedy as beyond the immediacy of the social, Wajda made *Hamlet* irrelevant, an evasion not an engagement. Wajda's Polish *Hamlet* rejected the work the play had performed in Russian culture, a culture in which the play had penetrated so deeply that, as William Morris wrote in 1888, 'Hamlet should have been a Russian, not a Dane.'[40]

NOTES

1. *Letters of Anton Chekhov*, ed. Simon Karlinsky (London: The Bodley Head, 1973), p. 36.
2. *Shakespeare in Europe*, ed. Oswald LeWinter (Harmondsworth: Penguin Books, 1970), p. 165.
3. For examinations of Shakespeare in other cultures, see particularly *Shakespeare and National Culture*, ed. John J. Joughin (Manchester: Manchester University Press, 1997).
4. *The Oxford Chekhov*, trans. and ed. Ronald Hingley (London: Oxford University Press, 1967), vol. 2, p. 240; Anton Chekhov, *Plays*, trans. Michael Frayn (London: Methuen, 1988), p. 66.
5. Thomas G. Winner, 'Chekhov's *Seagull* and Shakespeare's *Hamlet*: A Study of a Dramatic Device', *American Slavic and East European Review*, 15 (1956), 106.
6. Winner, 'Chekhov's *Seagull* and Shakespeare's *Hamlet*', p. 107, n. 6.
7. See Harai Golomb, 'Hamlet in Checkov's [sic] Major Plays: Some Perspectives of Literary Allusion and Literary Translation', *New Comparison*, 2 (1986), 74–75. Golomb explores the problem of retranslating this passage into English on pp. 77–78. Intriguingly, the same passage is to a considerable extent bowdlerized in Boris Pasternak's translation in the 1940s as 'To loll about in a greasy, crushed bed, to wallow in the perspiration of vice, to take pleasure in your own downfall'; see Anna Kay France, *Boris Pasternak's Translations of Shakespeare* (Berkeley: University of California Press, 1978), p. 36.
8. See A. P. Sumarokov, *Selected Tragedies*, trans. Richard and Raymond Fortune (Evanston, IL: Northwestern University Press, 1970).
9. Quoted in Ernest J. Simmons, *English Literature and Culture in Russia (1553–1840)* (Cambridge, MA: Harvard University Press, 1935), p. 206. See also D. M. Lang, 'Sumarokov's "Hamlet": A Misjudged Russian

Tragedy of the Eighteenth Century', *Modern Language Review* 43 (1948), 69.

10. On Catherine II's own translations of Shakespeare, see Ernest J. Simmons, 'Catherine the Great and Shakespeare', *PMLA*, 47 (1932), 790–806.

11. See Simmons, *English Literature and Culture in Russia*, p. 222.

12. Quoted in Yuri D. Levin, 'Russian Shakespeare Translations in the Romantic Era' in *European Shakespeares: Translating Shakespeare in the Romantic Age*, eds Dirk Delabastita and Lieven D'Hulst (Amsterdam: John Benjamins, 1993), p. 77.

13. Quoted in Levin, 'Russian Shakespeare Translations', p. 81.

14. See Simmons, *English Literature and Culture in Russia*, pp. 230–32.

15. Quoted in Eleanor Rowe, *Hamlet: A Window on Russia* (New York: New York University Press, 1976), p. 43. See also Levin, 'Russian Shakespeare Translations', pp. 84–88.

16. Rowe, *Hamlet: A Window on Russia*, p. 45.

17. Rowe, *Hamlet: A Window on Russia*, p. 45.

18. Quoted in William Shakespeare, *Hamlet*, ed. H. H. Furness (New York: J. B. Lippincott, 1877), vol. 2, 273.

19. Manfred Pfister, 'Hamlets Made in Germany, East and West' in *Shakespeare and the New Europe*, eds Michael Hattaway, Boika Sokolova and Derek Roper (Sheffield: Sheffield Academic Press, 1994), p. 79.

20. The dedication is not present in the first edition but is in the 1877 edition.

21. Furness reprints Freiligrath's poem in a translation by Furness's sister in vol. 2, 376–78, in the 114-page sequence devoted to German Shakespeare criticism.

22. Quoted in Rowe, *Hamlet: A Window on Russia*, p. 56.

23. Rowe, *Hamlet: A Window on Russia*, p. 59.

24. Rowe, *Hamlet: A Window on Russia*, p. 59.

25. Chekhov, *Plays*, trans. Frayn, p. 288.

26. Hingley, *The Oxford Chekhov*, pp. 291–92.

27. Ivan Turgenev, *Sketches from a Hunter's Album*, trans. Richard Freeborn (Harmondsworth: Penguin Books, 1990), p. 300.

28. Anton Chekhov, 'In Moscow' in Anton Chekhov, *Letters on the Short Story, the Drama and Other Literary Topics*, ed. Louis Friedland (London: Vision Press, 1965), p. 315.

29. Winner, 'Chekhov's *Seagull* and Shakespeare's *Hamlet*', pp. 103–04.

30. On *Hamlet* and *The Seagull*, see Winner, 'Chekhov's *Seagull* and Shakespeare's *Hamlet*'; Golomb, 'Hamlet in Checkov's [sic] Major Plays'; Robert Porter, '*Hamlet* and *The Seagull*', *Journal of Russian Studies*, 41 (1981), 23–32; Tom Matheson, 'Hamlet's Last Words', *Shakespeare Survey*, 48 (1995), 113–21; T. Stroud, '*Hamlet* and *The Seagull*', *Shakespeare*

Quarterly, 9 (1958), 367–72; Hanna Scolnicov, 'Chekhov's Reading of *Hamlet*' in *Reading Plays*, eds Hanna Scolnicov and Peter Holland (Cambridge: Cambridge University Press, 1991), pp. 192–205.

31. John Gielgud, *Early Stages* (rev. edn, London: The Falcon Press, 1948), p. 84.

32. Hingley, *The Oxford Chekhov*, p. 67.

33. See *Tolstoy on Shakespeare*, trans. V. Tchertkoff (New York: Funk and Wagnalls, 1906), and George Gibian, *Tolstoj and Shakespeare* (The Hague: Mouton, 1957).

34. Quoted in Gibian, *Tolstoj and Shakespeare*, p. 22. Cf. its later formulation in the essay: 'it is as clear as day that Shakespeare did not succeed and did not even wish to give any character to Hamlet, did not even understand that this was necessary.' (p. 74)

35. Printed with the English translation of Tolstoy's essay, pp. 127–65.

36. *Tolstoy on Shakespeare*, pp. 93–94.

37. Nikolai Okhlopkov, 'From the Producer's Exposition of *Hamlet*', in *Shakespeare in the Soviet Union*, eds R. Samarin, *et al.* (Moscow: Progress Publishers, 1966), p. 182.

38. Quoted in Pfister, 'Hamlets Made in Germany', p. 76, n. 1.

39. On Wajda's work see Marta Gibinska, 'Polish Hamlets, Shakespeare's *Hamlet* in Polish Theatres after 1945', in *Shakespeare and the New Europe*, pp. 159–73.

40. Quoted in Rowe, *Hamlet: A Window on Russia*, p. xv.

Translation and Self-translation through the Shakespearean Looking-glasses in Joyce's *Ulysses*

RICHARD BROWN

There are several concepts of Shakespearean translation that might offer us a way into the reading of James Joyce's *Ulysses* and, not least, into the chaotically elliptical but brilliant discussions of Shakespeare that take place in the 'Scylla and Charybdis' episode of that book.[1] A reading of *Ulysses* confronts us with Joycean multilingualism but also with the need to examine issues of cultural translation and of the reading and rereading of Shakespeare in the European cultural contexts of the period during which *Ulysses* is set and of Joyce's own life.[2] It is well known that Joyce can offer the reader a kind of diachronic modernist 'translation' of some aspects of Shakespeare into the circumstances of modern urban life, as well as a generic translation from drama into prose fiction. *Ulysses* conjures a 'translation' of Homer's *Odyssey* into Shakespeare's *Hamlet* and *vice versa*.[3] To see *Ulysses* as a work of Shakespearean translation may also invite us to explore the senses in which, and the extent to which, Joyce dramatizes his central artist figure Stephen Dedalus in terms of a self-translation into Shakespeare.

Typically for *Ulysses*, the discussion of Shakespeare in the 'Scylla and Charybdis' episode begins *in medias res* and the English reader, at least, might be struck by the continental European perspectives into which we are thrown from the start. Thomas Lyster, the 'quaker librarian', contributes to the discussion with a reference to Goethe's novel *Wilhelm Meister*, in which a translation and a performance of *Hamlet* take place. In it, the focus is on the character of Hamlet and his character is read as being that of an ineffectual dreamer, incapable of meeting the demands placed upon him by a difficult political situation. Lyster extrapolates that Hamlet is 'a hesitating soul taking arms against a sea of troubles' (*U*, 9.3–5). We might say that, in Goethe, Hamlet becomes translated into the terms of German Romanticism and that the German Romantic idea of Hamlet provides a specific historical and cultural starting point for the discussion. From the outset, the reader is confronted with a perspective on a perspective, which maintains and develops the sense of cultural particularity and of cultural diversity that is so important to *Ulysses* throughout.

From the perspective of the new century, Romanticism was only one among such historically located cultural positions and it is one whose aspirations to totality are quickly punctured in Stephen's interior monologue. He imagines an impromptu diachronic 'translation' of *Paradise Lost*, which mixes a popular sentimentalized '*Sorrows of Satan*' with a line from Canto XXI of Dante's *Inferno*, to create a grotesque Anglo-Italian portrait of Milton's hero:

> Orchestral Satan, weeping many a rood
> Tears such as angels weep.
> *Ed egli avea del cul fatto trombetta*
> [And he made a trumpet blast from his arse]. (*U*, 9.34)

Such a mixture of Milton, Dante and Corelli is symptomatic of Stephen's attempt to produce a modern synthesis of cultural allusions that is still, as yet, incomplete but which also informs his considerations of Shakespeare.

George Russell, the well-known Dublin mystic and man of letters who appears in *Ulysses*, makes his entry into the conversation (which is distinctively idealizing and spiritualizing) by referring to Shelley and to Plato and to the French Symbolist painter Gustave Moreau. He also introduces a continental European note that seems significant for the episode as a whole but, this time, it is located in a different period of cultural history. Invoking Mallarmé, he introduces a more contemporary perspective and that, in turn, prompts Richard Best, the assistant director of the library, to refer to Mallarmé's prose poem '*Hamlet et Fortinbras'*, in which the intellectual and the man of action are contrasted as symbolic types.

Still more interesting is his reference to a brief but intriguing note written by Mallarmé after a visit to a provincial theatre performance of *Hamlet* and ultimately published as a long footnote along with Mallarmé's fragments of theatre criticism, under the heading *Crayonné au Théâtre*.[4] This note takes up his distinction between Hamlet and Fortinbras as contrasting types but it also contains a particularly striking phrase, that is recalled here by Best, in which Mallarmé describes the character of Shakespeare's hero, presumably at that moment in Act Two Scene Two where he feigns distraction through reading: '*lisant au livre de lui-même*' (reading his own book/or, perhaps, reading the book of himself).

The performance is given a subtitle, to which Mallarmé refers: '*Hamlet ou le Distrait*' (Hamlet or the madman). This seems to inspire a French Symbolist version of Hamlet, seen as distracted rather than as dreamy or as ineffectual in the Romantic mode, perhaps anticipating the more modernistic concern with psychology and with pathological mental states that characterizes much work on Hamlet after Freud. Stephen quickly contributes a further modern retranslation of the phrase—a Kiplingesque one—calling Hamlet an 'absentminded beggar'. The phrase '*lisant au livre de lui-même*' marks Hamlet as self-conscious and self-obsessed and as being engaged in an unusually self-absorbed activity of reading. At any rate the phrase sticks in the mind and significantly introduces the idea of reading as in some sense a reflection of the selfhood of the reader, which offers a suggestive angle on Stephen's search for analogies to his own situation in Shakespeare's plays (and has provided clues for subsequent criticism of Joyce[5]).

The other French reader of Shakespeare who informs the discussion is Ernest Renan, whose enthusiasm for Celtic culture perhaps explains his presence in the thinking of John Eglinton, known to Joyce as a writer on Celtic themes. Eglinton refers to Renan's enthusiasm for the 'spirit of reconciliation' (*U*, 9.396) in the later plays and this sense of the late plays as a distinct grouping within the oeuvre, with a particular atmosphere of their own, becomes essential to Stephen's connection between the plays and the circumstances of Shakespeare's life.

A little later in the discussion Stephen alludes to Ernest Renan's rereading and indeed rewriting of *The Tempest* in his play *Caliban* where the three symbolic figures of Prospero, Caliban (*'être informe, a peine dégrossi, en voie de devenir homme'*; an ill-formed being, barely cultivated, in the process of becoming human) and Ariel (*'fils de l'air, symbole de l'idéalisme'*; son of the air, symbol of idealism) are offered as the three most profound of Shakespeare's creations.[6] Stephen's elliptical thought about 'Patsy Caliban, our American cousin' (*U*, 9.756–57) links *The Tempest* to the discovery of America, in a way that adds a further dimension to Renan's focus on the character.

Individually, each of these fragmentary references to European versions of Shakespeare may be rich sources of interpretative suggestion. Their repetition and accumulation appears to have a variety of functions besides providing a genuine sense of Joyce's own polyglot intellectual brilliance and a unique kaleidoscope of potential analogies and ideas. It serves, in one sense, to satirize the cosmopolitan intellectual pretensions of a Dublin literary society of the early 1900s that had excluded Joyce himself as a young man and had forced him to emigrate before he could develop his literary career. Stephen performs fragments of his theory to the assembled company but, at the same time, he is himself a kind of Hamlet inasmuch as he is distracted and repressed into a subordinate role as messenger, passing Mr Deasy's letter on the subject of the foot and mouth disease to Russell for possible publication in *The Irish Homestead*. Eglinton (the editor of the literary magazine *Dana*) meanwhile boasts of getting Synge to write for him and Russell is gathering a collection of the work of the younger poets of the day to which Stephen has not been invited to contribute.

Stephen, at the earlier mention of *King Lear*, has parodically imagined the bearded Russell as a version of the Celtic sea god Mananaan McLir (*U*, 9.190–91). In several ways during the scene the allusions to Shakespeare may be thought to have developed the analogy between his situation and that of Hamlet that was established by his stark final thought, 'Usurper' (*U*, 1.744), and by the comparisons between the Sandycove Tower and Elsinore (*U*, 1.567–68) in the first episode. But at this point in the text, he apparently sees himself as a kind of literary Cordelia, whose writing, like Cordelia's affection for her father, is the most deserving but is neglected nonetheless (*U*, 9.313).

This discussion of Shakespeare seems pointedly located in its time and, as it occurs in the National Library of Ireland, inevitably raises debates about Irish national culture that predated the political independence of Ireland at the turn of the century. Lyster invokes an Anglo-Irish literary context when he connects Stephen's thoughts about the love triangulation of the sonnets to readings by 'Irish commentator' George Bernard Shaw. More direct cultural nationalist pressure on Stephen might be posed in terms of a desire to, as it were, 'translate' Shakespeare into Anglo-Irish, that is, to produce a literary figure of Irish origin and aspirations equivalent in stature to that of Shakespeare in order to legitimate the claim for Irish national independence. In this vein, George Moore is invoked as the likely figure to write a 'national epic' after the manner of *Don Quixote* (*U*, 9.309), itself another text whose 'translation' *Ulysses* might be said to achieve through its latter-day mock-heroic protagonists.

Eglinton regrets that the 'young Irish bards ... have yet to create a figure which the world will set beside Saxon Shakespeare's Hamlet' (*U*, 9.43–44). Though Joyce's creation of Stephen Dedalus, especially as he appears in *Ulysses*, might now be thought by many readers to be exactly one such figure, and, according to Harold Bloom, Joyce and Shakespeare rub shoulders at the heart of the post-evaluative Western literary canon,[7] Stephen himself apparently has no wish to take on this role directly and Eglinton's question is ignored as George Russell changes the subject, suggesting that a narrow nationalist agenda cannot effectively resolve the many aspects of the discussion.

Later in the debate Eglinton regrets that no-one has claimed that Shakespeare was Irish (*U*, 9.519–20). This would appear to be ironic at a number of levels. Firstly, Matthew Arnold's *On the Study of Celtic Literature*, a work which sits clearly behind the discussion in the library, *did* argue that Shakespeare's natural imagery aligned him to the supposed 'Celtic' note in poetry that was so fetishized by *fin-de-siècle* literary tastes.[8] Secondly, the historical John Eglinton (W. K. Magee) was, in fact, so little of a nationalist that he left Dublin and his post in the library in 1922 in protest at the establishment of the Irish Free State.

The collage of cultural traditions through which Shakespeare is read in the episode has a further element when Eglinton, reacting to Stephen's suggestion that Shakespeare drew the character of Shylock from his own experience, challenges him to 'Prove that he was a jew' (*U*, 9.763). Stephen jokily responds: 'He was made in Germany ... as the champion French polisher of Italian scandals' (*U*, 9.166–67). This glimpse of the Jewish Shakespeare reminds us that Joyce was delighted by the theory of Victor Bérard that *The Odyssey* was a semitic text and thus one that united what Matthew Arnold had proposed as contrasting 'Hellenic' and 'Hebraic' cultural strains. Stephen's thinking during the episode deconstructs binarist notions of cultural identity in favour of a complex and extreme sense of the self as built of a fragmentary pattern of possibilities that are analogous to dramatic roles: 'Wait. Five months. Molecules all change. I am other I now.' (*U*, 9.205). That national, cultural and ethnic identities are seen as unstable should therefore be no surprise to us and it is a tribute to Joyce's acute sense of literary history that this aspect of the debate may best be understood in contemporary quasi- or post-Arnoldian terms.

Arnold defined criticism as a disinterested pursuit of excellence beyond the boundaries of nation and Joyce's literary Dubliners are indeed men of Arnoldian cultural ambition in this respect. Joyce himself, in the years of his life that followed this fictionalized moment, became a resident in a variety of mainland European countries, where this Arnoldian goal was not so much a difficult desideratum as it was an inevitable fate. Furthermore, the process of cross-cultural broadening became a two-way negotiation for him and, in his own personal circumstances, Joyce often found himself at the other end of the project: communicating, explaining and 'translating' English literary excellences to other national audiences and in the terms of other cultural traditions.

So to unravel the Shakespeare discussions in 'Scylla and Charybdis' even in the quasi-Arnoldian terms of the literary culture in 1904 may be to miss further significant points about the work of 'translation' that it represents. Though set in Dublin in 1904, the episode was written in Zürich during the First World War, after Joyce himself had been resident in continental Europe for more than a decade. During this time he had lectured on Shakespeare to a mixed European audience in Trieste and whilst in Zürich he was to become involved in the establishment of an English Theatre company, the English Players, as well as frequenting the Pfauen Theatre (and its nearby café), where English plays and plays in English were occasionally performed. A study of the principal Zürich newspaper of the time, the *Neue Zürcher Zeitung*, reveals that Shakespearean production was an important part of the cultural fare in the city, including productions of *Othello*, *King Lear* and, at one point, a so-called '*Fastnachtspeil*' entitled '*Was ihr wollt*' (recalling *Twelfth Night* but, also, since '*Fastnacht*' is Shrove Tuesday suggesting, perhaps, a carnivalesque quasi-Shakespearean comic play). Most significantly there was, during 1916, a production of Shakespeare's *Troilus and Cressida* that Joyce himself attended, as brief hints in Ellmann's biography and Frank Budgen's memoir indicate.[9]

Indeed the production of this play, which we can trace to April 1916, may well have been a more significant experience for Joyce than either account suggests and would have provided him with much relevant discussion of Shakespeare in a specific European cultural context. In addition to the production of *Troilus* itself, there was some discussion on and around April 23rd of the three-hundredth anniversary commemorating Shakespeare's death. The *Neue Zürcher Zeitung* included, as well as a review of the production on Monday, 17 April, articles about the anniversary (18 April), about the Shakespeare holdings of the Zürich Stadtsbibliothek (23 April) and a timely and relevant discussion about Shakespeare's attitudes to war (25 April 1916).[10]

So the European character of the Shakespeare theory in the episode not only serves as a reconstruction of the quasi-Arnoldian discussions of the 1904 period, but also responds to Joyce's own particularly transient and cosmopolitan cultural situation and particularly to the complex cultural situation of Zürich during the war years.

The fragmentary nature of the European traces of the discussion in the episode significantly echoes aspects of the fragmentary notes that survive from lectures that Joyce gave in Trieste in 1911 that, like the discussions in 'Scylla', seem to have focused both on *Hamlet* in detail and on a range of other plays in the context of Shakespeare's life and times. In notes for these lectures Joyce showed that he was aware of the complex history of Shakespeare's reception in mainland Europe, especially in France and Germany. He apparently discussed with his students the strong objections to Shakespearean drama that emerged from European neoclassical critical tastes, not least from Voltaire, who declared Shakespearean drama to be the 'fruit of the imagination of a drunken savage'.[11]

The fact that Shakespearean drama apparently flouted unities of time, place and action that were prescribed by Aristotle, let alone the strict division between comic and tragic genres, had created well-known problems for the reception of his plays from the eighteenth century. Samuel Johnson's Preface to the plays is perhaps best read as a defence of them against such charges, and other well-known eighteenth-century critical essays, such as the *Essay on the Writings and Genius of Shakespeare* by Elizabeth Montagu, explictly took issue with Voltaire.[12] The trace of this debate is evident in Joyce's early 'Drama and Life' essay which slights Shakespeare from a neoclassical perspective, though Stephen's theories of possibility and actuality in *Ulysses* notably redeem Shakespearean multiplicity in pseudo-Aristotelian terms.

It was, however, not just in terms of dramatic genre but also in its relation to Homeric epic historiography that English Renaissance literature showed a divergence from Classical Greek traditions and this is nowhere more evident than in *Troilus and Cressida*. As Kenneth Palmer explains in his Arden edition of the play, Shakespeare's version of the Troy story, like Chaucer's, partly draws its roots from Dares Phrygius (a Trojan) and Dictys Cretensis (pro-Greek).[13] Before the rediscovery of Homer, which in English terms we might broadly associate with Chapman's translation of his works that began to appear during the 1590s, the story had less of a single focus from the Greek perspective and this aspect of it was further reinforced by the tradition in Caxton and Lydgate which traced the origins of the British people not to Classical Greece but, through Aeneas, to Troy.

For Shakespeare, as for Chaucer, the siege of Troy is focalized through the story of the Trojan Troilus, rather than through the heroic exploits of the triumphant Greeks. Shakespeare's Greeks frequently appear in a less than heroic posture. Achilles 'in his tent/ Lies mocking our designs' (I.iii.145–46) and 'Ajax is grown self-willed' (I.iii.198). Nestor and Agamemnon, though more responsible, are ineffectual and even Ulysses, whose speech on the necessity of order is the most frequently quoted part of the play, seems either too philosophic or else too conniving to be a hero in the ideal sense. It was no doubt Shakespeare's deviation from the Greek perspective that inspired the Zürich reviewer of *Troilus* to choose to begin by sketching the play's relation to its Homeric and Chaucerian backgrounds.

Troilus, closely contemporary with *Hamlet* but still more deeply problematic in terms of its structure and ideas, is a play which is hardly amongst the most popular in the repertoire. It is, however, listed prominently alongside the better-known tragedies by Stephen and Joyce's probable knowledge of this performance has important resonances, though in Ellmann, as in most subsequent Joyce criticism, its implications are usually overshadowed by his more famous and delightfully farcical involvement with the English Players in the production of Wilde's *The Importance of Being Earnest* in the following year, which ended up in an argument about a pair of trousers.[14] The fact that everything Joycean has its funny side shouldn't prevent us from getting things in perspective or from seeing Joyce in terms of his positive enthusiasm for Shakespeare rather than of the unfortunate farce of his disagreement with the British Consulate at the time.

Joyce's one reported comment on the play, inspired by this performance, as reported by Frank Budgen, Stanislaus Joyce, Georges Borach and Richard Ellmann, concerns the character of Ulysses himself, either as a character 'who kept his dignity throughout', or perhaps even as one grudgingly admired by the play's most cynical character, Thersites.[15] According to Budgen, he admired the performance of Thersites by an actor called Karsten whose performance is also considered worthy of mention in the newspaper review.

At first sight Joyce's Ulysses, Leopold Bloom, might be said to share many of the complex and ambivalent resonances of Shakespeare's. As a character he shares something of the circumspection and guile of Shakespeare's Ulysses as well as his taste for philosophizing, though, of course, Bloom shows traces of many other versions of Ulysses too, including Homer's, Charles Lamb's, Dante's, Samuel Butler's, Victor Bérard's, and Tennyson's.

We may find other possible Joycean interests in the play beyond the representation of this one character. Bloom also suggests something of the sexual inadequacies of Troilus and, at times, both in fantasy and reality, may be seen to be playing the role of Pandarus in terms of the relationship between Molly and her lover Blazes Boylan. Joyce's Stephen, in his somewhat overdeveloped delicate sensitivity, his sexual idealism and his naivety in a complex political situation is another powerful 'translation' of Troilus. Molly Bloom's strength of character suggests the strong women characters of certain of Shakespeare's plays, especially in terms of Stephen's theorizing about them. Like Shakespeare's Cressida she is the mistress of her own sexual agency and this is the aspect of *Troilus and Cressida* that is most clearly remembered in Stephen's reference to the play in 'Scylla and Charybdis', where it appears as a part of a 'hell of time' in a tragic phase defined by Shakespeare's supposed marital estrangement (*U*, 9.401).

The treacherous tragicomic atmosphere of the play is suggestive as a model for the conflicting voices and value systems of modernist *Ulysses*, though, of course, Shakespeare's play takes on the matter of *The Iliad* whilst Joyce's novel that of *The Odyssey*. In *Ulysses*, Joyce's Dublin takes on some of the agonistic character of Shakespeare's Troy as well as of the First World War, not least in the 'Scylla and Charybdis' episode with its high-flown theorizing and in the subversive sick humour of Buck Mulligan who is something of a cynically jokey and irreverent version of Shakespeare's bitter fool Thersites in this scene, though it is perhaps worth noting that Joyce apparently also aligned Thersites with the 'I' narrator of the 'Cyclops' episode.[16]

It is moreover very tempting to read the nuances of Joyce's novel in terms of the complex translations of the Troy story as a whole through English and European cultural traditions, and to suggest that it was the issues and problems of cultural context and cultural synthesis, of 'translating' the Shakespearean into the Homeric and the Homeric into the Shakespearean versions of the Troy story, that must have come to occupy him in his work on the parallelisms that underpin the narrative of *Ulysses* during the period after seeing the play. The comments Joyce made to his Swiss student and friend Georges Borach that were recorded in the diary he kept for 1 August 1917 and are quoted at length by Ellmann seem especially interesting in this regard.[17] Whilst they confirm Joyce's sense of the origin of his idea for the narrative of *Ulysses* as being in his boyhood enthusiasm for the heroic anti-heroism of the character, their description of that character as engaged in a political debate with the other Greek heroes and as 'the only man in Hellas who is against the war' seems directly reminiscent of the Shakespearean version of the story as we might imagine it being performed in neutral Switzerland at the height of the carnage of the First World War.

By October 1917, as Ellmann's account confirms, Joyce had taken Nora and children to Locarno and it was whilst he was there that he finally wrote a working version of the first three episodes of the Ulysses story that had haunted him since his days in Rome, mailing them, suggestively enough, to Claude Sykes who was to become Joyce's collaborator in the English Players venture when he returned to Zürich and to his more comfortable apartment there in the new year. There would seem, then, every reason to connect the idea of his ambitious linking of Homer and Shakespeare to this encounter with *Troilus and Cressida*.

It seems, moreover, right to record the contemporary discussion of Shakespeare and war that took place in the Zürich paper at the time, obviously relevant to a production of *Troilus and Cressida* during the First World War with all the crises that its mass carnage represented to the values and ideals of that time and at a time in the war when its outcome still lay in the balance. Here, after all, is a play set in wartime, where the loyalties of both sides in the conflict seem to have become forgotten and confused in the general chaos and where heroism itself, and the issues of value that seem to go along with it, are irretrievably problematized. The painful anti-romantic love story of Troilus and Cressida themselves, who are only brought together by the machinations of Pandarus and are then divided by tragic circumstance, as well as the bitterly satiric comic figure of Thersites, create the distinctive atmosphere of the play, as do the high-flown philosophic discussions of the heroes that seem undercut by all that is around them. As Terry Eagleton puts it (with not a little sense of Stephen's 'nightmare' of history): 'barren history is the narrative *Troilus and Cressida* has to deliver, as both sides struggle to remember what it is they are fighting about, and as, beyond the dramatic conclusion, the war drags on.'[18]

Troilus and Cressida was produced in the Spring of 1916 before the battle of the Somme, whilst the German positions on the Western Front (simultaneously reported in the paper) were strong and the Allied advances that were to be so costly barely underway. By Joyce's return from Locarno in early 1918 the balance of the war was tipping decisively in favour of the Allies, making the atmosphere for a more celebratory kind of English theatre. Frank Budgen's account of the work of the English Players in Zürich clearly shows the political edge of producing plays in English in wartime. In the aftermath of the costly, almost pyrrhic victories of Ypres and Passchendaele, which had been enough to bring the United States into the war, Joyce felt obliged to 'do something for the Allied cause'. (He would have been eligible for military service were it not for a promise he had made to the Austrian authorities on leaving Trieste.) The impetus was also more strongly personal (with his brother in an Austrian gaol and his friend Thomas Kettle lost in the fighting) and less ambiguous for Joyce than the political pressure of the 1904 Dublin context.[19] As it turned out, the English Players themselves kicked off their repertoire with Wilde's Anglo-Irish play *The Importance of Being Earnest* and their gesture to Shakespeare was to have a go at Shaw's biographical burlesque, *The Dark Lady of the Sonnets*, for which Joyce wrote the programme notes. But by then Joyce had already begun those first three episodes of *Ulysses* and the larger 'something' that may be found in that book was underway. If the instinct of the English Players was to work their informal cultural ambassadorship by opting for a modern quasi-Shakespearean comedy, rather than for such a problematic play as *Troilus and Cressida*, then we might say that, by all but omitting the war and by turning the love tragedy inside out, *Ulysses* also makes a modern comedy out of one of Shakespeare's most bitterly tragic plays.

Ulysses in this guise may furthermore emerge as a more directly political work in the sense of its being—like a production of *Troilus and Cressida* in wartime Zürich—an anti-war work but also in the sense that it, like *Troilus and Cressida*, may be seen as a profound work of cultural synthesis or 'translation' in which the constructed parallelisms between Shakespeare and Homer suggest resonances and repercussions of linkage that go deep into European cultural history, suggestively linking Homeric and Virgilian as well as English and European traditions of representing the Trojan war, thus imagining a pan-European and pacific epic vision on an ambitious scale.

For Joyce's artist character Stephen Dedalus, however, the intellectual problem of 'translation' may be defined not only as one of how to translate Shakespeare into a European context or tradition or of how to translate Homer into Shakespeare but also as how to translate his own individual experience and artistic aspirations into artistic productions, and this, despite his reluctance to rise to Eglinton's bait, he sometimes seems to construe as a problem of how to translate himself into Shakespeare. That this project might be seen to have its Arnoldian aspect too should not be overlooked, since for Arnold the moral value of literature and of the criticism of literature was defined as a kind of self-translation. The reader engages in literary education and culture in order to define and project not the ordinary self but what Arnold, in *Culture and Anarchy*, called a 'best self' and since Shakespeare may be defined as among the 'best' of authors then this best of selves might be thought, in quasi-Arnoldian terms, to be quite credibly attainable as some kind of translation of the personal self into a self definable through Shakespeare, or perhaps even as Shakespeare.[20] Arnold is parodied in *Ulysses* (as indeed he might be said to have been in Wilde) yet he is deeply present in both authors nonetheless.

Perhaps inevitably, Shakespearean drama itself gives us the verbal pretext for referring to this highly serious Arnoldian type of self-betterment as a kind of 'translation'. In Shakespeare's poetic English the words 'translate', 'translated' and 'translation' occur fourteen times in all and in none of these uses does the most familiar modern sense (which the *OED* gives as 'to turn from one language into another') predominate over a range of other apparently more metaphorical meanings (though they are actually more faithful to the root sense of 'carrying across' that the word 'translate' shares with the word 'metaphor').[21] Of all the plays it is in *A Midsummer Night's Dream* that the word appears most often: when Helena begs to be 'translated' into Hermia in order to capture Demetrius's affection (I.i.191); and of course when the comic figure of Bottom wearing an ass's head is said to have been 'translated' in the words of both Peter Quince (III.i.122) and of Puck (III.ii.32). For many readers of the play, its 'translations' both reinforce the magical and fairy-like theme of transformation and also have a more serious educative and transformative aspect. The lovers' confusions are resolved, enabling their true desires to emerge and Egeus, as well as Titania and Bottom, in their different ways, are translated into wiser or at least more self-critical characters.

How appropriate it would seem then, that this play is one closely associated (thanks to his famous 1935 film version) with the director Max Reinhardt, whose Berlin Theatre company toured Switzerland and performed in Zürich during the early months of 1917. Reinhardt contributed greatly to the staging of the modern European naturalistic drama that Joyce had enjoyed and then in turn to more expressionistic innovations. Hauptmann (whom Joyce had translated), Ibsen (Joyce's first hero) and Strindberg (whom Joyce somewhat distrusted) were among the plays in the repertoire around the time of the Swiss visit.[22] However, not unlike Joyce, Reinhardt was at this time developing a major Shakespearean obsession, especially with *A Midsummer Night's Dream* (of which he mounted some fifteen productions in all) and it is not impossible that a performance or discussion of the play took place at the time. For Reinhardt it was the fantastical and imaginative qualities of the play that attracted and stimulated his growing fondness for elaborate stage spectacles, though his film version significantly recasts the play as an anti-Fascist allegory.

Though the play is not built as explicitly into Stephen's theory as it might have been (with Oberon as jealous husband or perhaps as ghostly father? Titania as erring wife? Demetrius and Lysander as warring brothers? the wood as place of exile?), Buck Mulligan does appear twice as 'Puck Mulligan' towards the end of the 'Scylla and Charybdis' episode and arguably performs his own 'mechanical' play in the 'Everyman his own Wife' skit. Stephen echoes Titania's complaint to Oberon about the blasted countryside in his thought 'Gone are the nine men's morrice' (*U*, 9.1168–69), that seems to point to the closure or imaginative exhaustion of his theorizing towards the end of the episode, but may also cast an anachronistic and rueful glance at the legacy of the trenches.

In 'Scylla and Charybdis', Stephen's intellectual endeavours transform him, for the moment, from the lowliness of his everyday circumstances to a higher Shakespearean level of critical and creative life that he evidently sees as his natural home. But, by the end of the episode, Mulligan's entrance has mocked and scoffed him back into his role as underdog once again. In this sense his theorizing also might be read in terms of the comic aspirations of the mechanicals in Shakespeare's comedy who 'translate' the classical tragedy of Pyramus and Thisbe into surreal and rather Joycean comic farce. It also shares something of the magical transformation and subsequent humiliation of Bottom as he is 'translated' in the play. That this parallel between Stephen and Bottom is more one of plot and less one of verbal echo or allusion than the parallels with Hamlet, Cordelia and Troilus that I have mentioned, should perhaps not deter us too much, since the episode is first and foremost a comedy and its trials better seen as an intellectual rite of passage than as a tragedy for Stephen.

At any rate, it may be in terms of Stephen's desire to translate himself into Shakespeare that we should understand the key element of biography that characterizes his thought. Stephen's contribution to the discussion of *Hamlet* begins with his distinctive take on the role of the ghost, which would seem to offer a 'translation' that diverges from the obsessive focus on the character of the Prince in both the German Romantic and the French Symbolist readings by suggesting that the authorial presence and therefore the interpretative focus of the play should be displaced onto the ghostly presence of King Hamlet, his father. His justification for this is biographical: Shakespeare was an actor and played the role of the ghost in the play.

Moreover, much of Stephen's thinking is characteristically derived from his theologically flavoured education, which was frequently much more explicitly moralistic than anything in the more secular criticism of Matthew Arnold. He quotes Thomas Aquinas, Aristotle and even Ignatius Loyola in his contributions and in his thoughts. Typically his entries into the discussion suggest a much deeper immersion than that of his interlocutors in Shakespeare's Elizabethan and Jacobean historical context and in his English Renaissance literary contemporaries.

Consequently, it is almost as a kind of Loyolan 'spiritual exercise' that Stephen imagines a Shakespeare engaged in the business of his everyday life:

> —Shakespeare has left the huguenot's house in Silver street and walks by the swanmews along the riverbank …
>
> Composition of place. Ignatius Loyola, make haste to help me! (*U*, 9.159–63)

From this develops the extraordinary biographical reading of the plays in terms of a set of characteristic marital and familial situations from Shakespeare's life, including a problematic marriage to an older woman and a series of intense sibling rivalries.

With notable exceptions, most modern Shakespeare criticism and scholarship has endeavoured to keep the plays and the life well separated from each other, not least because our knowledge of Shakespeare's life is based on so few verifiable details and because the plays themselves deal with such a broad range of historically and geographically dispersed subjects. It became, of course, familiar at the end of the nineteenth century to argue (and it is even sometimes still popular to entertain the view) that the plays were not even written by Shakespeare himself but by, as Joyce puts it, 'Rutlandsouthamptonbaconshakespeare or another poet of the same name' (*U*, 9.866). Modernist critical theory (at least in the person of T. S. Eliot) argued strongly for the separation of 'the man that suffers from the mind that creates'.[23] Yet there was something of a renewed vogue for investigating the life of Shakespeare at the start of the twentieth century and Joyce's reading shows him to have followed the debate closely enough and drawn on it for the episode. Moreover, we might argue that Stephen's translation of Shakespeare and discussion of the art in terms of the life opens the door for the complex process of his reading of the plays not as actor nor even as critic in the conventional sense, but in such a way as to enable the translation of his own life into that of the high post-Arnoldian creative artist that he wishes to become.

The pattern of Shakespeare's life as it is reinvented by Stephen and applied to the plays he mentions is well enough known. It is based on details from a number of contemporary biographical works but, as a fragmentary narrative, it has most in common with the structural scaffold that underpins *Ulysses* as a whole and that is the narrative of *The Odyssey*. Shakespeare's early marriage to Ann Hathaway and his long residence in London apart from her is the first point of reference through which the stories can be translated into one another but in this version she is not a 'Penelope stayathome' so much as a sexually active woman whose infidelities are portrayed in those of Cleopatra, Venus (in *Venus and Adonis*), Gertrude and Cressida in the plays. The apparent developmental pattern of Shakespeare's writing (through phases suggested by the early comedies, the middle tragic period and a final period of reconciliatory comedy) echoes the pattern of travel and return in Homer's epic, so that the one is seen in terms of the other in a mode of constructed analogy that might indeed be suggestively construed as an act of translation.

This cluster of associations and concerns finds one of its most richly compacted and suggestive images in the 'Circe' episode where the vision of Shakespeare in the brothel mirror may be said to reflect their life experiences and especially their sexual anxieties and their evasive modernist identities in his:

> *(Stephen and Bloom gaze in the mirror. The face of William Shakespeare, beardless, appears there, rigid in facial paralysis, crowned by the reflection of the reindeer antlered hatrack in the hall.)* (*U*, 15.3821–24)

Shakespeare himself appears at this point in the text to taunt them in a clichéd spoof of Elizabethan English. 'Thou thoughtest as how thou wastest invisible', he says as if to taunt them into the recognition that there is no more evading capture or revelation through the mirror of Shakespearean drama for them than there is for Shakespeare's Claudius in the play scene of *Hamlet*.

It is as individuals locked in the difficult circumstances of everyday life that this Shakespeare reflects them, rather than as creative artists or intellectuals. However, in the figure of Shem in Book 1, Chapter vii, of *Finnegans Wake*, Joyce more explicitly attempts to formulate the sense that it is the fate of the writer to have his own ambitions as author reflected through the figure of Shakespeare. Shem's drunken boast in that passage of the *Wake* is that he is:

> aware of no other shaggspick, other Shakhisbeard, either prexactly unlike his polar andthisishis or procisely the seem as woops (parn!) as what he fancied or guessed the sames as he was himself ...[24]

From this extraordinary location, which is apparently presented as being neither exactly distinct from Shakespeare nor as being precisely the same as him, Shem even more wildly boasts that he 'would wipe ally english spooker off the face of the erse' (*FW*, 187.6–7). Posed in some ways as a barroom braggart and 'low sham', the figure of Shem also perhaps suggests an extreme culmination of the Arnoldian processes of cultural translation and self-translation that, I have tried to argue, are present behind Stephen's Shakespeare theorizing in 'Scylla and Charybdis'. But his curious formulation of the idea of the artist as himself engaged in a creation by identification with Shakespeare does at least make explicit the necessary element of difference or of dis-identification that must also be involved.

To see Stephen's Shakespeare theory in *Ulysses*, though it was set in a virtual Dublin 1904, in terms of the real world of Zürich in 1916–18 is to mark a difference between Joyce's practical ambitions and Stephen's more idealized, Arnoldian and even tragicomic ideals. It can, as I have tried to argue, help us to see the episode as a kind of Shakespearean translation, in the sense that it draws on a variety of continental European traditions for reading Shakespeare and in the sense that, for all its universality, it selected and performed various aspects of the life and work for a particular audience in a particular and highly charged historical situation.

Though the theory most explictly addresses *Hamlet* and aspects of Shakespearean biography, we might approach an understanding of it in its context if we recall contemporary performances of *Troilus and Cressida* and allusions to *A Midsummer Night's Dream*. To do this is to find a place for Joyce in the history of Shakespearean translation and performance that turns out to be another natural home for his work. And to look at his work through the lenses of these two particular plays can enable us to highlight characteristically Joycean themes of the tragedy and futility of war and of the problems of artistic aspiration in the modern, or at least, post-Arnoldian world.

NOTES

1. Joyce, *Ulysses* (Harmondsworth: Penguin Books, 1986), pp. 151–79. Subsequent references to *Ulysses* are to this edition in episode and line number format, and included in the text of this essay.

2. I am particularly indebted to Inga-Stina Ewbank's essay 'Shakespeare Translation as Cultural Exchange' in *Shakespeare Survey*, 48 (1995), 1–12 and to the work of Fritz Senn on Joyce and translation, especially *Joyce's Dislocutions: Essays on Reading as Translation*, ed. John Paul Riquelme (Baltimore and London: Johns Hopkins University Press, 1984).

3. This essay is in part intended to complement some of my arguments in '"Shakespeare Explained": James Joyce's Shakespeare from Victorian

Burlesque to Postmodern Bard' in *Shakespeare and Ireland*, eds Mark Thornton Burnett and Ramona Wray (London: Macmillan, 1997), pp. 91–113, where a listing of some of the extensive and growing body of critical work on Joyce and Shakespeare can also be found.

4. Stéphane Mallarmé, *Oeuvres Complètes* (Paris: Gallimard, 1945), pp. 1557–58.

5. The most extensive discussion of Joyce and Mallarmé remains David Hayman, *Joyce et Mallarmé* (Paris: Les Lettres Modernes, 1956). For a recent use of the phrase, see Michael Patrick Gillespie, *Reading the Book of Himself: Narrative Strategies in the Works of James Joyce* (Columbus: Ohio State University Press, 1989).

6. Ernest Renan, *Caliban: suite de la tempête*, ed. Colin Smith (Manchester: Manchester University Press, 1954).

7. Harold Bloom, 'Joyce's Agon with Shakespeare' in *The Western Canon* (New York: Macmillan, 1994), pp. 413–31.

8. Matthew Arnold, *On the Study of Celtic Literature* (London: Everyman, 1976), p. 126, where Arnold writes: 'Shakespeare, in handling nature, touches this Celtic note so exquisitely, that perhaps one is inclined to be always looking for the Celtic note in him.' Passages of Arnold's work relating to the 'Celtic source' of much of English poetry and to Shakespeare's natural imagery were selected by George Saintsbury in his *History of English Prose Rhythm* (London: Macmillan, 1912), pp. 413–14, a work that Joyce knew and used extensively in his composition of *Ulysses*.

9. See Richard Ellmann, *James Joyce* (Oxford: Oxford University Press, 1983), pp. 412 and 416 and also p. 459n where the reference is made to a performance of the play in German. Frank Budgen's *James Joyce and the Making of 'Ulysses'* (Oxford: Oxford University Press, 1972) records a remark that also relates to this visit to the play (p. 169).

10. The *Neue Zürcher Zeitung* appeared in several editions for each day. The issue numbers referred to here are 614, 616, 644, 657 and 659.

11. See William H. Quillian, 'Shakespeare in Trieste: Joyce's 1912 *Hamlet* lectures', *James Joyce Quarterly*, 12 (1974–75), 7–63 and 'Composition of Place: Joyce's Notes on the English Drama', *James Joyce Quarterly*, 13 (1975), 4–26. Voltaire's remark is to be found in one of Joyce's transcribed quotations in these notes and see my argument about them in the article quoted above.

12. *Eighteenth-Century Essays on Shakespeare*, ed. D. Nichol Smith (Oxford: Clarendon Press, 1963) and *Shakespeare the Critical Heritage*, ed. Brian Vickers, especially Vol. 5, 1765–74 (London: Routledge, 1979).

13. William Shakespeare, *Troilus and Cressida*, ed. Kenneth Palmer (London: Methuen, 1982), pp. 26–30.

14. Ellmann, *James Joyce*, pp. 412–13, and of course Tom Stoppard's *Travesties* (London: Faber, 1978). Thomas Faerber and Markus Luchsinger

provide further local research in *Joyce in Zürich* (Zürich: Unionsverlag, 1988) but, unfortunately, no further information about the performance.

15. Budgen, *James Joyce and the Making of 'Ulysses'*, p. 169; Ellmann, *James Joyce*, pp. 412, 416–17 and 459n.

16. Ellmann, *James Joyce*, p. 459n.

17. Ellmann, *James Joyce*, pp. 416–17.

18. Terry Eagleton, *William Shakespeare* (Oxford: Backwell, 1986), p. 63.

19. Budgen, *James Joyce and The Making of 'Ulysses'*, pp. 200–01. For a recent sense of the First World War context for *Ulysses*, see Robert Spoo, '"Nestor" and the Nightmare: The Presence of the Great War in *Ulysses*' in *Joyce and the Subject of History*, eds Mark A. Wollaeger, Victor Luftig and Robert Spoo (Ann Arbor: University of Michigan Press, 1996), pp. 105–24.

20. Matthew Arnold, *Culture and Anarchy* (London: Smith, Elder, 1893), p. 56: 'The great thing, it will be observed, is to find our *best* self, and to seek to affirm nothing but that.'

21. John Bartlett, *A Complete Concordance of Shakespeare* (Basingstoke: Macmillan, 1979), p. 1598.

22. Reinhardt's visit is mentioned by Ellmann. For a fuller discussion of his work, see J. L. Styan, *Max Reinhardt* (Cambridge: Cambridge University Press, 1982).

23. T. S. Eliot, 'Tradition and the Individual Talent' in *Selected Essays* (London: Faber, 1980), pp. 13–22.

24. James Joyce, *Finnegans Wake* (London: Faber, 1939), II.21–25, p. 177.

Self-Translation and the Arts of Transposition in Allan Hollinghurst's *The Folding Star*

ALISTAIR STEAD

> —And why do you go to France and Belgium, said Miss Ivors, instead of visiting your own land?
> —Well, said Gabriel, it's partly to keep in touch with the language and partly for the change.[1]

> 'Do you speak Serbo-Croat, Archie?'
> 'No.'
> 'Then I'll translate.'[2]

Some texts—one thinks, almost at random, of *Ulysses*, *Shame*, *Rites of Passage*—insist on a reading through translation more than others. They may be thematically oriented toward issues of translation; they may be more cryptographic in texture. It is my contention in this essay that Allan Hollinghurst's second and, so far, best novel, *The Folding Star* (1992),[3] is a tragicomic gay romance which is concerned in many ways with translation itself as well as with various kinds of 'shadowy transposition'.[4] Translating intriguingly across sexual orientations (straight, gay), cultures (English, Belgian) and periods (principally, two *fins de siècle*, the 1890s and the 1990s), Hollinghurst projects Edward Manners, his gay narrator-protagonist, as translator in both material and metaphorical senses: as a teacher of English to foreigners, as an articulate reader of works of art, and pre-eminently as a passion-driven subject caught up in the project of transfiguring himself and others.

The Folding Star is a serious parody of a Symbolist fiction.[5] Presided over in Symbolist fashion by the complementary myths of Narcissus and Hermes, it is narcissistic, since its focus is intensely subjective and self-conscious; hermetic, since it is steeped in secrecy and the temptation to withdrawal. Both figures may represent translators: Narcissus, because the modern literary translator, highly subjective, strives after self-expression, contemplating his own likeness in the pool of art;[6] Hermes, because, as messenger or interpreter between worlds, especially between the living and the dead, he is a god of communication, associated with commerce and secrets.[7] More specifically, the book is in part a 'transposition'[8] of *Bruges-la-Morte* (1892), a once famous novella by the Flemish Symbolist poet Georges Rodenbach, whose life it now extends through discreet imitation,[9] and a transformation of aspects of the life and art of Fernand Khnopff, the Flemish Symbolist who furnished the frontispiece to the first edition of his friend Rodenbach's text.[10] It draws on other Symbolist writers and painters: principally, Huysmans, Maeterlinck, Redon, and Régnier (who supplies the foreboding epigraph). The heterosexual passion of Rodenbach's leading character, Hugues Viane, and of Khnopff, painter of mesmeric images of *femmes fatales*, transmigrates into the *fin-de-siècle* artist, Edgard Orst, in order to counterpoint the homosexual erotic compulsions of the novel's contemporary narrator. In his translation of literary and pictorial materials, Hollinghurst implicitly critiques the mystifying and dehistoricizing hermeticism of the Symbolism of Rodenbach and Khnopff with shocking candour, wit, and historical perspective.[11] Yet he simultaneously exploits its cult of introspection, elaborate correspondences, subtle evocation and calculated indecisiveness, and, most significantly, literary Symbolism's privileging of the medium of language.[12] Like Rodenbach's novella, this book is the work of a poet,[13] and the greatest talents of the Symbolist movement in Francophone literature, Mallarmé and Valéry, pertinently regarded poetry as untranslatable. In this context, lack of direct reference to either *Bruges-la-Morte* and Khnopff, or of translation of Régnier's poem, inevitably foregrounds questions of what has been translated, what is left untranslated, and what may be untranslatable.[14] In a word, we are faced with *enigma*, a Symbolist preoccupation with the *inexplicable* which the title, *The Folding Star*, most pressingly invites us to inspect.[15]

Translation, in the restricted sense, may appear to play only a minor part in this novel. But it is the oddness of translation, variously defined, which is conspicuous. 'Odd' selects itself primarily because 'odd' and 'oddly' are percurrent in this novel, mostly connoting wonder and strangeness, cumulatively reinforcing the focus on what is difficult, or impossible, to translate. Outstandingly, 'odd' characterizes the pivotal figure of the unstable Luc, the seventeen-year-old Belgian youth whose paradoxically 'odd-lovely' appearance fascinates the thirty-three-year-old Edward (p. 154). Not accidentally, the daunting three-tiered Belfry, associated with his tall blonde idol (his surname, Altidore, is 'a gothic belfry in itself', p. 16), is the 'odd construction' central to Edward's 'Bruges' and hints at the book's odd, triptychal, construction, an intersemiotic transposition of Orst's favoured pictorial form, the Symbolist secular parody of a late medieval Flemish altarpiece.[16] 'Odd' sorts naturally with Edward's dislocation, his openness to mystery, and, more exclusively, his sensitivity to all that's queer. Just as we see the meaning of 'queer' pass from 'odd' to 'gay', as Edward gradually realizes that a stranger's handshake is a sexual invitation (I 'held it for a queer moment longer', p. 257), so 'odd' crosses over from 'strange' to 'queer'. For example, when an English researcher visiting 'Bruges', whom Edward immediately suspects is a rival, asks directions of Luc, the narrator apparently interprets the enquirer's ambiguous explanation for his curiosity as a coded declaration of homosexual interest: 'How dare he foist his special odd interests on the boy?' (p. 118) More generally, the 'odd interests' of the gay protagonist himself may have a doubly defamiliarizing function for any straight readership, as they present the world from the 'odd angle' of the commonly marginalized figure (the medieval tourist attraction re-viewed from gay bars and cruising grounds) and satirize heterosexual norms (the 'semisedation of hetero expectations' exhibited by Edward's old schoolfriend, now family man, Willie Turlough, p. 238) by demonstrating society's strangeness.[17] Elsewhere, the gay man's incredulity before the straight world may seem overstated

(p. 292). His replaying of the Symbolist-inspired dilemma of withdrawal or engagement entails a perpetual oscillation between romantic monogamy—fantasies of 'the couple'—and actual transient pleasurings in 'the scene' which is difficult to divorce absolutely from heterosexual analogues. His undoubted sexual orientation still leaves space for respectful, even affectionate relations with heterosexuals (among them, his parents, their friend Mirabelle, his pupil Marcel, and his confidante Edie). His anxiety that he might sound 'like some creepy old hetero' (p. 62) balances against his consciousness of seeming 'pained and creepy' (p. 401) when suspected of being gay by Luc's straight friend Patrick Dhondt. While he may consider that some pornographic videos hold up a 'distorting hetero mirror' to homosexual fantasies (p. 393), Edward has already had to concede that he has been 'oddly excited' by the proliferating images of Orst's heterosexual monomania in his paintings, finding that something 'perverse' in their obsessiveness compensates for indifference to masculine beauty (p. 69); they become translatable, that is, into queer sensibility.[18]

Now 'odd' is explicitly conjoined with 'translated' in what seems merely an occasion for passing humour. Edward by chance re-reads *Careful, Mary!*, a novel by his 'comical-tragical' great-aunt Tina in which she muddled Bermondsey with Belgravia so that 'the "Bermondsey set" were like figures out of Thackeray oddly translated to the era of Victrolas and racing Bentleys'. There is a sense in which Edward's 'Bruges', the half-real, half-imaginary setting of his story, is also 'a topsy-turvy world' of confusing inversions (p. 46), and that Edward follows in her eccentric footsteps. Later, he does confess: 'this country ... to me it was a dream-Belgium, it was Allemonde ...' (p. 379). He has fallen into, and for, a translation, an odd translation into the high Romantic or mystifying Symbolist terms of the 'dream-terrain of sunless forests and ruined towers' (p. 175) inspiring Orst's series of prints, 'The Kingdom of Allemonde'.[19] Edward's Allemonde, like expatriated Tina's 'private fantasy of England' (p. 47) making stranger an already strange land, invests his story with the dim apprehension and melancholy eroticism of Rodenbach's verse and prose, of Khnopff's paintings and engravings.

Mid-text, we find another explicit and related mention of

translation. Edward's feelings on falling in love for the first time have been confirmed by the music of Janáček whose life, on the record sleeve, was, however, 'cryptically condensed and obscured by translation' (p. 242). 'Obscured by translation' is partly a characteristically witty throwaway (about technically inaccurate renderings). It chimes with Edward's mastery of languages, his pedagogic fastidiousness about the English of his Belgian acquaintances; it might also imply that translation *generally* obscures, being only approximate and as often as not leaving something seriously unexpressed; and, beyond this, translation might even be wilfully contrived to obscure. This is 'imaginary idiom', after Edward's phrase for Patrick's amusing solecism, 'that merry goose hunt' (p. 401), describing the vain search for the missing Luc. ('A wild-goose chase' has been accidentally transfigured; the incongruous 'merry' now traduces by a kind of intralingual translation the romantic quest for the 'wild'—that is, 'gay', mistranslating 'merry'—'goosed' youth).[20] But imaginary idioms may be designed: the 'secret language' of Paul and his Jewish schoolfriends, or the private 'language world' of Edward and his camp schoolfriend Graves who paraded French neoclassical preciosities, 'plonkingly translated into English' (p. 209). Such exclusiveness confirms George Steiner's contention that 'a major portion of language is enclosure and willed opaqueness'.[21] Graves's gesture becomes paradigmatic of the potential for textual 'inversion', where translation takes on a Symbolist aura of the cultic and may be imbricated with homosexual strategies. Edward's impassioned response to music, for instance, was stimulated by his transforming love for someone whose nickname, Dawn, is an odd *and* obscuring translation, since, by absurd misidentification, schoolboy Ralph is lumbered with the name of a poem by Gordon Bottomley.[22] Here distinctions between art and life have been blurred (as in Orst's mythologizing and Edward's exaltation of Luc), as much as those between conventionally masculine and feminine. Hunkily homosexual Ralph is, nevertheless, as Dawn, complicatingly feminized for life; the name is universally accepted and, in spite of its humorous possibilities, embraced quite seriously by his lover, who responds sensually to an admixture of the 'feminine' in his men, notably in Luc.[23]

The final explicit mention of translation in the book also has a musical reference. Edward is outraged upon hearing an aria from Act 1 of *The Magic Flute* being mangled by muzak at a seaside hotel. Publically, exhibitionistically, he identifies the music in German: '*Dies Bildnis ist bezaubernd schon*'. Privately, sentimentally, he recalls hearing 'on a childhood morning' his late father singing it, 'in the old Dent translation': '"O loveliness beyond compare"' (p. 377). Yet the German might be Englished more accurately as, 'This portrait is bewitchingly beautiful'. Probing, therefore, beyond the already subtle entwining of love for the dead father (who has haunted him all that day) with Mozart's music and Dawn (the song was heard originally in the morning; a feminine beauty is apostrophized), we might correlate the way Tamino, charged with saving Pamina, falls in love with her through her picture and the way Edward's second great love, whom he imagines to be rescuing from various threats, is mediated through a photograph. Obscured by the translation, then, is the sad unMozartian return, when the protagonist is despairing of finding Luc, to the illusive form of the very inception of his romance, the translated image.

Edward's story (like translation itself) abounds in gaps and gaffes. His self-assessment is almost accurate: 'My life seemed to be one of understandings based on sex and misunderstandings based on love' (p. 283). 'Almost', since he is still radically confused, continually translating sex into love and vice versa. For instance, Luc has been innocently feminized by the romantic symbolism of the Mozartian allusion, but, seductive and unchaste, has conversely to be perceived, once Edward has revealed that his own 'secret' middle name is Tarquin (p. 267), as a kind of *Luc*rece, victim of a rape incited, in Shakespeare's retelling of the legend, by a word-picture of the unseen beauty.[24] In any case, through uncovering such possible skewings of translation, readers are stimulated to explore the book's substantial concern, often comic, sometimes bitterly ironic, with misconstruction and misidentification as it affects its deeply ambivalent protagonist.

But I wish to approach this concern largely through the concept of *self-translation*, demonstrating some arts of transposition by which this is realized, since it is the most obvious fictional premiss of *The Folding Star* and chief source of misconstruction in the book. The concept may be understood at first as a material transporting of the self to elsewhere, a literalizing of Michael Wood's 'translation does involve travel and difference'.[25] Thus, Edward Manners resembles the teacher-protagonist of Joyce's 'The Dead', in making a point of visiting Belgium and France. From September to late December, Manners takes up residence in 'Bruges', where he undertakes, in separate sessions, the private tuition of two Flemish youths, Luc and Marcel (son of Paul Echevin, widowed curator of the Orst museum), and nurses the hope of fulfilling a vaguely defined ambition to write. More obscurely motivated than Gabriel Conroy's, his move abroad is still an evasion. Edward's 'capricious little exile' (p. 7) will, ironically, recast the 'planned escape, involving another man, a change of identity, a flight to another continent' (p. 302) which he speculatively attributes to Jane Byron, the Scottish mistress and muse-model to Orst, who disappears, presumed drowned, in the sea off Ostend, which, in turn, may well correspond to the design or destiny of Luc, the ephebe of Edward's dreams, last seen at Ostend. Self-translation may have been inspired by needful assertion of independence (from home or destructive relationships), but the hints at a suicidal impulse in the counterpointed Jane and Luc suggest his enterprise is 'melancholy, frantic or foredoomed' (p. 200). For Edward, a drifting, unpartnered gay man in his early thirties, drinking too much, hyperconscious of a thickening waist and wasting time, this is to be a serio-comically desperate '"last mad fling before old age sets in"' (p. 163) and a fresh start: romantically, since, even before he sets foot in Belgium, he is infatuated with Luc; artistically, since he seeks to return to the aborted plans of his adolescence when as a budding poet he found inspiration in the evening star (pp. 212, 216), the folding star of the title, which, as the double-aspected Venus, blends both his erotic and aesthetic interests and emblematizes what is to be the ambiguous nature of his experience.[26] But, Narcissus-like, he cannot escape himself. For all his sexual conquests and his aesthetic responsiveness, his adventure apparently founders on rejection of the carers (Cherif's love, Paul's altruism) and accommodation of the careless (Matt's opportunism, Luc's irresponsibility).[27] In the middle section of the book, *Underwoods*, he has to return to England for the funeral of Dawn, his first (and probably truest) lover, regretful memories of whom begin to infuse his current preoccupation with Luc.[28] The intertitle picks up on 'the dreamy underwoods of love' (p. 224), the remembered romance, but intimates how the section functions as the foundation, the 'emotional fulcrum of the whole work' (p. 282), to borrow the language used by Paul to describe the seascape panel of Orst's triptych, which appears to Edward to feature that folding star which is his own, and the novel's, central symbol.[29] His ties to his anxious mother (through regular correspondence) and his beloved dead father (a professional singer whose integrity is a pervasive unheeded rebuke) betray his dependency. By the end of the book, when he has lost the compulsively pursued Luc, he seems to be fated to return home, as estranged as ever; his 'real environment', a 'sense of desolation' (p. 231).

Self-translation may also be given a metaphorical interpretation, derived from an older, spiritual sense of translation as the passage to a higher state. Edward transplants himself in order to renew himself as dedicated lover and 'some kind of artist' (p. 33). Yet his insistence—'I'm a writer' (p. 273)—is manifestly hollow. That the novel itself is the creative fruit of the whole affair is doubtful. Edward appears to be a lapsed *poet* and is never self-consciously writing autobiography. On the contrary, his unspecified literary project dwindles into humble subsets of translation: correcting the English of the catalogue of Orst's work prepared by Paul and inventing pornographic responses for the sleazy business of Matt, one of his temporary bedfellows. His most noteworthy literary production is an 'unguarded' obscene love letter to Cherif. Arguably, his literary aspirations are radically displaced, partly into intersemiotic translation, art criticism (or the translation of a translation),[30] for he transposes works by Orst into brilliantly evocative, though unwritten, impressions; partly, into the entranced attention that an artist like Orst would expend on his models, transforming Luc into a work of art, fantasizing about 'the icon of his extraordinary face' (p. 68), responding to him in the transposed, proximate forms of photographic and cinematic images. Yet the ambiguity of this transpositional art—and Luc's curious physical appeal—inheres in the descriptive terms: his distinguishing upper lip looking as if 'finished off impatiently with a palette knife' (p. 29); his whole appearance, like 'a slightly kitsch piece of work' (p. 58). The disciplined Orst, purblind and half paralysed, has still been able to create works of art, whereas Edward's voyeurism precludes such formal transmutation of his material passion. Revealingly, he neither paints—Dawn draws *him*—nor photographs—he merely steals the negatives of seaside snaps of Luc: he is the scopophile *par excellence*, the narcissistic spectator of Merleau-Ponty: 'caught up in what he sees, it is still himself he sees ...'[31]

The accent falls more heavily on Edward's endeavour to translate himself into—that is, to adopt the exalted persona of—a 'passionate pilgrim' (more in the Shakespearean than the Jamesian sense, a devoted lover more than the beglamoured tourist to an ancient masterwork).[32] Much of the novel exploits the sacramental/chivalric lexicon of adoration ('pilgrim', 'shrine', 'saint', 'miracle', 'vigil', and so on), rehearsing motifs of mystical Symbolism.[33] Significantly, 'pilgrim', derived from *peregrinus* (Latin), meaning 'away from home'—hence 'translated'—shades from 'alien' into 'odd'. Myopic Edward's humorous reference to a 'short-sighted pilgrim' (p. 21) suggests an identification that he confirms by comparison of his disappointment at not finding Luc to the reluctance of an unhealed pilgrim to leave the shrine (p. 117). His attempted self-transformation is, however, sabotaged by many compromised references. The most radical subversion comes with Edward peering in at the 'mud and rubble' behind the vulgar façade of a ruined hotel called 'The Pilgrimage and Commercial' (pp. 3–4) near the nightmarish church of St Vaast, haunt of 'painted ladies' (p. 292), as if all high dreams are come to this, contamination with dereliction and commerce, as pilgrim-Edward will succumb in turn to cold-hearted Matt, dealer in pornography and fetishized schoolboy underwear, to ageing (turning 34), possibly to disease.

This exalted register mediates both Edward's passion and the aestheticism of Orst, whose art drew inspiration from 'childhood pilgrimages' to the old family home (p. 277) and who hoped to make of his Villa Hermès a 'shrine to his own calling' (p. 185). Although his art is represented as passion translated, it too is subject to demystification. Paul will notably demur at Edward's interpretation of the experimentally reassembled Orst triptych as tracing 'a kind of spiritual journey' (p. 282), not just because the sequencing of panels is in doubt. The outward attributes of fused erotic and artistic devotion in the paintings of Orst's mistresses—first Jane, then Marthe—pass from suggestions of oppression (a suspicious fascination with the legend of the chained, sacrificial Andromeda) to exhibited photographic proof of sadistic exploitation. In Edward's case, the pilgrim's aspiration is transmitted most compellingly through sublime imagery of height and light, borrowed from adolescence but intensified through his Orst-oriented experience. He took his poetic inspiration from the folding star ('high in the west', p. 216) and, at the climax of his lovemaking with Luc Altidore, he has 'a high starlit sense of it as the best moment' of his life (p. 337). But the dreamy rhetoric of verticality (the star) is periodically translated into nightmarish vertigo (folding), a condition to which Edward is peculiarly prone and which has traditional psychoanalytical associations with sexual anxiety. 'Bruges' is full of intimidating church towers, the real or imagined ascent of which induces in Edward intense sensations of giddiness and displacement.[34] As usual, Orst's pictures supply correlative images analogizing his story with Edward's, most obviously proposing that Luc is to Edward as Jane is to Orst. On the one hand, Orst's final illustration to his subversive *fin-de-siècle* transposition of the medieval legend of the False Chaplain may represent Edward's identification with a towering sexual obsession, and, on the other, Orst's print where 'a man stumbled down a spiral ramp into deepening darkness' (p. 174), anticipating his syphilitic decline, may forecast Edward's succumbing to AIDS. Edward's visions of love and art, reflecting the names of his principal lovers, Dawn (first light) and Luc (cf. Latin: *prima lux*, daybreak; *lucifer*, morning-star), are constantly depicted as 'luminous',[35] but tend to end, like his afterthoughts on that embarrassing scene at the hotel, in deepening darkness (p. 378). His effort at self-translation, then, gives 'the romance of myself' ('the romance of my new life', as Edward puts it, with a hint of Dantesque parody, p. 13) and only up to a point that countervailing 'account of myself' which might be said to recognize responsibly untranslated, unidealized reality.[36] It is by night or in bleak daybreaks, rather than in glimmering twilights, that the disconsolate 'account' may be detected, commonly couched in cadences compounded of nostalgia and resignation which read like 'prosifications' of Larkin.[37]

Failures in self-translation often relate to the widespread practice of self-dramatization, impersonation and renaming. Reclusive Orst's self-mythologizing Villa Hermès contains a statue of Andromeda, conspicuously symbolizing his ambiguous fixation on the legend and dictating the stay at the Hotel Andromeda which leads to Jane's disappearance. Wim's naming himself 'Matt', after Matt Dillon, glosses over amorality, while Edward's flustered self-identification, as porn star Casey Hopper, parodies those renamings as translations into some higher sphere. So many renamings are imposed, *resented* translations, like Rodney Young's. 'Pudging' Edward repeatedly, by a paramnesiac trick or '*conversion downward*',[38] translates the name of his 'pushy', but enviably fit, rival into 'Rex Stout' or 'Ronald Strong', a translation rebounding on himself, now distastefully comparable to the regularly rebuffed 'Strong' (p. 322) and shockingly successful in his sex-line impersonation: 'I seemed to be turning into Rex Stout' (p. 391).[39] To transfigure himself Edward may need, like Orst, to make others over, whether in vestimentary translation (vainly reclothing shabby Cherif) or in imagination (indulging his ineffectual fantasy of commuting others, like the blonde waiter at the seaside hotel, into Luc). But, donning the missing Luc's clothes, he sees in the mirror only 'a flushed impersonator', his idol's 'clumsy simulacrum' (pp. 348, 352), and faces the folly of his self-translating endeavour: 'Each second that I gave up to becoming him only took him further from me' (p. 349).

Edward's reluctantly disclosed middle name, Tarquin (p. 267), prefigures the vindictive taking of Luc in a manner which parallels Orst's abuse of Marthe (sublimated in art, grossly displayed in secreted photographs). Such transgendering refractions appear in the 'the translation of the simile'.[40] Sometimes comparison represents flirtation with homosexual monogamy—Edward responds to being introduced by Luc 'as if I were someone he wanted to marry' (p. 146); sometimes, a suspect feminization—'like my firmly benevolent mother' (p. 270). Heterosexual comparisons tend to ridicule ('like some difficult old widower', p. 417). But among myriad shaming likenesses (from 'buffoon' to 'stripper'), self-translation into old age incurs most distaste. 'This little old city' (p. 7) is the city of dreadful age, reverberating with his panicky pursuit of golden youth.[41] His desire for Luc is patently complicated by envy, 'a hopeless need simply to be seventeen, to be half my age at the wondering outset' (p. 344).[42]

The Folding Star works through the 'curving together' of more than one pair of stories (p. 178), like Paul's and Edward's, and correspondence between person or place often depends on acts of translation. 'Edward' almost translates 'Edgard', and the doubling of Dawn/Luc reticulates spaces through rewordings of Dawn as Aurora (Latin), the goddess's image adorning the Pavillon de l'Aurore (French), where *at dawn* Edward seeks Luc's most probable place of refuge and hopes to take vicarious possession. Secret places, locked, recessed, or derelict, house erotic transactions, their interrelation betrayed in transcodings: thus, the 'Pilgrim' tent shared with Dawn (a 'pavilion' was originally a tent, a figure in Psalms for a secret place), echoing the disused Pilgrim and Commercial hotel, points to the 'darkened pleasure-dome' of the Hermitage's pavilion, and thence to the Pavillon de l'Aurore, a remnant of 'adult pleasures and delusions' (p. 369) more probably reflecting Edward's own history 'like a locked and rotting pavilion' than Luc's (p. 144).

The Folding Star is narrated by a translator.[43] Although Edward teaches in English, converses in English with well-educated Belgians, and reads articles by and about Orst in English, he is represented as fluent in the two official languages of Belgium.[44] Surprisingly expert in his grandmother's Dutch, he speaks Flemish well with 'an English Dutch accent' (p. 132), brings (never consulted) French and Dutch dictionaries to 'Bruges', and has 'rehearsed and updated' his Flemish by reading newspapers

(p. 15). But Edward's self-translation as translator from the Flemish is another oddity. When Edward has to explain in French what is in the *Flemish Post* to his new working-class boyfriend, the French Moroccan Cherif, we 'hear' neither Flemish nor French. 'The text and the story speak different languages.'[45] Told that people speak these languages, we very occasionally hear some untranslated French, from Cherif's *tuyau d'incendie* (p. 306) to Paul's quoted '*esprits de silence*' (p. 379).[46] Cultivated Edward scatters French around in consistency with the cultural dominance of French in Belgium. Flemish, however, is virtually absent, confined to the names of a few characters like Dhondt and placenames like Grote Markt. Luc, for instance, resides on Long Street (p. 16), whereas in another English novel set in Bruges, the street is given its 'correct' name, *Langstraat*.[47]

Hollinghurst is manifestly faking knowledge of Dutch/ Flemish in order to empower his protagonist, already officiously supplying missing English words for foreigners. Edward's near-perfect command of languages colludes with desire for control. His tormenting vision of truant Luc, rumoured to have been involved in a louche card game on a Norwegian ship, in 'a ring of blond sailors in singlets, who exchanged glances and chatted about him [Luc] in a language he couldn't understand' (p. 101) dramatizes the relation of (queer) sex and linguistic power. Edward, unusually confessing to translational breakdown, accounts for Luc's disappearance by 'a glitch in our polyglot pillow talk' (p. 343), but the 'master', already 'half victim' (p. 27), realizing that sexually he can teach Luc nothing (p. 336), will have to admit complete inversion: 'I seemed to be my pupil's pupil' (p. 396). Initially, he has presented Luc's language as a comic translation, anachronistic 'spiffing English', his apparent linguistic innocence conflicting with his tutor's experienced mixture of the frankly sexual ('hard-on'), specifically gay ('contact numbers'), and camp ('bollocksy'). Finding it is 'both a comfort and a sadness to live so much more than him [Luc] in a world of metaphors and puns' (p. 339), Edward inhabits the 'fallen' world of intralingual translation, of euphemism ('gigolo' for 'rentboy', p. 343), of the pornographic idiom, 'both direct and archly metaphorical', of 'love-poles' penetrating 'love-holes'

(p. 127), and of that Nabokovian and erotically charged playing with Luc's name (focusing, in Symbolist mode, on language as a concrete medium[48]), which smuggles into innocuous conversation the 'lolling monosyllable' (p. 89) via 'Gluck' and 'Lucasta' (p. 93) and delights in the 'dream-palindrome' of 'Luc's cul' ('the two round cheeks of it and the lick of the s between', p. 178).[49] This transpositional sporting also transcends the narrator's conscious 'nonsensing and spoonerising' (p. 178) and, like implausible language-fluency, grants an apposite dream-reality to a halfway Symbolist text. Its echolalia and anagrammatism expose Edward's unconscious, its odd re-arrangements of syllables and letters falling appropriately perhaps into the Ciceronian rhetorical category of 'inversion', glossed by Kenneth Burke as 'transposition, metathesis, *conversio*'.[50] So Brugge may be plausibly, though silently, metathesized into 'bugger'. Luc's name by comparable dream logic haunts the text metamorphically in the 'secret identifications' of 'luck', 'lucid', 'pluck', 'reluctant', etc.[51] Thus, on his first bar visit in 'Bruges', Edward notices Luc's prototype ('a boy with thick fair hair and a long rather mouthy face—it must be a local type') accompanying an older man who 'couldn't quite believe his luck ...' (p. 5). Luc's odd surname, Altidore, exercising 'its glimmering romance' (p. 16), happens to be an anagram of 'idolater' (*idolâtre*), applicable as much to Luc's worship of heterosexual Patrick and queer Matt as to Edward's of Luc.[52] The surname emerges significantly when Edward is showing Luc's photo to his shadow self, the doomed drug addict Rose, anagrammatically 'Eros'.[53]

Reflecting complex self-division, Edward's language-world ranges from allusive eloquence to racy directness, from 'starlit Sphinx' (p. 35) to 'grateful sphincter' (p. 255). For Edward's pupils, communication in English seems drastically simplifying. Marcel lapses into Flemish to say something serious or shocking. Luc appears to sum up 'a private matter' 'in another language' more ambitiously (p. 60), but his unconsciously revealing botch ('I just want to get out of here and start all over again from scratch bottom', p. 327) is translated empathetically by Edward as 'I do know what you mean. Maybe that's why I'm here and not in England' (p. 327). A confessed misreader of faces, too (p. 87), including Luc's, he misses or extenuates Luc's delinquency and equivocation about sex. Luc volunteers nothing about an attack on asthmatic Marcel, attendance at a psychiatrist's, an 'orgy on the *Arctic Prince*' (p. 181), a former schoolfriend's crush on him, or his own thwarted passion for Patrick. Edward may laugh at Luc's wonderful queering of Shakespeare ('the course of true love never did run straight', p. 322), but it is precisely about homosexuality that Luc appears most disingenuous and treacherous: 'I think that guy Matt must be gay' (p. 323), he opines about someone with whom he has already been to bed.

Untranslated and untitled, the epigraph may be considered an epitome of intentional preservation of the unreachably private, like Orst's 'desire not to be too intimately known' (p. 186). Régnier's Symbolist poem is doubly mystified, as a displaced work about mysterious translation. It is the second lyric in '*Quelqu'un songe de soir et d'espoir*' (Someone dreams of evening and hope), one of the poetic sequences which compose his outstanding Symbolist collection, *Tel Qu'en Songe* (As if in a dream) (1892).[54] Grim and sonorous, it resembles a condensed dream itself, a subtle sound play which Hollinghurst's English sometimes emulates very effectively.[55] The personified winter winds' sinister translation of the disillusioned adolescents of a coastal town (nameless kin to the 'dead' and 'deserted' city of Rodenbach and Khnopff) is a kind of rape, suggesting a coming-to-terms with adulthood or mortality. The poem's oneiric motifs are transposed into Hollinghurst's bravura evocations of season, wind, town, and the omnipresent sea, and its 'plot' is displaced into Luc's curious consorting with foreign sailors and that unexplained flight which draws Edward ineluctably to Ostend to mourn his 'disappeared'. This epigraph, the emblematic threshold to a book that imitates and transposes Symbolist art,[56] anticipates distinctive epiphanies, like Edward's 'memory' of Dawn swimming, his Allemonde vision, and sombre submission to loss in the last paragraph—all liminal moments, enacted on the sea's margin.

Orst's 'reports from a world of dreams' (p. 69) match Edward's recountings of dreams and daydreams about Luc. Privileging the hermetic over the hermeneutic functions of language, Edward rarely analyses the content of his elaborate and sensual oneiric transpositions, although, in desperate quest for Luc, he comes to realize that, as dreams have turned into brute reality (a dream of being told that Luc had been possessed by Matt has proved woundingly true because something unconsciously known all along, pp. 252, 420), reality is now 'dream-like, implausible, only to be accounted for by the subtlest symbolic analysis' (p. 364). The transpositional nature of the dream seems impressed upon experience: 'rather as one place in a dream becomes another' (p. 367), his penetration of the Pavillon shadowed by an earlier Luc-inspired illicit entry into a house. Edward's descriptive rather than psychoanalytical procedure leaves it to the reader to translate, in a Proustian reading backwards or from the reverse side, what in the dream is secreted in a distorting mirror image or strange inversion.[57] Edward gives us the cue in calling 'Luc's cul', which reverses Luc's 'spiritual' and 'aesthetic' name—Luke—to accentuate his fundamental sexual attraction, a dream palindrome.[58] So Edward's postcoital dream, of fair Luc being displaced by dark Dawn, is followed by one where he is degraded to excluded voyeur of Luc's subjection to a marine gangbang at Mr Croy's sauna. Finally, despairing of recovering Luc, he dreams of taking him to meet Bottomley, whose poem 'Dawn', identified with Edward's early love, is in the dream called 'Mud', set to music by Finzi and sung by Edward's father (p. 373). The dream, too complex to analyse fully here, entangles art, love, and loss, and appears to admit that Luc can never be part of Edward's life (in it, the youth is self-abusing, attracted to another, vanishes), except as echo of his haunting loves, his father and Dawn.

Dream language, like Symbolist art, is 'a secret language we may hear, but never satisfactorily reproduce'.[59] Edward draws on the Orstian vocabulary of the 'inscrutable' and 'ineffable', 'the unknown and the unknowable' (p. 278) and comes to prove on the pulses 'the stark unknowability of others' (p. 400), whether it is his father's, Dawn's, or Luc's. As Edward concludes about his father, 'Almost everything he knew and felt had never been spoken, never sung, never known to another soul' (p. 243), and about Dawn's moment of desire for him, 'No one ever knew, no one ever will know ...' (p. 255). Symbolist descriptions of time and place open up seams of deep, rarely completely articulated feeling, moments escaping Edward's full consciousness, as when a suddenly remembered overambitious ascent of a church tower when he was very young ends, on hearing his father's serene singing, in untranslatable tears (pp. 14–15). They often sympathize with Orst's elucidation of his art's 'underwoods', 'the imponderable harmonies of childhood' (p. 278), and, like many occasions of Mr Manner's recollected singing, allude to the Symbolist theory that music carries the unparaphrasable affect most directly. Edward habitually works imaginatively on provocative gaps in his knowledge of others: visualizing the solemn deathday of Orst; envisaging his father entertaining his messmates by moonlight; 'remembering' young Dawn, afloat and 'thinking of me' (p. 255). Yet his intuitions can be parallactically undermined: Paul gives an account of the far from dignified end of Orst, and the euphoric 'quick undertow of possibility' supposedly felt by the seaborne Dawn is transposed into 'the desolate undertow of success' of Edward's postcoital *tristesse* after bedding Luc (p. 335).

I shall conclude by highlighting two distinctive transpositional devices for conveying the limits set to Edward's ability to translate. Mediating his experience of 'lost love' through recall of treasured poems, he quotes an unattributed quatrain that supposes the Ovidian metamorphosis of the loved one ('you') into a bird that sings 'in all the unknown tones/ Of all that self of you I have not heard' (p. 361). He has, in fact, repeatedly misheard, or refused to hear the significance of what touches him nearly, like Marcel's revelation that Luc has never been interested in girls, or Agustino's apprehensions about 'drugs, pornographic films, disappearances' (p. 168). Supremely, it is 'wild goose' Luc, 'unknowable' to his mother (p. 18), who has not been heard: 'There was something camp, mischievous about him that I hadn't heard before' (p. 330), Edward reports, increasingly unsure about tone. When Luc is told about Dawn's fatal crash, Edward perceives that 'Something had touched him' (p. 268), then takes at face value talk of car accidents, missing what might well be Luc's unvoiced anxiety about AIDS, of which Dawn was dying and of which, probably through unprotected sex with others (the sailors, Matt), Luc fears he too might die.

Finally, that Edward is an enigma to himself comes across in that strange temporal transposition at the heart of the text (pp. 248–51), when seventeen-year-old Edward appears as 'a haunted fore-echo' of himself at thirty three (p. 343). At 'Luc's discovering age' (p. 62), the vulnerable youth suddenly encounters an unfamiliar man, his older self, who seems to offer, first, sexual contact, and then, consolation, since his father is dying. Edward's 'eerily privileged visit to his younger self',[60] in a fold of time, is a prime example of 'abortive mimesis', a postmodern textual strategy for producing an effect of undecidability, disrupting the illusionary continuum by introducing a logically impossible, vertigo-inducing situation.[61] The odd narrative discourse goes *untranslated*, in that there is no authoritative explication of the moment, and, in this uncanny meeting, the younger Edward cannot 'hear' the time-travelling stranger. Incapable of recognizing himself, translated thus across time and confirmed in homosexual identity, he ironically feels 'lost and utterly unknown' (p. 251). Hence the most devastatingly defamiliarized vision of the narrator. Before, he has had to read himself translated into another's real or imagined deflating idioms: 'A very mysterious man' drunkenly singing and swearing (p. 166), or 'the man who went mad and raved against the music' (p. 378). Now there is dazzling equivocation about who reads whom, in an intriguing variant on the double which Keppler calls 'the second self in time', where different phases of a single existence are brought into fantastic confrontation.[62] Homosexual variants on the figure are remarkably common in the later twentieth century,[63] and Hollinghurst's version exemplifies 'the pederasty of autobiography', as the autobiographer can now look back on the younger self, from whose attitudes he is now sufficiently removed, with 'retrospective affection'.[64] But, if callow Edward suffers from myopia (not acknowledging what he is, distancing himself, with Dawn, from 'queers' like this stranger), his 'mature' self, however compassionate, still lacks vision, engaged twice over now, we come to see, in confused and ineffectual striving to enfold (shelter or seduce?) a seventeen-year-old 'star'.

NOTES

1. James Joyce, 'The Dead', *Dubliners* (Harmondsworth: Penguin, 1992), p. 189.

2. Rex Stout, *Over My Dead Body* [1940] (Harmondsworth: Penguin, 1955), p. 17.

3. Allan Hollinghurst, *The Folding Star* (London: Chatto and Windus, 1994). Subsequent page references are to this edition and are included in the text of the essay.

4. Hollinghurst's phrase for Graham Swift's equivocal style in *Waterland*: 'Of Time and the River', *The Times Literary Supplement*, 7 October 1983, p. 1073.

5. Parody is a potentially serious transformation of an antecedent text, not necessarily a satirical or mocking one (cf. Gérard Genette's *Palimpsestes* [Paris: Seuil, 1982]). Hollinghurst parodies more than one genre, transposing aspects of *Villette*, *Lolita* and *Death in Venice*.

6. Renato Poggioli, 'The Added Artificer' in *On Translation*, ed. Reuben A. Brower (Cambridge, MA: Harvard University Press, 1959), p. 139. Edward's rooms are overlooked by St Narcissus, the school from which Luc has been expelled. Aware of both straight/Christian (crusader bishop) and gay/pagan (boy-flower) implications of the plurisignificant myth, he vehemently rejects Freud's 'narcissist theory of gay attraction. I've always loved it with people who are different from me' (p. 156). In fact, Edward's passion for Luc tends to blur the boundary between same-sex love as analogous to self-love and the identity of the two. According to Bertrand Marchal (*Lire le Symbolisme* (Paris: Dunod, 1993), p. 109) much Symbolism seems to be a variation on the myth of Narcissus. The novel shares the Symbolist preoccupation (of Rodenbach and Khnopff) with watery reflections and mirrors. Edward is constantly self-conscious about his reflected image.

7. The god of secrets tops Orst's retreat, the Villa Hermès, and Edward's 'secret garden' in 'Bruges' contains what might be an erotic herm, the very hesitation in identification ('And there was something I couldn't quite see ...', p. 14) epitomizing the divine liminality.

8. Gérard Genette, *Palimpsestes*, p. 237, uses the term to signify the 'serious' transformation of an antecedent text.

9. The debt to Rodenbach's *Bruges-la-Morte* (Bruxelles: Jacques Antoine, 1977), unacknowledged in the book, is admitted in interview (see Matthew Pateman, 'Rising Star', *Leeds Independent Student Paper*, 24 June 1994, p. 17). I quote from the translation by Philip Mosley (Paisley: Wilfion Books, 1986). The 'Introduction' and Appendices A and B to Mosley's edition of *Georges Rodenbach: Critical Essays* (London: Associated University Press, 1996) indicate many transpositions—into play, opera, *roman noir*, film. Gloomily lyrical and densely atmospheric, this 'study of

passion' (p. 1) furnishes the model for Hollinghurst's subplot, the story of Orst. His prototype Hugues Viane, suicidally grief-stricken on the death of his beautiful wife, settles in Bruges where he finds her image in the labyrinthine 'dead city'. His attempt to make over an English dancer, Jane Scott, whom he convinces himself closely resembles his dead love, ends in her mockery causing him to strangle her with his dead wife's preserved hair. Only slight traces remain of literal translation: Orsts's first love is *Scott*ish *Jane* Byron and an English journalist's description of his condition as '*un veuvage précoce*—a premature widowhood, indeed' (p. 183) recalls: '*Mais le veuvage avait été pour lui un automne précoce*' (Rodenbach, p. 23).

10. Fernand Khnopff (1858–1921), like his compatriot Rodenbach (1855–98), was deeply impressed by Bruges, his childhood home, and his dreamy image of it in '*Une ville abandonnée*' ('A Deserted Town') (1904) matches Rodenbach's. Both celebrated silence, solitude, secrecy, reflections, and deserted old Flemish towns. Though typically Flemish in rooting Symbolist fantasy in regional particularity, they were part of the Belgian avant-garde, internationalists as translators of 'English' culture (Carlyle, the Rossettis, *Edgar* Allan Poe and *Edward* Burne-Jones, close friend of Khnopff and, fictionally, Orst). A dandyish cult figure, like Orst, Khnopff cherished his Des Esseintes-style privacy in a self-designed retreat. The translucent-eyed androgynous figures of his pictures, apparently based on his sister, suggest the perversity in Orst's art.

11. *The Folding Star* maps the 1990s onto the 1890s via the counterpoint of Edward (would-be writer) and Edgard (Symbolist painter), contextualizing subjective and esoteric impulses in both, and establishing a cultural comparison between the contemporary English homosexual (still living somewhat apart and under the shadow of AIDS) and the Belgian heterosexual (intensely secretive and dying from syphilis). 'I'd been incurious about every history but one', concedes Edward, infatuated with Luc (p. 288), hence slow to appreciate parallels between Orst and himself.

12. On Symbolism, see Robert L. Delevoy, *Symbolists and Symbolism* (London: Macmillan, 1978), and Lee McKay Johnson, *The Metaphor of Painting: Essays on Baudelaire, Ruskin, Proust, and Pater* (Ann Arbor: UMI Research Press, 1980); on Belgian Symbolism, Paul Gorceix, *La Belgique Fin-de-Siècle* (Bruxelles: Complexe, 1997), and Khnopff, *Impressionism to Symbolism: The Belgian Avant-Garde 1880–1900*, eds MaryAnne Stevens with Robert Hoozee (London: Royal Academy of Arts, 1994) and Robert L. Delevoy, Catherine de Croes, Gisele Ollinger-Zinque, *Fernand Khnopff* (Bruxelles: Cosmos Monographies, 1987).

13. A selection of Hollinghurst's verse appeared in *Poetry: Introduction 4* (London and Boston: Faber and Faber, 1978).

14. Similarly, the main setting, a composite, is named neither *Bruges* nor *Brugge*, the namelessness following Mallarmé's Symbolist aesthetic of suggestiveness.

15. For Paul Ricoeur, as for Mallarmé, the symbol is an enigma: 'The enigma does not block intelligence but provokes it: there is something to unfold, to unwrap in the symbol ...' (*De l'Interprétation: Essai sur Freud*, Paris: Seuil, 1965, p. 27). The symbolic title is a figure of *implication* (folding in), drawing overtly on adolescent Edward's reading of poems by Milton and others referring to his favourite twilight hour when the sheperd should 'put the sheep all safely in the fold'. But as, in the story, pastoral care yields to urban carelessness, so implication demands *explication*, 'the unfolding star' of *Measure for Measure*, IV.ii.219.

16. The tripartite division of a book in love with threes translates the form of Orst's disassembled triptych '*Autrefois*' (In the Past), a title fitting Bruges, '*La ville d'autrefois*' of Rodenbach (p. 45), and accumulated recognition of the presence of the past, but also loosely modelled on Khnopff's triptych '*D'Autrefois*' (1905). In Orst's *rifacimento*, the Virgin Mary, traditionally the centrepiece, is displaced (p. 278). Although his model-mistress, more *femme fatale* than madonna, becomes the iconic substitute, the central panel is now the Rodenbachian 'deserted town', scene of Edward's desolating idolization of Luc (an Orstian 'temptress' or the Virgin's descendant).

17. White, 'Foreword', *The Faber Book of Gay Short Fiction* (London: Faber and Faber, 1991), p. xi.

18. The practice of 'inverted' reading, analysed by Marcel Proust in describing the reading habits of homosexual Baron Charlus, '*l'inverti*' who has to translate omnipresent heterosexual fiction into his own terms ('Time Regained', *Remembrance of Things Past*, III, trans. Andreas Mayor, London: Chatto and Windus, 1981, pp. 948–49), is Edward's when he tries thus 'to convert' Orst's heterosexual perversity (p. 292).

19. Allemonde is the setting of the Flemish writer Maurice Maeterlinck's Symbolist drama *Pelléas et Mélisande*, published in the same year as *Bruges-la-Morte* (1892).

20. 'Wild' generally puns on Wilde, connoting homosexuality. A shrine and a seaside resort named mischievously after St Ernest keep Wilde in mind.

21. *After Babel: Aspects of Language and Translation* (London: Oxford University Press, 1975), p. 285.

22. Gordon Bottomley, 'Dawn', in *Poems and Plays* (London: Bodley Head, 1953), p. 56.

23. Girls' names attach themselves to desirable males, openly to Ralph, covertly to Luc (Lucasta, Lucrece). Edward nicknames Pieter, a tattooed rentboy, Rose, alluding to *The Rose Tattoo* (1950), an ostensibly heterosexual romance by the gay Tennessee Williams which involves conscious duplication of (male) idols. Both Luc and Rose repeat something of Jane Byron's fate, already redolent of the imaging of the dead wife in *Bruges-la-Morte*, which Gaston Bachelard said we could interpret as 'the *Opheliazation*

of an entire city' (*Water and Dreams: An Essay on the Imagination of Matter*, trans. Edith R. Farrell, Dallas: Dallas Institute of Humanities and Culture, 1983, p. 89). Luc looks especially attractive in feminizing gear (p. 139) and glamorous when casually dressed, 'like Garbo playing a tramp' (p. 266). While hermaphroditic or androgynous beauty was a perverse cult among Decadent and Symbolist artists (cf. Simeon Solomon's 'Dawn', 1871), contemporary gay critics, like Alan Sinfield and Jonathan Dollimore, argue that to link the feminine to the homosexual does not constitute an insult to either.

24. 'Lucrece' in William Shakespeare, *The Poems*, ed. F. T. Prince (London: Methuen, 1969), ll. 8–12.

25. *The Magician's Doubts: Nabokov and the Risks of Fiction* (London: Chatto and Windus, 1994), p. 144.

26. 'The folding star', suggesting simultaneously 'an embrace' and 'a soundless implosion, something ancient but evanescent' (p. 216), the protective enfolding of love as well as its collapse and dissolution, is here the 'Sweet Hesper-Phosphor, double star' of Tennyson's homoerotic elegy for Arthur Hallam (*In Memoriam*, cxxi), a masculinized merging of morning and evening stars, identifying as in a Freudian dream apparent opposites, Edward's twin loves, Dawn and Luc.

27. Caring (looking after, watching, sheltering, enfolding) and not caring are important themes (and criteria) in the book, contrasting Edward's parents, Edie, Colin, Paul, with Edward, Luc, and Matt, who 'cared about nothing' (p. 420). Cf. Hollinghurst's critique of Peter Ackroyd's *Hawksmoor* as 'almost wholly untouched by altruism or responsibility', *The Times Literary Supplement*, 27 September 1985, p. 1049.

28. From the death of Dawn, now recognized as 'the motor of my grandest feelings and most darting thoughts' (p.200), Edward pointedly intermeshes him with Luc (pp. 252, 265, 268, 339–40, 342, 373).

29. The book's transposition of the painting's panels (from 'reflected face-deserted town-empty seascape' into 'finding Luc-returning home-losing Luc') makes two important points: what is central to Edward's *autrefois* is his adolescence (the common, his dying father, sexy Dawn); and this triptychal form inscribes 'almost a circle', a folding back on itself, where Edward tragically repeats himself.

30. See Lee McKay Johnson, *The Metaphor of Painting*, pp. 213–14 (on Pater).

31. M. Merleau-Ponty, *The Visible and the Invisible* (Evanston: Northwestern University, 1966), p. 139.

32. The pastoral lyric xii (beginning 'Crabbed age and youth cannot live together' and ending 'Age I do abhor thee/ Youth I do adore thee') included in the 1599 miscellany 'The Passionate Pilgrim', customarily attributed to Shakespeare (*The Poems*, p. 163), is more pertinent to Edward's problems

than Henry James's 'A Passionate Pilgrim'. Nevertheless, the novel makes several witty allusions to James, most indirectly, through mischievous reincarnation of Mr Croy, Kate's disgraced—probably queer—father, from *The Wings of the Dove*, as mythical owner of a male sauna, frequented by 'wild' Edward (pp. 83, 97, 362–63).

33. The pilgrim, probably Dantean too (*'lo nuovo peregrin d'amore'*, l. 4, *Purgatorio*, viii: 'the new pilgrim of love'), recurs in Symbolist productions, from titles of collections of verse (Jean Moréas, 1891) and prose (Rémy de Gourmont, 1896) to Burne-Jones's *Love Leading the Pilgrim* (1896). Rodenbach famously made Bruges a place of aesthetic pilgrimage.

34. For example, pp. 11–12, 132, 159–62, 328, 395. Alfred Hitchcock's *Vertigo* (1958), the most distinguished cinematic transposition of Rodenbach, based on the psychological thriller, *D'entre les morts*, which Pierre Boileau and Thomas Narcejac derived from *Bruges-la-Morte*, has had an impact here, with its conspicuous use of the tower to explore psychosexual tension. 'Vertigo' is on one occasion associated with camera movement and voyeurism (p. 108).

35. 'Luminous' repeatedly figures in yearningly lyrical evocations of love (pp. 79, 123, 242, 340) and art (p. 278).

36. Allan Hollinghurst, *The Swimming-Pool Library* (London: Cape, 1988), pp. 4–5.

37. The term for transpositions from verse to prose used by Genette, *Palimpsestes*, p. 246.

38. Kenneth Burke's 'exorcism by misnomer', in *Terms of Order*, ed. Stanley Edgar Hyman (Bloomington: Indiana University Press, 1964), p. 63.

39. Rex Stout (1886–1975), creator of the massive Nero Wolfe, a Holmesian polymath solving crimes without leaving his house (see my second epigraph). Since 'Stout' is inquisitive but fit, Edward's animus operates deviously, probably associating 'Rex' with the Rexists, Flemish fascists and Nazi sympathizers ultimately responsible for the 'murder' of Orst (p. 384).

40. Allan Hollinghurst, reviewing Craig Raine's 'Martian' poetry, in *London Review of Books*, 20 August–2 September 1981, p. 14.

41. Greg Woods, in Chapter 1 of *Articulate Flesh: Male Homo-eroticism and Modern Poetry* (New Haven and London: Yale University Press, 1987), argues reasonably that anxiety about ageing and passion for youth are not exclusively gay concerns.

42. A travesty of Octavio Paz's conception of translation as 'an act of love' inspired by desire to participate in a creative making over. Josephine Balmer, 'Alexandria in a dingy alleyway', *The Independent on Sunday*, 26 July 1998, p. 26.

43. Hollinghurst has translated Racine's *Bajazet* (London: Chatto and Windus, 1991).

44. Official languages (dialects) of Belgium are French, spoken by the Walloons in the south, and Flemish (almost identical with Dutch) spoken by the Flemings in the north. French tends to be the language of the upper classes, and Flemish that of the man in the street. German is a third (minority) language.

45. Michael Wood, *The Magician's Doubts*, p. 144.

46. Quoted from Redon by Hollinghurst in his review, 'The Prince of Mysterious Dreams: The "Peculiar inward narrowness" of Odilon Redon', *The Times Literary Supplement* (14 April 1995), p. 17. Redon's 'deliberately and testingly obscure' '*noirs*' may lie behind Orst's late 'white' paintings.

47. Flemish dialogue in Pamela Hansford Johnson's *The Unspeakable Skipton* (London: Macmillan, 1959) also sustains her comic realism.

48. Lee McKay Johnson, *The Metaphor of Painting*, p. 2.

49. Vladimir Nabokov's Humbert Humbert famously games with the heroine's name in *Lolita* (1959).

50. Kenneth Burke in *A Rhetoric of Motives* (New York: Prentice-Hall, 1953) quotes from Cicero's *De Oratore* (Book III), translated by H. Rackam (p. 68).

51. Kenneth Burke, *Perspectives by Incongruity*, ed. Stanley Edgar Hyman (Bloomington: Indiana University Press, 1964), p. 146.

52. Luc's admirers are 'idolaters' (p. 60). Edward's idol may recall Shakespeare (Sonnet 105) but the homosexual may merge with a more general *fin-de-siècle* fetishism. See Bram Dikstra's *Idols of Perversity: Fantasies of Feminine Evil in Fin-de-Siècle Culture* (Oxford: Oxford University Press, 1986).

53. Cf. Vladimir Nabokov, *Ada* (Harmondsworth: Penguin, 1971), p. 288. 'Eros qui prend son essor! Arts that our marblery harbors: Eros, the rose and the sore.'

54. Henri de Régnier (1864–1936). *Oeuvres de Henri De Régnier*, V (Paris: Mercure de France, 1925), p.201. In prose translation: 'In winter, the great winds from overseas pass through the town like bitter strangers. Grim and pale, they gather in the squares, and their sandals scatter sand on the marble flagstones. As if with rifle butts in their strong hands, they batter the awning and the door behind which the clock has stopped dead. And the bitter adolescents have gone away with them toward the sea!'

55. The sound of the key word, '*la mer*' (the sea), reverberates through the poem in the circular rhyme-scheme ('*outremer*', '*amers*', '*amers*', '*mer*'). Hollinghurst keeps the waters beating through his text, literally and symbolically ('sea-heave of lust', p. 332; 'a black undertow', p. 133) and also replays syllables (like 'or' in the key words, Orst, Dorset, Altidore, Aurore, adore), forging secret identifications. The poem's circularity is mirrored variously in *The Folding Star*.

56. Each picture in Orst's liminal art—his masterpiece 'La Porte

Entr'ouverte' makes 'a mystic threshold' of his repeated image of the doorway (pp. 66–67)—opens 'the little door' upon mystery (p. 278), which is Redon's phrase, 'une petite porte ouverte sur le mystère', quoted (untranslated) in 'The Prince of Mysterious Dreams', p. 17.

57. See Proust, *Remembrance of Things Past*, pp. 932, 933.

58. St Luke, patron saint of painters, is represented as painting the Virgin Mary in a triptych in Bruges, while, in the context of Edward's teaching of Wordsworth, the Luke of 'Michael' may be recalled, dwelling pastorally in the cottage called 'The Evening Star'.

59. 'The Prince of Mysterious Dreams', p. 17.

60. Allan Hollinghurst, *The Spell* (London: Chatto and Windus, 1998), p. 189.

61. John Mepham, 'Narratives of Postmodernism', in *Postmodernism and Contemporary Fiction*, ed. Edmund J. Smyth (London: Batsford, 1991), p. 151.

62. C. F. Keppler, *The Literature of the Second Self* (Tucson: The University of Arizona Press, 1972), p. 172.

63. Benign co-presence of older and younger selves occurs in Roeland Kerbosch's film of Rudi Danziger's *For a Lost Soldier* (1992) and Tom Stoppard's *The Invention of Love* (1997); a sadistic assault, in Juan Goytisolo's masterpiece *Count Julian* (1970). The asexual endeavour to 'pick oneself up' in Edward Thomas's 'The Other' becomes in Thom Gunn's 'Talbot Road' a sexual encounter.

64. Edmund White, in the *Paris Review* interview (1988), reprinted in *The Burning Library: Writings on Art, Politics and Sexuality* (London: Chatto and Windus, 1994), p. 253. Hollinghurst appears more sceptical about the love being 'curative'.

Translation in the Theatre I: Directing as Translating

SIR PETER HALL
in interview with Mark Batty (3 June 1997)

Mark Batty You're known specifically as a writers' director, and you have yourself commented that ideally the author should be present when you're dealing with his work and that it is a privilege to be in the head of genius when working on a classic play. Given these views, what relationship do you like to have with a translator of the work of a non-living author?

Peter Hall I think the problem always with translation is that you inevitably feel as if you're looking through frosted glass at the original, that you can't quite get at the absolute. I've always been terribly disturbed by Ibsen translations which seem to me to vary from the obviously almost pedantic accuracy of the Oxford ones to the over-colloquial, sloppy, 'he's really a soap opera writer' of Michael Meyer. And the precision has never seemed to me to be there. Years and years ago when I embarked on *John Gabriel Borkman*, John Russell Brown, who was a colleague at that time at the National, suggested that I should meet Inga-Stina Ewbank, whom I knew of as a Shakespearean but not as an Ibsenite; we met and we got on. The great thing about working with her is that she has an unrivalled knowledge not only of Norwegian, and of Swedish obviously, but also of English, and of the darker recesses of these languages. And it's not really a question of the literal meaning. Anyone can come up with that, it's the subtext, it's what is underneath the text that you need to be led to. So we did *John Gabriel Borkman* together; she did a literal, I did a speakable version of the literal and passed it back to her. She amended it where she felt I'd strayed too far, and it went back and forth between us about four or five times. It ended up as something which we were both willing to endorse, as a representation of Ibsen and as something which we thought had poetic validity on the stage at that particular moment, which was the 1970s. Ralph Richardson, who played Borkman, found it genuinely poetic, especially the last act, and said that he felt very comfortable in it. Now the reason for that success was also that Inga-Stina attended rehearsals. I encouraged her to attend rehearsals as much as possible; she would sit with the Norwegian text and, as I dug into the English subtext, she would check if the Norwegian subtext was the same. There's one very strange thing about Ibsen and his vocabulary as a dramatist, which is quite hard to convey in English; Norwegian is a language with a very small vocabulary and Ibsen creates word clusters, for each player, which he uses obsessively. Now, he uses them obsessively, partly because the characters *are* obsessive and are locked into dilemmas which won't move, but also because the language doesn't provide any synonyms—so he makes a weakness into a strength. English, which is loaded with alternatives, makes translators drunk with the possibility of varying meanings slightly. You have to avoid that temptation. Otherwise, you absolutely lose the obsessive quality. As a consequence, having worked on *John Gabriel Borkman*, *The Wild Duck* and *The Master Builder* with her, I couldn't contemplate Ibsen at this point without Inga-Stina because I wouldn't be able to get underneath the text. So I find myself very lucky in having met her and worked with her. We are now toying with a version of *Little Eyolf*, and Inga-Stina is doing *Love's Comedy* with Ranjit Bolt, who works with me a lot. Ranjit's collaborating with her on that production because it's a play in verse and it needs real versifying.

MB Are there not occasions where one could legitimately permit oneself to fall for the temptations of the English language to improve, perhaps, perceived weaknesses in a foreign text?

PH It is a real rough one this. Translators tend to be either contemptuous of the original author, because they want to make it modern and speakable and dramatic, or so slavishly pedantic about what *they* think the author originally meant that they give something that is stilted and dead. Translation *is* adaptation which is why every masterpiece has to be done every twenty or thirty years; there is no such a thing as a definitive version.

MB When one is dealing with a classic, you cannot avoid adaptation, as it is no longer possible to present the original play. When, for example, you mounted the *Oresteia* there was clearly no way you could capture what those plays might have meant for the citizens of ancient Attica.

PH The *Oresteia* is obviously a very extreme example, because the further you go back in time the more difficult it is. You are dealing with a theatre community and a society at a time when the signals would have been quite different: what an actor said or did would have meant something quite different to the audience. I mean Ibsen isn't that far away from us so we have some understanding; but, even then, Ibsen lived in the white-hot revolution of Naturalism so that if somebody actually lit a lamp on the stage, or drew a curtain, it was so unusual that it had a metaphorical meaning. It has no such meaning for us now, people light lamps and draw curtains all the time. It's what we consider the normal theatre. The poetry of Ibsen's great naturalistic dramas is very much based on the symbolism of naturalistic behaviour and that is all dead to us.

MB There is also a concern, is there not, with trying to capture the cultural differences? In *John Gabriel Borkman* the references to nature, as something that has an effect on us internally, are perhaps lost to us in England, since we don't have that sense of the huge outdoors that exists in Norway and Norwegian culture.

PH No, we don't live in tiny mountain-locked towns many, many difficult journeys away from each other. No, you have to recognize it and try and find some equivalent, some element in the work you're doing which gives something of that to an audience. It's terribly hard. All one can say is that the really great playwrights, and after all there aren't very many of them, go on speaking although the signals obviously are changing. Aeschylus speaks to us, Shakespeare speaks, Ibsen speaks, Chekhov speaks, but there are hundreds and thousands of dramatists who say nothing to us now.

MB I'm very interested in the notion that a director, in engaging with a dramatic text and bringing it to life on stage, is performing an operation similar to that of a translator bringing a text into a new language. Inga-Stina wrote of Geoffrey Hill's translation of Ibsen's *Brand* that its success was not in how faithful it had been to the original, line by line, but more in its rendering into English of the spirit of the work. A director also works at capturing the crucial something that has been inspired in him or her by the text, rather than at verbal accuracy, which is perhaps less essential.

PH I'm not sure it's something that's inspired in him or her by the text, because that gets you into subjective interpretations. I'm really not very interested in most directors' feelings about a play. What I would like is for them to try and take the essence of the play and find a way of conveying that essence to their audience. That sounds simple but it's very, very hard. And it's not to do with being subjective, and it's not to do with being pedantic. The fact that Shakespeare wore modern dress, because all the people in his plays were costumed in Elizabethan clothes, doesn't mean that modern dress signifies the same thing to us at all. It doesn't, not remotely. For Shakespeare's audience, that was the way people dressed in the theatre; that was all there was to it. They put on a cloak and said they were Roman—and they were Roman. They didn't know what Romans looked like. We do. So what do we do? We have to find something which is the essence of Rome. But I do think that a director's job is partially like a translator's when he's dealing with an old classic. There are many aspects of a director's job which are an extension of that, obviously. The development of the actors, editing what they do, making sure that what they do are things that are genuinely creative rather than clichéd, and all that, but the essential point of why you're doing a play and what you're trying to communicate, I would suggest, is terribly like the act of translation. I wouldn't make great claims for myself as a writer but I've written all my life—articles, books about the theatre, and so on, and lots of adaptations, and film scripts, and these Ibsen plays with Inga-Stina—so I am terribly interested in dialogue and how dialogue operates, and that's something to do with the ear as much as anything else, just how the phrase sits. And there's an awareness, I suppose, that this language has to be spoken. I think that many translators don't understand that particular quality of speakability which is really why I've done the job myself. It was an extension of being a director as far as the Ibsen plays were concerned.

MB Extending the notion of speakability, which should be the supreme quality of a dramatic translation, there is also a dialogue being sought in the theatrical contract between the actors and the audience, and one hopes that an artist would be able to transmit something theatrically, whether that be a message or a question. Perhaps this is why the theatre has always served as a place where life is translated. Though it has become a cliché to say that the theatre reflects life ('holding a mirror up to nature'), to what extent does one engage in theatre because one is driven to comment on life, society and culture and how does that inform the way that we work? Are we behaving selfishly or selflessly in trying to appropriate something before we transmit it, as one does when one translates or directs?

PH I would have said that it is only of academic interest to put a play on the stage if it doesn't speak to the audience of now. Therefore, in my view, no classic is worth reviving unless it has contemporary validity, otherwise it remains dead. Now you can argue about what that means, but it doesn't mean saying, 'Hey, we can put *Romeo and Juliet* in leather jackets and on motorbikes', which to me is a simplification, and it doesn't say that *Romeo and Juliet* has extraordinary things to say to us about love and about racism. It simply makes the play a cartoon, if you do that kind of modernity. But, on the other hand, unless there is contemporary relevance about what the play is dealing with, what point is there in doing it? And plays do go in and out of … fashion is the wrong word, they go in and out of *communicability*. So that, for instance, at this particular moment, it is possible to do Granville Barker. I actually don't think it would have been possible to do Granville Barker thirty years ago because of the particular nature of his writing, the extreme ambiguity of it, the extreme precision, almost like Henry James had got it right in the theatre. Audiences were not conditioned to listen or to respond in that style. Now, after forty years of Beckett and Pinter, they are. So there's a change, and that change obviously is going on all the time. I think that we've begun to understand, and certainly Inga-Stina has very much helped me understand this: Ibsen is not that grim, dogmatic northern sage. That was a pose he liked to adopt in his later years. He's actually mordantly funny, full of very black comedy, and the realization wasn't really possible until Britain was subjected to the mid-century 'Theatre of the Absurd' and Joe Orton. Joe Orton has made Ibsen possible, the essence of Ibsen. Before that, Ibsen was stuffy; he wasn't shocking. I think he's very shocking.

MB And yet, in order to render a classic play for a contemporary culture, it is, as you have already said, a form of adaptation. You have to, in some way, respond to something that you see in the play that relates to modern culture. How can one avoid being subjective?

PH You shouldn't put it there and you shouldn't, I think, wilfully unbalance the play. It's always a debatable point what an author's intentions were but it is quite clear, for instance, that *Coriolanus* is a very sophisticated political play in which neither the right, nor the left, nor the middle, has the final approval of the author. But it is possible to do *Coriolanus* as a left-wing tract, or a right-wing tract, or as a plea for moderation in the middle. Those are all, to my mind, deceptions, and they are all bendings of the play which you really shouldn't do. *Coriolanus* is a very complex piece where everything is in balance with everything else, but you do actually have to go into the political obsessions within it, so where do you draw the line? It seems to me you have honestly, by scholarship, understanding, reading and considering it as a performance piece, to look at a play and try and evaluate what you think the author meant. When you've done that you have to try and say to yourself, 'Does what the author intended have any relevance or meaning to the audience I'm going to do this play for?' If it doesn't, don't do the play. If it does, 'Can I do it without actually warping the author's intentions seriously?' Then, I think, you have your brief to do the play but you should not adapt it. Of course, we all think that we're right whatever we're doing. In the 1960s, I did all Shakespeare's history plays. I was very obsessed and very struck by Shakespeare's analysis of political hypocrisy, and the fact that it's not so much that power corrupts as that you have to be corrupt in order to get power in the first place. I think it's a terribly realistic portrayal of politics. Yet, that was in the 1960s, when I was rehearsing *The Wars of the Roses* (which was a big cycle I did at Stratford for Shakespeare's quatercentenary) and Jan Kott's *Shakespeare our Contemporary* was published. So something was obviously in the air. What I was feeling and thinking and doing, and what Kott was writing, were pretty much in the same area, but he didn't know about me and I didn't know about him. So these things go in fashions, in waves, in *zeitgeists* but, over the last twenty years, there has been an increasing elevation, both in opera and in theatre, of directors' theatre. Now, directors' theatre—in the sense that what we're interested in is not what the author meant, not what the audience want to apprehend of what the author meant, what we're interested in is the director's subjective response to this material—is something that, frankly, doesn't interest me at all.

MB Following the logic of what you are saying, would it be true to state that you view a translator, and therefore a director, since we've made that connection, as a kind of surrogate author?

PH Yes, absolutely. Absolutely, and it's a heavy responsibility. It's not something you just say, 'Well, you know, we can cut that and alter that'.

MB You don't think one can take more licence with a dead author?

PH No. Less. I think, less.

MB In the sense that they have to be respected?

PH No. You have a responsibility. I don't mind silly-ass directors saying, 'Let's cut the first scene of *Hamlet*, we don't need it', but I wonder what Shakespeare would actually say. And I wonder also—we have a very strange culture—if we actually said, 'Well, we don't need the prelude to *Tristan and Isolde*, let's cut it'. There would be riots in the opera house yet we cheerfully cut the first scene of *Hamlet*. I mean, 'Shakespeare, money for old rope, you don't need Shakespeare', and they *do* cut.

MB What of the canon is there left to do? Do you have any agenda in terms of the kind of plays that you're interested in now? What is there left to do of worth from the Scandinavian stage, for example?

PH Well, I'd like to do Strindberg. I've never done Strindberg; and I'd like to go on doing Ibsen. I've just done *The Seagull*, so obviously I'm about to do some more Chekhovs, but I don't really think about what's left to do. There's a lot of plays I'd still like to do, and I suppose my appetite for plays shifts and changes within the currents of what I've tried to describe to you. I've always thought, for instance, that *An Ideal Husband* is the most subjective of Wilde's plays. Although it's always been written off as a melodrama with a few epigrams in it ('Pity it's not *The Importance of Being Earnest*'!) I've always thought that buried inside it was a deeply subjective play about Wilde's own position in society as a blackmailed homosexual. When I finally did the play with that in my mind and found that, line after line, speech after speech, it worked as a consequence. The production was then hailed as a revelation. It wasn't really a revelation because the play had been sitting there for a hundred years as it was. I didn't bend it.

MB Is this, ultimately, the function of the director—to finish the work? The dramatist produces the script but there is still that leap to the stage.

PH The director has got to finish the work on the stage and he has a heavy responsibility to the author, in my view. Otherwise he becomes the author himself. He can do an improvisation, he can do a piece of theatre that is not writer-driven. I think, though, if you have the privilege of spending a couple of months of your life in the head of Ibsen, or in the head of Mozart, you owe a little bit of, not respect, but responsibility to try and understand what they were driving at.

MB What is the role of the translator in the rehearsal process? What particular problems might arise? Could there be problems with other members of the crew, given the directorial aspects of translating and the responsibility felt towards the author?

PH No, not at all. What it really means is that it's very good to have somebody of intelligence and perception there in rehearsal who can say, 'But in Norwegian underneath this speech there is a definite feeling of ...' Actors pick that up and it helps them. It's helpful, even if the actors don't speak a word of Norwegian, to hear Inga-Stina, for example, say a speech in Norwegian with a certain emphasis. It's all helpful and, you know, if one gets into areas of motivational behaviour or emotions which are contrary to the text, she can blow the whistle.

MB What about the italicized text, the stage directions, and how the stage is to be dressed? Should a translator ideally have the kind of relationship with designers that a director might?

PH Well, one of the problems about Ibsen's stage directions is that he said he wrote his plays to be read and made his money by their being published, one coming out every two years. The plays slightly incline towards the novel anyway, and the problem about stage directions for an actor is that they describe the result, the end of the process, they don't describe how they got there.

Where it says 'angrily', it doesn't say why he or she is angry, so the actor puts on a generalized anger and never actually finds out what's going on inside the person. So it's terribly dangerous, stage directions are terribly dangerous; on the whole, I treat them religiously, but I keep them away from the work process.

MB That must be very awkward with an author such as Samuel Beckett. If you take *Waiting for Godot*, there are some fifty or so adverbs directing the actors how to speak in a text otherwise bare of indications.

PH Yes, his stage directions are fascinating precisely because they describe the result and not the process. I knew him very well, and I've worked with him a lot, and I know how misleading that can be. You have to find the reality which can then be described in that way. All that is actually making the same point that I think Inga-Stina has been an extension of me as a director, and I hope that I've been an extension of her as a translator. I think that's why our relationship has been very happy and very smooth and truly collaborative. The old myth that the first thing the director must do is shut the author—and certainly the translator—out of the rehearsal, and then change it all himself, I mean, to tell you the truth, that's all rubbish.

Translation in the Theatre II: Translation as Adaptation

JOHN BARTON
in interview with Mark Batty (12 June 1997)

Mark Batty You've done a great deal of work in the theatre that has involved intricate reworking of texts. You have worked in collaboration with Inga-Stina Ewbank on a number of Ibsen's plays, for example. How do you see the work you have done on adapting and translating texts in relation to your primary role as a director? Are these activities extensions of that role or separate interests?

John Barton What is adaptation and what is translation? The categories seem to me very blurred, and I wonder if this may not be Inga-Stina's view also when looking at particularly knotty plays. She has worked with me probably as much as with Peter Hall, though often on very different material. I have always found her sense of theatre as strong as her literary and scholarly side, and I, too, honour her for her collaborative work in preparing translations and in the rehearsal room, which is still something too rare among many academics. I agree with and respect Peter's position, and I, too, believe that directing itself is an act of translation, and that any production is going to be a directorial adaptation anyway. I know that much of such adaptation is bad and can pervert the author, and I have occasionally fallen into that trap. But I believe that what I've done has often also helped to make the author's intention, not mine, work better in the theatre. So if you ask me to talk in general terms about adaptation and translation, I can only answer in terms of the different kinds of adaptation and translation I have done, and the motives behind particular attempts, which are hardly ever the same.

MB I'd be interested, first, to discuss with you the impulses that lead you into adaptation. Do you go about putting together texts to create an adaptation as a kind of frustrated writer? Or, is it more from the point of view of a director who has an acute awareness of what works and who wants to improve a play, to allow it to follow its own line?

JB I think both, without doubt both. I'm not sure I know what kind of beast I am. I direct, I adapt, I translate, I do versions and also translations, though I don't know foreign languages. I've done the texts of a lot of foreign plays myself, rather than ask a writer to tackle them, because I thought I might be able to treat them more simply, and I realized that the need for textual scrutiny in detail would help me to know the plays better and more deeply—indeed, for the same reasons that Peter gives. So I set out with purist motives rather than otherwise. But sometimes, only sometimes, another urge or instinct overtakes me and, if I think it is not a distortion, I will try it out. Perhaps this comes from my being a mixture of categories and ingredients. Thinking about all the adaptations I've done, around twenty, I realize they are all of different kinds, and attempted for different reasons.

MB What qualities do you look for in a translation of a foreign classic?

JB Peter is quite right: everything has to be retranslated every few years. So if there is no translation to hand which satisfies me, I prefer to do my own rather than work through an intermediary. I tend to start on them by working through as many existing translations as possible, and then consulting the experts about the textual cruces, the same as I'm doing with the Greek plays I'm working on at the moment. But all sorts of peculiar problems are apt to come up. I decided to do my own version of *Three Sisters*, which is a relatively simple naturalistic text, so I looked through five or six translations, and they were virtually identical, except at about half a dozen points where they were completely different. When that happens in Russian, Greek, Spanish or whatever, one can be sure there's a problem. For example, when Masha gets drunk at the end of Act One in *Three Sisters*, in Russian she speaks a proverb: 'life is raspberry coloured'. So one could see why every translator had done different things with it. We tried out a number of possibilities in rehearsal and, after weeks and weeks, we decided that 'life is raspberry coloured' was the best solution, because everybody in the scene could look at Masha and play the reaction that she was being silly and drawing attention to herself. We ended up by taking a purist position and preferring the literal translation! There are no absolute rules, beyond seeking and testing out what works, what's viable. So I've not got the very precise approach that Peter has, though I respect it as the right habit of mind and starting-point. I react differently to different texts. With *Three Sisters* I felt that the more recent translations were actually not as good as the supposedly out-of-date ones, like William Archer's, because those early translations had more sense of period than some modern versions. In the recent *Ivanov* at the Almeida, words kept cropping up in the translation which wouldn't have been used in that period or society. I didn't want to be pedantically 'period', but I wanted to suggest, gently, something of how the characters might have talked then, so I changed very little. My one rule is always to prefer Anglo-Saxon words to Latinate ones, because they sound more timeless.

Recently I did a much more challenging English text, Byron's *Cain*. It is the only play of his that was not performed in the nineteenth century. One of the reasons why it has never been done is that he wrote very loose blank verse, and it would be very difficult for an actor to learn, speak, phrase and control the text as it stands. I reorganized it quite a lot but I wouldn't dream of doing that with one of Byron's more achieved plays.

MB So your own approach, then, is only activated within a production or a translation when you perceive something faulty? You say you wouldn't do it with an achieved play and yet many of the plays you have worked on, including Shakespeare and Ibsen, are recognized classics.

JB But surely some plays are more achieved than others. That is why we knocked about *The Wars of the Roses* all those years ago. We may have been wrong because people have since solved the Henry VI plays without adapting. They've found ways of changing scenes round and cutting them. I thought Adrian Noble's *The Plantagenets* was a very good version; he didn't add new lines but he'd done a mass of cutting, transposing and reshaping. When Peter and I did *The Wars of the Roses* way back in 1963, we agreed at the outset that there had to be a version involving some adaptation, though he reacted very strongly against that sort of thinking very soon afterwards, probably rightly. To me, it's all to do with thinking, 'That bit won't work, there's something missing', or 'That won't trigger an emotional response from the audience, or work in the mouth of modern actors'. How I react depends entirely on a particular play. My initial intention is usually to reinforce and clarify rather than to alter, and I wish my instincts and experiences were as sure and certain as Peter's. Philosophically, I agree with every word he says, but, in practice, something else happens to me when I encounter a text. We share the same starting-point, a deep interest in the text itself; but, as I work with the actors, I become more and more concerned with how what we are doing is going to work in performance, and I begin to ask myself questions like 'Are we taking the audience with us?' or 'Will they listen at a given point to a text which I care very much about?' When such feelings come, I often make adaptive changes during the rehearsal process itself.

MB Can one justify cutting or reworking a text in any way at all if you perceive the spirit of the play, for example, in terms of its other non-textual elements?

JB Don't you have to cut *Hamlet*? I personally believe you must, because an uncut version tires an audience and people get restless and stop listening to the harder or less important bits. I was a textual adviser on the Franco Zeffirelli film of *Hamlet* [1991], and he'd been told that, if he didn't cut it drastically, it would be too expensive and they would only fund him up to two hours and ten minutes. So I said, 'That means you've got to cut 1100 lines.' I happened to have cut *Hamlet* myself at least four times in the past: for Peter Hall's first production, then Trevor Nunn's, and then my own (no textual rewrites whatever), besides an early television version by Peter Wood which had to be very heavily condensed. So I had some sort of evidence to go on, and said to Franco, 'I've nothing to offer you interpretatively; *you're* directing the film, and your views are different from mine, so all I can help you on is to suggest what you mustn't cut and what you've got to cut. I think regretfully, for instance, that you've probably got to cut the opening scene because it will save seven minutes if you're keen to include the Reynaldo scene.' He did so, and he wanted to do a number of interesting things which he had to earn, as it were, by cutting other things. That was the working process, two men reacting to a basically pragmatic pressure. Where should one take an interval in *Hamlet*? And should there be one interval or two? In theory you always have one; but, if there's only one in *Hamlet*, the odds are it's going to be after two and a quarter hours and I don't believe an audience can take or enjoy more than an hour and a half of it. That's a directorial decision, but it amounts in practice to a major text-change which is not Shakespeare's.

Cutting is one of those grey areas which I don't like to theorize about. And I'm hesitant about talking in such a dogmatic way because I know I am talking of a habit of mind which is potentially very dangerous. It can lead to the most appallingly perverse work. A lot of directors want to seize on a bit of material and make their own conceptual statement; they are not actually interested in digging into Shakespeare but prefer overlaying his text with some contemporary obsession of their own which they feel easy with. I call it, 'How to put on a play without actually doing it!' There was an extraordinary *Macbeth* on TV recently, done in modern dress in a council house [*Macbeth on the Estate*, BBC2, 1997] and it was very silly, but I'm sure the director [Penny Woolcock] believed she was unlocking

Shakespeare. I would claim that I'm much more purist than most directors because I'm very, very meticulous about the text. The basic instinct of a primarily conceptual director, whose sensibilities are visual, social and political, is deliberately and callously to adapt his or her material so that it fits his or her own interests. If you say to him or her, 'But that's not what the text is saying here', he or she is not interested. I believe that it is possible to be both rigorous and imaginatively free, and I try to find that balance.

MB Is there any difference between taking an extreme interpretative stance with a play and doing the kind of adaptive work you are known for? Is it possible to take on a play as your own, as its director, without abusing either text or author?

JB Yes, often, but what about bits that are normally cut in the theatre? The Hecate scenes in *Macbeth*, should one be 'purist' about them? Should one restore the third act in *The Importance of Being Earnest*? There are hordes of examples where something in a supposedly sacrosanct text is peculiar: biblical scholars know that strange errors have been found in that publication also. So it's not surprising that some loose ends turn up in most Shakespeare plays. Is alteration necessarily an abuse? If people don't know a difficult text, I feel at times that I've got to help the audience in little minor and modest ways. There's often the question of adding something. Maybe it's just a slight rewording. But sometimes I do go further, and, now and then, probably go over the top. I've gone wild on one or two productions but normally I've proceeded very cautiously. I found myself drawn into a very controversial *King John* because I got interested in the two source plays, *The Troublesome Reign of King John* and *King Johan*, and I wanted to work some of that material in. I was rightly attacked for it, but I don't feel particularly defensive about it, as the play still exists in its original form for others to pick up again.

MB You have also relocated 'lost' text into a number of your productions, text taken from the play's manuscript but rejected for the first performances. What draws you to such material, which, for the most part, must have been rejected by the author himself? Is that something a dramaturge will point you to, or do you seek it out yourself?

JB I look for it myself. I don't do terrific amounts of background reading but if I feel, on a close reading of the text, that there is something not quite right somewhere, then I look in a scholarly edition and sometimes come across bits of material which seem not only useful but extremely valuable. I remember when working with Inga-Stina on *The Pillars of the Community*, that I used material from Ibsen's manuscripts that is absent from the printed version and did so with her full support. With *Three Sisters*, there were five very minor such bits, but a sixth was absolutely major, and I'm amazed that nobody's ever picked it up. It seems so obvious. I'd always wondered why, at the end of *Three Sisters*, Masha, being Chekhov's favourite among the sisters, had the shortest speech. Well, in the original she didn't. There was an extraordinary little passage which Olga Knipper didn't like or wouldn't play, so Chekhov cut it and it's never been performed. I asked about Russian versions and was told, 'Never been done'. Yet there's this wonderful bit where she uses the metaphor of the birds which have been mentioned as the characters philosophize in Act Two—the birds go on flying and life goes on, and no one knows why. It's not only a poetic passage, but absolutely integral to the play. It is surely worth keeping an eye out for such nuggets of gold.

MB You also make use of transposition. What use does that have as an adaptational tool, other than for trying to make the chronology clearer, or for placing an argument earlier in a play? Or is transposition more a question of fine tuning rather than adaptation?

JB Transposing not only whole lines, but sometimes whole scenes, very often unlocks more than any piece of cutting or any addition. That can lead to major changes of impact, and that is surely a form of adaptation too. Once again I cannot generalize about it, but I proceed pragmatically. My guiding principle is to make the text work on an audience; that is what matters most to me, and if I can't make it work, or I feel there's a real problem of meaning or communication, then maybe I do something. For me, that's the way it starts. In *Peer Gynt*, for example, I began by moving a number of couplets or a quatrain or two—oddball lines from some odd place, because they were acknowledged to be in an odd play anyway. Perhaps *Peer Gynt* is the greatest and most obvious example of *required* adaptation, a play that was never written for the theatre and which was presented for years in a crudely cut form with Ibsen's approval. Peter Hall once said to me that he's never liked the play because he didn't understand it. When I was invited to do it in Norway, I felt exactly the same and it was made worse by my inability to understand actors rehearsing in Norwegian. So I had to make the play clear to myself in order to cope and direct at all. This led to massive adaptation, mostly done during rehearsals. There were songs which the dramaturge based on stray bits of the text itself and one major insertion from Ibsen's manuscript. I remember that Inga-Stina herself approved the end production as a valid version, perhaps because that way of handling a particular text is something she approves of. We have worked on a number of shows together; and, when we did Strindberg's *A Dream Play*, she told me that nobody had ever brought that play off and it wasn't quite clear, even to her, what Strindberg was doing, particularly at the end. So his was an even more open-ended play. I don't think I rewrote much but I know I knocked it about a lot, and there were certainly important adaptive transpositions. When I questioned her, there were a lot of things that she didn't want to lay down the law about, because she also thought that the play didn't work as it stood. I found in fact she was thinking very much in the way I was, trying to solve problems rather than being academically purist, and, in the end, we just about made it work because of the various modifications we made to the text. She also thought that *The Vikings at Helgeland* was not viable today without drastic reworking and she was right behind all that we did with it in Bergen. And it was Inga-Stina, too, who put me onto Ibsen's rejected manuscript when I did *The Pillars of the Community* at the RSC in 1977. Above all, she agreed that, if I were tackling *Peer Gynt* and was told that it had to play for no longer than three hours, I would have to adapt boldly, albeit carefully. I decided to put in bits that had never been played in Norway, though I did not discover that until well into rehearsal. An old lady who came to see it—and it was her thirty-sixth *Peer Gynt*—said, like many others, that we played a lot of text which they had never seen, and, one in particular, which had never, never been done.

MB Is this the scene with Solveig's father?

JB I found that scene a major help in storytelling terms, but also because it was full of character potential for the young Peer and Solveig's father (who doubled with the Button Moulder). But the Norwegians were worried about it because Ibsen had only roughed it out, and they told me it was not very well written. So our dramaturge ironed out the text skilfully, and pretty well everybody agreed it was a good and valuable scene that helped make sense of the whole play. I also did, in some form, include every scene in the play, however truncated, whereas for years and years they had just done the first three acts. It was quite normal in Norway to cut the fourth act completely, but I was fascinated by the possibility of integrating it fully and of clarifying its highly ambiguous meaning. I saw one or two of their old prompt books in which they'd cut big hunks whereas I had cut little bits, little bits all the time. They seemed to welcome my approach and felt that they themselves were following the play more easily. All these were very much directorial choices and, as the full text lasts over six hours, it was probably the most drastic surgery I have ever undertaken, but the play did cohere. Like Peter, I'd never liked the play because it's so sprawling but I felt, when all was done, that for the first time I'd come to understand and really love the play. It all sprang from having to make it clear to myself and the actors, and from having to make choices about cutting. *Peer Gynt* is the perfect example of a category of play which I call a Flawed Masterpiece. It's wonderful, one of Ibsen's greatest plays, but as he didn't write it for the theatre, it remains an oddball.

There is another act of adaptation I should mention: the putting together of two texts of the same play, either in English or in translation. Any director of *King Lear* or *Hamlet* has to make choices about the different surviving texts of the play. He may prefer one to the other, or he may quite validly conflate. I've done that two or three times, for example, Granville Barker's *Waste* and Calderón's *Life's a Dream*. I don't know Spanish, so I went through five existing translations of that play. They seemed to me too even in style and somewhat dated, so I decided to do my own version in blank verse. I felt that what I'd done provided a viable English equivalent, but that it was no good in the comic sections, particularly those involving Clarion the clown. Then suddenly Adrian Mitchell sent me a version he had done for the National, but which they had not been able to use. I asked him if I could put our two versions together. He said, 'Sure', and I did so, and the result was exactly half his text and half my own. Sometimes there was a long section from one of us, and sometimes I jumped from my blank verse to his short lines and rhymes to keep the ball rolling and to sharpen the mood changes. That was one extreme form of both translation and conflation. I did another quite different one with the Granville Barker. Peter has just done *Waste* [in 1997] and I directed it about ten years ago. There's a major textual problem with the play, because there are two completely different versions, one written in 1907 and another in 1926. Each has exactly the same situations and characters but no two sentences are quite the same. Peter looked at my version but decided, sensibly enough, to do the 1926 text because it's clearer in places and is, presumably, the author's preferred version. The political references here are less difficult to follow than in the 1907 text. But I thought that both versions had huge virtues, so I wanted to conflate them. As it's still in copyright, I had to get permission to do so from the Estate, as represented by an intelligent and sensible academic, Marjorie Morgan. She disapproved on the whole but I persuaded her that, provided it wasn't published, it would increase interest in the play and wouldn't do it any actual harm. I am grateful that she let me go ahead. I went through it with a fine toothcomb and didn't write anything in at all. I preferred one sentence to another, or one little bit of dialogue to another, and the result was half 1907 and half 1926. The whole came together and flowed as one.

MB In many ways, it would seem, by adding your own pieces and by cutting pieces out from these sprawling masterpieces, or re-pasting snippets from old manuscripts, you are displacing the author whilst at the same time wanting to clarify what the author has attempted to do. You're doing two things: you're placing yourself as adapter and director in the author's position but you are also doing that in order to bring out whatever the author has put there in the first place, and to translate that visually. How can you reconcile that apparent contradiction?

JB By embracing it. All great theatre involves contradiction. And I believe that all directing involves some form of adapting, even if one tries not to do it in any rough-handed way. We haven't yet mentioned the main elements that make any performance of the text an adaptation, whatever the director sets out to achieve. Though the text is for me both the starting-point and the goal, it is transformed by what the *actors* do and what they themselves believe, and by the overlay of evocative and powerful suggestion which a *designer* provides with setting and costumes. These elements are never entirely under a director's control, nor can they be, nor should they be. I suspect that the act of casting is the most drastic form of adaptation. *Three Sisters* provides a very obvious talking point here. Two acting questions always come up in that play. There's always a great debate among the sisters: 'What is the portrait of the sisters' father going to be like? Will it feel right?' That matters a lot to them. So when they are first shown a portrait, they will probably say, 'But that's not our father. It feels wrong.' An even better example is the question, 'Do Masha and Vershinin go to bed together?' I said that there was no textual evidence one way or the other. I think that, because Chekhov knew his job, if he'd wanted us to know about that, he'd have put it in in some way or given us a hint. As I could find no such hint, I challenged the actors to find one. Since they were the two who were playing the relationship, they certainly needed to decide for themselves whether they had been to bed together or not, and if they did, whether it was after Act Two or Act Three. I left it to them and said they didn't even have to tell me. Of course, they did need to go into it, though I felt it was irrelevant because the audience were not going to know anyway and it's not in the text. Subtext may be vital to bring something to life where there is nothing explicit in the text, but it can be a dangerous distortion to invent one and treat it as if it is authorial. With classical plays, it is wisest to assume the author only put in what he wanted to. If I am honest, though, I must confess that I am not always sure myself what the author is doing. But actresses and actors have to make choices and cut through; they cannot avoid it and my job is to help them. There have been many times in various plays where it wasn't clear, to me at least, quite what the author was up to. So I think my main motive in modifying the text is simply, 'How do we make this work with a modern audience in performance? Are we going to lose them or bore them or confuse them? How are we going to make it clear?' Now it may be a matter of staging, or the actors themselves may sometimes solve something which I had thought a huge problem. We all know we must take the audience with us and, above all, we must tell the story clearly. If we are to make them listen, we must never impose an image that is either irrelevant or positively contradicts the text itself.

MB Looking at the processes of directing and translating, it strikes me that what is fascinating about the theatre, but also fascinating about translating, is that the theatre is made up of rhythm, motion, momentum, darkness, colour and some words, whereas the text attempts to capture all that in words alone. Is that not where the translating power of the director comes in?

JB I think design is a major part of the process of adaptation, perhaps more strongly than anything to do with the text. As soon as the curtain goes up, the stage set imposes and defines. It makes a statement over and above the actor who is in front of, and enclosed on three sides by, whatever setting is provided. Today, most directors depend more and more on their designer. So do I, but I always want to be selective and not have too much, so that the audience can focus on the actor. My main passion is working on the text as the centre of the experience I am trying to communicate. I've got to make people listen. I suppose the truth would be that I am often drawn to a play that specifically invites or requires that. I think also that the different fashions of academic approach are interesting here. In Shakespeare scholarship, it's rather out of fashion at the moment to be particularly interested in the texts, both as a whole and in detail, and people are much more interested in scholarly issues in other areas, often loosely related. Not many academics these days base their work on a close reading of the text. Instead they build or challenge some selective concept around it. I expect that fashion will change again. The same kind of volatility exists in academic contexts as it does in the theatre, though it's of a very different kind. I get very suspicious when somebody says, 'I have got the right answer here; I have solved it.'

MB Has your great involvement with Shakespeare and your great knowledge of his works defined your overall approach to directing? In Shakespeare, the text gives everything, it offers images and dictates how it should be spoken, and what kind of energies can be created from it. Does your emphasis on obeying the text stem from this involvement?

JB The text thing is by far the most important thing to me with any play. If a play is entirely in rhyme, with images and similes, one's got the same ingredients at work as with Shakespeare. The actor has to find and coin a simile in the moment, to express it as his own. I try not to tell him that it's there because it's 'poetic' but that his character expresses himself in that way. But the text in performance is inevitably transformed into something different from the text on the page. There are a lot of things that I believe about Shakespeare that I have found apply equally to *Peer Gynt*. If I'm watching a run-through and I think, 'I'm getting lost there', then the audience is going to get lost, or if the performance feels boring, or if we're not making what is being played clear and real and human, then we need to go through the text and sort out what is wrong.

MB How much does your interest in some of these issues that we've discussed derive from the fact that what you've managed to do is marry the academic side of you, the fascination with language and analysis, with the theatrical side, the fascination with how one renders a text on stage?

JB I find that difficult to talk about. It's obviously convenient to label people and talk of their academic or their theatrical side, or their imaginative side, or their analytical side. It's perfectly valid, but I don't think I fit quite together in those terms. I relate to the text as intensely as I can and sometimes a bit of knowledge which one might put under the heading 'academic' (though it certainly wasn't something I knew when I was in academic life), would feed into something and sometimes not. Very little of any adapting or translating that I have done has academic roots. For instance, the example I've taken from *Three Sisters* is derived from simply looking in the main scholarly edition, and finding somebody else's discovery. It immediately lit up the whole play for me because I'd already thought that the birds were a key metaphor in it, so I seized on that. My reasons were perhaps a mixture of theatrical, literary and even bibliographical ones. I don't think that Chekhov had particularly wanted to cut Masha's speech, so that seems a valid act, both of adaptation and interpretation. But we're talking about an area that finally is very subjective, aren't we? I mean, one can either take a position I respect, Peter's very firm, clear view, or one can adapt with as much caution as possible. But if one lacks that clearness of thinking, then of course there's a danger of tumbling into a perverse solution, and I recognize that only too clearly. I think that my somewhat shifting position is somewhere in between these two alternatives. I react violently to any director's imposition which seems to me modish or perverse or, as often happens, plain stupid because he or she has basically not done his or her homework, nor engaged with the text itself. So, finally, I'm not even sure that, in looking into these different questions, I can end up by categorizing at all. Directing a play will always be part guesswork and a continual battle to harmonize one's own reaction to the text with the reactions of the actors themselves. Though a text may be a fixed thing (it often isn't), the performance of that text is by definition infinitely volatile. And any form of adaptation is likely to be as ephemeral as its performance is.

Notes on Contributors

MARTIN BANHAM is Emeritus Professor of Drama and Theatre Studies at the University of Leeds and editor of *The Cambridge Guide to Theatre*.

JOHN BARNARD is Professor of English Literature in the School of English at the University of Leeds. He is the author of *John Keats* and edited *The Complete Poems* for Penguin Classics. He is the General Editor of Longman Annotated English Poets.

JOHN BARTON is a writer and director who co-founded the Royal Shakespeare Company with Peter Hall in 1959. As Assistant Director (1960-1991), he has directed and adapted many plays, including the ground-breaking *Wars of the Roses*. Since 1991 he has been an Advisory Director. His publications include *Playing Shakespeare* (1984).

JONATHAN BATE is Leverhulme Research Professor and King Alfred Professor of English Literature at the University of Liverpool. The most recent of his many books are published by Picador: *The Genius of Shakespeare* (1997), *The Cure for Love*, a novel (1998), and *The Song of the Earth* (2000).

MARK BATTY is Lecturer in Theatre Studies at the University of Leeds. His research interests include twentieth-century French theatre, translation for the stage and the director's role in the process of play authorship. He is currently working on the translation of various Swedish plays. A book on Harold Pinter is forthcoming.

RICHARD BROWN is Senior Lecturer in English at the University of Leeds. He is the author of *James Joyce and*

Sexuality (1988), *James Joyce: A Postculturalist Perspective* (1992) and founding co-editor of *The James Joyce Broadsheet*. His current work is on James Joyce and English Literature.

MARTIN BUTLER is Professor of English Renaissance Drama at the University of Leeds. He has recently edited the collection of essays *Re-Presenting Ben Jonson: Text, History, Performance* (1999), and is a General Editor of the Cambridge Edition of the Works of Ben Jonson (in progress).

SHIRLEY CHEW is Professor of Commonwealth and Postcolonial Literatures at Leeds University. She has edited *Arthur Hugh Clough: Selected Poems* (1987) and co-edited *Unbecoming Daughters of the Empire* (1993). Her articles include work on R. K. Narayan, Ama Ata Aidoo, Daphne Marlatt. She is currently writing a critical study on Anita Desai.

KELVIN EVEREST is Bradley Professor of Modern Literature at Liverpool University. He has published *Coleridge's Secret Ministry* (1979), *English Romantic Poetry* (1990), and a number of articles and edited collections on topics and writers in English Romanticism. He is currently editing the Complete Poems of Shelley.

DAVID FAIRER is Professor of Eighteenth-Century Literature at the University of Leeds. He is the author of *Pope's Imagination* (1984), *The Poetry of Alexander Pope* (1989), and editor of *Pope: New Contexts* (1990) and *The Correspondence of Thomas Warton* (1995). With Christine Gerrard he has edited *Eighteenth-Century Poetry: An Annotated Anthology* (1999).

SIR PETER HALL has been Director of the Arts Theatre; Founder and Director of the Royal Shakespeare Company; Artistic Director of Glyndebourne; and Director of the Royal National Theatre. His many productions for The Peter Hall Company (formed in 1988) include a landmark season of 13 plays at the Old Vic in 1997.

GEOFFREY HILL, formerly Professor of English (University of Leeds) and currently University Professor of Literature and Religion and Co-Director of the Editorial Institute (Boston University), has worked closely with Inga-Stina Ewbank on a stage-version of Ibsen's *Brand* (National Theatre, 1978). His latest volume of poetry is *The Triumph of Love* (1998).

PETER HOLLAND is Director of the Shakespeare Institute, Stratford-upon-Avon, and Professor of Shakespeare Studies at the University of Birmingham. His most recent book is *English Shakespeares: Shakespeare on the English Stage in the 1990s* (1997). His articles include work on Chekhov, Stanislavski, Shakespeare, Garrick and English pantomimes.

LYNETTE HUNTER is Professor of the History of Rhetoric, University of Leeds, and co-editor of the Arden Third Edition *Romeo and Juliet*. Her earlier work is centrally concerned with rhetoric as a way of assessing moral, social and political implications of texts, and she is currently researching the rhetoric of gesture.

ELDRED JONES is Emeritus Professor of English at the University of Sierra Leone (Fourah Bay College) and editor of *African Literature Today*.

PETER LICHTENFELS has worked extensively in British theatre as an artistic director, and both in the UK and internationally as a director. Author of a performance edition of *The Merchant of Venice*, he is currently co-editing the Arden Third Edition *Romeo and Juliet*. His recent research has focused on developing a vocabulary that will allow textual editors to make use of performance elements such as mask, breath, movement and voice.

DAVID LINDLEY is Reader in Renaissance Literature at the University of Leeds. His most recent publications include *The Trials of Frances Howard* (1993), an edition of *Court Masques* (1995) and essays on the politics of music in the Renaissance. He is currently editing *The Tempest* for the New Cambridge Shakespeare.

GAIL MARSHALL is a Lecturer in English at Leeds University. She is the author of *Actresses on the Victorian Stage: Feminine Performance and the Galatea Myth* (1998) and articles on George Eliot, Ibsen, and late-Victorian theatre. She is currently working on a study of Shakespeare and Victorian women.

LEONÉE ORMOND is Professor of Victorian Studies at King's College, London University and has published widely on Victorian and Edwardian literature and painting, with books on George Du Maurier, J. M. Barrie and Tennyson. She is the author, with Richard Ormond, of a critical biography of Frederic, Lord Leighton.

RICHARD SALMON is a Lecturer in the School of English, University of Leeds; his research interests lie primarily in the field of nineteenth-century literature, and he is the author of *Henry James and the Culture of Publicity* (1997).

ALISTAIR STEAD is Senior Fellow in English at the University of Leeds. He is co-editor of *James Joyce and Modern Literature* (1982) and *Forked Tongues? Comparing Twentieth-Century British and American Literature* (1994). He co-edits *The James Joyce Broadsheet* and has published essays on Henry Green and Janette Turner Hospital.

ANDREW WAWN is Reader in English and Icelandic Studies at the University of Leeds. His recent publications include *The Iceland Journal of Henry Holland* (1989), *The Anglo Man: Þorleifur Repp, Philology and Nineteenth-Century Britain* (1991), and *Northern Antiquity: The Post-Medieval Reception of Edda and Saga* (1994).

STANLEY WELLS is Emeritus Professor of the University of Birmingham and General Editor of the Oxford Shakespeare. He edited *A Midsummer Night's Dream* for the New Penguin Shakespeare.

Index of Names